A Tribal Order

A Tribal Order

Politics and Law in the Mountains of Yemen

BY SHELAGH WEIR

THE BRITISH MUSEUM PRESS

Published in Great Britain in 2007 by The British Museum Press
A division of The British Museum Company Ltd
38 Russell Square, London WC1B 3QQ
www.britishmuseum.co.uk

A catalogue record for this book is available from the British Library
ISBN-13: 978-0-7141-2579-4
ISBN-10: 0-7141-2579-2

Printed in the United States of America

♾ The paper used in this book meets the minimum requirements of
ANSI/NISO Z39.48-1992 (R1997) (Permanence of Paper)

In memory of Ernest Gellner

Contents

CHAPTER EIGHT
Conflict and Violence 190

PART III
The State-Tribe Relationship

CHAPTER NINE
The Qāsimī Period 229
CHAPTER TEN
The Ḥamīd al-Dīn Period 256
CHAPTER ELEVEN
The Republican Period 284

Conclusions 307

APPENDIX 1
Chronology of Events Affecting Rāziḥ 315
APPENDIX 2
Catalogue of Rāziḥī Documents 321

Notes 343
Glossary 355
Bibliography 359
Index 375

List of Figures

List of Tables

Preface

This book is based on seventeen months' fieldwork on Jabal Rāziḥ in the far north of the Republic of Yemen, where I spent from March to October 1977, October 1979 to May 1980, and January and February 1993. The "ethnographic present" therefore refers to that period. Throughout my fieldwork I lived in the tiny "town" or *madīnah* of al-Naẓīr, the main settlement of a tribe in southern Rāziḥ. During my first two stays I maintained a semi-independent household; and on my third I lived *en famille* in the house next door. The *madīnah* was an ideal fieldwork base. It is socially and occupationally heterogeneous. Men prominent in tribal and government affairs were among my neighbors. And visitors came from far and wide to its lively weekly market. I did most of my research in and on the tribe of al-Naẓīr, one of the ten small tribes of Rāziḥ, partly because I wanted to understand one community well, and partly because travel was difficult in the mountainous terrain. There were no motor tracks during my first fieldwork in 1977, and although the construction of a trans-Rāziḥ track and feeder tracks had begun by 1979, travel remained slow and most places could still only be reached on foot. Although I traveled widely in Rāziḥ and visited the neighboring tribal region of ʿUqārib, therefore, my deepest firsthand knowledge is about the tribe of al-Naẓīr, and I describe the tribal system of Rāziḥ mainly from that perspective.

No-one in Rāziḥ spoke English, so all my fieldwork was conducted in Arabic. The local dialect, or language, is extremely unusual, and was always a difficulty, but some male informants could switch registers to a form of Arabic I could understand more easily. My linguistic struggles were greatly helped by Bonnie Glover Stalls, a specialist in Arabic dialects, who accompanied me to al-Naẓīr for two months in 1979 to study spoken Rāziḥī, and has continued to provide helpful advice. I was also aided in the field by Cynthia Myntti, who came for a month in 1977 to do a health study, and by Ian Dunn and Michael Dunn, who visited for a month in 1977 to make a film. Ian also kindly helped me map the *madīnah* and tribal territories during a second short stay in 1980. Apart from these visits, I was unaccompanied during my fieldwork. Being a lone foreign woman was an advantage. I could cross the gender divide as no man could do, and women could visit me without prejudicing their reputations. I explained that I was studying "customs and traditions" and "history," and this was accepted.

This research was conducted under the auspices of the British Museum, where I was curator for Middle Eastern ethnography at the former Museum of Mankind. I initially intended to study crafts (Weir 1975), and I made a collection of artifacts for the Museum. I was also interested in the local economy, on which I have previously published (Weir 1985a, 1985b, and 1987). Then at the start of my second visit, in 1979, a dispute broke out between al-Naẓīr and a neighboring tribe. This breakthrough event, which I describe in Chapter Eight, opened a fascinating window on tribal law and politics, which thereafter became my primary focus. Hitherto I had understood the tribal system largely through my informants' abstract and idealized descriptions; now I saw tribal politics being practiced, and tribal law being implemented, and glimpsed the richness and complexity of this system. This dispute also first alerted me to the immense importance of documents in Rāziḥī culture. I discovered that hoards of scrolled papers were preserved in peoples' homes, and realized that this was an anthropological treasure trove. By a stroke of luck two Naẓīrīs owned photocopiers which ran off portable generators, and during my second two visits I was able to copy more than three hundred and fifty papers spanning nearly four centuries. A short catalogue of most of these is provided in Appendix 2, and they are referenced in the text with the prefix D. I regret that it has been impossible to translate or reproduce many of these fascinating documents in this work because of lack of space, but I plan to do so elsewhere, and the reader is meanwhile referred to Weir 1996.

Most of the documents I copied are pacts and treaties among and between tribal groups, between tribes and state authorities, and among the ruling elite themselves. Whenever problems arose, men gathered (as they still gather) to resolve them, and recorded their decisions, judgments, and agreements in handwritten papers which they preserved for future reference. These documents are an invaluable primary source, for they catch local people "inscribing" their own system for their own purposes at different periods. They provide a wealth of information about tribal political and legal matters. Because they are usually dated, and invariably name the participants of the meetings at which they were written, they also make it possible to track individuals and groups, and their relationships, back through time; however, they only rarely and briefly provide information about events such as would facilitate a narrative history. Overall, the documents testify to the predominantly contractual basis of political relations in Rāziḥ, and to remarkable continuities in structures and practices, both of which are major themes of this work.

Throughout my fieldwork I gathered social information indiscriminately while participating in everyday life and special occasions. I also collected data by more formal methods: photography, tape recordings, censuses of selected settlements, and surveys of occupations, land-ownership, and the market of al-Naẓīr. With local help I also did preliminary translations of documents—a difficult task which has continued over subsequent years, and delayed the completion of this work. This variegated material has allowed me to present my themes and arguments with an eclectic mixture of formal description and analysis, quotations from informants and documents, and narratives of events and cases based on documentary evidence and informants' accounts. Stories had undoubtedly been adjusted in their countless retelling to fit current concerns; but Rāziḥīs are politically sophisticated, and their accounts reveal a refreshing absence of mystification about how their system operates, and are filled with information and insights. Although my authorial overview of the tribal system of Rāziḥ undoubtedly differs from that which any local person would produce, I hope that Rāziḥīs who one day read this book will recognize the picture I paint as true in essentials to their own understandings.

Acknowledgments

I would like to thank all the Rāziḥīs who helped me during fieldwork for their immense kindness and generosity. I am particularly grateful to the women of Bayt Manṣūr ʿAlī and Bayt Aḥmad Muḥammad Jubrān, the shaykhs of Ilt Faraḥ, and members of Bayt Abū Ṭālib. I am also indebted to all those who allowed me to copy their family documents, and to Aḥmad Muḥammad and Ṣāliḥ Misfir ʿAbūd for allowing me free use of their photocopying equipment and paper.

Three Naẓīrīs made such major contributions to my research that I consider this work theirs as much as mine, though I should stress that they bear no responsibility for my views and mistakes. Aḥmad Muḥammad Jubrān was a constant source of advice and information, including during two visits to London he made in 1981 and 1991, at my invitation, in order to help me with my research. Without Aḥmad's brotherly support and uplifting wit, and the kindness of his wives, ʿAjībat Aḥmad and Ḥamāmat Aḥmad, I might well have floundered. Sharaf Muḥsin Abū Ṭālib generously devoted all his free time for several months to helping me decipher and understand local documents. I will never forget his patient commitment to this thorny task, nor the unfailing good humor with which he and his wife, ʿAjībat Ḥusayn, welcomed me almost daily into their home. I did not meet Khālid ʿAbdō al-Rāziḥī until I had finished my fieldwork. On discovering that he was a fluent English speaker, I invited him to London in 1994 and 1995 to work with me, and he skillfully and patiently helped me with translations of tapes and documents throughout his time as a student at SOAS in 1996–97, and during short visits I made to Yemen in the late 1990s. No anthropologist could possibly have been blessed with better helpmates than these.

My fieldwork was financed by the British Museum, and I am grateful to my former colleagues, the late William Fagg, Jean Rankine, and John Mack, for supporting my project at crucial stages, and to Sarah Posey and others for covering my work during my absences. Muḥammad al-Mākhadī suggested al-Naẓīr as a fieldwork base, and kindly furnished me with personal introductions. I also received official support and kindness from Qāḍī Ismāʿil al-Akwaʿ, and Dr. Yūsuf ʿAbdallāh, former Directors of Antiquities, and Dr. Aḥmad al-Marwānī, former Director of the Centre for Yemeni Studies. I must also thank those who gave me hospitality in Sanaa during various visits: the late John Baldry, Claudia Cooper, Sarah Soulsby, the directors of the American Institute of Yemeni Studies, John Mandaville and Noha Sadek, and the director of the Institut Français, Franck Mermier. I have greatly benefited from being able to compare and contrast my material and ideas with those of fellow anthropologists who were speedier than I in writing up their Yemeni research, and I pay tribute to their pioneering work. I am also indebted to many colleagues and friends who commented on various drafts during the long gestation of this book: the members of ARSTAG, Linda Boxberger, Sheila Carapico, William Donaldson, Ian Dunn, Robert Fernea, Elizabeth Fernea, Michael Gilsenan (who kindly agreed to supervise my thesis late in the day), André Gingrich, Ianthe Maclagan, Tim Morris, Martha Mundy, Cynthia Myntti, John Peterson, Hugh Roberts, Susan Wright, and Dan Varisco. I have also benefited from discussions with, and information provided by, Najwa Adra, Ḥusayn al-ʿAmrī, Isa Blumi, Gabriele vom Bruck, Steven Caton, Paul Dresch, Bernard Haykel, Tomas Klaric, André Korotayev, Thomas Kuhn, Gerhard Lichtenthäler, Wilferd Madelung, Emanuel Marx, Brinkley Messick, Venetia Porter, Mikhail Rodionov, the late R. B. Serjeant, Muḥammad al-Sharafī, Bonnie Glover Stalls, Charles Tripp, Janet Watson, Zayd al-Wazir, Lisa Wedeen, John Willis, Muḥammad al-Zulfa, and Leila al-Zwaini. All are, of course, absolved from blame for the remaining inadequacies.

I would lastly like to thank the Middle East Center of the University of Texas for sponsoring this book, and Annes McCann Baker at the Center, and Wendy Moore and Leslie Tingle at the University of Texas Press for all their help. I am also grateful to the Society for Arabian Studies, the British Yemeni Society, and the Seven Pillars of Wisdom Trust for contributions toward the production costs, and to the Leigh Douglas Memorial Fund, the British Academy, and the British Council in Sanaa for financing visits to London by Aḥmad Muḥammad and Khālid Abdō. Robert Travis of Graphein drew the excellent maps and diagrams.

This work is based on a thesis for which I was awarded a doctorate by London University in 2004. I dedicate the book to my original thesis supervisor, the late Ernest Gellner, whose incisive criticisms of early drafts, faith in the importance of my subject, and unfailing encouragement over many years made me feel my project was worthwhile, and gave me confidence to continue. I deeply regret that he did not live to see my work come to fruition, but hope it lives up to his constant admonitions to write clearly and remain true to my data.

Note on Transliteration

I have used the system for transliterating Arabic of the *International Journal of Middle Eastern Studies* for both written and spoken words, with modifications in order to render certain features of the unusual Rāziḥī dialect (Behnstedt 1985, 1987; Watson et al. 2006). Since *tā marbūṭah* is pronounced as well as written, I invariably write it. As elsewhere in Yemen, spoken Rāziḥī has lost the contrast between *ḍād* and *ẓā*, which is reflected in the documents; common words such as *ḍumanā* (guarantors), for example, are written with either letter. I have therefore followed the standard Arabic spelling for such words. I write *al-Naẓīr* throughout, although the spelling *al-Naḍīr* was adopted in local and official documents from the mid-twentieth century. The pronunciation of both /ḍ/ and /ẓ/ is as an emphatic voiced interdental fricative similar to an emphatic version of /th/ in the English word *this*. I have usually written the definite article as /al/ even when transcribing speech, although it is rarely pronounced as such in Rāziḥ; I have rendered diphthongs as /ay/ and /aw/, although they are pronounced as monothongs (long vowels); and I write *qāf* as /q/, although it is pronounced /g/, and use /ch/ for the Rāziḥī sound as in the English *chat*. I have used Anglicized versions of common words and place names such as *Quran* (not *Qur'ān*) and *Sanaa* (not *Ṣanʿā'*), and have not italicized well-known Arabic words.

Currency

In the 1970s and 1980s Rāziḥīs used two currencies: the Saudi *riyāl* (SR) (*riyāl ʿarabī*) for small, everyday transactions, and the Maria Theresa dollar or thaler (MT$) (*riyāl faranṣī*) for large transactions such as land and house purchases and brideprices. By the 1990s the national currency, the Yemeni *riyāl* (YR) (*riyāl jumhūrī,* "republican riyal," as they call it), had become the sole currency in Rāziḥ. Exchange rates fluctuated greatly from the 1970s–1990s, so I sometimes provide the U.S. dollar equivalents.

Abbreviations

BS	brother's son (nephew)
FBS	father's brother's son (cousin)
FBD	father's brother's daughter (cousin)
FF	paternal grandfather
FFF	paternal great-grandfather
MB	mother's brother (maternal uncle)
b., bin	son of
CYDA	Confederation of Yemeni Development Associations
LDA	Local Development Association
YAR	Yemen Arab Republic

A Tribal Order

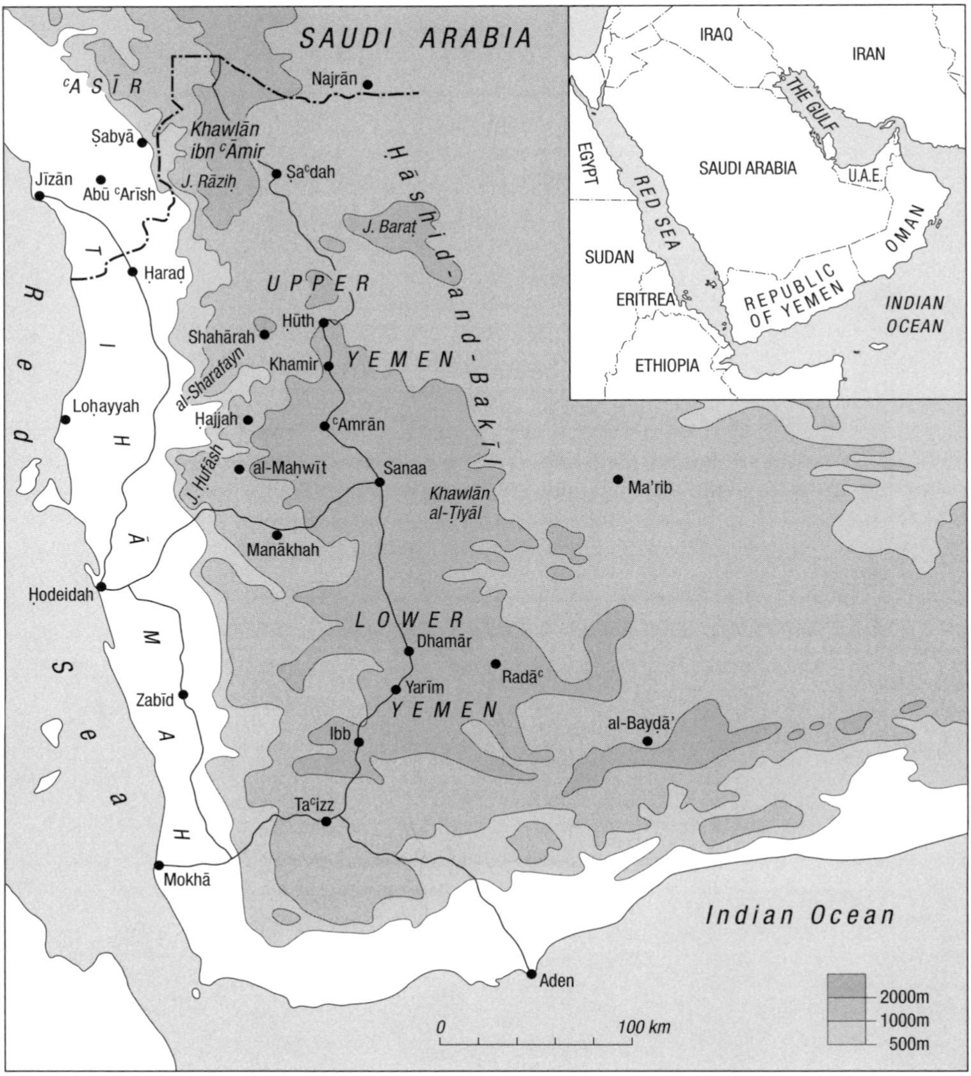

FIGURE 0.1
Map of west and north Yemen

Introduction

This book describes the politico-legal system of small tribes of farmers and traders which have existed on Jabal Rāziḥ, in much the same form, for at least four centuries, and considers their historical relationship with a continuous succession of religious rulers and the present republican state. Throughout the book I have addressed fundamental questions of governance. What are the key political groups, and how are they conceptualized? What accounts for their size and positions? How are power and authority distributed and exercised, and curbed or resisted? How are disputes settled and order restored, how effectively, and in whose interests? And how are the institutions, principles, rules, and procedures for maintaining law and order sustained and reproduced, or changed? These issues are especially compelling when a political system exhibits, as does that of Rāziḥ, remarkable structural and cultural continuities, and an apparently abiding concern for containing and resolving conflicts and minimizing violence.

The entities usually called "tribes" found throughout rural North Africa and the Middle East are diverse polities. Anthropological attempts to formulate a detailed, universally applicable definition have therefore invariably fallen foul of exceptions.[1] Some anthropologists of Yemen have therefore employed the term *tribe* without defining it,[2] or have opted for a less loaded term, such as *community*.[3] We need to categorize and label, however, in order to discuss, differentiate, and compare sociological phenomena, and the term *tribe* is still a useful portmanteau term, I believe, for territorial polities whose members share a common allegiance, which exist in a matrix of similar polities with which they have relations, and which have always been potentially or actually formally subordinate to some kind of "state," also, of course, a problematic term. These minimal criteria at least distinguish "tribes" from other sub-state entities, such as "ethnic groups" or "peoples," which are not necessarily political organizations; from political parties which are not territorial; and from state-administrative units which do not interact politically, and whose members owe allegiance only to the state. At the same time, my general formulation deliberately invites description of tribal features which vary through space and time, and which should always be empirically determined, if possible, for different regions and periods.

Among important variables are economies. Not all tribes are nomadic or transhumant, as some have assumed or implied (Gellner 1981:24, 89; Asad 1986; Eickelman 2002:46). Many in Afghanistan, Iraq, Iran, Morocco, and Algeria, and most in Yemen, comprise populations of settled farmers. Tribes also vary in their criteria of membership and idioms of identity. Many are conceptualized as large descent groups, but others place greater emphasis on idioms of place and leadership. If we wish to understand political action, therefore, we need to avoid thinking of tribes as invariably comprising "large kin groups, organized and regulated according to ties of blood or family lineage" (Khoury and Kostiner 1991:4), and to be alert for other organizing principles.[4]

Much of Yemen is divided into mostly sedentary tribes, and has been since antiquity; the only major region which seems never to have been tribally organized surrounds the towns of Ibb and Taʿizz in "Lower Yemen." Anthropological studies show that while the tribes of Yemen share a similar political culture, especially those of the northern highlands ("Upper Yemen"), they also vary regionally in size, forms of identity, and modes of organization.[5] Unfortunately, as Gingrich (1993) notes, this has been obscured by homogenizing generalizations about "the tribes of Yemen." Such approaches not only mask diversity, but also fail to address the environmental and historical factors underlying it. Dresch even explicitly denies the relevance of ecology for understanding Yemeni tribes, the structures of which he portrays as sets of cognitive categories on a linguistic model.[6] But tribal groupings are more than systems of definition or classification which can be analytically divorced from their varied contexts as he implies.

Yemen is a land of dramatically differentiated topography, climate, and ecology. Some tribes have territories in arid regions of marginal agriculture and widely scattered populations; others occupy fertile, well-watered regions, produce surpluses and cash crops, and are densely populated. Some tribes occupy easily traversed plains, others steep, inaccessible mountains. Tribes also vary in their proximity to, or remoteness from, major towns and trade routes, and the peripatetic centers of past states. All such factors have, I contend, affected the sizes of tribes, how they are organized, and their inclination and ability to solve their problems peaceably or violently in different historical circumstances. The tribal relationship with local or colonial states was also contingent on environmental factors. Some tribes were too poor or remote to attract rulers, and could evade or resist their control; others were strategically or economically attractive to states, and were forced or induced to submit. The kind and degree of state control, and the policies and methods of different rulers, also affected tribes. It is therefore essential to examine each tribal system on its own terms, and within its particular geographical, economic, and historical context, as I have attempted to do in this book. This is not, I should stress, to argue for some kind of economic or political determinism. On the contrary, I see tribes as polities created, maintained, or changed by people acting, individually or collectively, in their own perceived interests, and striving to achieve concrete goals. With this in mind, I have throughout emphasized the instrumental and administrative aspects of tribal politics and state-tribe relations, and tried to show how people construct and operate their system, resist or comply with its dictates, and compete for power, prestige, and the rewards of office.

The dominant anthropological model of tribal political organization in the Middle East and North Africa when I embarked on fieldwork was "segmentary theory."[7] This attempts to explain the maintenance of order in so-called "acephalous" societies which lack (or are assumed to lack) permanent governmental institutions. The ideal-type "tribe" of this theory comprises a population which usually claims patrilineal descent from a common eponymous ancestor, and is subdivided into a hierarchy of "nested" lineages or "segments" named after subsequent ancestors. Although anthropologists use various labels to differentiate these tribal "segments" (typically, in ascending order, family, lineage, clan, tribe, and confederation), the segmentary model insists that these structures are essentially homologous—that each comprises more or less egalitarian kin groups which replicate in all but size those of which they are part, or into which they are divided. Above all, and this is the crux of the theory, no segment has specialized or permanent political functions—there is no "crucial level of social organization" (Gellner 1981:117; 1991:109).

The fundamental concept of segmentarism as a theory of politico-legal action is that of "balanced opposition." In the absence of effective leaders, order and the balance of power are maintained by collective action: equivalent groups at different levels of the system mobilize in response to threats, then dissolve when they abate. This happens, of course, in many societies, but in segmentary societies it is *this mechanism alone* which operates. The action groups typically take is violent revenge or "feud," and conflicts are resolved by temporary mediators with little power—a role for which Gellner notably argued holy men ("saints") are specially qualified, in Muslim societies, because of their religious prestige and political neutrality.[8] But peace is temporary, and dormant feuds are repeatedly resuscitated. The segmentary model has been challenged by several anthropologists, and many think it now defunct.[9] It retains explanatory power, however, for societies lacking specialized order-maintaining institutions, has a degree of fit with what some anthropologists have observed, especially among nomadic tribes, and remains useful as an ideal type for comparative purposes.

As we shall see, the tribal system of Rāziḥ shares several characteristics with segmentary systems: it comprises nested groups (though they are not homologous); political relations are expressed in kinship idioms; collective responsibility is fundamental; groups can take revenge; and mediation is centrally important, including by religious specialists. But Rāziḥ *has* a crucial level of organization, its long-lived tribes, and other stable governmental institutions: dynastic leadership; administrative and judicial structures; written laws, and specialized personnel and procedures for their enforcement; and durable alliances based on contracts and treaties reflecting interests, not genealogical connections. All these features are incompatible with the segmentary model.

My research therefore led me to adopt an alternative, geo-political approach to understanding the tribes of Rāziḥ, which I eventually conceived as tiny sovereign domains, each governed and represented by leaders with constitutional authority and powers of office. The concepts of tribal governance and sovereignty have a long history in the anthropology of different countries and continents (see Dole 1968; Vincent 1990:42–46), but have been under-used in studies of North African and Middle Eastern tribes. This might be partly because key polities are often small, unmarked by dedicated buildings, and have governmental practices which can seem "rudimentary" and "informal" from the (sometimes condescending) perspective of members of modern states (see Vincent 1990:46; Gledhill 2000:11). It might therefore be necessary to focus closely on individual communities and families in order to find "government," as Mundy (1995) has notably demonstrated for another area of Yemen. Tribal governance has also been insufficiently recognized because, as Munson (1989) and Hugh Roberts (2002, 2003) have argued, some anthropologists have been blinkered by segmentary theory, with its anarchic and agonistic vision of tribal societies. They have therefore tended to see tribesmen more as warriors to be mustered in battle than as citizens subject to the same jurisdictions. Like the citizens of states, however, and as the evidence from Rāziḥ shows, they can be either according to circumstances.

State-Tribe Relations

Rāziḥ lies due west of the northern plateau town of Ṣaʿdah, and due east of the Red Sea port of Jīzān. It is a fertile and populous region with a productive economy based on agriculture and trade; it bestrides an important trade route across the northern mountains; and in the west it commands the coastal plain (the Tihāmah). For fiscal and strategic reasons, therefore, it has probably attracted some kind of supra-tribal or "state" control since antiquity—perhaps even since Sabaean times in the mid–first millennium BC.[10]

Rāziḥ has experienced great cultural continuity in state governance. Since the birth of Islam in the seventh century, it has known nothing but Muslim regimes, and from the foundation of the Zaydī-Shiʿite state in Yemen in the late ninth century until Rāziḥ joined the Republic after the 1960s Civil War, it was usually under some kind of Zaydī *dawlah*—a polysemic term which can be translated as "state," "regime," "ruler," or "government," according to context. The only major interruption to Zaydī rule was seven decades of Ottoman occupation from the mid-sixteenth to the early seventeenth century. For over three centuries thereafter, Rāziḥ was ruled by members of the Qāsimī dynasty, whose founder initiated the Zaydī insurrections which eventually ousted the Ottomans from Yemen. For periods it was under the main Zaydī-Qāsimī rulers (sing. *imām*) based in various highland seats including Sanaa. At other times it was part of dissident imāmates or *dawlahs* based in Ṣaʿdah. And for long periods it was under locally based *dawlahs*. It will be noted that, in common with the rest of North Yemen, Rāziḥ has never been colonized by a European power.

Zaydī *dawlahs* were very different from the Weberian-western model of states. None had sole jurisdiction, nor a monopoly of the legitimate use of force, within the domains they claimed and aspired to rule. All were also weak in human and material resources, and had tiny, highly personalized administrations which mainly aimed to administer sharīʿah law, collect taxes, and preserve or expand their own hegemony; and the tribes which constituted most of their domains had substantial politico-jural autonomy and were well armed. These Zaydī domains also fluctuated in size as tribes and territories were won or lost, and it was not until the twentieth century that the Zaydī imāmate gained fixed, if contested, borders.

In Rāziḥ these weak and fissiparous *dawlahs* were superimposed on relatively stable tribes, which functioned as the prime and constant units of state governance. Rāziḥīs referred to this composite polity by the collocation "state-and-tribe" (*dawlah-wa-qabīlah*). As I will show in Part III, by their policy of indirect rule, imāms and other religious overlords reinforced the tribal system of Rāziḥ, both ideologically and instrumentally, by accepting it as the principal and legitimate form of local governance, and by co-opting and exploiting its structures and practices for their own fiscal, legal, and military purposes. At the same time, they caused modifications in tribal structures, and triggered changes and disturbances in the tribal system by strengthening or weakening particular leaders, tilting local balances (or imbalances) of power, and creating or exacerbating conflicts of interest.

I touch on aspects of the state-tribe relationship in Rāziḥ throughout the first two parts of the book, which focus mainly on tribal politics and law, but have deferred detailed consideration of the state-tribe relationship in a historical context until last, after the tribal system has been described. I have taken the expulsion of the Ottomans from Yemen as my starting point for this more chronological treatment, partly because it was a major juncture in local and national history, and partly because the earliest Rāziḥī documents I found date back to that period.

TABLE 0.1. RULERS OF RĀZIḤ, SIXTEENTH TO TWENTY-FIRST CENTURIES

Dates	*Rulers*
1540s–1613	Ottomans
1613–c.1650s	Main Zaydī imams
c. 1650s–c. 1714	Imams of Ṣaʿdah
1714–1870s	Semi-independent principality
1870s–1909	Main Zaydī imams
1909–1914	Idrīsī of ʿAsīr
1914–1971	Main Zaydī imams
1971–1990	Yemen Arab Republic
1990–present	Republic of Yemen

PART I

The Tribal System

CHAPTER ONE

Environment and Economy

Jabal Rāziḥ is a high massif which lies on the western edge of the Yemeni highlands overlooking the coastal plain (Tihāmah) of the Red Sea next to the border with Saudi Arabia. Rāziḥ has impressive natural defenses. Jabal Ḥurum (alt. 2790m), its highest summit, which is crowned by two fortresses, guards the only pass into the massif from the north or east. The deep gorge of Wādī Khulab creates a formidable barrier with the Khawlān massif to the southeast. And in the west and south the slopes of Jabal Rāziḥ plunge from summits of over 2500 meters to meet the Tihāmah at an altitude of about 500 meters. Here the culture of "the highlands" (*al-jabal*) gives way to the very different culture of "the plain" (*al-sahal*), as locals call the Tihāmah. *Sahalī*s follow the Shāfiʿī *madhhab* of Sunnī Islam, not the Zaydī *madhhab* of the highlands. Their dialect, dress, furnishings, and ceremonies also contrast with those of the highlands, and many have African ancestry—most obviously manifested in their physical appearance and circular thatched huts.

Jabal Rāziḥ has many rocky ridges and summits, and is deeply dissected by steep-sided watercourses, though permanent streams are few. Nine tribes have their territories in this steep and rugged terrain, and another occupies Jabal Ghamar, a lower mountain to the east. These ten tribes comprise the distinct tribal region of Rāziḥ, the main focus of this book. Fringing the Rāziḥ massif to the west and south is a chain of lower mountains and foothills with altitudes of less than 1300 meters. These are the territories of the six tribes of another tribal region, ʿUqārib, which have close relations with Rāziḥ and will also figure prominently in this account. Along the western edge of the ʿUqārib hills runs the Yemeni-Saudi border. From there the ʿAsīr Tihāmah inclines gently westward for sixty kilometers to meet the sea (see map page 88).

Rāziḥīs regard themselves as part of a wider tribal region they call Khawlān ibn ʿĀmir, which includes most of northwest Yemen and part of Saudi ʿAsīr.[1] Khawlān ibn ʿĀmir has had several alternative names, historically, depending on the speaker's standpoint. The famous tenth-century Yemeni geographer, al-Hamdānī, writing within the Arab genealogical tradition, called it "the land (*bilād*) of Quḍāʿah" or "Khawlān b. Quḍāʿah" after a probably mythical ancestor, and educated Rāziḥīs familiar with his work still quote that name today. Ottoman governors and the Zaydī imāms referred to it as "Khawlān Ṣaʿdah" or "the Province of Ṣaʿdah" after the northern town from which it was invariably ruled. And southerners call it "the northern Khawlān" (Khawlān al-Shām), to distinguish it from Khawlān al-Ṭiyāl near Sanaa, or simply "the north country" (*bilād al-shām*)—an epithet synonymous, for many, with "the back of beyond." For Rāziḥīs, however, "the north" (*al-shām*) is ʿAsīr, and the back of beyond is what they call "the south" (*al-yaman*)—the vast region beyond the mountains on their southern horizon, which few ever visited before the late twentieth century. Even in the 1970s men visiting the capital, Sanaa, were said to be "away in *al-yaman*," and only gradually has *al-yaman* primarily come to mean the republican state. Similar compass terms are used within Khawlān ibn ʿĀmir. Rāziḥīs call the plateau where Ṣaʿdah lies "the east" (*al-mashriq*), and historically referred to states or rulers (*dawlahs*) based there as *dawlat al-mashriq*. And *mashriqīs* refer to Rāziḥ as "the west" (*al-maghrib*).

In the 1970s and 1980s, Jabal Rāziḥ, Ghamar, and ʿUqārib together comprised "Qaḍā Rāziḥ," a sub-province of the Province of Ṣaʿdah. Other sub-provinces likewise corresponded to tribal regions of Khawlān ibn ʿĀmir: Khawlān, the massif southeast of Rāziḥ; Jumāʿah, which extends across the mountains north and east of Rāziḥ and into the plateau (and includes a major tribal region called Munabbih); and Ṣaḥār (where Ṣaʿdah lies) on the plateau south of Jumāʿah. The fifth sub-province of the Province of Ṣaʿdah corresponded to another distinct tribal region called

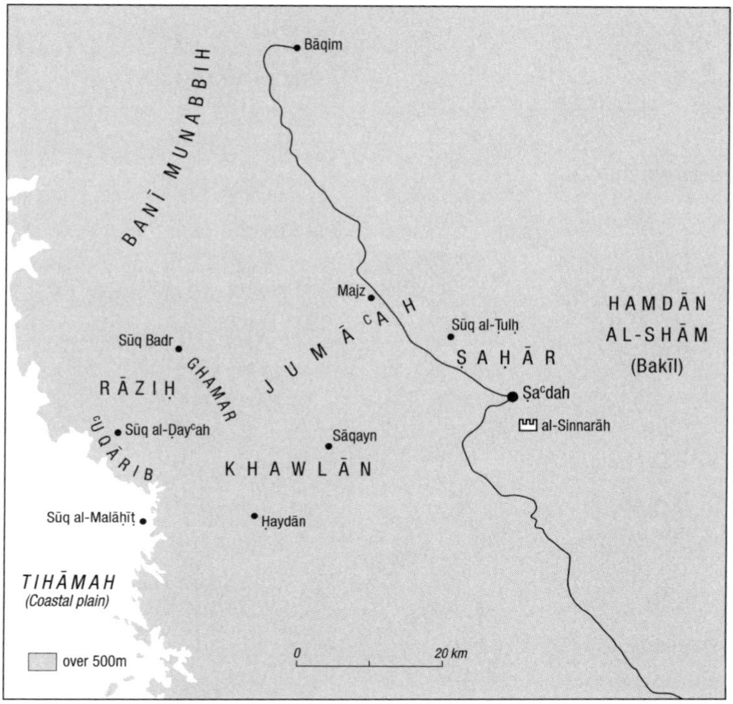

FIGURE 1.1
The tribal regions of Khawlān ibn ᶜĀmir

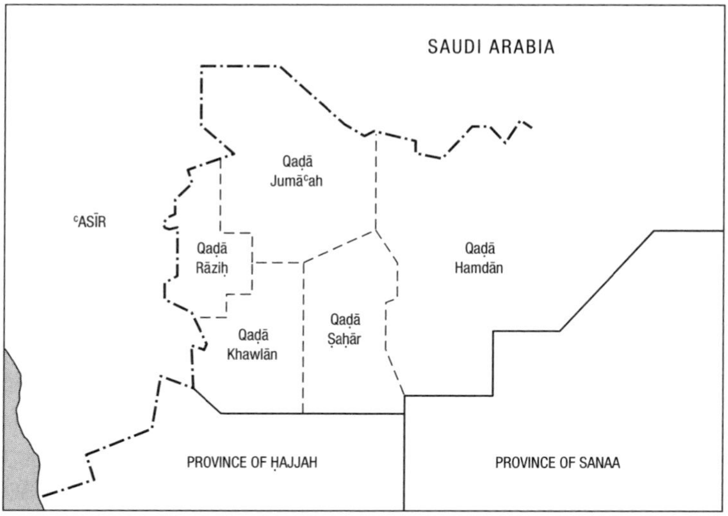

FIGURE 1.2
The sub-provinces (sing. *qaḍā*) of the Province of Ṣaᶜdah, late 1970s

Hamdān al-Shām, "the northern Hamdān," which is part of Bakīl—one of the two large tribal groupings, often named in tandem as Ḥāshid-and-Bakīl, which occupy much of the high plateaux of North Yemen and their mountainous margins.

Climate, Agriculture, and Population

Because of its exposed position and high west-facing slopes, Jabal Rāziḥ receives the full onslaught of the southwest monsoons which bring rain to Yemen, in good years, between March and May and during the main rainy season between July and September. These moisture-laden winds flow from the Red Sea across the hot Tihāmah plain with little precipitation. The *sahal* is therefore mainly pastureland for sheep and goats, and most agriculture is concentrated in the floodplains of the wādīs which dissect the mountains.[2] Rainfall is also sparse in the hills and low mountains of ʿUqārib, where livestock rearing is economically more important than on the heights, and millet, maize, and sorghum (*dhurah*) are also grown. *Jabalīs* disparage the people of the *sahal* and ʿUqārib for their greater dependence on animals, and their small dwellings, referring to them disdainfully as *badū*—meaning "less civilized"—and exalt their own massive houses, intensive agriculture, and heavy involvement in trade as evidence of superiority.[3]

On hitting the western escarpment, the warm winds rise and cool, and precipitate most of their rain above an altitude of about 1300–1500 meters. Northwesterly winds can also bring rain to Rāziḥ between December and February.[4] The heights of Jabal Rāziḥ therefore receive a relatively high mean annual rainfall of 700–1000mm. As important for agriculture are the clouds which swirl up from the coast in the afternoons, especially in winter, cocooning the summits of Rāziḥ in damp mists, depositing dew, reducing evaporation from the soil, and protecting crops from harsh sunlight. No wonder Rāziḥīs boast, "Our land has divine blessing (*barakah*)," meaning the rain with which God rewards the pious. But they are also acutely aware that their subsistence and prosperity are precariously dependent on capricious nature, and have painful memories of droughts and famine when the rains failed.

The heights of Jabal Rāziḥ, within the main rain-belt, are spectacularly clothed in long flights of terraces (sing. *jillah*); "there is no land which its people cannot tame," as the local saying goes. Rāziḥīs understandably eulogize the awesome architectural achievement on which their livelihood de-

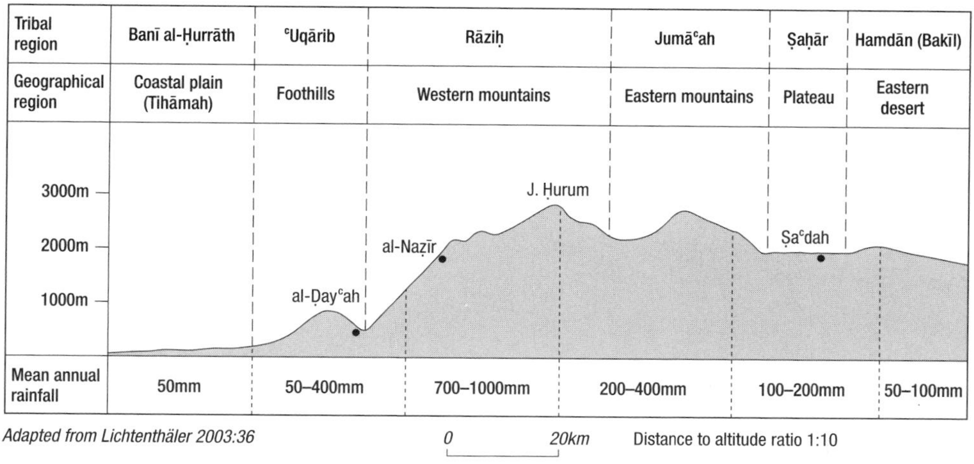

FIGURE 1.3
Cross-section through the northern highlands of Yemen, showing rainfall

pends, and tell of herculean competitions between legendary terrace-builders who hewed the stones, built the retaining walls, and lugged the infill earth from the lower slopes. Terraces demand constant toil and vigilance. They can become waterlogged during storms, causing breaches in walls and earth-falls onto lower terraces; and violent floods (sing. *sayl*) can sweep them down the mountainsides. Rāziḥī landowners are therefore legally obliged, in tribal law, to maintain their terraces to protect those below.

A variety of crops flourish in different parts of Jabal Rāziḥ according to variations in altitude and micro-ecological conditions (Weir 1985a). The staple grain crop is sorghum (*dhurah*), which is grown throughout the massif, and is sown in April, after the start of the spring rains, and harvested in October when the stars of Ursa Major (*ᶜallān*) appear (see Varisco 1994:70). Sorghum is (or was historically) the major subsistence crop of Rāziḥ, as of all highland Yemen, because it is drought resistant, its grain can be preserved for two or more years in underground silos (sing. *madfan*) or (nowadays) oil barrels, bread and porridge are made from its head, and its leaves, stalk, and roots provide fodder and fuel. Secondary grain crops, winter wheat (*burr*) and barley (*shaᶜr*) are sown on the sorghum terraces in December and reaped in February or March.[5] Major cash crops—banana, coffee, and qāt (*Catha edulis* Forssk.), a mild stimulant chewed socially throughout Yemen (Weir 1985a and 1985b)—are grown on the rain-exposed slopes in the west and south of the massif. Apricots, peaches, aromatic herbs, and a variety of greens and legumes are also cultivated on the heights, and papayas, mangos, limes, lemons, and citrons at various altitudes of the western escarpment.

Only the most precipitous slopes in the fertile upper reaches of the massif are left unterraced and uncultivated. These small "wild" (*qafarah*) areas are important sources of fodder for domestic animals. Because of the dearth of pasture, animal production has always been small scale; most households keep or kept one or two cows, mainly for their milk products and dung, and up to four or so sheep, and a few landowners and ploughmen a bullock. After centuries of woodcutting and house-building, only a few scattered trees stand among the terraces; all domestic firewood (*ḥatab*) must therefore be fetched from the *qafarah* areas of thorny scrub in the lower reaches of the mountains.

East of Jabal Rāziḥ, rainfall decreases, and even neighboring Ghamar, in the rain shadow of the massif, cannot sustain the variety of crops grown on Jabal Rāziḥ, though sorghum, wheat, and barley flourish there (Gingrich and Heiss 1986:77). In the mountains of Jumāʿah the climate becomes even more arid, agriculture more limited, and the population perceptibly smaller. About sixty kilometers from Rāziḥ, as the crow flies, the mountains descend to the arid high plateau (alt. 2000m), the territory of eastern Jumā ʿah and Ṣaḥār, which is mostly pastureland for goats and sheep, with small areas of grain and fruit cultivation (most famously grapes) in walled gardens and along wādīs.[6] The population of this region is also sparse and scattered, with a large minority concentrated in the ancient walled town of Ṣaʿdah, the provincial capital. At the eastern margins of the plateau the agricultural economy of the highlands gradually gives way to the nomadic or semi-nomadic pastoralism of the deserts of inner Arabia.

Population and Land

The population of Qaḍā Rāziḥ at the time of the first and probably most accurate national census in 1975, shortly before my fieldwork, was about 32,300, of which roughly 24,000 lived on Jabal Rāziḥ, 5000 on Jabal Ghamar, and the rest in the hills and mountains of ʿUqārib.[7] The area of Jabal Rāziḥ is probably around 200 km^2, so the density of population in relation to the whole mountain is possibly over 100 km^2, and is certainly much greater in relation to the intensively cultivated upper slopes where most settlements are concentrated. Ghamar, with a large territory of perhaps 100 km², has a much lower density of population, as does ʿUqārib. The population of Jabal Rāziḥ has been constantly augmented, historically, by immigration from poorer areas. This overall drift is attested in the oral histories of countless Rāziḥī families, and has its mirror image in Yemen's arid regions, where people remember the poor seeking a living in the more prosperous western mountains during times of scarcity.[8]

The high population of Rāziḥ puts great pressure on land, and virtually every patch and plant in the agricultural zone is (mostly individually) owned, and protected by law. All types of land and permanent plantings, including trees, are partible for inheritance or sale. Some land, including *qafarah,* is also dedicated to a permanent charitable beneficiary such as "the poor," a mosque, or a cemetery as a religious endowment (*waqf*). By comparison with other fertile areas, this is probably less than 5 percent of arable land.[9] Some hamlets also claim exclusive usufruct of small *qafarah* areas, but the more extensive *qafarah* below the densely settled heights are true commons which anyone may exploit. In accordance with the Quranic injunction, spring water (*ghayl*) for drinking is regarded as a common resource for the public good, but the owners of certain terraces below springs and *sayl* channels have contractual rights to a time-share of their water for irrigation.[10] Arable land varies in value according to position and planting; thus Naẓīrīs boast, "We have terraces of coffee, banana, and qāt in so-and-so wādī," meaning that they own well-watered land with permanent cash-crop plantations (*maghāriṣ*). The value of such prime terraces is roughly three times that of grain land (*ḥarth*). As in other fertile areas (Messick 1978:26), terraces are individually named, and are often very old; one mentioned in a land-sale contract of 1605, for example, still existed in the same place and with the same name in 1980 (D1605).

Land is mostly acquired by inheritance or purchase. The preciousness of land as the fundamental source of livelihood is reflected in the contrasting values placed on selling it, which is slightly reprehensible because it deprives one's heirs, and purchasing it, which is prestigious; a common expression of admiration is *khalaf wa shafaʿ*, meaning "he procreated abundantly, raised his children well, and accumulated land." Land was and is, nevertheless, regularly sold outside the family, especially (as mentioned) to survive through hard times, or to raise capital for house-building or marriage expenses. Land could also be lost by pawning it against a fixed-term loan and failing to redeem it, or could be forfeited to pay criminal compensation.

A person's landholdings are often dispersed in different places, though they are usually near their homes—people dislike traveling far to work or guard their land. The Islamic law of preemption (*shufʿah*) accords co-owners, or the owners of adjoining holdings, first refusal on purchase, and this principle is extended to try and prevent members of other tribes, or "foreigners" (*min khārij*) as they are called, from buying land in a tribe not their own (a custom called *juwārah*).[11] Most land within each tribe is consequently owned by its resident members. But there is always some owned by "foreigners" who acquired it by purchase or inheritance. This sometimes leads to the kind of inter-tribal problems that the *juwārah* custom seeks to avoid.

Land is relatively evenly distributed on Jabal Rāziḥ (Weir 1985a). This serves the interests of tribal and state governance alike; it is vital to both that households produce surpluses which can be siphoned off in taxes, and in subscriptions toward politico-legal fines and expenses. In contrast to the situation in other regions, however, land-ownership is not a criterion of "tribal" (*qabīlī*) status.

Landholdings in Rāziḥ are generally small, averaging about two hectares of arable land per household in 1975, and substantially less in the most densely populated, cash-cropping areas such as al-Naẓīr.[12] Although some men periodically accumulated larger landholdings, the latter were scattered through the mountains and in the Tihāmah foothills, not consolidated in one area, and were not perpetuated over generations so as to create a stable, land-based class system. This applies throughout the northern highlands of Yemen, and is largely due to the application of Islamic inheritance law, which divides property among several relatives.[13] Although Rāziḥīs endeavor to maintain the integrity of family holdings, chiefly by persuading women to cede shares to their male relatives, by brothers making their patrimony a joint estate (*khushrah*), or by making their land a "family *waqf*" (*waqf dhuriyyah*), the overall trend is for property to become fragmented over time. The superior ability of wealthy, ambitious men to contract multiple marriages (serially or polygamously), and therefore generate more heirs than men of modest means (who are mostly monogamous), also undermines the ability of elite families to conserve large holdings.

There are therefore no permanent, large estates in Rāziḥ worked by communities of socially inferior laborers as in Lower Yemen and the Tihāmah.[14] Neither do powerful plateau shaykhs own land in Rāziḥ as they do in other western mountains.[15] Such estates were often created by imāms who secured the loyalty of shaykhs and other clients by granting them land,

and the recipients were able to control their distant properties through local agents (*wakīls*) because the regions concerned were relatively accessible, had weak or no tribal organization, and were controlled by plateau-based states.[16] This phenomenon is therefore presumably absent in Rāziḥ because of its inaccessibility, its strong tribal system, and its long history of locally based semi-independent *dawlah*s.

Exports and Imports

Both local and long-distance trade have always been vital to the Rāziḥī economy because of its varied crops and other products, and its production of cash crops for export. By far the most important export crop, historically, was coffee. The misty, well-watered conditions of southwest Rāziḥ are ideal for coffee cultivation, and its bean is widely noted for its superior flavor.[17] Rāziḥ also lies near the northern limits of coffee production in Arabia, and close to ports and markets in ʿAsīr from whence coffee was historically shipped abroad, or transported northward by camel train. It was therefore probably in the vanguard of the coffee trade as it developed during the second half of the sixteenth century, and coffee was certainly being cultivated in Rāziḥ by the early seventeenth century.[18] During the heyday of the coffee trade, which lasted until Yemen lost its international monopoly in the 1720s, money flooded into coffee-producing areas such as Rāziḥ, enhancing general prosperity, augmenting the wealth and power of the local mercantile and political elite, and creating attractive pickings for tax-collecting states. Hundreds of local men must also have worked in the coffee trade as farmers, pickers, huskers, merchants, or transporters.

Despite the decline in the Yemeni coffee trade in the mid-eighteenth century, Rāziḥī coffee remained significant for overland trade and taxation into the nineteenth century, and was still being exported to ʿAsīr, Hijaz, and Najd in the 1930s.[19] And although coffee is no longer a major cash crop, beverages made from the bean (*ṣāfī*) and husk (*qishr*) of coffee remain important for domestic consumption and hospitality rituals within Rāziḥ, and sacks of beans are still offered as formal gifts to dignitaries.

From the mid-twentieth century, and most dramatically since the 1970s, qāt has become Rāziḥ's major export crop. Qāt has probably been cultivated in Rāziḥ—initially on a small scale for elite consumption—for as long as coffee (Weir 1985b:76–78). In contrast to coffee beans, however, which can be stored for months and exported long distances, qāt leaves are highly perishable; they wilt within two or three days of picking, losing their appearance, flavor, and mildly stimulating effects—and consequently their value. Before the advent of motor transport in the late 1970s, therefore, Rāziḥī qāt was traded only to the plateau and the Tihāmah; but afterward it could be marketed as far as Hodeidah and even Sanaa. Improvements in transportation coincided with a huge nationwide increase in demand. After the great hike in oil prices in 1973–74, Yemeni migrants earned high wages in Saudi Arabia, which pushed up Yemeni wages. This new prosperity caused an explosion of consumerism, including a national efflorescence in qāt consumption. Prices soared, and enormous revenues flooded into Rāziḥ, where qāt cultivation doubled—mainly at the expense of grain. This qāt boom, like the earlier coffee boom, created work for many Rāziḥīs as pickers, packers, and transporters. However, the qāt industry favored small-scale marketing by numerous small traders, and did not become as concentrated in the hands of a few big merchants as had happened in the coffee trade (Gerholm 1977:55; Weir 1985a, 1985b).

Rāziḥ also formerly exported grain (mainly sorghum) and bananas (Philby 1952:496); bananas are still sent to Saudi Arabia. Banana plants also gained extra commercial value from the 1970s because their stems and leaves are used to pack qāt (Weir 1985a). Aromatic herbs, used for medicine, personal decoration, and for scenting homes in ʿAsīr, are also a lucrative cash crop, though they only thrive on high, cool slopes. Rāziḥ's other main exports, hides and stoneware (*naḥt*), are the products of small artisanal industries. Tanning has recently ceased, but salted skins were still being exported to the coast in the traditional bales of twenty (*khūrajah*) in 1980. Rāziḥ is also famous for its stone cooking utensils and oil lamps produced in the mines of al-Izid and al-Shawāriq (tribes in southern Rāziḥ), which have probably been traded throughout southwest Arabia since antiquity.[20]

Rāziḥ imported a variety of commodities from neighboring regions and abroad in the past. From the Tihāmah came grain, animals for meat, sesame oil, tobacco, matting, basketry, perfume, pottery, salt, lime and plaster, and cloth. From overseas, via Jīzān and Hodeidah, came sugar, tea, paraffin, matches, guns, ammunition, silver including coins, incense, snuff crystals (*duqduqah*), ceramic coffee cups (from China), and cloth, clothing, and a variety of brassware and utensils from Persia, India, and eastern Asia.[21] Animals were also imported from the mountains of Jumāʿah. And from or via the plateau in the east came fruits, especially grapes, raisins, pomegranates (from Ṣaḥār), and dates (from Najrān), acacia bark (*qaraḍ*) for tanning, iron for agricultural implements (from the ancient, now defunct, ironworks near Ṣaʿdah), hides in transit to the Tihāmah, sheepskins, handwoven rugs, blankets, and men's waistcoats of goat hair and wool, and (from villages near Ṣaʿdah) colorful baskets for displaying food and storing valuables. Some of these products were unable to compete with the foreign foodstuffs and commodities which flooded Rāziḥī markets from the 1970s, but others survived or even flourished.

Trade Routes and Markets

Goods are distributed within Rāziḥ through a network of weekly markets which spans the whole region, and forms a zone of intensive local trade. The steep terrain provides limited choices for routes and marketplaces. Although some were occasionally shifted short distances for political and security reasons, therefore, most seem to have stayed in much the same places for centuries. This is reflected in past efforts to pave and step difficult paths, and build wayside pools and shelters for travelers. Legend attributes much of this herculean labor to a divinely inspired philanthropist who paid builders with leaves which miraculously changed into coins. The overall stability of Rāziḥ's patterns of trade underlies the stability of its tribes, which are responsible for controlling and protecting the trade routes and markets within their respective territories. Markets are prestigious for shaykhs, and enhance their power and influence, and they usually live beside them. Those without a market in their tribe therefore sometimes try to inaugurate one, but lacking viable catchment areas, they tend to fail.

Markets are so spaced that no settlement is more than an hour or so's walk away from at least one, enabling shoppers to return home in time for the main midday meal.[22] It is shameful for men to eat in public because it suggests that their wives have withdrawn their services—a common method of protest. In common with other western mountains (Maclagan 1993:55), there were therefore no cafes in Rāziḥ until the advent of motor transport, when a few opened to serve outsiders. There was once a large warehouse-inn (*samsarah*) in al-Naẓīr where traveling merchants could stay, but most now stay with friends or in a mosque; markets often have mosques beside them to serve and attract visitors. Rāziḥī merchants used their own or friends' houses to store and bulk their goods.[23]

Until the late 1970s most sūqs were just areas of open ground where traders spread their wares. Some had small stone booths, and each had a special area for tethering pack animals, for sheep and cattle awaiting sale,

TABLE 1.1. THE WEEKLY MARKETS OF QAḌĀ RĀZIḤ BY TRIBE, 1980

	TRIBE	*DAY*	*SITE (if named)*
RĀZIḤ			
	Banalqām	Wed	al-Sifl
	Banī Asad	none	
	Banī Maʿīn	Wed	
	Banī Rabīʿah	Sat	Shaʿārah
	Birkān	none	
	Ghamar	Tues	Badr (Rishwayn)
		Fri	(Sawādī)
	al-Izid	none	
	Munabbih	Mon	Shaʿbān
	al-Naẓīr	Sun	*madīnah*
		Thurs	*madīnah*
	al-Shawāriq	Tues	
ʿUQĀRIB			
	Ālat al-ʿUṭayf	none	
	Banī ʿAbīd	none	
	Banī Ṣafwān	Thurs	Ḥijlah
	Banī Ṣayāḥ	none	
	al-Waqir	Fri	al-Ḍayʿah
	al-Wuqaysh	none	

and for butchers to do their work. During the consumer boom of the mid-1970s to the mid-1980s, these simple spaces were physically transformed by a flurry of shop-building (Weir 1987). But the rhythm of trade remained unchanged; sūqs were still empty most of the week, then filled with traders and a bustling throng of visitors on market days. Markets are important centers for male socializing, exchanging news, and political activities. There was once a special "chatting place" (*masmar*) in the marketplace of al-Naẓīr where traders gathered after trips, and—leaning on special stones—compared prices and enacted comic versions of their transactions. Men also routinely consult tribal leaders and judges in markets. And shaykhs make public announcements (sing. *ẓāhirah*) there, sometimes preceded by drumming to alert people's attention.

The topography of North Yemen dictates a distinctive pattern of long-distance trade. Two parallel routes run longitudinally down the plateau and

FIGURE 1.4
Market day in *madīnat* al-Naẓīr, 1977

the coast, and these are linked by a series of transverse routes which run roughly east-west across the mountains. One of the latter leaves the plateau near Ṣaʿdah in Ṣaḥār, winds through the mountains of Jumāʿah, branches off to run through the Khawlān massif, then arrives at Badr in Ghamar, the major entrepôt between Jumāʿah and Rāziḥ. From there the route enters Jabal Rāziḥ through its northeastern gateway, skirts Jabal Ḥurum, winds through the most important internal markets of Sūq Shaʿārah and Sūq al-Naẓīr, then plunges down the slopes of al-Naẓīr to Sūq al-Ḍayʿah in the ʿUqārib foothills. This was for centuries a vitally important transit station for the exchange of products between the highlands and the Tihāmah, and for transferring loads between mountain donkeys and camels, which cannot deal with coastal conditions, and coastal animals which are adapted to walking on sand but cannot climb. The Tihāmah entrepôt was not always at al-Ḍayʿah. In pre-Islamic times, and for centuries thereafter, it was sited—though not necessarily continuously—at al-Bār, which is now in the lower reaches of Naẓīrī territory.[24] During the nineteenth and early twentieth centuries it was shifted back and forth between various other sites in the foothills, including al-Ḍayʿah, because of insecurity on the coast. And in the 1920s it returned to al-Ḍayʿah, where it remained until its apparently final demise in 1985 (see Chapter Eight).

From al-Ḍayʿah the trade route continues west to Jīzān and places north, and south to Hodeidah via al-Malāḥīṭ, Khawlān's Tihāmah entrepôt at the mouth of Wādī Khulab.[25] The tribal regions of Ṣaḥār, Jumāʿah, Khawlān, Rāziḥ, and ʿUqārib, are thus joined by permanent arteries of trade. This, I argue, is a major factor underlying the politico-legal identity of Khawlān ibn ʿĀmir.

Travel on foot or with donkeys or camels between Rāziḥ and other regions was arduous and time-consuming. The journey from Rāziḥ to Ṣaʿdah in the east or to Jīzān in the west took two or three long days, from Ṣaʿdah to Sanaa a week, and from Rāziḥ to Hodeidah two weeks. Motor transport therefore revolutionized trade, and spelled the virtual demise of centuries of animal transport. Construction of the first surfaced road between Sanaa and Ṣaʿdah began in the early 1970s and was completed in 1979. And a rough trans-highland track to connect the plateau near Ṣaʿdah with the coast via Rāziḥ was begun in 1976, had reached the edge of Jabal Rāziḥ by 1977, but was not completed until 1981 because of funding problems and disputes over the route it should take through the massif. After this Rāziḥīs could reach Ṣaʿdah, Jīzān, and even Sanaa within one long day. After the completion of the Tihāmah highway in the 1990s, Hodeidah was also only a day away.

Settlements

The population of Rāziḥ is dispersed in hundreds of tiny hamlets of up to twenty or so houses which are dotted over the upper slopes of the massif, many perched on rocky promontories above sheer drops or long steep flights of terraces. The sizes of hamlets and houses correlate with the density of population, as shown in Table 1.2, which compares the most heavily populated tribe of Qaḍā Rāziḥ, al-Naẓīr, with the average for the sub-province.

Past concern for security is evident in the fortress-like structure of houses and their close configuration in settlements, and also in the existence of privately owned watchtowers, known as "outposts" (sing. *khārijah, ṭārifah*), which guard vulnerable slopes and tribal borders. Many summits in Jabal Rāziḥ and ʿUqārib are also crowned by forts built or rebuilt by the Ottomans, imāms, or other rulers, proclaiming the region to have been a pre-

FIGURE 1.5
Donkeys climbing through the mountains, 1979. *Madīnat* al-Naẓīr is on the horizon.

TABLE 1.2. SETTLEMENT PATTERNS IN QAḌĀ RĀZIḤ, 1975, AND IN SIX HAMLETS IN AL-NAẒĪR, 1980

Region	*Pop.*	*Settlements*	*Houses*	*Houses/ settlement*	*Pop./ settlement*
Qaḍā Rāziḥ	32,300	579	4,394	7.5	56
al-Naẓīr	1,045	6	79	13	174

Sources: Steffen et al. 1978: 62 (for Qaḍā Rāziḥ); fieldwork census, Oct. 1979–Feb. 1980
Note: Population figures include men temporarily working abroad

cious domain which was repeatedly contested by competing *dawlahs*, and sometimes ruled by force.

The two largest settlements in Qaḍā Rāziḥ are al-Qalʿah and the "town" (*madīnah*) of al-Naẓīr, both of which are strategically situated on the main trade route through Jabal Rāziḥ, and historically associated with state power. Al-Qalʿah (meaning "the fortress") is in "northern" (*shawāmī*) Rāziḥ, and lies at 2200 meters altitude southwest of Jabal Ḥurum. In 1975 it had a population of about four hundred people occupying nearly sixty houses (CPO 1978:80). States have always had their center (*markaz*) in or near present-day al-Qalʿah, although (according to oral history) the original eponymous fortress was built only in the early eighteenth century. The Governor of Rāziḥ always resides at al-Qalʿah; judges of Islamic law hold court there; the fortress houses a garrison of police and the local jail; and the grain tax, which was collected in kind, was stored until recently in its cavernous underground silo.

The *madīnah* of al-Naẓīr (my fieldwork base) is in "southern" (*yamānī*) Rāziḥ, and is the largest settlement in the sub-province, with a population (at the time of my census in 1980) of about nine hundred people living in over seventy houses. This little "town" sits on a high ridge of the western escarpment at 1800 meters, and has a large marketplace with a capacious "Friday" mosque, the largest in Qaḍā Rāziḥ, at its edge.[26] Although this settlement grew large, heterogeneous, and busy enough to merit being dubbed a *madīnah* only in the mid-twentieth century (Weir 1986), it has been a commercial, religious, and political center for centuries.

Al-Qalʿah and *madīnat* al-Naẓīr are both more socially and occupationally differentiated than other settlements. Al-Naẓīr, for example, contained members of about thirty agnatically unrelated patronymic groups in 1980, and members of all three status categories (to be described in the following chapter).[27] It would be mistaken, however, to characterize either in terms of a rural-urban dichotomy. They are essentially rural settlements, set among terraces many of which are owned or farmed by their residents; and they are tightly integrated by economic and social ties with their surrounding hamlets.

Houses

The traditional houses of Jabal Rāziḥ are towering stone mansions up to five storeys high, with small, shuttered windows and massive wooden (or nowadays metal) doors. On the windowless ground floors are byres for cattle and sheep, storerooms for farming equipment, seed grain, fodder, and traders' stocks, and sometimes a stone rotary quern—a relict from before mechanical flour mills were introduced in the 1970s. Old houses also have an underground grain silo (*madfan*) for storing sorghum—a vitally important hedge against periodic shortages in the days before the importation of foreign grain. From the entrance a gloomy stone staircase leads off at each landing to one or two rooms. The smaller rooms (sing. *khalwah*) are

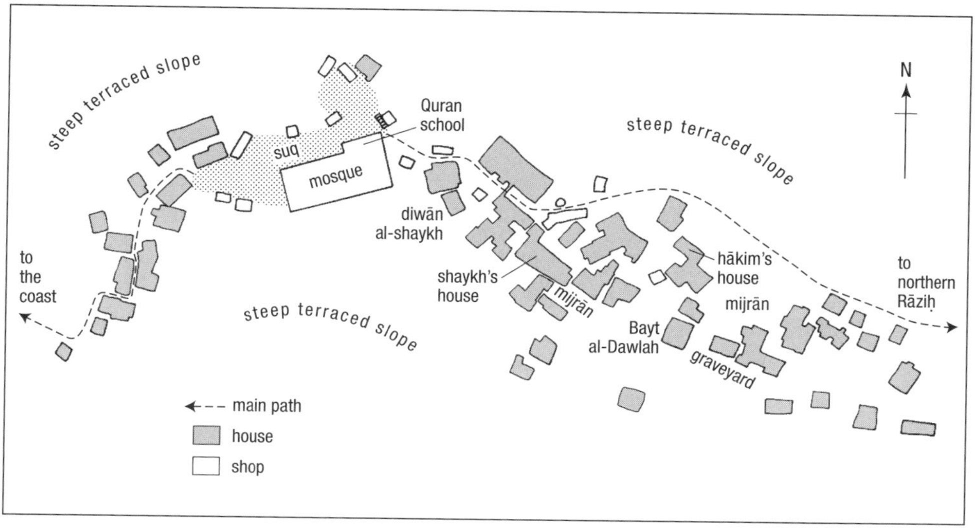

FIGURE 1.6
Plan of *madīnat* al-Naẓīr, 1977. Source: Survey by Ian Dunn and Shelagh Weir, 1977

FIGURE 1.7
View of *madīnat* al-Naẓīr, 1977

controlled by married women who hold the key; there they keep their dowry jewelry and clothes locked in trunks, entertain female friends, sleep with their children, and receive their husbands at night. Larger rooms (sing. *dīwān*) are used by the whole family for eating, socializing, sleeping, and putting up guests. Men also conduct their business there, or in a grander room (*mafraj*) on the top storey with large decorative windows—a recent architectural fashion copied from Sanaa. Rooms are sparsely furnished with rugs, mattresses, and cushions. Near the top of each house are one or more dingy, smoke-blackened kitchens (sing. *daymah*) and large jars or tanks of constantly replenished water. On the flat roofs above, women wash and dry clothes, drape bedding to air, spread grain and coffee cherries to dry, and thresh and winnow grain.

Houses are the main permanent way of displaying wealth, as distinct from the main transient ways—giving guests lavish meals, or conspicuously consuming top-quality qāt. Politicians and big merchants, who all "work from home," therefore generally have bigger houses than others; the three largest mansions in al-Naẓīr, for example, were built in the nineteenth century by the governor of southern Rāziḥ, the shaykh of the tribe, and a big coffee merchant, ʿAbdallāh ʿAlī (whose house is pictured in the first color plate). The first two were still inhabited by descendants of their original owners in the 1980s, and the third had been fragmented by inheritance, and housed six unrelated households—*sic transit gloria*.

Houses are tightly clustered in settlements, and sometimes abut to form large, asymmetrical complexes with internal connections. Beside them are yards where cows are tethered, manure is heaped "to cool," firewood is stockpiled, and huts are placed for storing sorghum stalks and boiling their heads (an important preservation method). Some households also own underground cisterns for storing rainfall runoff, either adjacent to their houses or on a nearby terrace. Settlements also have common spaces (*mijrān* or *manāfis*) for threshing and winnowing grain, and where circumcision ceremonies and other public gatherings are held; some also have graveyards and tiny neighborhood mosques.

Households

The primary units of landowning and of production and consumption are patriarchal households (sing. *bayt*). These are always named after the senior male (*rāʿī al-bayt*)—for example, "*bayt* Muḥammad" meaning Muḥammad's household, or (if they constitute an extended family)

"Muḥammad's compound" (*ḥawsh* Muḥammad). There is also a small minority of households headed by widowed or divorced women of independent means, for which there is no corresponding title—reflecting the cognitive and actual dominance of patriarchal units. Patriarchal households are based on the conjugal relationship, and depending on their stage in the life cycle and the economic circumstances of their adult males, comprise a man, his wife or wives, their unmarried children, their married sons and their wives and children, and elderly relatives, such as a widow of the former household head. Men can establish their own households only once they have independent means—typically after inheriting land and other property from their fathers or another relative, but sometimes earlier if they secure independent employment.[28]

Households are defined as eating from the same kitchen, and the inauguration of a new household is marked by the creation of a new kitchen, or simply by the installation of a separate oven on a landing. Thenceforth, household members provide for themselves and cook and eat apart—sometimes at different ends of a room which was formerly jointly owned, but is now in divided ownership.[29] If families expand, the house is extended vertically or laterally, or men hive off and build elsewhere, often selling their share in the house to a brother who remains. People prefer to keep houses in exclusively family ownership, and most are inhabited by agnatically related households, some of whom can be renters. Because of the fragmenting effect of Islamic inheritance law, however, houses and their associated properties are often under multiple ownership. For this reason, and because of demographic pressures and immigration, about a tenth of houses in densely populated al-Naẓīr contain unrelated households. The average household size for Qaḍā Rāziḥ as a whole in 1975 was about 6 persons, including temporarily absent workers, and the average number of households per house in ʿUqārib was 1, in Ghamar 1.2, and in Jabal Rāziḥ 1.3.[30] In the tribe of al-Naẓīr, however, the most densely populated in Rāziḥ, the average household size in 1979–80 was 6.6 persons, and households averaged nearly 2 per house (see Table 1.3).

Most households depend on farming their own or others' land, and a large minority on trade, craft-production, or the provision of specialized services. Some non-farming occupations are full-time, while others provide only occasional employment and minor income; some are also restricted to low status categories (see Chapter Two). Rāziḥīs who pursue non-farming occupations tend to live in areas of commercial agriculture, and near major

TABLE 1.3. RESIDENCE PATTERN IN SEVEN SETTLEMENTS IN THE TRIBE OF AL-NAẒĪR, 1980

Settlement	*Pop.*	*Houses*	*House-holds*	*House-holds/ house*	*Pop./ household*	*Pop./ house*
The *madīnah*	877	71	123	1.7	7	12.4
Ilt Rāshid	334	22	44	2	7.5	15.1
al-Farq	218	18	41	2.2	5.3	12.1
Ilt al-Burmī	136	11	17	1.5	8	12.3
Shibāb	137	12	24	2	5.7	11.4
Qulal al-ʿUqab	138	8	22	2.7	6.2	17.2
Shaṭūr	82	8	12	1.5	6.8	8.2
Totals	**1,922**	**150**	**283**			
Averages				**1.9**	**6.6**	**12.6**

Source: Fieldwork census, Oct. 1979–Feb. 1980

markets. For that reason, only half the men surveyed in the tribe of al-Naẓīr claimed land or farming as their *main* source of income, though many of the rest gained some income from agriculture—for example, from leasing out a few terraces or from seasonal labor. Men also derive income and capital from renting out vehicles, rooms, and shops, and from brideprice payments (always high in relation to wages) when they marry off daughters. Rāziḥī men are generally extremely enterprising and hardworking; as in other cash-cropping areas (see Gerholm 1977: 66), many engage in several occupations simultaneously, or successively through the year; and as new economic niches opened up during the 1970s, they rapidly and eagerly filled them. From the late 1970s, a large minority of men, mainly youths, took laboring jobs in ʿAsīr, the proceeds of which went chiefly toward marriage expenses, house building, or trading investments (see Weir 1987). However, work and wages in Saudi Arabia dwindled from the mid-1980s, and ceased abruptly when the Saudi government expelled its Yemeni guest-workers after the 1990 Iraqi invasion of Kuwait.

There is a relatively rigid, gender-based division of labor in Rāziḥ, with little overlap between male and female tasks. Muslim men are legally obliged to provide for their households and have the right to be served, and women have the right to be supported and the duty to serve. Rāziḥī prac-

TABLE 1.4. MAIN SOURCES OF INCOME OF A SAMPLE OF 450 MEN IN THE TRIBE OF AL-NAẒĪR, INCLUDING THE *MADĪNAH*, OCT. 1979 – FEB. 1980

Main source of income	*Number*	*%*
Land (178/39%) or agricultural labor (49/11%)	227	50
Shopkeeping, general trading	121	27
Qat trading	42	9
Services	54	12
Driving	33	7
Working in Saudi Arabia	55	12
[of which multiple responses]	[−82]	[−17]
Totals	**450**	**100**

Note: Informants were asked for their main occupations or sources of income. The sample represented just under half the males over age 15 in the tribe of al-Naẓīr at the time of the first national census in 1975. A sample excluding the *madīnah* would have shown a higher proportion of men dependent mainly on farming.

tice conforms to this injunction. Men are responsible for most agricultural tasks: building and repairing terrace walls; clearing landfalls; working the soil; sowing, planting, and tending crops; irrigating terraces; and threshing and winnowing grain with draught animals (though women help using flails and trays). Men also virtually monopolize commercial agriculture, trade, craft work, and service occupations.

Women are responsible for child care, managing the household stores, chopping wood, food processing, cooking, washing clothes and utensils, and tidying and cleaning; and before the introduction of motorized mills in the 1970s, they spent hours a day grinding flour. Women also care for domestic animals, and milk cows and churn milk to make buttermilk (*ḥaqīn*) and clarified butter (*saman*)—a prestigious domestic product which is flaunted at feasts. Their main agricultural tasks are weeding, growing legumes and green vegetables for domestic consumption, and harvesting sorghum and storing its grain, stalks, and leaves. They also pick coffee and fruit for the household, and pack qāt for market. A minority of mainly low-status women peddle pottery, fruits, and other commodities around weekly markets, or run tiny shops in their houses to serve other women. But with these exceptions, women do not trade or even shop unless they are bereft

FIGURE 1.8
Ploughing a large terrace in al-Naẓīr, early 1977

of menfolk, for men decree the sūq and commerce to be exclusively male domains.[31]

Women's three most onerous tasks outside the house are fetching fodder, water, and fuel. These regular expeditions (sing. *barāḥah*) demand immense strength and stamina because of the steep terrain and the distance of sources from settlements. Not for nothing is the common female greeting "*Quwwah!*" meaning "May you be strong!" Girls and younger women fetch drinking water from springs in deep clefts several times a day. If their household has animals, they collect fodder from precipitous *qafarah* slopes about five days a week. And until recently most made astonishingly arduous treks to fetch firewood from the *qafarah* areas over a thousand meters below their settlements twice or three times a week. These prodigious female tasks were therefore substantially alleviated from the late 1970s by the widespread building of household cisterns, the trucking of water and firewood along the new motor tracks, and the advent of bottled gas.

It will be evident that the maintenance of households requires a huge investment of time and effort. Almost all the productive activity which is essential to people's livelihoods and sheer survival is labor-intensive and physically demanding. Every capable member must therefore pull his or her weight, including children.

Economic Relations

Few households are self-sufficient in labor or resources. All therefore depend on a variety of partnerships and exchanges to manage their affairs and tide them over crises.[32] If landowners have non-farming occupations, or inadequate family labor, they lease terraces to tenants called "partners" (sing. *sharīk*) for a specified number of years and a proportion of the crop. In 1980 Naẓīrī sharecroppers usually paid the owner half the crop (in cash or kind) on irrigated land and land planted with cash crops, and one third on rain-fed grain land, and were also responsible for all inputs such as manure and seed, as well as for paying the canonical taxes "off the top" of the crop (before the division).[33] Animals are also sharecropped. Cows can be leased out for an agreed proportion of their calves, milk, and manure, and people sometimes buy a calf or lamb jointly, and share its products or meat according to their respective inputs—something often done in anticipation of ʿĪd al-Aḍḥā, the religious Feast of Sacrifice. Laborers (sing. *shāqī*) are hired for short-term labor needs, such as for ploughing, picking coffee (December–February), and harvesting and packing qāt (all year round), the daily wage being determined by the going rate and the worker's skills.

There is no evidence that sharecroppers or wage laborers ever constituted a dependent and subservient economic or social class in Rāziḥ as in regions with major and enduring inequalities in landownership such as the Tihāmah and the Taʿizz-Ibb region.[34] Neither is any stigma attached in Rāziḥ to being an agricultural tenant; in fact landowners are often also *sharīks* or *shāqīs*, typically working a neighbor's terraces as well as their own. As elsewhere in highland Yemen, the relationship between landowner and agricultural laborer is therefore often one of social equals.

The whole spectrum of trade and artisanal industry is characterized by a similar diversity of working relationships based on wage employment, or on partnerships (sing. *shirākah*) for small-scale capital investment and profit-sharing. Although most economic enterprises are household or family based, it is also common for non-kin to be employed as *shāqīs* to compensate for deficits in family labor at peak periods such as ploughing or harvest times. Individuals also enter into partnerships to share the profits (or losses) from trade, transportation, butchery, building, or running shops, artisanal workshops, flour mills, or generators. It is customary to offer credit in commercial transactions, so wholesalers, retailers, service providers, transporters, and customers are also bound to one another by multiple ties of indebtedness.[35] These relationships frequently cross-cut descent groups (clans) and status categories. Partly because of the difficulty of travel in the steep terrain, however, most economic interaction takes place between people who live near one another; proximity, common interests, and mutual trust and liking can be more important than ascriptive ties. People also prefer to forge economic links with members of the same tribe because disputes are more easily settled internally than when they become "inter-tribal." Striking evidence of this preference was provided by my survey of the market of al-Naẓīr, which showed the overwhelming majority of shopkeepers to be Naẓīrī (see Table 1.5).

Everyday economic relations are governed by principles of generosity and mutual aid which are among the primary ideals of "tribalism" (*qabyalah*) (Adra 1982, 1985). Every act and gift is noted and evaluated, and failure to reciprocate can weaken the relationship. People constantly cooperate in countless informal but vitally important ways—exchanging food and water, carrying goods and messages for one another, and, most important, lending each other money, agricultural and other equipment, draught animals, and labor. These exchanges, called *ʿārah-wa-baddah,* were particularly important in the past when cash was short, or household labor was insufficient for urgent tasks such as harvesting, carrying tree trunks to building sites, or clearing collapsed terraces. A herald (*dawshān*) then beat his drum in the sūq or other announcement place, and the "crier" (*muẓhir*) called for help. If he could afford it, the recipient would reward

TABLE 1.5. RESIDENCE OF SHOPKEEPERS IN THE MARKET OF AL-NAẒĪR, EARLY 1980

Residence	*Number*	*Percentage*
The *madīnah*	60	42
Other Naẓīrī settlements	73	52
Neighboring tribes	5	4
Not known	3	2
TOTALS	141	100

Source: Fieldwork census

his helpers by slaughtering an animal and giving them a meal. But people often volunteered their help without immediate reward, knowing that others would help them in similar circumstances.[36]

Another form of mutual help, called *chawī,* based on verbal agreement and trust, involves farmers exchanging days of labor.[37] People also clubbed together to help those whose livelihoods were threatened by calamities. One custom involved the owner of a bullock or camel which had died severing its tail, and placing it under a stone in a reception room; the gathered men would then subscribe toward buying him a new animal. Such mutual aid is fundamentally based on a sense of common interest, and the principle of delayed or generalized reciprocity. This is evident, nowadays, when cars fall off the perilous new motor tracks (which they often do), when other drivers immediately gather to haul them back. A procession of men passed by one day to rescue a car, and when I asked my companion if he was going to help, he replied, "No, I don't have a car." If he *had* felt part of this local Automobile Association, he would have automatically joined the helpers.

Women are particularly dependent on reciprocal relationships with their neighbors. Female neighborhood groups are visible every morning when small processions of women set off to fetch water, fodder, and firewood together, and every afternoon when they huddle in their yards or houses to relax and chat after their main chores are done. Neighborhood women share their yards and woodpiles, lend each other utensils and labor, give food or water when reserves run low, take care of each other's children, and help out with domestic work when their friends give birth, fall sick, go away to visit relatives, or prepare feasts. This interdependence is expressed in the wry saying, "Weddings [are enjoyable] for the families but a bother for the neighbors." These cooperative ties are fundamentally based on proximity, and although neighbors are often related because of the dominant pattern of spatially close marriage (see Chapter Three), are equally strong between unrelated households. Each household is therefore enmeshed in a dense web of inter-dependence with its close neighbors, and is attached by looser strands to other hamlets in the same area of the mountains. This is the tightly woven fabric from which tribes are constructed.

CHAPTER TWO

Social and Political Inequality

The people of Rāziḥ are differentiated and ranked according to several criteria, innate and ascribed, with profound effects on their potential for wielding power or influence. Men monopolize the politico-legal sphere as a taken-for-granted gender right, while discriminating among themselves on the basis of age, descent, and occupation. A minority of men is therefore socially and politically advantaged, while a majority of men, and all women, are disadvantaged or subordinated. This chapter outlines, in necessarily schematic fashion, the values, rituals, and behaviors which express and sustain this institutionalized inequality, with particular focus on those pertinent to understanding the politico-legal system of Rāziḥ.

From Boyhood to Manhood

Small boys are defined as "ignorant" (sing. *jāhil*), but from around the age of six they start acquiring moral, social, and religious sensibility (*ʿaql*). Thenceforth they are expected to start behaving like responsible adults, deferring to older males, helping their fathers at work, and eschewing female social gatherings. At around this time their fathers present them with their first dagger set (*jihāz*, literally "equipment") comprising a curved, steel dagger (*jambiyyah*) in an angled sheath attached to a broad belt. Daggers are the quintessential symbols of masculinity, and

FIGURE 2.1
Men doing a dagger dance during a circumcision ceremony, *madīnat* al-Naẓīr, 1979

the focus of great interest and attention. They have histories, pedigrees, and reputations; hilts, scabbards, and belts are often expensively decorated with silver and gold; and blades are kept sharp and gleaming so that they glint when youths wave them during dances.[1]

Soon after receiving their daggers boys are circumcised during theatrical and noisy ceremonies (sing. *khiṭān*). These are usually held at the annual "Feast of Sacrifice" (*ʿīd al-aḍḥā*) when Muslims are enjoined to slaughter animals to invite God's blessings during the coming year. The ceremonies are usually shared by several age-mates (sing. *sāyir*) who are invariably neighbors and sometimes related, and are always held in an open space, such as a threshing-floor, adjacent to their homes. Each ceremony is thus identified with a particular hamlet or neighborhood, and binds friends and playmates in a public drama of high emotion and stoically endured pain.

In the Naẓīrī ceremonies I witnessed in the late 1970s, the boys to be circumcised performed dagger dances (*yidarrimū*) for two or three days before the main ceremony. Then early on the first day of *ʿīd,* before an audience of older men, children, and heavily veiled women ("offstage" on the rooftops), youths (*shibāb*) gathered from other hamlets and formed a large revolving circle (*ḥalīqah*), stepping and bobbing in unison while poetic

FIGURE 2.2
A circumcision ceremony, *madīnat* al-Naẓīr, 1979

cheerleaders exchanged rhyming badinage in high-pitched chants (sing. *maghrad*), poking fun at each other's hamlets (see Caton 1990). At intervals men fired guns in celebration, then the boys were led into the circle, deftly circumcised to the deafening crackle of gunshots and firecrackers, then whisked off to their houses for their wounds to be tended, whimperers being exhorted to "Be manly!" (*tarajjal*). The youths continued their stomping and poetic ripostes, then walked in procession to the marketplace, where they performed line dances (*baraʿ*, *muthallath, murabbaʿ*) in threes and fours, waving their daggers in unison, and flaunting their vigor and grace (see Adra 1982); then they entered the mosque for midday prayers. Later the boys' fathers entertained friends and relatives to a banquet, then socialized while chewing qāt. That same afternoon the boys' female relatives and neighbors brought them small gifts of money—one of the many reciprocal exchanges by which women sustain local networks.

Through the symbolism of place, dance, poetry, and hospitality, circumcision ceremonies clearly reflect and reinforce key aspects of the social order of Rāziḥ: age and gender hierarchies; the value of friendships with peers and neighbors; and the identities of neighborhoods, hamlets, and tribes. The large gathering, and the mocking banter of the men in the *ḥalīqah,* which would be grossly insulting between members of different tribes, flaunted their intimacy, solidarity, and numbers to visitors invited from "abroad" (*min khārij*), while glossing over divisions and conflicts. Rāziḥīs see circumcisions as primarily religious ceremonies, however, and take for granted their "tribal" meanings as part of the natural scheme of things.

Circumcision ceremonies mark the beginning of the transition to manhood, an essential part of which is the acquisition of religious knowledge (see Caton 1990:26–27; Messick 1993). Fathers teach their small sons the rudiments of Muslim doctrine and prayer rituals at home, then encourage them to attend the mosque, where they are beckoned into line and copy the prayer movements of the men. And a minority of boys who can be freed from work, or whose families have a tradition of religious scholarship, study the Quran with scholar-jurists (sing. *faqīh*). A boy's completion of the Quran is celebrated with a small ceremony called the *khaṭṭāmah,* from the verb meaning "to seal and complete," in which he recites from the holy book while joining in a procession with fellow students between the Quran school and home. Like circumcision ceremonies, therefore, the *khaṭṭāmah* ceremony links home, locality, and religion (see Messick 1993:81–82).

At puberty boys sport obligatory mustaches, and when they are fully fledged "youths" (*shibāb*), grow small beards. This is seen as both a religious obligation and a sign of manhood—specifically men's social and physical strength. Men who shave while living outside Yemen therefore regrow their hair before returning to avoid being ridiculed as emasculated and "weak" (*ḍaʿīf*). Related to this, men's faces and heads are the symbolic locus of their integrity and authority. It is a serious insult (*ihānah*) to touch another man's head (except when joshing with intimate friends), and especially to seize his beard, which is a repository of his dignity and

FIGURE 2.3
Graduates of the Quran school, *madīnat* al-Naẓīr, 1977. The Quran teacher, the *faqīh* Ḍayf Allāh Manṣūr (*right*), his son (*left*), and Sharaf Muḥsin Abū Ṭālib (*center*), the then school director, are standing behind.

integrity (*sharaf*). When a man makes a promise, he grasps his beard, or strokes his finger down his cheek, saying "by my face" (*fī wajhī*). Facial metaphors are also much employed in politics; tribal leaders, for example, are often referred to as *wujīh al-qabīlah,* literally "the faces of the tribe," best translated as "the tribal authorities" or "representatives of the tribe." *Shibāb* also discard the skullcaps of childhood, and after a period when they often go bareheaded (perhaps as a sign of "modernity"), they begin to wear turbans as symbols of mature manhood. Turbans represent status and authority, and are important instruments of persuasion during political and legal negotiations.

Men (sing. *rajul* or *rajjāl*) should be strong (*qawī*) and assertive—especially *shibāb,* the epitome of the masculine ideal. People particularly admire the physical strength and stamina of farmers, traders, and builders, and the rhetorical strength of tribal leaders, whose forceful, clever speeches can promote their followers' interests. An important way men demonstrate their strength is by manifestly controlling their women. The marital relationship therefore makes men vulnerable; wives can be discreet about their husbands' weaknesses, or as Maclagan (1993) describes, can subvert their pretensions by gossip and insubordination. Men especially dread their wives' publicizing their poverty, which is considered an especially shameful condition.

Daggers denote status category (see below), and the *qabīlī*-style dagger worn upright at the front is explicitly equated with masculine virtues, and especially with the imperative to appear invincible. Once they become *shibāb,* therefore, men generally wear their daggers whenever they go out in order to project their masculine strength. As one explained as he buckled on his *jihāz* to visit the sūq: "I *must* wear it or people will think I'm weak (*ḍaʿīf*)." This does not, however, mean that daggers are often used aggressively; on the contrary, they are mainly used for mundane cutting tasks. There are strong sanctions against hot-headed physical aggression, and bloody violence is rare and abhorred. Daggers are associated more with the *maintenance* of order than its desecration, for they are routinely given as pledges of submission to legal process. Similar significance and constraint apply to guns; they also symbolize strength and violence, are expensive prestige items, and are deposited as legal sureties. They are not, however, identified with their owners as daggers are, and are usually kept locked away in trunks along with money, letters, documents, and other valuables. Guns are mainly "worn" for important inter-tribal meetings or confrontations, when they represent the tribe's political and military might; and they are invariably fired in jubilation during ceremonies. Less often, they are used in defense and war. But firing with hostile intent in peacetime is strictly forbidden in tribal law.

Men ideally marry shortly after puberty, depending on family means. The groom's side must make several payments to legalize a marriage: a brideprice (*difaʿ*) to the bride's father, which is seen as compensating him for the loss of her labor, and which is paid in three or more annual installments; a dowry (*mahr*) of jewelry to the bride, which she keeps if divorced; and a small money gift (*shibrah*) for the bride's mother, which acknowledges the great importance in this culture of the mother-daughter bond. The groom must also present his bride with a trousseau (*kiswah*) of clothing and other articles, but in contrast to elsewhere in Yemen (Mundy 1995:126–138), the bride's father does not endow her with anything.

Marriage expenses have always been hefty, so fathers formerly arranged and financed their sons' marriages. However, when young men started earning high wages in Saudi Arabia in the late 1970s, responsibility for funding marriage shifted onto them. At the same time, as throughout Yemen, there was rampant inflation in marriage payments fueled by wage rises and profits from qāt exports. This had political implications. By demanding high brideprices, the paternal generation was effectively siphoning off a high proportion of young men's wages, and thereby reducing the potential threat the latter's newfound economic independence might have posed to their own social and political dominance.[2]

The bride's father distributes part of the *difaʿ* in small money presents (sing. *sharṭ*) to her paternal and maternal uncles and their sons, and to selected other relatives and friends, including milk siblings. These gifts help maintain and perpetuate the agnatic relationships which constitute hamlet-based clans, the most important groups below tribes, and the affinal and neighborly relationships which link clans and hamlets within tribes, and tribes within Rāziḥ. Both the donation and reception of these gifts are discretionary. If men accept the *sharṭ,* they and their women must visit the bride with small money gifts on every religious feast-day thereafter, and during the forty-day period of work-free pampering she enjoys after childbirth. But if they refuse the *sharṭ* or are not offered it, inter-family relations are weakened. Marriage is therefore a moment for structural adjustment.

Marriage does not substantially affect a youth's standing. Until he acquires the means to become a "household head" (*rāʿī al-bayt*) in his own right, which is usually after he inherits from his father, he remains subordinate to the senior men of his family.

Older men are supposed to embody a calmer, wiser, more conciliatory strength than the more headstrong and frivolous *shibāb,* and to be pillars of the community from among whom the elders and shaykhs of their tribes are chosen. When their hair grays and their bodies weaken, they finally transform into "old men" (sing. *shaybah*), and retire from manual labor to be supported by their sons. However, political and legal specialists tend to work to the end.

From Girlhood to Womanhood

Girls begin doing adult tasks around the same age as boys, and are likewise admired for their ability to work hard. Men say "Better a strong woman than a pretty face." Women are also proud of their strength, boasting of the loads they carry and the distances they climb. As girls approach puberty they start avoiding male spaces and gatherings where women are not allowed: qāt parties, political meetings, public ceremonies, mosques, and markets (although exceptions are made for women without men who must do their own shopping, and for low-status peddler-women). Although men disparage women's religious knowledge and practices, piety is as important to them as it is to men. Girls learn to pray from their mothers, who do so regularly in the home, and girls and women fast during Ramaḍān and at other times. Before the republican era, however, almost all girls and women were illiterate.

Small girls are modestly dressed in miniature versions of adult clothing—bonnets and dresses when small, then later headscarves, and long dresses over ankle-length trousers. Small variations in women's outfits once indicated a woman's region or tribe, but these were submerged by the glittery new fashions of the 1970s. Trousers symbolize women's inherent impurity, and their potential for disgracing men; men therefore sometimes invoke them, or even display them, to insult their opponents during the melodramatic rhetoric of political confrontation. As girls approach puberty, they smear their faces with green leaf juice—a distinctive Rāziḥī custom which is protective and cosmetic. Most, except low-status women, also don all-concealing opaque black veils outside the house, signaling their readiness for marriage (a custom which has become more widespread since the 1970s). They do not, however, hide their faces from male agnates and affines, milk siblings, or close neighbors.

After marriage, a girl is handed over into the safekeeping of another family, who might be unrelated, and starts working for a new household and interacting with new neighbors. It is these changes, and not the sexual or reproductive aspects of marriage, which are most emphasized in the small commensal rituals and processions of the wedding (*hōd*).

A girl's primary socio-political identity and affiliation are unchanged by marriage. She continues to be named after her father—for example "Fāṭimit Muḥammad," meaning "Fāṭimah daughter of Muḥammad"—and remains a member of her natal clan and tribe, and ideally politically loyal to them. This means that her close male agnates, in the first instance, and by extension her clan and tribe, retain responsibility for her welfare and protection. If her husband maltreats her, for example, her father or brothers should intervene or take her back. These rights and responsibilities are also reflected in the marriage rituals and exchanges. The substantial brideprice and trousseau acknowledge a girl's social value, and dignify and legitimize submitting her into the care of "strangers," which would otherwise be shameful (this obviously varies according to the social distance between the families). As important, the bride's relatives *deliver* her to the groom's home during the wedding; the groom's side does not *take* her. Because giving is coercive in this culture, demanding appropriate reciprocation, this means the wife givers retain the upper hand with regard to her subsequent fate.

Most women are debilitated early by their unremitting labor and childbearing, and are generally worn out by their forties, when they are defined as "useless" (sing. *ʿajūzah*); there is little compassion for physical frailty in this tough culture. Women are committed to drudgery by the demanding environment, and by the dominant masculine ideology; any man who helped with "female" tasks would be severely ridiculed. Women's potential for improving their positions is also undermined by the fact that, as elsewhere in Yemen (Mundy 1979, 1995), their brothers or husbands often gain control of their inheritances.[3]

Women's Role in Politics

Women are barred from playing any formal or public roles in the politico-legal system. They cannot be tribal leaders or legal specialists, and they are disenfranchised with respect to the fundamental rights and duties of most men—choosing leaders, contributing to collective expenses, and engaging in military action. They must also rely on men to represent their legal interests. And they are excluded from the places where men conduct business and exchange news—mosques, markets, and male qāt parties. This is disempowering symbolically, by implying women's inferiority, and practically, by restricting their access to information—although women strive to overcome this disadvantage by incessant questioning and surveillance.

Men justify women's political subordination on the grounds that they are innately "deficient in good sense, piety, and inheritance." Rāziḥī women, for their part, lack the education to create an alternative political ideology which imagines female emancipation or equality, and therefore regard male domination as natural. Although men casually denigrate "women" in general, however, they implicitly concede their knowledge and wisdom by seeking and often heeding the advice of those close to them. Women therefore influence men, and not only their relatives; they can also act as moral arbiters in tribal affairs, and sometimes goad their men into military action by loud ululations, or (unintentionally ironic) cries of "Are you all *women*!"

Despite being relegated to the wings of public affairs, behind the scenes and downplayed by men, women also play vital practical roles in the politico-legal process. The most important is in food preparation. Food is as important to meetings and litigation as it is to socializing and rites of passage. The prestige and influence of leaders and officials depends, in part, on providing generous hospitality for important visitors; and reconciliation between disputing groups is invariably sealed by shared banquets. This all depends on substantial female labor. Behind every prominent man who sweeps in to his guests bearing baskets of bread and bowls of food with an effortless flourish is a small, invisible workforce of women from his own and neighboring households whose combined exertions are essential to his performance and success. In addition, women have the vital task of supplying food, water, and other necessities to men on guard duty or at war.

Women also sustain the neighborhood relationships which are vital to all men by countless daily gestures of reciprocal sociability and generosity. They also mediate their children's marriages, and influence the dominant pattern of spatially close marriage by their eagerness for their daughters to intermarry with friends and close to home. And they deliberately forge permanent, intimate "milk" relationships with unrelated families, including those of inferior or superior status, by suckling their babies, which precludes intermarriage, but enables their children to behave like close agnates or affines. If a woman is an inadequate friend and neighbor, therefore, both

FIGURE 2.4
Cafe woman making bread for customers, Ghamar, 1977

she and her husband are socially impoverished, and a politically active man could scarcely function.

It follows that one of the most powerful acts of protest a wife can perform is to "flee" (*tifirr*) to her natal home if her husband displeases her. He must then persuade her to return with apologies and gifts, and lodge a gun-bond with her father or brothers, and sometimes slaughter an animal, to show contrition and intent to mend his ways. This institutionalized withdrawal of labor and services (found throughout the Middle East) debilitates a man's household, and publicly humiliates him by showing he cannot control his wife. As Maclagan (1993:214) notes, such female defiance also undermines and demystifies the image men wish to project of their own self-sufficiency by exposing their dependency. The denial of dependency in symbiotic relationships is an important theme in Rāziḥī culture, extending from gender relations at one end of the spectrum, to state-tribe relations at the other.

Women also play an important, though more passive, political role as objects of marriage exchanges. In contrast to the situation in much of the Middle East, Rāziḥīs state no preference for marrying paternal cousins (FBD/FBS), and the small proportion of such marriages that occur should be understood as part of the general pattern of spatially close marriage.[4] On the Naẓīrī evidence, most marriages take place within the same tribe, and most of those between members of the same or neighboring settlements. This must be partly attributed to property considerations, especially if a girl stands to inherit a nearby building or terraces (see Mundy 1995), and partly to the immense importance of economic partnerships and neighborhood relations. Political considerations are an additional factor. Men expect their affines, as much as their agnates, to help them in disputes, so prefer them close at hand. Spatially close marriage strengthens ties between the people of the same and neighboring hamlets (who are often already agnatically related) and helps consolidate localized clans. The minority of extra-tribal marriages are mainly contracted by traders, and members of the tribal and religious elite, who further their particular economic and political interests by creating wider affinal connections.

Inter-tribal marriages have special political significance because "affinal rights and obligations" (*ḥaqq al-ḥasab*) are generalized to tribes—all of whose members are regarded as classificatory affines. All the men of a woman's natal tribe are thus considered to be in loco parentis to her, and hold the men of her husband's tribe collectively responsible for her welfare. Women married into other tribes are called *ḥamāyil* (sing. *ḥamīlah*), which connotes "responsibility"; women therefore metonymically symbolize the identity of tribes, and their collective liabilities. This is manifested in the fact that when a man visits another tribe, he should pay a courtesy call on any nearby house inhabited by a *ḥamīlah* from his tribe, and the latter can formally complain to her shaykh if a man shirks this duty. This custom reminds an exogamously married woman, and her husband's family, of her natal tribe's enduring concern for her welfare. It also helps maintain her primary political loyalty, and means that each tribe has a small female "fifth column" in other tribes. This is important during inter-tribal strife when *ḥamīlah*s can shelter fellow tribesmen, or provide them with "intelligence."

The generalizing of affinal relationships to entire tribes is demonstrated and reinforced by the hospitality etiquette of circumcision ceremonies. If the boy's mother is a "foreigner" (*min khārij*), instead of his father inviting her male relatives casually, as when they are from the same tribe, he must send them a formal, written invitation (*kafāl*). Provided this is properly worded, and sent in good time, it is benevolently "accepted" (*maqbūl*), and only one or two representatives attend the ceremony—typically the boy's maternal uncles (*akhwāl*). However, if the boy's father defaults on this courtesy, it is considered an insult—not only to his affines, but to their

TABLE 2.1 MARRIAGE PATTERNS IN THE TRIBE OF AL-NAẒĪR, 1980

Residences of husbands of 370 ever-married women from six Naẓīrī hamlets and the *madīnah.*

Husband's residence	***Number***	***Percentage***
Same settlement	91	24.6
Close settlement (up to 20 mins. walk away)	154	41.6
Same tribe, more distant settlement	34	9.2
Bordering tribe in Jabal Rāziḥ	51	13.8
Other tribe in Jabal Rāziḥ	21	5.7
ʿUqārib tribe	2	0.6
Khawlān	10	2.7
The *mashriq* (Ṣaʿdah region)	3	0.8
Elsewhere in Yemen	4	1.0
Totals	**370**	**100%**

Source: Fieldwork census, 1979–80

entire tribe. The offended family reacts by notifying its shaykh, he musters "large numbers" of other tribesmen, and they all descend on the ceremony uninvited, and stay with the boy's father for several days. Though they sometimes bring sheep with them, to show they mean no harm, they still inflict expense and ridicule on their hapless host. As we shall see, such coercive demands for hospitality are common in the politico-legal sphere.

Male "Honor"

Men's reputations are extremely precious to them, and are highly vulnerable in this face-to-face community with its acute sensitivity to deviation (Messick 1993:179), efficient dissemination of information, and predisposition to defamation. The ideal man should be pious and law-abiding, and fulfill his social, legal, and political duties to his family, clan, and tribe. He should also be hospitable and generous, reciprocate invitations and favors, and honor his debts. Wealth is therefore very important—to the extent that the poor are socially almost invisible. During my census, a man asked, after naming the residents of his house: "There are also some poor people; do you want them too?" The ideal man should also manifest his ability to protect and control his vital interests. This is the core concept of *ʿarḍ* or "honor." To preserve their *ʿarḍ,* therefore, men should present a hard carapace, especially to strangers, so as to deter verbal or physical abuse against themselves or the people and things which most matter to them. And if the latter are threatened, they must act decisively to restore their appearance of strength. Men's honor can be impugned by attacks on any component of their honorable selves, but three are metonymically exalted to special iconic status—their daggers, landholdings (*arḍ*), and women—any damage or insult to which most seriously threatens a man's honor (*ḥatak ʿarḍōh*). Daggers must be especially carefully safeguarded because, as we have seen, daggers maketh man. A man is incomplete, symbolically emasculated, without his dagger; his honor is dented if he loses it or has it stolen, and is severely injured if it is seized. Damage to land, the ultimate source of livelihood, is also extremely grave, even if caused by its owners' own neglect. Men's honor is most profoundly compromised, however, if they fail to prevent their women from misbehaving, or from being verbally or physically abused by other men.

Because men regard women as inherently and irrevocably weak, and easily led astray by sexual predators, they should monitor and control them. But they cannot exercise constant vigilance because women regularly range beyond their surveillance for work and social reasons. Female nature and mobility therefore render men permanently vulnerable, and give women a particularly powerful symbolic role in relation to men. Women are a paradox. They have extremely high social and economic value; their labor and services are indispensable; they are vital for building up and reproducing their husbands' households and clans; and they bond men and groups and help define their identities. At the same time, wittingly or unwittingly, they constitute a perennial threat to men's honor at the heart of every household.[5]

Daggers, land, and especially women are therefore simultaneously valuable and dangerous; they are quintessential ingredients of a man's reputation, which depends on strength and means; and they are also potential sources of his disgrace because they can expose his vulnerability. Precisely because these entities are metonymically elevated as sacrosanct embodiments of men's honor, men can be most easily dishonored through them. This negative, dangerous aspect of the things which most powerfully constitute *ʿarḍ* is crystallized in the momentous epithet *ʿār*. No English word expresses the notions of danger, extreme vulnerability, and sacred inviolability which are concentrated in the term *ʿār,* which is so laden with emotional significance that a man can barely utter it without lowering his voice, grasping his beard, and meaningfully stroking his finger down his face. If a man's wife is insulted, he can menacingly warn, "Beware, you are slurring my honor!" (*tatakallam ʿalā ʿārī*). And if he disregards the insult, he can be disparaged as "having no shame" (*mā maʿōh ʿār*); he has disgraced himself by his unwillingness or inability to defend his "honor," meaning his fundamental interests. It follows from the male construction of femaleness that, though women can disgrace men by their scandalous behavior, they cannot themselves possess *ʿarḍ* or *ʿār.*

The above notions of maleness, like those about *ḥamīlah*s, are generalized to clans and tribes. Their members, resources, and collective interests are considered inviolable, and any threats, insults, or attacks they suffer are held to damage the entire group. Just as men's ability to protect their individual *ʿarḍ* is a test of their honor and manhood, therefore, so is the ability of tribes to protect their collective *ʿarḍ* or *ʿār* a test of their political integrity and strength. Tribes are therefore rendered particularly vulnerable by their women, whose ambiguous natures and regular forays across tribal boundaries pose a permanent threat to the peace—in a manner of speaking, they are a disaster waiting to happen. If a woman is harmed while "abroad," then the honor of her whole tribe is violated; its vulnerability, a chink in its armor, has been exposed, and the situation can only be redressed by decisive action to restore its invincible façade. A peaceful resolution of the crisis is more difficult than for any other offense, and some of the most devastating inter-tribal conflicts have been provoked by attacks on women while they were visiting other tribes.

Status Categories

Men's professional and political fortunes are profoundly affected by their birth-ascribed status and clan membership, which influence or determine their choice of work, restrict or enable their access to power, and qualify or bar them from tribal or government office. All Rāziḥīs occupy almost immutable positions in a status hierarchy which is primarily based on the culturally powerful principle of patrilineal descent, and is similar (though not identical) to the stratification systems found elsewhere in Yemen.[6] There are three principal status categories or strata (*tabaqāt*) in Rāziḥ: a religious aristocracy of *sādah* (sing. *sayyid*), who comprise roughly 5 percent of the population; "tribespeople" (*qabāyil,* sing. *qabīlī*), who comprise about

90 percent of the population; and a diverse category known generically as "butchers" (*jazr*, sing. *jazzār*), who form the remaining 5 percent of the population.[7] Because of their specialized occupations, most *sayyids* and butchers are concentrated in and around the *madīnah* of al-Naẓīr and al-Qalʿah.[8] In contrast to the situation in other regions of Yemen, however, there are no specially protected religious enclaves (*hijar*, sing. *hijrah*) mainly or exclusively inhabited by *sayyids* who devote themselves to religious pursuits (al-Akwaʿ 1996). In Rāziḥ, *hijrah* protection and privileges are conferred on individuals or families, not entire settlements. People of different status categories also live cheek by jowl in the same hamlets, and even houses, and are buried in the same graveyards (see Table 3.3, page 76).

When asked about their *tabaqāt*, Rāziḥīs of all categories invariably offered the above three-tier model of their social hierarchy, spontaneously explaining, for example, that *sayyids* are "on top," *qabīlīs* "in the middle," and butchers "at the bottom." Butchers had internalized this model which disadvantages them; a woman of that category once spontaneously informed me: "We are the third creation (*khalq al-thālith*)." Another once politically important status category, which stands apart from this tripartite formulation, is that of hereditary jurist-administrators (*quḍā*, sing. *qāḍi*), who are considered of *qabīlī* stock, but were formerly ranked above other *qabīlīs* because of their descent, learning, and roles in the imāmic state. There were also once slaves (*ʿabīd*) in Rāziḥ, owned by a few wealthy *sayyids* prominent in public affairs, who lived *en famille* in their households, and performed menial and agricultural tasks, allowing *sayyid* women (*sharāyif*) to be secluded, and men to concentrate on learned occupations. Though slaves were of African appearance, they partook of the high status of their owners. All were freed or sold in the mid-twentieth century when slavery became illegal. However, there are people of conspicuously African descent in the Tihāmah and foothills still called *ʿabīd*, though they are purportedly "free," some of whom are henchmen of ʿUqārib shaykhs. The few Jewish families of Rāziḥ emigrated to Israel around 1950, though some individuals stayed and converted to Islam.

Geographical Origins

Rāziḥīs imagine themselves as being a land (*bilād*) of people descended mostly from immigrants.[9] Immigration is usually discussed as an exclusively male phenomenon, though men sometimes arrived (and still arrive) with wives and children. According to clan traditions, most immigrants were seeking work in agriculture or trade, a few were refugees from debt or punishment for crimes, and some were wandering scholars (*muhājirīn*) who came to study or teach in Rāziḥ's mosques where they could be supported by alms (sing. *ṣadaqah*). Many men who came to Rāziḥ as government officials also stayed.

A poor male immigrant typically integrates into Rāziḥī society by first becoming the protégé (*jār,* pl. *jīrān*) of a wealthy, influential patron such as a shaykh or tribal elder, and by extension, of his clan and tribe. In return for shelter, sustenance, and legal protection, such *jīrān* provide their patrons with labor or other services, increase their supporters, and enhance their prestige as bestowers of protection and largesse. Because of their client status, and lack of local property and kin, *jīrān* are construed as politically and socially "weak" (*ḍaʿīf*), and are exempted from the full obligations of tribal citizenship. If they need help, they can approach their patron, saying, "I am your protégé" (*anīh jārak*), and he should take them under his wing. But once they start working and have means, he might exhort them, "Be manly about it" (*tarajjal lōh*), meaning, "You can stand up for yourself now." Thereafter they start contributing to collective expenses, and typically marry a local girl, acquire their own home, and are spliced into the tribe by bonds of locality and affinity. Eventually they either assimilate into their patron's clan, or build their own. The politico-legal distinction between weak, poor, and dependent new immigrants and "strong" (*qawī*) established residents with property, connections, and civic liabilities is expressed in the composite term *jār-wa-qarār.*

More affluent or high-status immigrants such as merchants, government officials, and religious specialists enter Rāziḥī society at a higher and more secure social level, their wealth, professions, and prestigious external connections, especially to state power, reducing their dependence on local patronage. Often their power and prestige also enabled them to intermarry immediately with local elites. Some *sayyids* and *qāḍis* were accorded *hijrah* protection by tribal leaders, but this privilege was selectively awarded to those whose learned qualifications and services were especially valued and needed, and was subject to negotiation and contract.

Clans

Members of all status categories belong to the descent groups which I call "clans" (sing. *bayt*) rather than "lineages" because their members cannot usually trace their genealogical connections to one another or to their putative founders (sing. *jidd*) (Tapper 1983:10; Barnard and Spencer 1998:58). In fact most men (apart from *sayyids*) can only name their fathers and grandfathers, whose given names are suffixed to their own to identify them. For example, the typical name Muḥammad Aḥmad Ibrāhīm means "Muḥammad son of Aḥmad and grandson of Ibrāhīm." Some men can also name their great-grandfathers (FFF). This is as far as most can go, and is sufficient to distinguish men from others, define their positions in their clans, and verify their status "abroad" (*fil-khārij*). The common Yemeni notion, familiar to Rāziḥīs, that people who can trace their descent back seven generations are socially superior does not therefore distinguish the *qabīlī* category from "butchers," because few of either category can.

Clan names are sometimes tacked onto personal names, like surnames, to indicate group membership; for example, "Muḥammad Aḥmad Faraḥ," meaning "Muḥammad son of Aḥmad of the Faraḥ clan." The distinction between grandfather's name and clan name is not, therefore, obvious in speech, but it is indicated in documents by the omission of *ibn* ("son of") before the clan name. The above name would thus be customarily written "Muḥammad ibn Aḥmad Faraḥ." This usage indicates that several generations have passed since the time of the ancestor, who has transformed from a remembered person into a label for a group.

The clan patronyms (sing. *kunyah*) of *qabīlī*s and butchers are usually prefixed by the term *ilt,* meaning "people." Thus Ilt Ibrāhīm means "Ibrāhīm's descendants." *Sayyid* clan names, by contrast, are always prefixed by the synonymous, classical-Arabic terms *āl* or *bayt*—for example, Āl Muṭahhar or Bayt Abū Ṭālib (the alternative names of the most prominent *sayyid* clan in Rāziḥ, which will figure much in this work). Leading *qabīlī*s sometimes copy this usage to put on airs. The shaykhs of al-Naẓīr, for example, sometimes refer to their clan as Āl Faraḥ or Bayt Faraḥ, instead of the more common *qabīlī* usage, Ilt Faraḥ.

Sometimes sub-clans which are dispersed in different hamlets are named after women, typically the different mothers of half-brothers, and therefore have matronyms instead of patronyms. This practice preserves the politically useful notion of their relatedness. Other clan names derive from their founder's place or tribe of origin. An example is a Naẓīrī clan, Bayt al-Hamdānī, founded by an immigrant tax official from Hamdān Ṣaʿdah, the prefix of which still resonates with its founder's prestigious connection with the former imāmic state. Over time, however, toponyms tend to lapse as the significance of external links fades, and clans are renamed after prominent men of later generations.

Clan membership is an extremely important aspect of individual identity and status, and creates significant inequalities *within* status categories which are glossed over by the simple tripartite model of the social hierarchy. People often spontaneously cite their clans to define their status or that of others; for example, "He's one of us (*minnanā*)—from Ilt Ibrāhīm." They also affirm or question the status of strangers by reference to their clans, as in "He comes from Bayt so-and-so, who are shaykhs in Najrān," or "He claims to be a *qabīlī*, but he's from Ilt so-and-so in Khawlān, who are butchers, so I wonder." It is not only that everyone in a clan is burnished or tarnished by the defining occupations—prestigious or despised—of its members, but also that clans vary greatly in size, ranging from one or two households up to thirty or so households and seventy men.[10]

Clans are corporate groups in the politico-legal sphere, so large clans have more clout. This applies to all status categories, including *sayyids*. Āl Muṭahhar (Bayt Abū Ṭālib) is the most powerful *sayyid* clan in Rāziḥ partly because of its impeccable religious and political ancestry, the fact that it once ruled Rāziḥ, and because of the high offices some of its members still hold. But its relatively large size (it boasted about thirty adult men in 1980) is also important in its influence. As one of its members spontaneously commented: "We used to be weak (*ḍaʿīf*) and need tribal protection, but now we are many we don't anymore." Clan size is especially significant within the *qabīlī* category because the shaykhs and elders of each tribe need large support groups, and enough men to ensure hereditary succession. The members of these large, leading clans comprise a superior stratum within their status category, just as leading *sayyid* clans do within theirs.

Descent and Origins

It is characteristic of Rāziḥī (and Yemeni) culture to distinguish between status categories, and between families and clans within each category, by reference both to their putative ancestors *and* to their natal *bilāds*—merging human and geographical origins in a usually timeless historiography. *Sayyids* thus define themselves as "northern" Arabians by citing their ultimate descent from the legendary Arabian ancestor, ʿAdnān, and thereby distinguish themselves from the "original" inhabitants of southern Arabia—the majority of the population—who, in this mythical genealogy, are descended from Qaḥṭān.[11] This predominantly learned construction also conforms with, and reinforces, *sayyid* claims to ancestral origins in the Hijaz.

More specific distinctions are drawn according to recent and traceable human "origins" (*aṣl*), often phrased as *al-ḥasab-wa-al-nasab,* meaning "relatives on both sides" and implying "of good stock." It is a common put-down, for example, to say, "He can't trace his ancestry." *Sayyid*s claim, and were historically accorded, superior status on the basis of their descent from (*yinsubū ilā*) the Prophet's daughter, Fāṭimah, and her husband, ʿAlī b. Abī Ṭālib.[12] Rāziḥī *sayyids* refer to themselves as Hashemites after the Prophet's great-grandfather (FFF), or as "the people of the [Prophet's] House" (*ahl al-bayt*). Many can also trace their pedigrees (also *nasab*) back to an illustrious ancestor of indisputable Fāṭimī-ʿAlawī descent such as an imām. Members of Āl Muṭahhar (Bayt Abū Ṭālib), for example, can recite by heart all their ten or so antecedents back to Imām al-Qāsim b. Muḥammad "the Great," famed for his anti-Ottoman *jihād* at the turn of the seventeenth century, and founder of the dominant ruling dynasty of North Yemen for the subsequent two and a half centuries. Some *sayyid* families also inscribe their family trees in their Qurans to help legitimize their claims—probably mainly to competing *sayyid*s (see Meissner 1987:166; Bruck 1991: Chap. 9, 232n13).

While claiming superior status to most of the population, *sayyid*s differentiate among themselves according to whether or not they are descended from former rulers, particularly Imām al-Qāsim, or are related to notable *sayyid* clans elsewhere in Yemen. A member of Āl Muṭahhar emphasized that Qāsimī *sayyid*s had earned their special positions: "The Yemeni tribes decided to give special protection (*qararū tahjīrhim*) to the progeny of Imām al-Qāsim as a reward for his campaign against the Turks." At the other end of the spectrum are many *sayyid*s with small families, limited education, and meager connections to noted *sayyid* clans who have no special position or privileges in Rāziḥī society.

Rāziḥīs generally venerate (*iḥtaram*) the concept of holy ancestry, but they do not indiscriminately revere all *sayyid*s, as has sometimes been implied.[13] They greatly respect (*sharraf*) those who are exceptionally pious, learned, and wise, and *sayyid* judges or governors who resist the temptations of office, and are fair and uncorrupt. But they criticize or even vilify *sayyid*s who fall short of the learned and religious ideals of their status or positions. In the past they also opposed those who abused political office and power. This reality of conditional loyalty is obscured by epithets such as "the Zaydī tribes."

*Qāḍī*s also claim prestigious external origins, though their category does not share a common apical ancestor like *sayyid*s (Bruck 1991:80–81.) The famous *qāḍī* family of al-Naẓīr, Ilt al-Judhaynah, for example, claims that their local founding ancestor, who was a noted Quran teacher, judge, and scribe of tribal agreements, originated from the Prophet's tribe, Quraysh. Local documents suggest that he probably came to Rāziḥ in the late eighteenth century, and his descendants followed the same occupations until the mid-twentieth century, when they "lost" their learning.

Most *qabīlī* and butcher clans are believed to have been founded by an immigrant from another Rāziḥ tribe, from the ʿAsīr Tihāmah, or from elsewhere in highland Yemen. In al-Naẓīr, for example, only two small *qabīlī* families (Ilt al-Qayyāl and Ilt al-Wālī) are said to be descended from the "original" (*aṣlī*) inhabitants of the tribe. Clan ancestors usually have hazy identities, and mainly function as labels for corporate groups and idioms for describing their political relations. Among themselves, *qabīlī*s attach no particular importance either to external or local origins. The few remaining men of Ilt al-Qayyāl and Ilt al-Wāli, for example, are the living embodiment of al-Naẓīr's antiquity, but are otherwise socially and politically insignificant. In general, therefore, *qabīlī* origins differentiate, but do not rank. The exceptions are shaykhly clans, whose founders are sometimes personalized and glorified. Shaykhs and certain elders can also recite pedigrees as long as those of *sayyid*s. Shaykh ʿAwaḍ Manṣūr Faraḥ of al-Naẓīr, for example, recited to me a string of antecedents, and a *sayyid* present, who had obviously been counting, exclaimed, "Nine!"

Butchers have similar attitudes to their origins to *qabīlī*s. However, members of the superior social categories disparage them behind their backs for their "lowly" ancestry, alleging (because some are dark-skinned) that they are of Ethiopian (*ḥabashī*) descent—a degrading suggestion according to the dominant skin-color aesthetic of Yemen. It is common for personal resentments to be expressed in hyperbolic rhetoric, and to be generalized from individuals to groups. Racist comments (which also occur between and among *sayyid*s and *qabīlī*s) do not, therefore, accurately reflect the nuances of relations between status categories any more than mysogynist comments do gender relations. Despite such routine derogatory comments, members of different status categories have close relationships based on neighborhood, religion, and shared economic interests. Neighborliness also conspicuously overrides (or masks) status distinctions at rites of passage, when it is important to have a good turnout. Status distinctions can also be transcended by a shared sense of tribal solidarity in the face of external threats.

Occupation

Like other Yemenis, Rāziḥīs valorize occupations, and link them with specific status categories, reflecting a cultural predisposition to regard skills and even character as somehow embodied and heritable.[14] The association between descent and profession is reinforced by the fact that fathers commonly instruct their sons; therefore occupations—including in politics and religion—tend anyway to run in families and clans. This favors some categories, and discriminates against others. Only persons of high *qabīlī* status can be tribal officials, and however large their clans or great their wealth, neither *sayyid*s nor butchers can hold tribal office. *Sayyid*s with *hijrah* protection are also in an ambiguous relation to the tribal system; they live within it, and are subject to its laws and protection, but they are simultaneously politically outside it because they are (or were, because this is changing) exempted from the defining legal, political, and military obligations of tribal membership. These exemptions do not, however, apply to butchers, who have the same duties as *qabīlī*s.

Most Rāziḥīs, whatever their status category, are farmers, and a large minority are traders. In contrast to the situation in most other regions, and presumably because of the long-standing importance of trade in the Rāziḥī economy, land-ownership (as mentioned) is not an absolute qualification for *qabīlī* status, nor do *qabīlī*s or *sayyid*s consider commerce or market work unworthy of their status.[15] Some high-ranking *qabīlī*s are, furthermore, blacksmiths, carpenters, grain measurers, qāt traders, and vegetable growers—work which no *qabīlī* would deign to perform in most of North Yemen, still less a *sayyid*.[16] Yet the most famous vegetable growers in Rāziḥ are *sayyid*s, known as "the greengrocer *sayyid*s" (*al-sādah al-qashshāmīn*), who cultivate in Wādī al-Muʿayan.[17]

There are, however, certain occupations which *qabīlī*s and *sayyid*s despise and could not take up without disgracing themselves and their clans. These are butchery, running cafes, pottery making, polishing *jambiyyah*s and making their scabbards, being a barber, tanning and working with hides, medicinal cupping, circumcising, and drumming and other music playing. Although *qabīlīs* and *sayyids* tend to lump the members of the lowest status category together as undifferentiated "butchers" (*jazr*), and deride them as "deficient" (*nuqqās*) because of their ancestry and professions, those who actually slaughter animals for a living, or who farm or trade, regard themselves as socially superior to tanners, cuppers, circumcisers, and musicians, whom they refer to by the derogatory terms *dawāshīn* or *muzāyinah*.

An interesting aspect of both butchery and circumcising is that both are denigrated by *sayyids* and *qabīlīs* as filthy, polluting activities, yet their products have immense social value. Circumcision creates proper Muslim males. Butchery creates meat—the most prestigious food, and essential for hospitality meals, and banquets to celebrate religious feasts, weddings, circumcisions, and political reconciliation. This seeming paradox intriguingly parallels gender attitudes. Men denigrate women for their innate characteristics, they think them polluted and polluting because of the blood of menstruation and parturition, and they strictly eschew women's work as shameful for men to engage in; yet they also deeply value, and fundamentally depend upon, women's productive and reproductive services. As we have seen, women are also key elements in the construction of key social and political relationships and collective identities. The above similarities suggest a common logic: that which is precious renders those who value and need it dependent and vulnerable, and threatens their strength and independence. They therefore neutralize the danger posed by their social inferiors by defining them as "weak" (*ḍaʿīf*) and "deficient" (*nāqiṣ*), "protecting" and controlling them, and maintaining their impotent subordination. The sexist and pseudo-racist attitudes of men in general, and of the superior status categories in particular, are therefore essentially hegemonic, and help maintain a status quo which serves their partial interests.

Sayyids are especially associated with the "religious sciences" (*ʿilm*)—the study of the classical Arabic language, theology, and sharīʿah law—which they believe it is their special duty to study and promote.[18] "It's incumbent upon *sayyids*," Zayd Abū Ṭālib explained, "to provide spiritual guidance (*irshād*), and to propagate enlightenment and culture (*nashr al-waʿī wa al-thaqāfah*). In return the tribes respect them, and accord them special protection and privileges." This vision reflected his own ideals and practice. Before the Civil War he had studied *ʿilm* for years in various Yemeni centers of religious learning, had held various official posts, including the governorship of Majz where he then was, and was regarded as a wise counselor and mediator in tribal disputes and matters involving the state. Rāziḥīs also admired him for his effective command of royalist tribesmen during the Civil War; *sayyids* can be esteemed for martial as well as scholarly prowess.

Sayyids who acquired learned credentials taught religion (*qaraʿ ʿilm*) in local mosques or at home, for which they received alms (*ṣadaqah*) or fees; or they made a living as freelance lawyers and mediators, implementing sharīʿah law, especially the complex rules of inheritance, and adjudicating in disputes. By these means some established influential positions. A notable example in al-Naẓīr is the *ʿālim,* Sayyid ʿAlī Ḥusayn al-Ḥūthī, who came to Rāziḥ from al-Ḥūth as a wandering scholar (*muhājir*) in the 1870s, and was venerated for his learning and piety. He lived in rooms which a Naẓīrī made *waqf* for him, married his daughter to a leading member of Āl Muṭahhar, and gained fame for his fair judgments and respect for tribal law. Other well-educated *sayyids* (and *qāḍīs*) secured government posts as governors, judges, treasurers, or secretaries, either within Rāziḥ or in other northern regions. Members of Āl Muṭahhar (Bayt Abū Ṭālib), whose ancestors (as mentioned) once ruled Rāziḥ, held many such posts under a succession of imāms, and continued to do so under the republic. In 1980 three were local judges (sing. *ḥākim*), others were their secretaries, one was director of education for Rāziḥ, and others were similarly employed elsewhere in the Province of Ṣaʿdah. At the other end of the spectrum are *sayyids* who have no scholarly, religious, or political ambitions, and who pursue the same occupations as *qabīlīs*.

Although their religious descent and formal education advantaged *sayyids* during the imāmate, they never completely monopolized the learned professions. Men of any status category, including butchers, could and can become religious specialists or "jurist-teachers" (sing. *faqīh*) by their own studious efforts. Such men often have the honorific *sīdnā* ("our master") prefixed to their names. Notable examples from al-Naẓīr are the *faqīh* and Quran teacher Sīdnā Ḍayf Allāh Manṣūr, who came from the plateau in his youth; and Aḥmad Sālim Shabūṭ, from a large "butcher" clan, who studied *ʿilm* with the son of al-Ḥūthi (who was also a scholar), then became a noted teacher in his own right. In 1980 he used to butcher in the mornings, then teach in the mosque in the afternoons. In such cases, people's respect for religious learning can override their contempt for lowly birth or occupation and make it irrelevant. Men cannot, however, alter their birth status by their scholarly accomplishments, nor automatically transmit their achieved standing to their sons (Bruck 1991:80–81). If the family tradition of religious learning lapses, so does the attached status. This happened to the *qāḍīs*, Ilt al-Judhaynah, who became déclassé when they ceased to pursue *ʿilm* in the mid-twentieth century, and are now regarded as ordinary *qabīlīs*—though their clan hamlet is still called Bayt al-Qāḍī.

Symbolic Expressions of Status

Before the Civil War dagger sets were the clearest visible indicators of male status. Daggers in Rāziḥ were worn in three contrasting positions: *qabīlīs* wore them upright in the center of their bodies, while others wore them in a slanting position, hilt to the fore, *sayyids* on their right hips, butchers on their left.[19] *Qabīlī* scabbards are also more angled than those of *sayyids* and butchers, and whereas the dagger hilts, scabbards, and belts of *sayyids* and *qabīlīs* could be richly ornamented, those of butchers were supposed to be unadorned. The *sayyid*-style dagger was also, and remains, closely associated with religious learning; *qabīlīs* and butchers who become *faqīhs* are not, therefore, considered to be dressing above their station by wearing slanting daggers to the right.

Other aspects of dress, especially headgear, also indicated male status.[20] *Sayyids*, *qāḍīs*, and *faqīhs* wore smoothly wrapped white turbans (sing. *imāmah*) which symbolized religious scholarship and were associated with state power. Most *qabīlīs* and butchers, by contrast, wore indigo turbans (sing. *ʿaṣābah*), while tribal leaders proclaimed their positions with voluminous turbans (sing. *shāl*) of lighter-colored, more costly fabric. Learned men also inspired "respectful awe" (*haybah*), and emphasized their prestigious, sedentary occupations, by wearing long white gowns with wide, trailing sleeves, and neatly folded shawls of luxurious fabric (see Messick 1993:165). Their educated speech also distinguished them from the majority of men, who could only speak the local dialect.

The encumbering, costly dress of the elite, and the patrician demeanor of its wearers, contrasted with the practical shirts, waistcoats of woven goat-hair, and short skirts (*fūṭah*) of indigo or colorfully striped cotton worn by most *qabīlīs* and butchers, which revealed their lower legs and arms, and conspicuously fitted them for strenuous work and striding through the mountains.

Under the republic, the significance of male dress as a status indicator has been eroded by the pressure, especially on *sayyids*, to appear more egalitarian, and by the popularity of new fashions such as western-style

FIGURE 2.5
The Quran teacher, Ḍayf Allāh Manṣūr, dressed up for ʿĪd Ramaḍān, 1979

jackets and Saudi-style shifts, especially among the *shibāb*. In particular, there has been a leveling of dagger symbolism, and now most butchers and *sayyids*, except for *ʿulamā*, wear *qabīlī*-style daggers.

Female dress before the Civil War mainly distinguished between *sayyid* women (*sharāyif*, sing. *sharīfah*) and the rest. *Sharāyif* veiled heavily outside the house, and were generally more secluded, and even in 1980 some *sharīfahs* were "hardly ever seen," and did not gallivant around afternoon tea parties like other women. Other female clothes were less concealing, and most women did not veil their faces in public until the mid-twentieth century, when the governor decreed that those living in the *madīnah* of al-Naẓīr should do so to protect their reputations from the increasing numbers of male visitors. Thereafter the custom spread, and became almost universal during the 1980s except among low status market women. This was largely due to the fashion influence of Sanaa.

Before the Civil War, and to an extent in the 1970s and 1980s, *sayyid* status was also affirmed and reinforced by terms of reference and address. People invariably addressed *sayyids* as "my lord" (*sīdī*) or "*al-sayyid* so-and-so," and *sayyids* referred to one another in speech and documents as *al-ṣanū*, meaning "noble brother." Members of other categories also greeted *sayyids* deferentially by kissing their knees or the hems of their gowns instead of exchanging the cheek kisses of social equals, and were reprimanded if they failed to greet them first when entering a room. Differences in ascribed status were also reinforced by seating patterns. *Sayyids*, shaykhs, and other notables were invariably accorded, or took, the most prestigious positions at the head of the room, and those of lower status sat further down, the humblest place being next to the door (see Gerholm 1977:180; Weir 1985b:130–135). The seating arrangements at women's social gatherings, by contrast, stressed community, not status, as in other rural areas (Maclagan 1993:261).

Marriage

Inequalities between status categories are maintained by strict marriage rules which have continued to be observed in Rāziḥ during the republican period. *Sayyids* maintain their social superiority by marrying their daughters exclusively to fellow *sayyids*, a practice they justify by invoking the religious doctrine of "equality of descent" (*kafāʿah fil-nasab*).[21] At the same time, leading *sayyids* preserve their ranking *within* their social category by giving wives only to fellow clan-members or to families of similar or

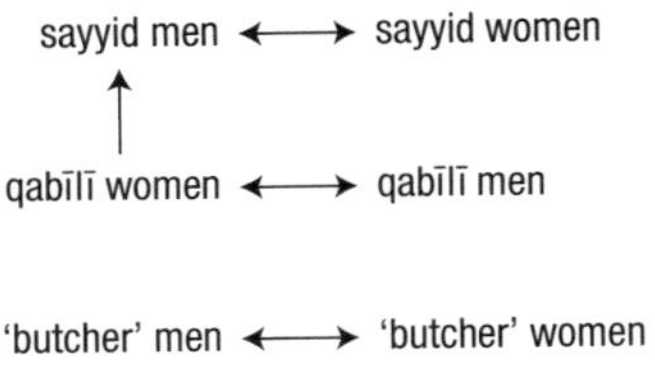

FIGURE 2.6
Marriage according to status category

superior standing. The most prominent and wealthy *sayyids*, notably leading members of Āl Muṭahhar (Bayt Abū Ṭālib), have also tended to intermarry, serially and polygamously, with leading *sayyid* clans outside Rāziḥ (especially where they held posts), with *sayyid* officials sent to Rāziḥ by various rulers, and with *qabīlī* notables such as shaykhs and big merchants. This strategy, which created politically useful connections between states and tribes, was not available to *sayyids* of modest means because of the expense of maintaining several families, and because *qabīlī* brideprices have always been twice or more those of *sharīfahs*.

Apart from the small minority of *qabīlī* women who marry *sayyids* hypergamously, *qabīlīs* marry exclusively within their status category. Leading *qabīlī* clans, like leading *sayyid* clans, also preserve their ranking and strength by a high rate of intra-clan marriage combined with strategic marital alliances with other leading clans—mainly within their own tribes and within Rāziḥ (see Table 3.2, page 73).

In contrast with other parts of Yemen, neither *sayyids* nor *qabīlīs* will intermarry with "butchers," who therefore comprise a completely endogamous category.[22] Because of the symbolic and instrumental importance of marriage and affinal relationships, the marital isolation of "butchers" ensures their social subordination and political weakness, and provokes bitterness over their seemingly immutable position at the bottom of the social pile. Nevertheless, they discriminate among themselves. Those who butcher, farm, or trade will not give their daughters to *dawshāns*.

Upward Mobility

Since birth status obviously cannot be denied within the natal community, upward mobility within the status hierarchy can only be achieved by moving to a distant region, inventing a better status, and hoping no one will check or care. Rāziḥīs realize that immigrants might have done this, and have a verb (*taqabyal*) for someone posing as a *qabīlī*. If they suspect a family is faking its status, they can prevent its advancement by refusing to intermarry with it; marriage is the crucial testing ground. In one case, an immigrant claiming *qabīlī* status was accused of being a "butcher" by someone who had visited his natal *bilād*. Challenged to "reveal his *qabīlī* grandfather," he failed, but was rescued from ignominious demotion by the shaykh of his adopted tribe. The latter announced in the sūq that he was an authentic *qabīlī*, and his family subsequently consolidated its position by marrying within that station—though leading *qabīlī* clans spurned their advances. Conversely, Bayt Abū Ṭālib (Āl Muṭahhar) have "kept down" a purportedly *sayyid* family (who "lost their family tree") by denying the authenticity of their claimed status, and rejecting their requests for brides—though they have taken their daughters in marriage. Status is therefore, to a limited extent and in special circumstances, in the gift of the religious and tribal elite, who can sabotage or aid social climbers.

CHAPTER THREE

The Tribes of Rāziḥ

Rāziḥīs have a strong sense of common identity based on inhabiting the same remote massif, and their limited contact, until recently, with other regions. A few Rāziḥīs traveled beyond their mountains for trade, for religious studies, to conduct the pilgrimage to Mecca, or to petition shaykhs or government officials. But in contrast to the people of poorer regions in the Tihāmah, Lower Yemen, and Hadramaut, few emigrated to work before the 1970s because they could make a living at home. Rāziḥīs were also too tied by agriculture and trade, and too far from state centers and most military engagements, to have provided a constant reservoir of mercenaries for the Ottomans or the imāms like the needier tribesmen of the plateau and South Yemen, many of whom spent long periods away from home.[1]

Rāziḥīs speak a distinctive dialect (or perhaps language) which is unintelligible to other Yemenis, and could be an isolate in Yemen (see Watson et al. 2006). They intermarry and trade mostly among themselves, rub shoulders in the same markets and mosques, and frequently encounter one another as they clamber through the mountains. They have also experienced the vagaries of the same climate, endured the same disasters, and been subject to the same rulers. And they share an intimate knowledge, which is social knowledge, of the same highly differentiated territory. All this creates a sense of community and distinction from other regions which transcends politics, and is what people have in mind when they refer to Rāziḥ as their "homeland" (*bilād*).

The Tribes of Rāziḥ

Rāziḥ also has a distinct geo-political identity. This is characterized as the sum of its parts—"the tribes of Rāziḥ" (*qubul* or *qabāyil* Rāziḥ), or "the people of Rāziḥ" (*ahl* Rāziḥ)—which means the same thing since inhabiting a tribe (*qabīlah*), like inhabiting a state, is an unavoidable condition of existence. "The people of Rāziḥ" is implicitly understood to mean the people of its respective tribes just as "Europeans" is assumed to mean the citizens of Europe's respective states. The tribes of Rāziḥ are remarkably old. Two (Munabbih and Banī Maʿīn) appear in a thirteenth-century chronicle.[2] And three others (al-Naẓīr, Birkān, and al-Shawāriq) are mentioned in a local document from the beginning of the seventeenth century, as is the alleged founder of the shaykhly clan of al-Naẓīr (D1605).[3]

The tribes of Rāziḥ are stable and effective polities partly because they are small and simply organized. It is difficult to estimate the size of tribal territories because of the steep terrain, but most are probably less than 20km^2 in area, including uninhabited *qafarah* land, except for Ghamar, which is much larger. And their populations, at the time of the first national census in 1975, ranged from under a thousand to around six thousand persons, of whom a quarter were adult men. Each tribe has a discrete and continuous territory (*arḍ, bilād*) with well-defined political borders (*ḥadd,* pl. *ḥudūd*), and is bounded by several others—referred to as its "neighbors" (*awthān*) or "abroad" (*fil-khārij*). Tribal territories therefore form a continuous patchwork which covers the entire region, and this adjoins similar patchworks in the neighboring tribal regions of ʿUqārib, Jumāʿah, and Khawlān. There is no land in this region which is not in a tribe.

The tribes of Rāziḥ are all similarly structured and governed. Each is composed of numerous patronymic (or sometimes matronymic) clans (sing. *bayt*) based in hamlets. Most are also subdivided into larger administrative areas which, following Mundy's (1995:23) apt usage, I will refer to as "wards." Wards vary in number and name between tribes, but whatever their nomenclature are invariably perceived as *fractions* of their tribes. The tribe of al-Naẓīr, for example, is subdivided into three wards known as "the Thirds of the tribe" (*athlāth al-qabīlah*), and named "the Upper Third," "the Middle Third," and "the Lower Third." Tribes are further subdivided, for specific purposes and variable durations, into smaller frac-

TABLE 3.1. THE TRIBES AND SHAYKHLY CLANS OF QAḌĀ RĀZIḤ

Tribal region	Tribe	Adjectival form	Shaykhly clan
Raẓiḥ	Banalqām	Yalqamī	Marhab
	Banī Asad ("Bakīl")	Asadī ("Bakīlī")	ʿAwfān
	Banī Maʿīn	Maʿīnī	Abū ʿAwthah
	Banī Rabīʿah	Rabīʿī	Falhān
	Birkān	Birkānī	ʿAfrīt
	Ghamar	Ghamarī	Ḥassān
	al-Izid	Izdī	Sarīʿ
	Munabbih	Munabbihī	Sālim
	al-Naẓīr	Naẓīrī	Faraḥ
	al-Shawāriq	Shāriqī	ʿAzzām
ʿUqārib	Ālat al-ʿUṭayf	ʿUṭayfī	Jabbār
	Banī ʿAbīd	ʿAbīdī	Farwān
	Banī Ṣafwān	Ṣafwānī	Ismāʿil (?)
	Banī Ṣayāḥ	Ṣayāḥī	Daʿaybil
	al-Waqir	Waqrī	Ghalfān
	al-Wuqaysh	Wuqayshī	Salāmah

tions—typically "quarters" or "fifths"—comprising clusters of hamlets and clans. Anthropologists usually illustrate such nested groupings with tree diagrams, but since these can misleadingly imply genealogical connection, I prefer to render those of Rāziḥ by a schematic map.

Clans, wards, and tribes are the principal structures of tribal governance, and have proper names and corporate identities which transcend the generations. Each tribe has an identical leadership hierarchy. At the apex is a hereditary chief, entitled *shaykh,* also referred to as "head of the tribe" (*kabīr al-qabīlah*), or "head of the market" (*kabīr al-sūq*) if his tribe has one, reflecting the great importance of trade in tribal politics. The shaykh "runs the tribe" (*yisawwiq al-qabīlah*) through a second tier of tribal officials, called the "notables" or "elders" of the tribe (*aʿyān al-qabīlah, kubār al-qabīlah*), who are chosen from other leading clans. The *aʿyān* assist and deputize for the shaykh (*yiqūmū maqām al-shaykh*), and represent and administer their clans and wards. Below them is a third tier of headmen (*umanā,* sing. *amīn*) who represent and administer hamlets. Shaykhs and elders together comprise the tiny government or parliament of each tribe.

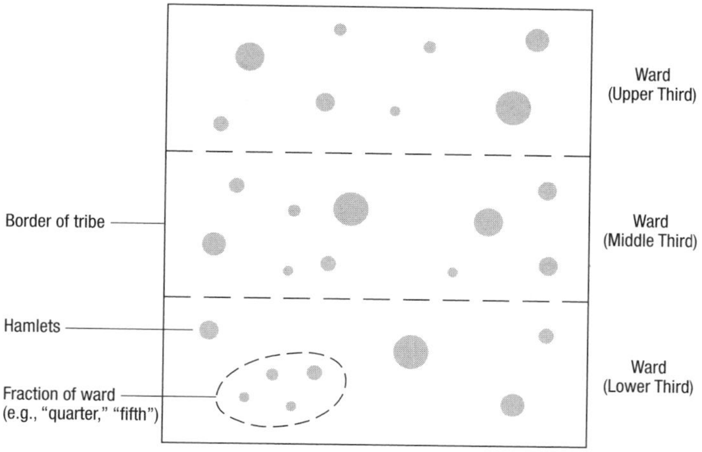

FIGURE 3.1.
Diagram of tribal structures (the example of al-Naẓīr)

A *sayyid* official made a spontaneous comparison with states: "It's like the President with his ministers. The *aʿyān* are like ministers (*wuzarā*), and the *umanā* are like deputy ministers. It's the same everywhere in the Arab world," he added. "Shaykhs and *aʿyān* solve problems." Shaykhs and elders can also be compared to foreign ministers, for they represent their tribes externally with other tribes and the state.

Rāziḥīs commonly describe their geo-political structures and relations using idioms of kinship and descent. They can say, for example, that a tribe is a "son of Rāziḥ" (*ibn* Rāziḥ), or "one of the sons of Rāziḥ" (*min awlād* Rāziḥ). This should be understood as a figure of speech for "one of the tribes which has historically occupied the same massif"; it is a statement of the regional identity and perceived permanence of the main local structures of governance. When pressed, people sometimes vaguely declared that their massif is named after "a man who was maybe the first to arrive," but "Rāziḥ" is neither personified in legends, nor vividly imagined as the ancestor of its tribes. It is predominantly thought of as a *place—bilād* Rāziḥ.

The same applies to tribes. Although some say that their tribe was founded by a man, especially if it has a patronym, no Rāziḥ tribe is regarded as a group of people mostly descended from a common ancestor; these polities are not defined by consanguinity. This even applies when the tribe has a patronym like Banī Maʿīn, literally "sons of Maʿīn." The term *banī,* here, just means "people" like *ahl.* The point to stress is that the members of that tribe do not imagine that they are all, or even mostly, literally descended from a founding ancestor called Maʿīn. Like all tribe names, "Banī Maʿīn" is essentially a label for a territorially based polity. Since the people of each tribe claim diverse ancestral and geographical origins, and belong to different status categories which observe marriage restrictions, they could not, in any case, logically imagine that they are all related, nor do they.[4] Furthermore, individuals or groups can defect or secede to (*inqātaʿ min*) another tribe politically without moving, and can reside in other tribes while retaining their original allegiance—like foreigners living abroad in state systems.

These practices create a distinction between political domains and human constituencies; a tiny minority of each tribe's residents "belong" politically to other tribes. In short, the population of each tribe is, and is acknowledged to be, heterogeneous, and no tribe has an all-encompassing genealogical framework according to which relations between its constituent members and groups are organized or rationalized.[5] If we understand genealogical schemes as systems of classification for political and administrative purposes, this is unsurprising. Sedentary people have less need to conceptualize their groupings genealogically than nomads, who generally have such schemes, because they live in fixed settlements. In the case of Rāziḥ, the dramatically differentiated landscape, with its many vantage points, and the hamlets conspicuously scattered over the steep mountainsides, are evidently sufficient for "imagining" its tribes and their subdivisions "on the ground," and keeping people's "addresses" in mind (Gellner 1981:33).

Clans

The largest groups in the tribal system of Rāziḥ based on an ideology of common descent are the localized patronymic (or sometimes matronymic) groups which I call "clans" (*abyāt,* sing. *bayt*). Clans are the building blocks of tribes, and are joined by strong cement. Each clan is composed of a variable number of households and extended families which are bound by numerous strands of friendship, neighborhood, agnatic and affinal kinship, and economic interdependence, and are linked to other clans, especially in the same vicinity, by similar multiplex ties. Clans are also conceived as being "built up" over time; indeed the whole concept of *bayt,* which also means "house" or "dwelling," implies something *constructed.* To extend the architectural metaphor, each tribe is an aggregation of many clans of diverse sizes, origins, compositions, statuses, and power, some forming the lower courses of the socio-political edifice, others crowning and dominating it.

Clans are the most important political and administrative units of the tribes of Rāziḥ. The *shaykh* and elders (*aʿyān*) of each tribe are chosen from its largest, most powerful clans by a system of hereditary succession which can justifiably be described as dynastic. Elders are chosen from the most eminent members of their clan by their fellow clan members in coordination with the shaykh of the tribe. "We choose them according to seniority," explained Shaykh ʿAwaḍ Manṣūr Faraḥ of al-Naẓīr. "And they must be intelligent, well off, and forceful." And the elders, representing their clans and wards, choose the shaykh from the tribe's shaykhly clan (*bayt al-mashīkh*).

All the tasks of tribal or state governance are devolved onto clans, which have collective rights and responsibilities in tribal law. Clans are also people's primary support groups. As mentioned, they have collective "honor" (*ʿarḍ*); insults or injuries to individuals are therefore deemed to affect their whole clan as well as their households, and its elders should ideally help them seek legal redress. Individuals can also enhance their clan's reputation by noble deeds, or sully it by their inaction or transgressions. Improper acts can therefore invite automatic rebuke from the elders and members of one's clan, so clans also function as instruments of social control and the maintenance of moral values.

The people of each tribe are closely identified with their shaykhs and shaykhly clans. This is facilitated by the fact that most of the latter have distinctive and exclusive patronyms (see page 68). Men are commonly described as the *aṣḥāb* of their shaykhs or elders, a term which can be translated as "followers," "supporters," "comrades," or "allies" in different contexts. Naẓīrīs are thus described, for example, as "the comrades of Ibn Faraḥ" (*aṣḥāb ibn Faraḥ*)—*ibn* (literally "son") meaning here "descendant" of Faraḥ, the eponymous founder of Ilt Faraḥ (their shaykhly clan). Even without the honorific *shaykh,* everyone in Qaḍā Rāziḥ knows that "Ibn Faraḥ" is the shaykh of al-Naẓīr, though they might not all know his personal name. Such usage implicitly takes hereditary entitlement for granted, and helps reinforce it. Shaykhly patronyms are therefore like titles of office. The same applies to the patronyms of elders, though they are not always so distinctive. This almost iconic association between tribes and their leaders' clans is analogous to the identification between groups and their putative apical ancestors in tribes based on an ideology of common descent.

It is also symptomatic of the way tribes are politically constituted—as a systemic, contractual relationship between leaders and constituents. As a "butcher" put it: "I can't imagine a tribe without its own shaykh and elders. It wouldn't be a tribe. A tribe *must* have this structure: a shaykh, *aʿyān, umanā,* and constituents (*afrād*), which," he added, "includes people of *all* statuses (*tabaqāt*)."

The discourse of tribal leaders misleadingly implies that each tribe is composed of only a few large clans—their own. When I asked leading Naẓīrīs to name the clans of their tribe, for instance, they invariably listed those from which their shaykh and elders are drawn. They would say, for example, "We have Ilt Faraḥ and Ilt ʿAbdallāh and Ilt Ibrāhīm and Ilt al-Ḥājj . . . " and so on, naming nine or more *qabīlī* clans, as though providing a comprehensive list. (Once a butcher piped in with his clan name, which my informant then politely included.) These same clan names also crop up time and again at the head of tribal agreements (*qawāʿid*), where the participants are often stated to be representing their clans, wards, or tribes depending on the range of the agreement. For example, a nineteenth-century pact between the leading men of the Middle Third of al-Naẓīr begins typically as follows:

> Attending (*ḥaḍar*) were those mentioned from the clans (*abiyāt*) of the whole Middle Third: [three names] from Ḥājjī-and-ʿAṭāsī; [two names] from Ilt Muḥammad; [two names] from Ilt Ibrāhīm; and [one name] from Ilt al-Zaharī. Each represents (*taqaddam ʿalā*) his whole group (*man ilayh*), whether recently arrived or established (*jār wa qarār*), dissident or compliant (*shādhdh wa bādhdh*). They are "brothers" (*akhwān*), and united in supporting what is right and tribal agreements (*mawāḍīn*). (D1887)

This gives the impression that the Middle Third then comprised only four clans (including the shaykhly clan, here named after its then leading subclan, Ilt Muḥammad). However, the true picture is that these were just the dominant clans of the Middle Third, which was then evidently divided into four administrative "quarters" (though this is not explicitly stated). Because of such elite representations, it was only once my acquaintance widened, and I had done a household census, that I realized many smaller clans existed which were silently subsumed, in speech and documents, under the administrative and political umbrellas of the larger, dominant clans from which leaders are almost invariably chosen.

TABLE 3.2. MARRIAGES OF 33 MEN FROM A LEADING NAẒĪRĪ CLAN, ILT IBRĀHĪM, 1977

	Within Ilt Ibrāhīm	*With leading Naẓīrī clans*	*With other Naẓīrī clans*	*With other tribes*	*With shaykhly clans in other tribes*	*Total marriages*
	11	5 Ilt al-Zaharī 5 Ilt ʿAbdallāh 4 Ilt Faraḥ 1 Bayt al-Hamdānī 1 Ilt Jarad	7	2 Birkān 2 Jumāʿah 1 al-Shawāriq 1 al-Shām 1 al-Yaman	1 Birkān 1 B.Rabīʿah 1 B.Ṣafwān	
No.	11	16	7	7	3	44
%	25%	36%	16%	16%	7%	100%

Leading clans help preserve their ranking and strength by a high rate of endogamous marriage (possible only when clans are sufficiently large), and by strategic marriage alliances with other leading clans within and without their own tribe. This is illustrated by the marriage pattern of men of the leading Naẓīrī clan, Ilt Ibrāhīm (Table 3.2).

As mentioned, most *qabīlī*s and butchers can name only two or three male ascendants. Few can therefore trace their connections back to the putative founder or ancestor (*jidd*) of their clan, or work out how their fellow clan members are genealogically related.[6] When I requested such information, men sometimes bashfully referred me to an elder of their clan who was rightly perceived as more knowledgeable. Such men have a vested interest in fostering the sense of kinship obligation to their clan which helps motivate men to perform their civic duties under the rubric of collective "honor." They are also experienced in propagating and "refining" genealogical information for personal political and administrative ends. As competitors in tribal politics they are concerned, by affirming the agnatic basis of their clan power-bases, to maintain and maximize their clans' corporate political identities, and resist the centrifugal forces of fission and dispersal. And as tribal officials charged with administering their groups, they need to delineate their spheres of authority. Such men were unable to produce detailed genealogies, but they *could* explain how the contemporary branches and households of their clan were related, and locate them in hamlets and houses. They also tended to stress prestigious connections with other leading clans. Thus when the poet Muḥammad Yaḥyā described his clan, the above-mentioned Ilt Ibrāhīm, he first mentioned the external origins of its eponymous ancestor; he then stressed its close ancestral relationship with the shaykhly clan, Ilt Faraḥ—a fact attested in a local document which he possessed; and finally he invoked the material reality and historical connections of Ilt Ibrāhīm's "first hamlet in al-Naẓīr," Shaṭūr, and explained how the present branches of the clan were generated:

> Ilt Ibrāhīm originated from Ḍarb Banī Shiʿbah [in ʿAsīr], like Ilt Faraḥ. Two brothers came—Faraḥ Ḥasan, who begot (*khalaf*) the shaykhs of al-Naẓīr, and Ibrāhīm Ḥasan [the founding ancestor of Ilt Ibrāhīm].
>
> Shaṭūr is a famous historical place. It once contained an old Turkish house built from small, square stones. Over two centuries ago it fell into ruins, and our *jidd* rebuilt it. This was Yahyā Ibrāhīm. And he begat Jābr Yaḥyā and Jubrān Yaḥyā and Aḥmad Yaḥyā, and the following *bayts* have all branched (*tafarraʿ*) from them . . . [He then named eleven contemporary families, including his own.] Imagine—all those came from one *bayt*! Twenty-five mansions (*qaṣr*) from one!

Co-existing with the descent ideology of clans is the recognition that they can absorb unrelated people. As one man put it: "Ilt Rāshid is divided into many families and places, and anyone can live among them and become a member of Ilt Rāshid." People also acknowledge that clans can merge (*yinḍumm*). The Naẓīrī clan, Ilt al-Ḥājj, for example, fused with Ilt ʿAṭās after the latter—which had existed with that name for at least three centuries—dwindled in size.[7] In the document quoted above (D1887), the two clans are still mentioned as a composite, but the name Ilt al-Ḥājj later became dominant, and the name Ilt ʿAṭās became obsolete as a clan name. Such merging or absorption appears to depend on contiguity; in other words, place trumps kinship ties and putative descent.

When clans grow too large for their elders to administer, or leading members move away after quarrels or for economic reasons, they can conversely divide into sub-clans and acquire new names. Then the link with the original clan is often still recalled, partly for administrative reasons, partly for status reasons (if it is a leading clan). For example, the four matronymic subclans of Ilt Ibrāhīm, allegedly named after the mother and co-wives of its eponymous founder, are always described as "part of Ilt Ibrāhīm," although they dispersed into different hamlets long ago. This is partly due to the efforts of leading elders to maintain memories of the link.

A clan can also be renamed when a powerful or wealthy man emerges within one of its branches, then imposes his authority over the whole group. This may take place in the man's own lifetime or in the next generation, especially when he leaves a large patrimony and many sons. But when this happens, people still recall the clan's previous name. For example, in the late nineteenth century the Naẓīrī clan, Ilt ʿIzzān (a name which first appears in D1658) was renamed Ilt ʿAbdallāh after the coffee merchant mentioned in Chapter One. A branch of the clan retained the patronym ʿIzzān, but in 1980 it was still subsumed under, and eclipsed by, the later patronym ʿAbdallāh; people said: "Ilt ʿIzzān is the same as Ilt ʿAbdallāh." In the 1990s, however, the name ʿIzzān again became prominent because that branch of the clan produced a major Zaydī scholar (*ʿālim*).

It is common for the contemporary name of a clan to be spontaneously linked to prior names in the way described, providing a short chain of two or three patronyms which can be traced back through tribal agreements for several centuries. This imposes a veneer of historical continuity and political stability onto a reality of some flux and change, benefiting contemporary power holders. Changes in clan names, and adjustments in clans, have therefore regularly taken place for demographic, administrative, and political reasons. But clans are, overall, remarkably stable structures—especially the large, dominant clans, the names and status of which are maintained from generation to generation, in mind and practice, by the efforts and ambitions of their leaders.

As Muḥammad Yaḥyā's explanation showed, clans are closely identified with particular hamlets, though there is rarely a tidy correspondence. Small clans might be concentrated in a single hamlet, but larger ones invariably have "offshoots" (sing. *naqīlah*) from their principal hamlets living elsewhere. Also, most hamlets, especially large, old ones, contain members of several unrelated families or clans, and the *madīnah* is especially heterogeneous (Table 3.3).

Large clans and their principal hamlets sometimes share the same name, like the Naẓīrī hamlet Ilt Rāshid—which actually contains five unrelated families, including members of its eponymous clan. More often, however, clan and hamlet names differ, and then they are used interchangeably or treated as virtually synonymous. For instance, people can equally say, "He's

TABLE 3.3. NUMBER AND STATUS OF AGNATICALLY UNRELATED FAMILIES/CLANS IN SEVEN SETTLEMENTS IN THE TRIBE OF AL-NAẒĪR, 1980

Settlement	*Pop.*	*Number of agnatically unrelated families/ clans by status category and origins*
The *madīnah*	877	19 *qabīlī* 5 *sayyid* 6 'butcher'
Ilt Rāshid	334	4 *qabīlī* 1 'butcher'
al-Farq	218	11 *qabīlī* 1 *sayyid*
Ilt al-Burmī	136	4 *qabīlī* 1 *sayyid*
Shibāb	137	9 *qabīlī* 1 *sayyid* 1 'butcher'
Qulal al-ʿUqab	138	2 *qabīlī* 1 *sayyid*
Shaṭūr	82	3 *qabīlī* 1 'butcher'
Totals	**1,922**	**70**

Source: Fieldwork census, Oct. 1979–Feb. 1980

gone to Ilt ʿAbdallāh" as "He's gone to Qulal al-ʿUqab" ("the rocks of the vultures"), the clan's main settlement. People also spontaneously identify clans or their offshoots by reference to their ancestral or satellite hamlets—as one might refer to the head office and branches of a business—and often point out, as Muḥammad Yaḥyā did, the "original house" of their founders. Clans are also identified with their members' individual landholdings, which are usually near their hamlets. Just as people equate the hamlet of Shaṭūr with Ilt Ibrāhīm, although it contains three other unrelated families, so they point to the terraces above the hamlet and say "That's Ilt Ibrāhīm land," although they are actually owned by members of various clans.

Clans and hamlets are similarly equated in popular historiography. Rāziḥīs think of the evolution of their tribes in terms of the establishment and expansion of dwellings and settlements, and the transformation of a forested, uncultivated wilderness into an agriculturally productive resource by the laborious construction of terraces. People often recall at whose behest houses were built, and mention the relative ages of houses and hamlets. Naẓīrīs, for example, regard two or three houses, still standing, as the "original" houses of their tribe, and those who built them as its "original families"—the aforementioned Ilt al-Qayyāl and Ilt al-Wālī, which have now dwindled to one or two families and men.[8] As the population grew by immigration and natural increase, they explain, the first six hamlets of al-Naẓīr were built. Trees were felled to provide rafters, doors, and shutters; more land came under cultivation; and yet more hamlets were created as men hived off from their natal settlements to live closer to terraces inherited or bought elsewhere, to be nearer the market, or to escape conflicts with neighbors—a process, they point out, which continues today. People thus conceive of a kind of genealogy of place. Houses begat hamlets, hamlets reproduced, and a tribe evolved.

Rāziḥīs take the great age of their system for granted. Though chronologically vague, their sense of historical longevity is realistically based on the material evidence of the built environment and local documents. Not only do houses, settlements, and terraces present an imposing aura of age and permanence, but the antiquity of many can be verified in dated sale papers. The names of tribes and clans also recur in countless dated agreements preserved in people's homes, especially those of tribal leaders and the descendants of former rulers. This evidence could, of course, be ignored, but heredity and precedent are revered in this culture, and the demonstrable historical continuity of groups and dynasties is valuable political capital and greatly emphasized—especially by shaykhs, elders, and leading *sayyids* who all have a particular vested interest in preserving the principle of hereditary entitlement. Shaykhs therefore insist that their clans are the "original, authentic" (*aṣlī*) shaykhly dynasties of their tribes, brandishing documents to prove it, and the members of other leading clans similarly assume and assert their right to supply the elders of their tribe as their forefathers did. Partly by their own efforts, therefore, shaykhs and elders embody the permanence as well as the contemporary identities of their tribes.

Tribal Sovereignty

It is vital for understanding the operation of the tribal system of Rāziḥ to appreciate that, within that system, its tribes are autonomous sovereign polities.[9] This is partially obscured, however, by the polysemic and homogenizing use of the term *qabīlah*. This is one manifestation of a typical feature of Rāziḥī (and Yemeni) linguistic usage: the custom of applying identical categorical terms to entities which share certain key characteristics, but which are sociologically distinct. An important example is the term *bayt,* and its synonyms, *ilt* and *āl* (which are used only in possessive constructions with proper names). "Bayt Muḥammad," the more common "Ilt Muḥammad," and the mainly *sayyid* (standard Arabic) usage, "Āl Muḥammad," can all refer to a household headed by Muḥammad, *or* to an extended family of several households with a living or recently deceased head named Muḥammad, *or* to a clan named after a long-deceased ancestor. Such varied usage disguises the fact that these are distinct kinds of structure. Households and extended families are usually ephemeral, in the sense that their names and identities do not necessarily survive the deaths of their male heads. Clans, however, are named corporate groups with permanent politico-legal identities which outlive their constituent families and transcend the generations. What the common terminology reflects is a shared ideology of agnatic descent, and that the structures it refers to are developmentally related and usually nested (though lone households and extended families exist which have not yet developed into clans, or which were once, but have since declined).[10] The point to stress is that people with local knowledge distinguish between different kinds of groups by the *proper name* (surname) to which the term *ilt, āl,* or *bayt* is prefixed, and from the context of an utterance.

The terminology of larger tribal structures is similarly polysemous. The term *qabīlah* is applied to a hierarchy of sociologically distinct, nested structures which, like *bayt*s, share a common characteristic—in this case, that they constitute some kind of politico-legal grouping or alliance larger than a descent-based clan.[11] Thus, while Rāziḥīs invariably refer to tribes as *qabīlah*s, they do not do so exclusively. When they want to stress or exaggerate the solidarity or status of other structures, they sometimes exploit the terminological ambiguity and refer to them as *qabīlah*s too. For example, men sometimes assert that their ward is a *qabīlah* because they are disaffected with their shaykh, and yearn to secede and become an independent polity. People can also refer to supra-tribal structures and alliances (to be described in Chapter Five) as "one *qabīlah*" in order to emphasize their political unity or common identity in particular circumstances; sometimes they even assert that the whole of Rāziḥ is "one *qabīlah*" for reasons of self-aggrandizement. It is such hyperbole, perhaps, which has led some anthropologists to describe Rāziḥ as "a tribe."[12] But Rāziḥ is not an autonomous polity or sovereign domain with political borders, nor does it have a leader with supreme and permanent *political* authority. Individuals and groups cannot therefore join Rāziḥ as they can its constituent tribes, because there is no such permanent, corporate polity to belong to or join, nor political "shaykh of Rāziḥ" to whom they can contractually attach themselves. Rāziḥ is not, therefore, by my definition, a tribe.[13]

The term *shaykh,* which basically means "leader," is similarly polysemic. As well as being the title for the chief of a tribe, it is also used as a generalized honorific for a shaykh's close agnates, and can also be applied to elders. This usage reflects the fact that tribal governance is both a cooperative and a competitive enterprise. Shaykhs are assisted by close relatives from their clans, who act as advisors and deputies, and form a ruling team of "shaykhs." At the same time, other relatives and unrelated elders contesting the shaykh's position can also dub themselves "shaykh" in order to exaggerate their own positions—especially with government officials, who are often ignorant of tribal structures and power plays.

Local terminology can therefore be confusing to an outsider, but Rāziḥīs themselves are well aware of the difference between a "real" *qabīlah* and a rhetorical one, and between the properly instituted, hereditary shaykh of a tribe on the one hand, and a relative of a shaykh, a pretender to the shaykhship, or a presumptuous tribal elder on the other, because they have intimate, insider knowledge.

The Tribal Constitution

The tribal leaders of Rāziḥ are accorded by their constituents, and by the leaders of other tribes, exclusive jurisdiction within their respective territorial domains with regard to the application of tribal law and the implementation of government demands. This applies regardless of whether transgressors are residents or "foreigners" (*min khārij*). It is the tribe in which a crime or fight takes place which determines primary responsibility for dealing with it, not the identities of the protagonists. For this reason, as we shall see, when people tell stories of crimes or conflicts, they invariably stress and prioritize their *locations*. This is not mere scene-setting, but essential information for understanding the dynamics and resolution of problems.

The leaders of each tribe are also responsible for protecting the interests of its residents and its resources, including most importantly its trade routes and market (if it has one). To that end, it is their right to allow or prevent access to their domains; as it is expressed in tribal agreements: "The opening and closing [of borders] is under the authority of tribal leaders" (*fatḥ wa taghlīq bi rā'ī al-kubār*). They also have the exclusive right and duty to represent their constituents in inter-tribal affairs and with the state. The corollary of this is that no shaykh has the right to exercise political authority outside his own tribe, nor to represent any tribe but his own unless specifically requested to do so by other shaykhs. All this is what I mean by "tribal sovereignty."

The constituents of each tribe, for their part, are "one summons" (*dā ʿī wāḥid*), meaning that they owe their shaykh political allegiance, should submit to his jurisdiction in matters of tribal law, and should unite "as one hand" (*yid wāḥidah*), in the local idiom, if he requires them to muster militarily. For this reason tribesmen are sometimes referred to as "fighting men" (*ḥarrābīn, muqātilīn*). Collective responsibility is fundamental in Rāziḥī tribal governance.[14] Shaykhs and elders allocate financial, legal, political, and military liabilities within their tribes according to agreed legal criteria, and their constituents are obliged to one another, as well as to their leaders, to contribute or mobilize. These principles of solidarity and mutual help are a legal extension of the basic values of "tribalism" (*qabyalah*), and are upheld by the principle of reciprocity and the rules and values enshrined in tribal law. Because the collective ideals of other Middle Eastern tribes have sometimes been portrayed as morally unconditional—"My brother right or wrong"—it should be stressed that the opposite ideal applies in Rāziḥ, where the support of one's leaders and fellows is conditional on one's law-abiding behavior (see page 166).

Tribal governance, like that of all polities, generates a variety of expenses, including fees for tribal officials, and the substantial costs and damages which arise from litigation, dispute settlement, and military action. One of a shaykh's main duties, therefore, is to collect financial subscriptions toward these liabilities, which none is wealthy enough to bear alone as in other regions.[15] The operation of this political system therefore absolutely depends on the material contributions of each tribe's members.

FIGURE 3.2.
Shaykh ʿAwaḍ Manṣūr conversing with the leading elder of Ilt ʿAbdallāh, Sawādī Ḍayf. He has just fired his gun to alert people for a subscription collection.

The vital and definitive obligation of tribal citizenship is therefore to contribute to the expenses of tribal governance, and to the liabilities of one's clan, ward, or tribe as clearly defined in tribal law. The fundamental importance of what I earlier dubbed "corporate subscription" (Weir 1986) is reflected in the fact that the most common epithet for a male member of a tribe is *ghārim* (pl. *gharrāmah*), literally "contributor to expenses"—roughly equivalent to "taxpayer" or "citizen" in states. A common idiomatic expression for "tribal unity," for example, is "subscribers side by side" (*al-ghārim janb al-ghārim*), meaning that each tribesman must *pay his share* as well as play his part in collective enterprises. The central importance of corporate subscription is also reflected in the plethora of special terms referring to the payment (or non-payment) of tribal dues, and the relentless repetition of mantras stressing the obligation to pay in documents and speeches. Among the main pledges a tribesman makes when he swears allegiance to a shaykh, for example, is that he will support him *fī farq wa ṭarq,* meaning that he will pay his subscriptions (sing. *farq*) and comply with their administration (*ṭarq*). When shaykhs make public announcements (sing. *ẓāhirah*), they also invariably preface them with a formulaic preamble reminding their constituents of these civic responsibilities.

Tribal Governance

The shaykhs and elders of each tribe combine roles which, in complex polities, would be separately assigned to the executive and the judiciary, but there is no "separation of powers" in Rāziḥ. Nor are there specific premises for conducting tribal business; shaykhs and elders all work from home, though shaykhs sometimes dedicate a special room (*dīwān al-shaykh*) to this purpose. Otherwise they deal with problems wherever they occur.

The main everyday task of shaykhs and elders is dealing with crimes, disputes, or any other problems which take place within their domains. This involves a variety of legal and administrative tasks: investigating accusations, intervening between disputants, apprehending offenders, organizing oath-taking, judging cases, and collecting and distributing subscriptions. Shaykhs are also expected to entertain important visitors on behalf of their tribes—an expensive and onerous task, though one which yields dividends in prestige and connections. Shaykhs also provide asylum (*wazā*) for refugees, though if they are criminals fleeing justice from neighboring tribes, tribal law decrees they "extradite" them to face their deserts.[16] Shaykhs delegate many governmental duties to the *aʿyān* of their tribes, who carry them out within their respective clans and wards, and in turn delegate tasks to hamlet *amīns*. As Shaykh ʿAwaḍ of al-Naẓīr explained:

> The shaykh has overall responsibility for the tribe (*mas'ūl ʿala al-qabīlah*), and he informs the elders (*aʿyān*) what needs doing, and each passes it on to those under him (*taḥt aydeh*). If it's an urgent demand, they jump to it. Or it might be a matter of solving a dispute or other duties. A shaykh is responsible for his tribe like an officer over his soldiers (*mithlmā al-ʿarīf ʿala al-junūd*).

In their capacity as law-enforcers, *aʿyān* are called "guarantors" (*ḍumanā*, sing. *ḍamīn*). Those with special responsibility for enforcing the security of the market and its trade routes, for example, are called *ḍumanā al-sūq*, "guarantors of the market." The *aʿyān* and *ḍumanā* of a tribe are often, therefore, the same men playing different roles.

Shaykhs, with their *aʿyān*, are also responsible for representing their tribes at inter-tribal meetings, where they are expected to promote their interests and forge useful alliances. When inter-tribal disputes cannot be solved by bilateral negotiation, and go to arbitration, shaykhs become advocates for their tribes, and assemble cases for the prosecution or defense which they present during litigation proceedings presided over by arbitrators—usually shaykhs neutral to the case. And when litigation and diplomacy fail, or outside threats loom, shaykhs must organize their men for defense or war. Afterward, the shaykhs and *aʿyān* orchestrate the peacemaking, and participate in the meetings at which the written settlement is negotiated and decided. Shaykhs must also liaise with the state on a range of matters, including order maintenance, tax collection, mobilization for military purposes, and (nowadays) censuses and development projects.

Meetings (*mawāʿīd*) within and between tribes are the archetypal activities of tribal governance, but they are so commonplace that men explaining their system often skated over them as too obvious for words. When they described political action, they tended to stress dramatic, devastating, and unusual events. But at the conclusion of exemplary or cautionary tales of famous tribal conflicts, the tape recorder sometimes caught a matter-of-fact, throwaway remark which referred to the most important, though narratively downplayed, component of any dispute: "... then we held meetings, wrote documents, and that was it." As such casual comments also take for granted, the decisions taken at tribal meetings are invariably recorded on paper, and copied for each main participant for their future reference.

These agreements, referred to generically as *qawāʿid* (sing. *qāʿidah*), meaning literally "fundamental regulations," create and affirm the principles, rules, and practices of tribal law, and stipulate the terms and conditions of the full spectrum of tribal relationships. They are thus the medium in which relations between the relatively stable corporate groups of Rāziḥī tribal society are conducted; and they textually constitute the identities and politico-legal functions of its various governmental structures. At the same time, agreements reinforce the status and positions of the political elite who participate in their compilation and are invariably named in them; and their names reciprocally lend authority and weight to *qawāʿid* (see page 72).

Qawāʿid have the same overall structure. They invariably begin by recording the representatives (*muqaddamīn*) who attended (*ḥaḍar*) the meeting at which they were compiled, each of whom is stated to be representing (*taqaddam ʿalā* or *qaṭaʿ ʿalā*) his "followers" (*man ilayh*), "tribesmen" (*qabāyileh*), or "group" (*jamāʿateh*), or more specifically his clan (*bayt*), ward (e.g., *thilth*), or tribe (*qābīlah*)—the proper names of which are often omitted because they are so well known. Representatives are then usually stated to have "affirmed and acknowledged" (*aqarrū wa aʿtarafū*) the terms or decisions of the agreement. These preliminaries reflect what Messick (1993:206), referring to sharīʿah documents, calls "the fundamental quality of presence" in the witnessing of words and deeds and judicial processes. They also show the great importance Rāziḥīs attach to the fact that leaders are making commitments on behalf of groups which consent to the terms and will support their implementation. As a Naẓīrī commented, "No one would dare say he represented his group unless he knew it was behind him."[17] The opening lines of *qawāʿid* are often followed by pledges of eternal unity (couched in customary idioms such as "brotherhood") and of adherence to sharīʿah as well as tribal law, and sometimes also express respect for prior agreements. Especially around the accession of new rulers, documentary preambles can also include fulsome expressions of religious piety and allegiance to the state.

After this introductory material follows the main substance of the document. This can vary greatly in length and content according to the complexity or gravity of the issues at hand. This matter is then followed by the names of the guarantors (*ḍumanā*) of the agreement. These are invariably shaykhs or elders, and fall into two principal categories: internal (or primary) guarantors (*ḍumanā al-razz* or *ḍumanā al-qudam*), who are always from the groups (clans, wards, or tribes) which are parties to the agreement; and external (or secondary) guarantors (*ḍumanā al-jidhū* or *ḍumanā al-radam*), who are always from groups which are *not* parties to the agreement, and which are structurally equivalent or superior to them. For example, the external guarantors of an agreement between clans or wards of the same tribe would typically be from other clans or wards of that tribe; of an agreement between two Rāziḥ tribes from one or more other tribes; and of an agreement between tribes of two different regions, from tribes of a third tribal region. A third category of guarantor, called *naṭū,* appears to have been co-opted on an ad hoc basis. An individual can call in any prominent man in his tribe or another to be his *naṭū* in a dispute, for example if the *ḍamīn* of his own clan is inadequate or away; or tribal leaders can co-opt one another as *naṭū*s in particular exigencies. Many tribal agreements from the imāmic era end with the formulae "guaranteed by internal and external guarantors" (*ḍumin bi ḍumanā razz wa jidhū*), and "whoever is co-opted should be recorded" (*man nuṭī kān ruqim*).

The significance of the above patterns of guarantee is that elders and shaykhs enforce the law and the terms of agreements within other groups as well as their own. This intra-tribal and inter-tribal cooperation in the maintenance of order is a fundamentally important characteristic of Rāziḥī governance.[18]

Qawāʿid conclude with the month and year of the agreement (the day is not recorded until the early twentieth century), followed by the names of the scribe (*kātib*) and witnesses (sing. *shāhid*). Scribes are often the sons of shaykhs working their apprenticeship, or men of *sayyid* or *qāḍī* backgrounds who specialize in penning tribal documents. Witnesses must be men of probity, and can be *sayyids*, *qāḍīs*, or *qabīlīs*. Butcher names rarely appear except when they witness agreements which specifically affect them. Each *qāʿidah* is thus topped and tailed by a veritable cast list of local dignitaries, inscribes some cross-section of the Rāziḥī political establishment, and reveals a facet of its workings. Important documents are also authenticated and endorsed at the head, above the text, by government officials, typically the local judge or governor, and (from the late eighteenth century) are sometimes stamped with an official seal. This final addition locks central governance onto tribal governance, and textually represents the hierarchical structure of the Yemeni state or local *dawlah* at the moment it was written (see Messick 1993: Chap. 12).

Tribal Territories

The size and disposition of tribal territories should be understood in relation to the practical problems of administering and protecting a scattered population in such extremely difficult terrain. Because shaykhs and elders are constantly petitioned in their homes, are summoned to the scenes of incidents anywhere in their tribes, and regularly meet to deal with problems, they and their constituents need to be mutually easily accessible. It is also desirable to conclude business within half a day—before or after the main midday meal—so that neither leaders nor plaintiffs need provide expensive hospitality. This means, in practice, that shaykhs should ideally live no more than two hours' walk or so from anywhere in their domains.[19] Travel considerations also apply when tribes are threatened from outside, and men must be mobilized and guard duty organized. For administrative and military reasons, therefore, the tribes of Rāziḥ are small, and fit into the landscape in a logistically logical way.[20] Thus each tribe occupies a discrete mountain or mountainside with cultivable slopes and water sources, and is bounded on most sides by divisive natural features such as precipitous slopes, rocky ridges, or deep clefts which separate settlements, impede travel, and facilitate defense.

The people of Jabal Rāziḥ categorize their tribes as being in "northern" (*shawāmī*) Rāziḥ or "southern" (*yamānī*) Rāziḥ—or simply "the north" (*al-shawāmī*) or "the south" (*al-yamāniyah*). This geo-political terminology reflects the direction of the main trade route through Rāziḥ, and the position of its two main gateways, control of which has always been of great political significance. These factors cause people to conceptualize their region and its tribes on a north-south axis, rather than (say) east-west. The bipartite division of Rāziḥ also has a historical basis in state rule. For strategic and administrative reasons, states usually governed Rāziḥ from centers in the north and south of the massif respectively (al-Qalʿah and al-Naẓīr), and divided its tribes into two districts named "the *shawāmī*" and "the *yamāniyah*." The earliest documentary mention of this division is in D1657.

The tribes of *shawāmī* Rāziḥ are Ghamar, which occupies a mountain of the same name east of Jabal Rāziḥ; Munabbih, which extends over several mountains; Banī Asad (nicknamed "Bakīl"), on Jabal Ḥurum; and Banī Maʿīn, which shares Jabal Ḥurum, and includes the adjacent valley of al-Ghōr. The tribes of *yamānī* Rāziḥ are Banī Rabīʿah, which occupies the

TABLE 3.4. THE TRIBES OF *SHAWĀMĪ AND YAMĀNĪ* RĀZIḤ

shawāmī *Rāziḥ*	yamānī *Rāziḥ*
Ghamar	Banī Rabīʿah
Munabbih	al-Izid
Banī Asad	al-Shawāriq
Banī Maʿīn	Banalqām
	al-Naẓīr
	Birkān

slopes around the well-watered valley of Wādī al-Muʿayan in the center of Jabal Rāziḥ; al-Izid, which curves along the highest crest of the escarpment; and al-Shawāriq, Banalqām, al-Naẓīr, and Birkān, which comprise summits and slopes at the top of the escarpment, and spurs, slopes, and wādīs which plunge to the Tihāmah. The ʿUqārib tribes similarly correspond to distinct natural formations; each occupies or shares one or more of the foothills or small mountains which fringe the west and south of the Jabal Rāziḥ massif (see page 22). They are also often assimilated to either *shawāmī* or *yamānī* Rāziḥ in speech, as they were administratively by past rulers.

Each tribe is closely identified with its unique and distinctive mountain territory—to the extent that place names and group names are virtually synonymous.[21] This is most obvious in the case of Ghamar, which is both the name of the tribe and its territory, and of tribes with toponyms such as Birkān, which means "two springs," and al-Shawāriq, which means "the place in the east," or with descriptive names like al-Naẓīr, which means "the beautiful place." However, the synonymity of territory and tribe applies equally to tribes with patronyms. Banī Maʿīn is both a place name and the name of a polity; thus someone can be equally said to "belong to" as to be "traveling to" Banī Maʿīn. Toponyms and patronyms do not therefore indicate different forms of political organization—one geographically based, the other genealogically based. Whatever their etymology, tribal names are just labels for polities and their territories.

The administrative and political constraints on the size of tribes help explain the absence of any legendary or documentary evidence of the tribes of Rāziḥ invading others or forcibly appropriating territory, or of any procedures for implementing such action. Such colonizing aggression would run counter to the entire ethos of tribal co-existence according to which shaykhs

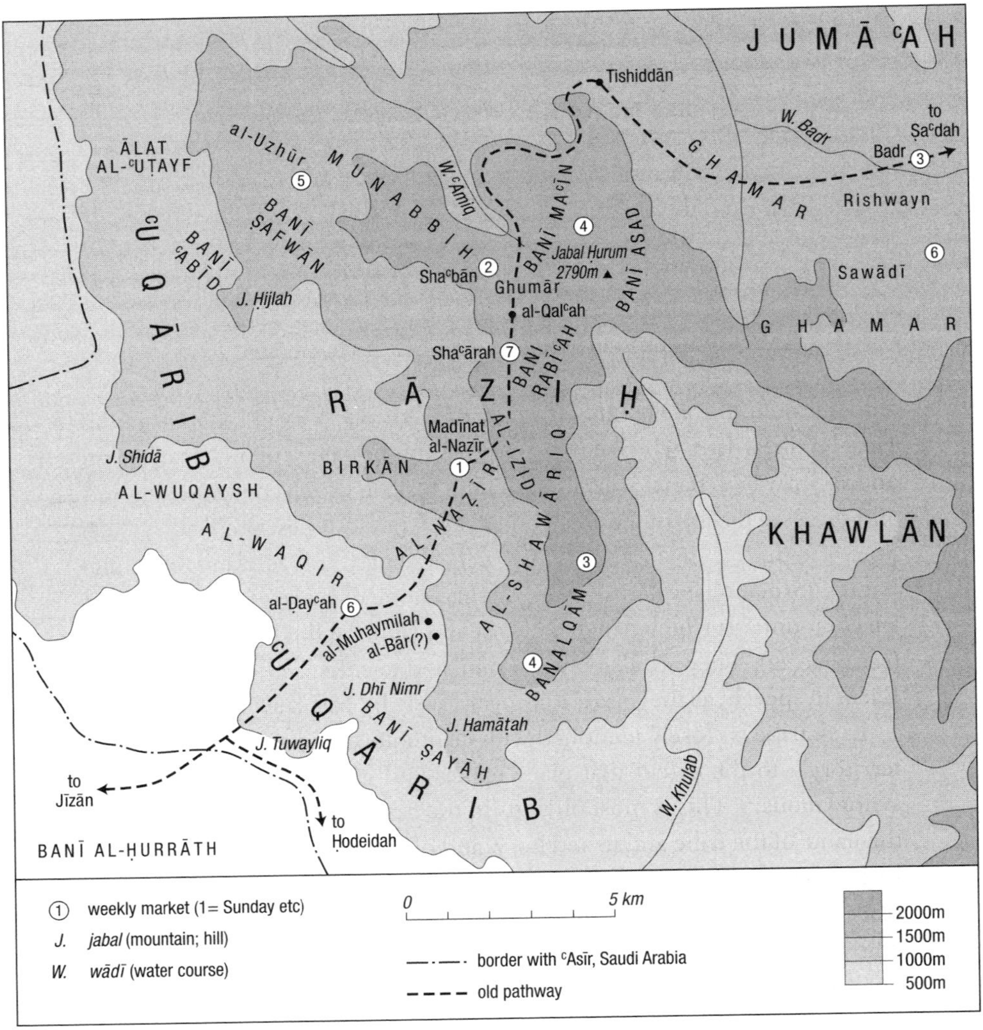

FIGURE 3.3.
Map showing the tribes of Rāziḥ and ʿUqārib.
Source: Surveys by Ian Dunn and Shelagh Weir, 1977 and 1979–80

officially and reciprocally recognize each other's sovereignty (though they might be covertly undermining it). Ambitious shaykhs certainly try to exert political influence over other tribes and their leaders, and they welcome new members—especially defectors—because they increase their support and prestige, but it is difficult for them to extend their physical domains without losing control. These tribes are not, therefore, units of territorial expansion. At an early stage in Rāziḥī tribe-formation, we can suppose, shaykhs competed and cooperated to carve out manageable domains, and apart from minor adjustments, that is more or less how they appear to have stayed.

Most tribes are subdivided into between three and five administrative parts (sing. *jizz*) which I call wards. As mentioned, these are perceived as fractions of their tribes, and can have fractional names, toponyms, or patronyms. The number and disposition of wards in each tribe are determined more by the size of its territory, its topography, and its settlement pattern than by the size of its population. This can be seen by comparing the neighboring tribes of al-Naẓīr and al-Izid, which—though their populations greatly differ—are both divided into three wards referred to as their "thirds" (*athlāth*). This is because their settlements are widely dispersed in relatively large territories. The wards of al-Naẓīr lie one above the other down the mountain of al-Naẓīr, as reflected in their names: The Upper Third (*al-thilth al-aʿlā*), the Middle Third (*al-thilth al-wāsaṭ*), and the Lower Third (*al-thilth al-asfal*). The "thirds" of the long, high territory of al-Izid range from east to west and have proper names: Banī Mālik (named after a leading descent group), al-Jabal ("the mountain"), and al-Gharbī ("the west"). The wards of other tribes are similarly based on their particular topographies and settlement patterns. Al-Shawāriq, for example, is subdivided into two wards: The Easterners (*al-sharqiyīn*) on the heights, and the Westerners (*al-gharbiyīn*) on the steep-sided spur which descends to the Tihāmah. On the other hand, although Birkān and Banalqām have comparable populations, Birkān lacks wards, whereas Banalqām is divided into "fifths" (*akhmās*). This can be explained by the contrasting terrains and settlement patterns of the two tribes. The settlements of Birkān are clustered on and around its relatively level summit and are therefore accessible to their shaykh, whereas the settlements of Banalqām are scattered down its steep, narrow territory from the summit of al-Ḥilf to the Tihāmah. The division of the tribe into several vertically arranged wards therefore facilitates its administration.

Because of the difficulties of governance in these mountains, there is a tendency for the wards of the largest tribes to be administered semi-autonomously, or for a ward to bid for independence. The large tribe of Ghamar (1975 population, 5300), for example, was usually represented as "one tribe" in inter-tribal affairs, but its two wards, Rishwayn and Sawādī,

TABLE 3.5. THE TERRITORIES AND WARDS OF THE TRIBES OF RĀZIḤ, 1980

Tribe (with estimated 1975 populations)	*Ward names*	*Location of wards*
Banalqām (1,100)	al-Ḥilf	Summit
	Ilt Marhab	Below summit
	al-Awsaṭ	Middle of spur
	Ilt al-Zāfir	Lower spur
	Ilt ʿAlī Sālim	Bottom of spur
Banī Asad (750)	none	
Banī Maʿīn (3,000)	al-Ghūr	Valley of al-Ghūr
	Āl al-ʿUlā	Lower, west slopes of Jabal Ḥurum
Banī Rabīʿah (1,500)	Walad al-ʿĀmrī	North
	Ilt Muḥammad	South
	Ilt al-Naẓīr	East
Birkān (1,100)	none	
Ghamar (5,300)	Rishwayn	Wādī Badr area
	Sawādī	Heights of mountain
al-Izid (2,500)	Banī Mālik	East
	al-Jabal	Center
	al-Gharbī	West
Munabbih (3,700)	Shaʿbān	North and summit
	Ghumār	East
	al-Qidd	North
	Ilt ʿAlī	and
	al-Uzhūr	West
al-Naẓīr (4,000)	Thilth al-Aʿlā	Top
	Thilth al-Wāsaṭ	Middle
	Thilth al-Asfal	Bottom
al-Shawāriq (1,500)	al-Sharqiyīn	East
	al-Gharbiyīn	West

seem to be administered relatively autonomously. Similarly, the large tribe of Munabbih is probably stretched to its functional limits—though this did not deter its ambitious shaykh from constantly trying to exert control over the neighboring tribe of Birkān. Evidence that the shaykh of Munabbih was probably over-reaching himself emerged during fieldwork, when the leading elder of the Ghumār ward of Munabbih was bidding for independence by strenuously asserting that it was a tribe in its own right, and he its rightful shaykh. The position of Ghumār has always been anomalous, however, because it is the site of the government center (*markaz*) at al-Qalʿah, and has historically supplied governors with police and soldiers—sometimes straining its tribal relationships, and feeding the ambitions of its leading clan. It has therefore occasionally behaved like an independent tribe—for example by being represented and accepting collective liabilities independently of Munabbih. However, on this occasion, its leader was thwarted because other shaykhs would not acknowledge Ghumār's independent status—such inter-tribal acknowledgment being one pre-condition of full tribehood. Al-Naẓīr, with its large population and far-flung settlements, is probably another maximally sized tribe, though there was no sign of it fragmenting in the 1990s.

Tribes are often identified by reference to their wards. Naẓīrī documents often state, for example, that the tribe's shaykh and elders represent "the Thirds of al-Naẓīr." The whole is pictured as the sum of its parts, and they are exclusively conceived as administrative fractions (not genealogical segments). Wards, like tribes, are of great long standing. Al-Naẓīr and al-Izid, for example, have each been divided into the same named "thirds" for at least two centuries. Other fractional divisions have appeared and disappeared historically as populations fluctuated, and in response to the administrative requirements of shaykhs or rulers. There were times, for example, when the Thirds of al-Naẓīr were subdivided, for specific purposes, into "fifths" (*akhmās*), and they are nowadays subdivided into "quarters," each quarter (*rubaʿ*) comprising a major hamlet and smaller neighboring settlements. So when the shaykhs and elders of al-Naẓīr list names and estimate contributions, they do so ward by ward, and within each ward "quarter" by "quarter" as they formerly did "fifth" by "fifth." As Shaykh Nāṣir explained: "These groupings are intended for accounting (*ḥisāb*)—for the purpose of subscription-collection (*mafraq*)." This included work for states, which appropriated and sometimes modified tribal structures for the purposes of tax collecting and law enforcement. This is reflected in the almost obsolete term *maktab* (pl. *makātib*), from the root "to write," which was once the state-administrative term for "tax-paying unit." Today it survives in Rāziḥ only as the term for the five wards of Munabbih, but it was once also applied to tribes (D1847b).[22] States also sometimes "created" their own fractions by recategorizing or regrouping tribes or their subdivisions. At some periods, for example, they grouped the tribes of Rāziḥ into "fifths," and also dubbed the major tribal regions of Khawlān ibn ʿĀmir its "fifths."[23]

The striking dominance of the "fractional principle" in the conceptualization of tribal structures is symptomatic of the huge importance of collective responsibility and corporate subscription in both tribal and state governance. Fractional subdivisions helped and help tribal leaders and states to calculate and allocate liabilities within their domains and among their constituents.[24] The point to stress is that a fractional term always reveals that a grouping is part of a co-liable whole in a particular context, but it does not connote a specific sociological entity nor reveal its administrative purpose or function. The characteristics and relationship of both part and whole must therefore always be determined by empirical historical and anthropological research.[25]

Borders

Because each tribe is a sovereign domain, it is of the utmost importance that its borders be demarcated and recognized. Neither the interests of leaders nor those of their constituents would be served by lack of clarity over rights and responsibilities. Shaykhs need to define the precise territorial limits of their jurisdiction. And everyone needs to know whom to turn to when problems arise—whether they are at home in their own tribe or "abroad" in others. Tribal borders are consequently well known and clearly marked by major natural features such as ridges and wādīs, and by smaller landmarks such as trees, rocks, and buildings. Some, as mentioned, are also overlooked by tall, circular watchtowers called "outposts" (sing. *khārijah* or *ṭārifah*).

The borders of tribes are portrayed as ancient, immutable, and sacrosanct, especially by politicians, who have a vested interest in the image and reality of permanence and stability.[26] Thus a Rāziḥī *sayyid* with wide governmental experience explained:

> Every border has been known since the division of the ancestors (*min qismat al-sābiqīn*). They can *never* be altered. They are all determined and

FIGURE 3.4.
Guard tower (*khārijah*) near the border between the tribes of al-Naẓīr and al-Izid

> well known . . . everyone knows his borders (*ḥadd*), his tribe (*qabīlah*), and his homeland (*bilād*).

And when I asked Shaykh Nāṣir Manṣūr, the co-shaykh of al-Naẓīr, whether it was ever possible to change tribal borders, he replied:

> Never! They can *never* alter the borders (*ḥadd*), nor shift land from one tribe to another . . . Even were there only five people left, they would still keep their own borders.

Despite these assertions, borders must have fluctuated historically. They could sometimes have shifted, for example, when border land was sold to a member of the neighboring tribe, or when houses or hamlets on a tribal boundary seceded politically to a neighboring tribe or gave land to meet crippling legal debts. Banalqām, for example, is supposed to have once given al-Shawāriq the land of al-ʿArḍ in the Tihāmah foothills in lieu of *diyah* (blood money) after a war. The southern boundary of al-Naẓīr with al-Waqir could also have changed when the site of the Tihāmah entrepôt, and responsibility for its protection and revenues, were shifted historically.

The practical and symbolic importance of borders is reflected in the existence of "security zones" (sing. *kufalah*) along certain stretches which are protected by special regulations to maintain the peace.[27] These zones are especially vulnerable to conflicts because the dwellings of different tribes are in close proximity, because they are traversed by paths between tribes, or because of their particular topography. The *kufalah* zone between al-Naẓīr and Birkān, for example, comprises two steep, facing slopes on either side of the wādī which forms the border between the two tribes in their heavily populated upper reaches. The *kufalah* zone between al-Naẓīr and al-Izid, said to have been created after a Naẓīrī shot an Izdī, similarly comprises two facing slopes dotted with hamlets, and where the steep gradients provide excellent vantage points from which men armed with guns can target the opposite slope. Some *kufalah* zones were therefore probably established or widened when guns became widespread in the nineteenth century.

Neighboring tribes created *kufalah* zones, or reaffirmed their regulations, either in anticipation of hostilities, or in their aftermath to prevent a recurrence. They then defined them with great precision:

> [Representatives of] al-Naẓīr and Birkān . . . affirm their guarantee of the *kufalah* to be described . . . it being a specified, bounded area which we define as follows: from the Well of Birkān and the terrace below it, which are included in the *kufalah,* up the slope from the well as far as the path, then on the level to the depression and the terraces along the wādī, then upward to the terrace called al-Maththar and from there as far as Ibn Maṭar's house via the large landfall [called] Qabaʿ, then on the level to the Mosque of Ibn ʿAydān, which is included in the *kufalah* . . .

and so on, in the same vein, until the circuit descends to its starting point at the Well of Birkān (D1892b).

The actual or potential violation of security zones therefore activates responses which reinforce the tribal order. Problems in *kufalah* zones can be seized upon or magnified by leaders in order to "mark" their domains, rattling their fences, so to speak, at their neighbors—provided they are confident in their case and in the backing of their tribe. Inter-tribal agreements such as the above which define *kufalah* zones in detail also symbolically accentuate the political significance of borders and territories, and reaffirm each tribe's sovereignty. Keeping borders and security zones in good cognitive repair is therefore comparable to maintaining genealogies in systems where tribes are defined as groups of people descended from a common ancestor.

CHAPTER FOUR

Tribal Leadership

We have seen that the tribes of Rāziḥ are constituted by a contractual relationship between hereditary shaykhs and their constituents. In order to understand the operation and longevity of this tribal system we therefore need to examine the institution of tribal leadership more closely, and especially to consider how certain clans have monopolized shaykhships (sing. *mashīkh*) for centuries, and how shaykhs gain, maintain, or lose power and influence. This chapter will explore these issues by focusing mainly on the shaykhly dynasty of al-Naẓīr, Ilt Faraḥ.

Origins and Legitimation

According to Ilt Faraḥ, their dynasty was founded by an immigrant from coastal ʿAsīr. The following is a composite of their legend of origin, which Shaykh ʿAwaḍ Manṣūr recounted to me on three occasions. It is typically ahistorical, and undoubtedly simplifies complex events. But it is realistic about the bases of shaykhly power: wealth, control of markets, and popular support.

> My ancestor (*jiddī*) came from Ḍarb Banī Shiʿbah about four centuries ago. He killed a man, then fled here with two brothers [who went elsewhere]. First he settled in Tuwayliq [a Tihāmah foothill], and built there and bought land. Then he moved to al-Bār [the former Tihāmah entrepôt], and bought

> more land there, and brought it to life. Then he moved to Baḍaʿah [another entrepôt site] and acquired our land in al-Muhaymilah. Later he came up to Khalaqah [halfway up Jabal al-Naẓīr] and acquired more land. All our land in those areas dates from then.
>
> People were coming from the *mashriq* at that time, and collecting [illegitimate] taxes like *ḍarībah*. My ancestor said, "How can you let those Ṣaḥār people tax you? This must not continue!" So they surrounded the house where the *mashriqīs* were staying, and slaughtered them by *jambiyyah* in one fell swoop. Those stones in the sūq are their graves.[1] I have old documents (*qawāʿid qadīmah*) about this.
>
> Then our ancestor moved up the mountain and built that old shaykhly tower-house (*ʿāliyat al-shaykh*) called Bayt ʿOthmān next to the sūq. Then he took over (*aḥtall*) al-Naẓīr, and acquired more land and built houses and settled here. And the people congregated around him and built houses and developed the land, and the tribe multiplied (*kutharat al-qabīlah*). Order and security were established, and the tribe flourished.

SW: Didn't they have a shaykh before your ancestor came?

> No, al-Naẓīr was just a forested wilderness (*qafarah*) then, and the people were lower down. They had no shaykh, they were ungoverned (*jāhiliyyah*).

In stressing the acquisition of land and houses (most still owned by Ilt Faraḥ) as the shaykhly ancestor's stepping-stones up the mountain and to tribal leadership, the story boasts of the material possessions which still underpin and symbolize shaykhly power—large landholdings (*māl,* "wealth") and the towering mansions (sing. *qaṣr*) from which they govern their tribes (see Mundy 1995:3). The story also shockingly depicts the ancestor's route to the top as saturated with criminal violence. In an inversion of the ideals of tribal law, the future upholder of tribal order is a killer fleeing justice, and gains power by murdering visitors. He redeems this disgraceful act, however, by dispatching the rapacious "easterners"—archetypically fierce tribesmen in Raẓiḥī folklore. This heroic act of liberation from oppression heralds a new era of peace and good fortune under Ilt Faraḥ's leadership. Before the ancestor arrived al-Naẓīr was just *qafarah* and its people were *jāhiliyyah,* the Quranic epithet for the supposedly ignorant and anarchic condition of the Arabs before the civilizing influence of Islam. Afterward the Naẓīrīs farmed the land and prospered; cultivation is metaphorically equated with order.[2] The story is thus a parable of the necessity for tribal governance. The message is clear: if you want to resist exploitation and flourish, you need to be politically organized. You need a shaykh and a tribe.

The eponymous ancestor of Ilt Faraḥ is first mentioned in a sale paper of 1605 (D1605), which Shaykh ʿAwaḍ had probably seen or knew about. This suggests that Ilt Faraḥ rose to power toward the end of the first and only Ottoman occupation of Raẓiḥ when the Zaydī imām was leading anti-Ottoman insurgencies, firearms were spreading, and wealth was flooding in from the coffee trade (see Chapter Nine). The shaykhly dynasty of al-Naẓīr, and others in Raẓiḥ, might therefore have been kick-started by patronage, subsidies, and arms from either or both rival states. Another, muted tale further suggests that Ilt Faraḥ violently wrested the shaykhship from Ilt al-Wālī, one of the "original clans" of al-Naẓīr, whose members were perhaps employed by the Ottomans (who called their governors *wālī*). A legendary war between Ilt al-Wālī and another old clan, which is related to Ilt Faraḥ, perhaps derives from that struggle for power, and the latter admit that the old woman said to have inadvertently caused this conflict was a member of their clan. They thereby gain credit for the existence of the mosque of al-Naẓīr, which she ordered to be built in redemption. The mosque bathes Ilt Faraḥ in religious respectability as well as attracting visitors. Various shaykhs have therefore added to it and, most recently, rebuilt it, using profits from trade, revenues from terraces near the marketplace which their ancestors made "*waqf* for the mosque," and with the help of men from different Rāziḥ tribes who volunteered their labor because they "considered it everyone's."

Dynastic Monopoly

The documents show that Ilt Faraḥ has monopolized the shaykhship of al-Naẓīr in apparently unbroken succession since the time of its eponymous ancestor until today, and other Raẓiḥ tribes have a similar pattern of long and continuous dynastic leadership. Once on track, shaykhly clans were evidently difficult to derail. This must be partially, or even mainly, attributed to the ideological power of the descent principle in Raẓiḥī (and Yemeni) culture—the conviction shared and religiously sanctioned by *sayyids* and imāms—that agnatic transmission of status and occupation is natural and proper. The longer a clan retained the shaykhship, therefore, the harder it would have been to challenge its claim to be the "real, authentic, original" (*aṣlī*) shaykhly clan of its tribe. Its hereditary right, once established as fact and confirmed in contracts and treaties, could be lost only if its wealth or numbers drastically declined.

Hereditary shaykhship is also preserved by the customary mode of succession. This falls into Lewellen's category of systems in which "[s]uccession is circumscribed by rules which restrict the number of contenders, while providing a sufficiently large 'pool of variability' . . . from which the fittest might emerge" (Lewellen 1992:55). Since there is no strict rule of succession such as primogeniture, there is invariably intense competition for office within shaykhly clans. While continuing to assert their entire clan's monopoly on the shaykhship, those in power try to narrow the field by asserting that only *their* branch or sub-clan is entitled to office. The half-brothers who were co-shaykhs of al-Naẓīr during my fieldwork, for example—Nāṣir Manṣūr and ʿAwaḍ Manṣūr—repeatedly asserted that the shaykhship of their tribe "can *never* leave Ilt Faraḥ," invoking their legend of origin and centuries of tenure. At the same time they insisted that only the direct descendants of their long-lived grandfather (FF), Shaykh Jubrān Qāsim (1853–1890s), were eligible within their clan. When I asked Shaykh Nāṣir: "Must the shaykh *always* be from Ilt Faraḥ?" for example, he erupted in his typically hyperbolic way:

> Yes!—but *only* from Bayt Jubrān! There are about seventy men now in Bayt Faraḥ, but [the following] are disqualified [he then recited the patronymics of six other branches of his clan]. All of those are prohibited except for Bayt Jubrān Qāsim. This would even be the case if there was only a *woman*! They proclaimed from the announcement place: "Britain has no queen but Elizabeth!" and even if there was only a *woman* left in Bayt Jubrān Qāsim, we would uphold her position too!

Shaykh Nāṣir's account of how his grandfather gained the shaykhship in competition with his cousin (FBS), Aḥmad Nāṣir, implicitly spurns the notion that anyone outside Ilt (Bayt) Faraḥ could legitimately aspire to the office. It also evokes the tension surrounding the transmission of power, and the importance to the tribe of choosing the right man—Jubrān Qāsim, in this account, whose suitability is accentuated by the story's magical realism. A woman with supernatural powers discerns the underdog Jubrān's hidden qualities, making his accession seem right and inevitable.

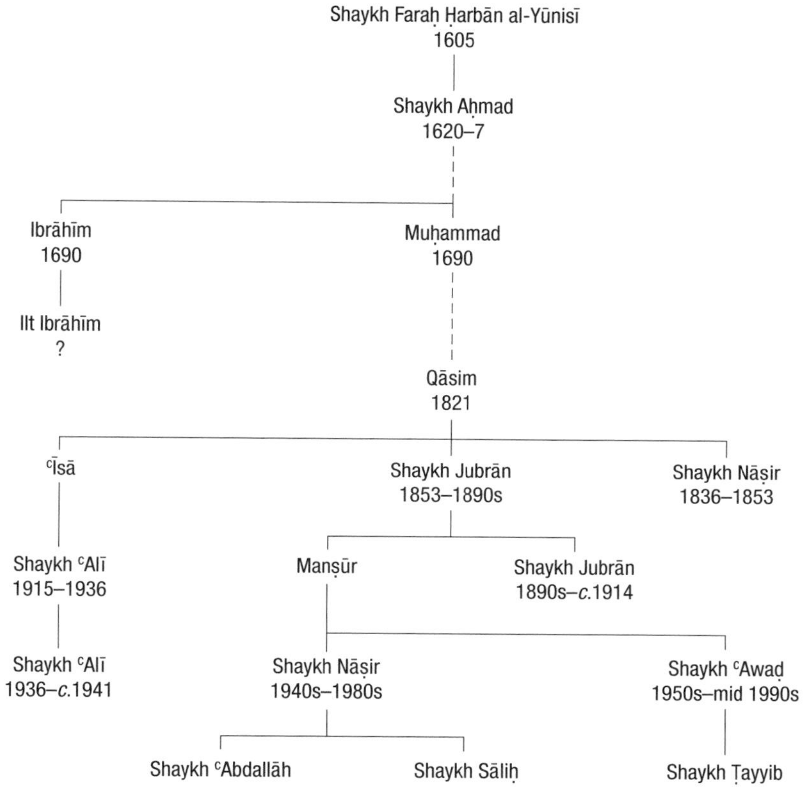

FIGURE 4.1.
Simplified genealogy of Ilt Faraḥ, the shaykhs of al-Naẓīr, showing the relationships of recent shaykhs. Dates indicate when they were politically active.

My grandfather Jubrān Qāsim and Aḥmad Nāṣir held meetings. Aḥmad was handsome as a bullock and strong as a bough, whereas my grandfather . . . [he shrugged, implying small and weak]. But fortune favored him. Aḥmad wanted the shaykhship, and they quarreled. The elders (*aʿyān*) intervened, and said: "The only solution is to go to Ibn ʿUrayj in Tishiddan" [in Ghamar].[3] So Aḥmad Nāṣir and his four guarantors (*ḍumanā*) and my grandfather and his four guarantors went to Tishiddan, where the shaykh served them goat.

The daughter of Ibn ʿUrayj was wise and thoughtful and told fortunes in sand. Her father moaned:

"The Naẓīrīs have burdened me with a big problem. I don't know which of those two to choose, and it's embarrassing."

"You must simply judge correctly," she said.

"But what should I say?" he asked. "They are equally respected."

"I will take them coffee," she replied, "and greet one saying, 'How are you, O shaykh?' *He* is the one who should be shaykh. I will know from my fortune-telling."

Aḥmad Nāṣir, tall and comely, was perched on a bedstead [the best place in the room] surrounded by the elders, and Jubrān Qāsim was hunched up alone behind the door wrapped in a shabby sheepskin. The shaykh's daughter entered, looked around, then went straight to Jubrān Qāsim and shook his hand, saying, "How are you, O Shaykh?" Then she greeted the others and left the room.

Her father stared at her with eyes wide as coffee cups.

"That shaykh will bring them good fortune and strength," she explained, "and they should only choose *him*. The one on the bed is from a useless *bayt,* and if they choose *him* they'll have unending strife."

The elders continued discussing their dilemma, and Ibn ʿUrayj brought them supper.

"God willing," he assured them, "we'll announce the verdict in the morning."

Next morning he gave them a good breakfast for their journey.

"Hurry up and give us your decision, O Ibn ʿUrayj," they said.

"You heard it last night!" he exclaimed.

"What do you mean?" they asked.

He explained it, then handed each one a document, guaranteed by guarantors, confirming that Jubrān Qāsim should be shaykh and no one should oppose him. So the Naẓīrīs returned home, and people greeted them with joyous gunfire, shouting: "Congratulations to our genuine shaykh (*al-aṣl*)!"[4]

The clan branches the "victors" define as ineligible for the shaykhship can be permanently excluded and become independent clans. The leading Naẓīrī clans, Ilt Ibrāhīm and Ilt al-Ḥājj, for example, are said to have once been part of Ilt Faraḥ, and appear to have broken away in the seventeenth century, although their elders remain at the heart of tribal governance—which is presumably why the connection is still "remembered."[5] Otherwise excluded branches remain in the clan, support or oppose incumbent shaykhs, and sometimes return to power. The latter happened after Jubrān b. Jubrān Qāsim was imprisoned in ʿAsīr in 1914 (though Shaykh ʿAwaḍ did not volunteer this information, which spoils his picture of uninterrupted succession in his own line). Whatever its internal rifts, the shaykhly clan shares an interest in preserving its dynastic entitlement, and closes ranks if it is challenged. These factors counter the fragmentary tendencies of shaykhly clans, and ensure that they remain large enough "pools of variability" to produce suitable leaders.

Shaykhly clans are so closely identified with their tribes that it is difficult for most constituents to imagine usurping them. It would be tantamount to annulling their tribe, and effacing its history and permanence. It could also prejudice its internal and external relationships and agreements, including the webs of guarantee and alliance in which all shaykhs are enmeshed. This motivates constituents to support their shaykhs, and shaykhs to support allied shaykhs, creating an overall propensity toward the reproduction of the dynastic status quo. Occasional challenges for the shaykhship from other clans therefore tend to be based on claims of superior, meaning anterior, "authenticity." This happened in al-Izid, where an elder repeatedly tried to wrest the shaykhship of his tribe from Ilt Sarīᶜ, claiming that his forefathers were the *aṣlī* shaykhs of al-Izid, and had lost the shaykhship after becoming poor and dwindling in size. After Ibn Sarīᶜ died in the early 1990s, this rival tried to persuade the government to acknowledge him as shaykh and award him the monthly stipend, and he passed through al-Naẓīr one day, en route to Sanaa, with a bag containing several nineteenth-century documents which he hoped would convince officials of his status. However, his efforts to oust Ilt Sarīᶜ failed, and the deceased shaykh was succeeded by his son. Ilt Sarīᶜ is rich and numerous, and has led al-Izid for at least two centuries (D1807a), so easily retained its dynastic monopoly.

Selection and Appointment

Shaykhs are selected by a quasi-democratic process which involves evaluation of each candidate's potential for carrying out his shaykhly duties effectively.[6] This tends to favor the sons of shaykhs because of the experience and knowledge they gain while helping their fathers. They also inherit hoards of *qawāʿid* and other papers, as well as the authority they confer and the commitments they enshrine—notions often invoked in documents. What everyone wants, above all, is a shaykh who will solve problems and disputes with the minimum of trouble and expense, and promote the tribe's welfare—including, some believe, by bringing rain (*barakah*) and crops. "A shaykh's leadership should be 'green,'" Shaykh ᶜAwaḍ explained. "One person can benefit the people," he added, "and another can sow dissension." Some shaykhs are also believed to have *jinn* informers, and to be protected from their enemies by magic potions.

Shaykhs should be knowledgeable about tribal law and politics, and capable of administering their tribes and dealing with other tribes and government officials. Both appearance and performance are important; the masculine imperative to act and look strong is multiplied for shaykhs. This is especially the case when they attend hostile inter-tribal meetings (sing. *mīʿād*)—a duty called "defense and confrontation" (*tuqā-wa-liqā*). In these challenging situations, they should adopt a bold, dignified, and uncompromising posture, and represent their tribes' interests persuasively and assertively "without their voices quavering," letting rip, when necessary, with rhetorical invective. When they are invited to arbitrate between men or groups within their own tribes, or between other tribes, they should also be able to weigh the evidence calmly and carefully, and pronounce fairly according to the dictates of tribal law. Whether in ruling, confrontational, or mediatory mode, a shaykh should ideally also be proficient in the terse Rāziḥī style of argument and oratory, and be able to reproduce, as appropriate, the special, code-like terms and phrases which encapsulate the key concepts of tribal governance. Politics is partly theater, and lines and delivery are equally important.

When shaykhs fall short of these ideals, their deficiencies are offset by the collective character of tribal governance; the "genuine shaykh" of each tribe is always acting in concert with his councils of relatives and elders who act as his advisors and deputies. The Naẓīrīs regarded one Rāziḥī shaykh, for example, as "weak and stupid" because he was new to office and ignorant of tribal law, and had a meek and ineffectual manner. His deficiencies were compensated for, however, by the fact that his chief counselor was a wise, knowledgeable, and experienced elder from another major clan. They also made fun of a shaykh who often garbled the specialized politico-legal language, but who was similarly sustained by his co-governing clique. As Shaykh ʿAwaḍ put it, "If a shaykh's no good, they just limp along until they find a better one." The fact that shaykhs are always part of a governing team, and not autocrats, helps the institution of shaykhship survive the inadequacies of individual shaykhs.

New shaykhs are installed after the incumbent shaykh dies, or when he becomes old and frail and "can no longer climb up and down," as one shaykh put it. Rivals then flaunt their abilities and garner support from

FIGURE 4.2.
Shaykh Nāṣir Manṣūr of al-Naẓīr and sons Ṣāliḥ (left) and ʿAbdallāh (right), 1979.

their own and other clans, and people take sides. This was happening in al-Naẓīr in 1980 when the co-shaykhs Nāṣir Manṣūr and ʿAwaḍ Manṣūr were becoming elderly and physically incapable of performing their duties. Both had trained their eldest sons for the shaykhship, and were pushing their candidatures. Some Naẓīrīs backed Shaykh ʿAwaḍ's eldest son for the post, but he was not interested. Shaykh Nāṣir's eldest son, Ṣāliḥ Nāṣir, on the other hand, was politically ambitious, had striven to acquire the requisite knowledge and skills, and had seized opportunities for self-promotion by asserting himself at meetings and formulating statements in the correct form of words. He also tackled two issues of burning local concern: the soaring cost of marriage and growing alcohol consumption. He summoned the shaykhs of Raẓiḥ to Shaʿārah, the traditional tribal meeting-place in central Raẓiḥ, and delivered a resounding speech which persuaded the delegates to try to limit the brideprice. He also organized raids on the homes of drinkers and their suppliers in al-Naẓīr. These popular actions helped ensure his appointment (though he died prematurely a few years later).

After canvassing their constituents, the elders of the tribe meet, and appoint the new shaykh (*shayyakhūh*). "They hold a celebration (*ḥafl*)," Shaykh ʿAwaḍ explained. "Then they say 'We witness what is in the documents of your father and ancestors, and you shall be our shaykh, and these *ḍumanā* will support you.'" Without this backing from the elders, shaykhs could not function; "a rod on its own is useless," as the saying goes.

The elders record their agreement to appoint a new shaykh in "shaykhship contracts" (*waraqāt al-mashīkh*), which implicitly confirm their positions as shaykh-makers, and their tribe's collective leadership. Those I copied all date from the twentieth century. These affirm the shaykh's allegiance to God and the state, reiterate his obligations to both state and tribe, including attending meetings with government officials and upholding tribal law, and record his pledge to fulfill them. Some also record how the shaykh will be paid, and allude to the reason for the new appointment. The contracts are usually drafted in front of the local judge, who witnesses and endorses their contents and the identities and probity of the signatories, and forwards them to the local governor for his information and endorsement. This ensures that the government stipend is transferred to the new shaykh, and reassures the governor of the continuity of responsible and loyal tribal governance. While respectfully acknowledging the state's superior authority, however, the documents also implicitly assert that the appointment of shaykhs is a tribal, not a state, prerogative. As Shaykh ʿAwaḍ declared: "The shaykhship depends on the wishes of the tribe (*al-mashīkh ʿalā rughbat al-qabīlah*)." Rulers appear to have accepted this too. They needed effective shaykhs to work through, and the latter could not function without grassroots legitimation and support. They tended not to interfere in the selection process, therefore, though they sometimes investigated charges of corruption, oppression, or maladministration (D1938b). The following extracts are from the 1936 contract of Shaykh ʿAlī ʿAlī ʿĪsā:

> Present were the elders (*aʿyān*) . . . [named] . . . representing the Upper Third, Middle Third, and Lower Third [of al-Naẓīr] . . . and they agreed to appoint (*aqdamū wa aʿqalū wa akbarū*) ʿAlī b. ʿAlī ʿĪsa Faraḥ as shaykh for everything which might afflict the tribe with regard to defense of territory, war and peace, and whatever might dishonor it. No one else must promote himself [instead] by making pronouncements or solving problems or opening [negotiations] without the shaykh's authority and the tribe's agreement. Any disobedience or betrayal of the shaykh, the tribe, or the government (*dawlah*) shall be the responsibility of the perpetrators, who will be disowned, and held liable for all the costs of their dissension . . .

> In return for his [government] stipend (*ijrah*), [the shaykh] must obey and submit to God's authority and that of the imām and his successor (*mawlānā amīr al-mu'minīn wa walī ʿahadeh*), and his officials and judges (*ʿummāleh wa ḥukkāmeh*), uphold their orders, requests, or prohibitions, and comply with their wishes together with others under imāmic rule (*ahl al-ṭāʿah*) . . .
>
> [The shaykh] must treat his tribesmen (*raʿiyyah*) equitably, be they weak or strong, closely related or distant, brother or comrade. He must be fair and unbiased when giving orders. He must not accept false witnesses against those accused, whether or not they are his relatives, and should accept only verified evidence. He must not take bribes nor tolerate offenses. And he should strive his utmost to benefit [the tribe].
>
> The shaykh pledges to accept responsibility for discharging the above-mentioned duties, and if he fails, [accepts that he] will forfeit his authority unless he puts the matter right and [accepts responsibility for] whatever expenses [his mistakes or misjudgments] caused. (D1936a)

The Material Bases of Tribal Governance

Tribal governance has always been officially subsidized from "above" by the state, and "below" by the tribes, both sources of material reward ultimately deriving from the surplus production of Raẓiḥ. Zaydī rulers defined shaykhs as among the *ahl al-ḥuqūq* (sing. *haqq*), meaning those to whom they delegated administrative tasks, especially in tax collection, and in return for which they paid them substantial stipends. Intra-clan competition for the shaykhship therefore often focused on which branch could legitimately claim to be the true *ahl al-ḥaqq,* which (like the shaykhship itself) was considered a hereditary right. Shaykhs also receive payment for their services from their constituents in the form of fees (sing. *ijrah*) skimmed "off the top" of the monies collected toward their tribes' liabilities; fines extracted from offenders; and subscriptions levied on an ad hoc basis for unexpected outlays they make on behalf of their tribes. Sometimes tribes also remunerated their shaykhs with fixed monthly salaries (D1931a). Shaykhs are also authorized in tribal law to appropriate land from transgressors when they default on major legal penalties. And they receive fees and expenses when they act as external guarantors or arbitrators for other tribes or their members.

Shaykhs disburse part of their income for various governmental purposes, such as paying for the services of messengers, drummers, and butchers, and to defray the heavier costs of defusing fights and crises and providing hospitality (*ḍayfah*) for official guests (*ḍayf al-dīwān*). The latter could be a burdensome duty in hard times, and was shared among the shaykhly family and the *aʿyān* of each tribe according to contractual agreements. In the late nineteeenth century, for example, Shaykh Jubrān Qāsim of the above legend and the elders of the Middle Third of al-Naẓīr agreed in writing to take turns entertaining official guests under the supervision of a "rotator" (*mudawwil*), and that anyone who defaulted would be fined double the expenses (D1887).

Shaykhs also share their income with their ruling team of fellow clan members and other *aʿyān* according to each man's contribution to tribal governance. This was also subject to contract. After Shaykh Jubrān Qāsim's death, for example, his five sons agreed to divide the shaykhly portion of the taxes between them in unequal fractions according to their respective responsibilities, with his successor, Shaykh Jubrān Jubrān, getting the largest share. They also agreed that:

> The responsibility for [attending] meetings and hostile confrontations (*mawāʿīd wa tuqā-wa-liqā*) should be divided in thirds . . . Manṣūr Jubrān will be responsible for organizing inter-tribal meetings, Jubrān Jubrān for sharīʿah matters, and Ḥusayn Jubrān for administering mosque and *dīwān* property [meaning the *waqf* which helped fund tribal administration]. And the upkeep of the *dīwān* will be divided between the [five] brothers in fifths. (D1905c)

People accept that shaykhs and elders should be reimbursed for their work and associated outgoings, but practice is perennially rife with dissension. Leaders quarrel among themselves about their shares of official income. And their constituents are always suspicious that their leaders might be "eating," in the local idiom, more than their legitimate portion. They are also alert to the possibility that, instead of solving problems, leaders might be fomenting them for their own benefit and plunging their tribes into unnecessary and expensive litigation.

Their official incomes helped shaykhs accumulate relatively large landholdings during affluent periods, especially, we can assume, during the coffee boom when they played a major part in collecting market taxes. Most of their land, like other men's holdings, is within their own tribes. Shaykhs, like others, protected some of their land from the fragmentary effects of Islamic inheritance law by making it *waqf*, and sometimes dedicated the pro-

FIGURE 4.3.
Shaykh ʿAwaḍ serving food to guests, 1979

ceeds toward the expenses of tribal governance. This helped support their dynasties, but also provoked intra-clan quarrels over rights to proceeds. In 1844, for example, Ilt Faraḥ quarreled over terraces their predecessors had made *waqf al-dīwān* to fund *dīwān al-shaykh* and rooms in the mosque. A member of Ilt Faraḥ claimed the land was his, the case went to litigation, the shaykh produced documentary evidence from earlier disputes confirming the terms of the *waqf,* and the adjudicating *qāḍī* supported his right to control the proceeds on condition he disburse them to the *dīwān* and mosque under the supervision of representatives of the three Thirds of the tribe (D1844b). Another quarrel broke out over the *waqf* in 1909 between Shaykh Jubrān Jubrān Qāsim and his brother, and the case went to the *ʿālim,* Sayyid ʿAlī Ḥusayn al-Ḥūthī. He decreed that *he* would assess and distribute the *waqf* proceeds, and the two brothers would be equally responsible for furnishing the *dīwān* with rugs and paraffin, and caring for visitors sent there from the mosque (D1909b). In 1977 the harvest from these terraces was still funding *dīwān al-shaykh,* but when the market dramatically expanded soon after, Ilt Faraḥ rented the land out to shopkeepers (Weir 1987). Then in the 1980s, when prices soared, they quarreled over the right to sell the land or build houses on it. Some must have succeeded, for a grand new shaykhly mansion and the first government telephone exchange in Rāziḥ now stand on the terraces (see page 305).

Family wealth gives shaykhs a hedge against the vagaries of income from state and tribe, helping them to meet their tribes' obligations and maintain their authority during lean times—for example by advancing fines and expenses in order to resolve problems, and collecting subscriptions later. Official and family income also enables shaykhs to enhance their prestige and influence by building imposing houses, furnishing their *dīwān*s well, providing guests with lavish hospitality, affording expensive transportation, and employing retainers. Shaykh ʿAwaḍ Manṣūr used to ride a prestigious white mule between his houses in the *madīnah* of al-Naẓīr and Khalaqah down the mountain, sometimes accompanied by guards. And Ibn Ghalfān, the shaykh of al-Waqir, has a retinue of black henchmen, known as "the slaves (*ʿabīd*) of Ibn Ghalfān." Since the 1980s, most shaykhs have also acquired impressive motor vehicles.

Wealth also helps shaykhs to make strategic marriage alliances within and beyond their own tribes. Men of modest means are deterred from multiple marriages by high brideprices and wedding expenses, pressure on domestic space, and the cost of new building. Most are therefore monogamous and only a small minority have two or more wives simultaneously.[7] But rich shaykhs can afford to marry serially and polygamously, and with leading families. Ilt Faraḥ pride themselves on their exclusivity in the marriage stakes, and its members have consistently intermarried with leading clans of al-Naẓīr and other Rāziḥ tribes. They have also given daughters to Bayt Abū Ṭālib, though (to their annoyance) their requests to marry *sharīfahs* have always been refused.

In a society with high rates of infant mortality and low life expectancy, polygyny increases a man's chances of rearing several children, which further enhances shaykhly power and helps ensure dynastic succession. As Shaykh Nāṣir pithily observed about a shaykh he disliked: "He's cowardly and bad. He doesn't protect his honor (*ʿarḍ*). And he's a weak character. But he's got lots of land and eight sons." Any man with many adult sons, and especially a politician, is a force to be reckoned with. A shaykh's power is also augmented by daughters, though this is downplayed. They are the medium for creating advantageous affinal connections; and they provide essential labor, including preparing the banquets which promote men's standing.

Consolidating Power and Exerting Authority

The position of novice shaykhs is initially precarious, with everyone critically evaluating their performance, and relatives often still vying for the office and its rights and privileges. Shaykh Jubrān Qāsim faced such opposition at the start of his "regime" in 1853. A collateral from Ilt Faraḥ, fulsomely named Jubrān b. Aḥmad b. Ḥasan Sharīf Faraḥ in the litigation paper (D1853a), contested Jubrān Qāsim's tax-collecting rights on the grounds of hereditary precedent, and the case was heard by a Tihāmah shaykh and an elder of al-Naẓīr. The opponents submitted documents going back more than one and a half centuries to support their competing claims, but the mediators ruled that *all* Ilt Faraḥ were *ahl al-ḥaqq*. Jubrān Aḥmad therefore persisted with his claim, but the shaykh decisively quashed his ambitions by calling in external guarantors to support his rulings, and meting out heavy penalties on his rival for challenging his leadership and insulting him in the sūq, and on those "who had tried to elevate Jubrān Aḥmad, desiring to resist the [true] shaykh's authority (*yurīdū al-qawmah fī wajh al-shaykh*)." He also divided the costs of settling this dissension between his rival, the latter's supporters, and his ward, "because no one from the Middle Third intervened to stop him, or took control, or seized sureties until after the expenses had been incurred." As we shall see in Chapter Six, it is obligatory for bystanders, and especially elders, to intervene in quarrels and restore law and order; in this instance, however, it was the political order, specifically Shaykh Jubrān's authority, which had been threatened. The shaykh also vigorously asserted his right to rule, and organize tax collection, by reminding the *ḍumanā* that . . .

> He [Shaykh Jubrān] should be honored and revered by the tribe according to the agreements (*ẓunnāt*) in his possession, and no one should oppose him because he is the leader of the whole tribe . . . And he affirms the calculations, terms, and guarantees (*al-ʿadd wa al-dhikr wa al-ḍumān*) in the agreements (*ẓunnāt*) and settlements (*fuṣūl*) in the shaykh's possession, whether old or recent . . . His family (*bayt al-shaykh*) is in overall charge of accounting to the *dawlah* for the canonical taxes . . . and the [*ḍumanā* of each of the] "fifths" are responsible for [collecting from] those under their authority. And whoever submits his taxes contrary to the shaykh's orders will be taxed twofold and bear all the expenses of mobilizing guarantors (*shallat al-ṣāḥib*) [to enforce the shaykh's wishes]. (D1853b)

The following month representatives of "all the fifths of all the Thirds of al-Naẓīr" affirmed their support and respect for Shaykh Jubrān Qāsim, and for his agreements and decisions. Such rivalries for the shaykhship are not always conclusively resolved, so two co-shaykhs can share power in an uneasy relationship of alternate competition and cooperation for years. This was the situation in al-Naẓīr, where Shaykh Nāṣir had shared the shaykhship with his younger half-brother, Shaykh ʿAwaḍ, for several decades—each supported by different factions.

A shaykh consolidates his "domestic" position by gaining the trust and confidence of the senior, experienced members of his own family, who act as counselors and share his shaykhly duties, and the elders (*aʿyān*) of the tribe who implement his instructions within their clans and wards. In order to retain the loyalty of this governing team, he needs to call tribal councils and consult them regularly, and to share official income with them equitably and according to prior agreements. To offset internal intrigues, he must also gain support among his tribe's largest clans—especially those on the margins of his domain which are the hardest to control and most likely to secede. This is achieved, among other ways, by intermarriage, hospitality, and discriminatory favoritism, for which the subscription system is an ideal

FIGURE 4.4.
Procession by members of the Upper Third of al-Naẓīr, to welcome Shaykh Nāṣir's son, Ṣāliḥ, home from medical treatment abroad, 1980.

tool. Shaykhs can exempt clans or wards from contributing to collective liabilities at the expense of the rest of the tribe, but not themselves.

The political support such means can garner was demonstrated in 1980 when Shaykh Ṣāliḥ Nāṣir returned to al-Naẓīr from a medical visit abroad. Members of the Upper Third ward of al-Naẓīr, which had recently been exempted from contributing to the inter-tribal litigation to be described in Chapter Eight, processed through the mountains to the *madīnah* yelling a high-pitched chant (*maghrad*) of praise. On arriving at Ṣāliḥ's house, their leader made a short speech expressing delight at his safe return, then presented him with three sheep and a sack of coffee beans, which he accepted, and thrust a wad of money at him which he ostentatiously refused. The sheep were slaughtered at the door, and the visitors were served coffee and later treated to a banquet. A member of the delegation told me that they had levied SR100 each from about fifty men to pay for their prestations.

Shaykhs also need to maintain the support of other tribal leaders, especially close allies, because their positions depend on them acknowledging their authority, inviting them to guarantee and witness their agreements, and helping them enforce the law. Tribal leaders also collectively help legitimate the whole notion of dynastic succession by their constant reference to other shaykhs as being from the "authentic" shaykhly clans of their tribes, and by invoking the historical relationship between their respective fathers and other forebears. Shaykhs can therefore undermine enemy shaykhs by denying their legitimacy and refusing to deal with them. The shaykhs of al-Naẓīr were doing this in 1980, when they were at odds with Ibn al-ʿAfrīt, the shaykh of Birkān, who was suffering internal dissension. They claimed his rival, a leading elder, was Birkān's "true shaykh," and that they would deal only with him. But long-standing hereditary entitlement, combined with strong support from al-ʿAfrīt's main ally, the shaykh of Munabbih, enabled the shaykh of Birkān to survive this challenge to his authority.

Protest and Rejection

As Maclagan noted with regard to Jabal Ḥufāsh, "Men in a strong position . . . can demonstrate their power by behaving shamelessly and getting away with it" (Maclagan 1993 : 292). This applies to some Rāziḥī shaykhs who are said to be serial adulterers, or to have used violence against opponents with impunity. But if they flagrantly abuse their positions and the moral code, they can severely damage their reputations and influence. This happened after an infamous incident within living memory.

A notoriously oppressive brother of the shaykh of al-Naẓīr publicly accused a poor laborer, Abū Ḥāmis, of failing to pay his debts. Provoked by this insult to his honor, Abū Ḥāmis killed him in a fit of rage, then owned up to government officials in al-Qalʿah. The Naẓīrīs offered to pay the *diyah* and pleaded for clemency, but their shaykh spurned compensation, demanded capital punishment, and even assisted in the execution. Women sang laments for Abu Ḥāmis, who was pitied as a victim, and the shaykh's reputation was irredeemably tarnished. His behavior so violated people's ideals of justice and mercy that, even years afterward, they were ashamed to describe it, muttering sadly, "Shaykh so-and-so once made a terrible mistake." This act lost that shaykh support within his tribe, and helped a clan rival gain ascendance.

If shaykhs consistently flout the ideals of leadership, or are bad for their tribes, they provoke dissension or rejection. The most common form of protest against an unpopular shaykh is to refuse to subscribe to collective liabilities or mobilize for direct action. If the elders of a rebel's clan or ward deem this action unjustified, they force him to comply with his obligations. But if his pretext is just, they support him, and their shaykh must modify his demands or policies. Tribal obligations therefore provide a barometer of a shaykh's authority and standing within his tribe (see Chapter Seven).

A more serious and institutionalized form of protest is for individuals, hamlets, or even wards to defect to another tribe (*inqaṭaʿ min qabīlah ukhrah*). This usually involves only the transference of political allegiance and responsibilities; most people are too tied to their houses and land to move physically.[8] As in state systems, therefore, a distinction is made between residence and citizenship, as mentioned in Chapter Three. Despite still living in their old tribe, defectors (sing. *shārid, quṭīʿ*) sever their political contract with its shaykh and constituents, and make a new one with another tribe and its shaykh. Defectors are described as "escaping from the authority" (*harab min taḥt*) of their former shaykhs, and receiving shaykhs are described as "giving them sanctuary" (*awzā-him*), meaning from political or legal oppression. "After that," Shaykh Nāṣir explained, "they are with us in everything. Whatever afflicts them afflicts us, and whatever afflicts us afflicts them."[9] He then recited key formulae of tribal membership: "That means that they are among the people of al-Naẓīr in war, death, upholding shaykhs and pacts, and that they pay subscriptions with us."[10] Their houses and land now also "belong," politically, to their new tribe, and their new shaykh can legitimately enter them to enforce the law, or invest them during inter-tribal hostilities, without abusing the sovereignty of the tribe in which they are situated. Receiving shaykhs thus also gain tiny territorial enclaves in other tribes when men defect to them. When border groups seceded to neighboring tribes, therefore, inter-tribal boundaries might (as mentioned) have shifted, although leaders—wedded to the notion of borders being immutable—denied this ever happened.

Defectors seek a fairer, less corrupt, and more effective leader who is also accessible, and so will not need heavy expenses for dealing with problems far from his domain. In the days of travel on foot, therefore, most defections were probably to neighboring shaykhs—though this could change with motor transport. When walking through the mountains, my companions would occasionally wave toward a hamlet and remark that it had defected to (*inqaṭaʿ min*) a neighboring tribe, usually spontaneously adding "and they pay with them now." During the Civil War, for example, residents of hamlets in Banī ʿAsad defected to the neighboring tribe of Banī Maʿīn. As Shaykh Nāṣir explained: "Those who defected to Abū ʿAwthah [the shaykh of Banī Maʿīn] still live in their houses on their land, but now they pay their religious taxes and tribal subscriptions (*yisallimū zakāh wa furūq*) to *him*

. . . and Ibn ʿAwfān [the shaykh of Banī ʿAsad] has no more claims over them for subscriptions or anything (*fī farq-wa-ṭarq walā shī'*)."

Whereas ordinary immigrants routinely join new tribes without formalities simply by setting up residence, defection is regulated and ritualized. The aspiring defector (or defectors) formally requests the shaykh of his choice to accept him into his tribe by presenting him with a gun surety (*rabākh*), and uttering the words "I place myself under your protection and authority (*anīh bō wajhak*)." The shaykh he has repudiated then has a statutory period of a month (formerly fifteen days) to "chase up" (*laḥaq*) his defector and persuade him back into the fold. In the nineteenth century, this task was delegated to the elders of the defector's ward (D1879a).

A weak or guilty shaykh might do nothing to retrieve his man so as to avoid exposing his own deficiencies, while another will pursue him assiduously in order to restore his personal reputation and authority or "face" (*wajh*). To retrieve a defector, a shaykh presents a "gun of justice" (*bunduq al-taʿdīl*) to the shaykh the defector wants to join which demonstrates that he wants him back, and that he is willing to submit to an independent assessment of his grievances (*ʿuwal*).[11] Shaykh Nāṣir compared this procedure to a woman's institutionalized "flight" to her natal home when she is dissatisfied with her husband:

> We [shaykhs] submit a "gun of justice" (*bunduq al-taʿdīl*) to the shaykh our defector fled to, then we and [the defector] submit our cases to that shaykh (*ʿāwalnā ʿand al-shaykh*). If the defector has a justified grievance (*ʿūlah*) against us, then it will be revealed. But if it's only a silly idea in his head, then he must return to us unsatisfied. It's like when a woman flees (*tifirr*) to her father because her husband has abused her rights, and he submits a "gun of justice" to her father.

If the shaykh appealed to uphold the defector's complaints, the culpable shaykh must pay the costs and compensate the defector. But if he finds for the defector's shaykh, the latter fines his defector for his defiance of authority, and charges him for all the litigation expenses. This happened in 1841 in al-Naẓīr. Certain Naẓīrīs tried to defect to other tribes to avoid obligations, and their shaykh summoned external guarantors (*ṣāḥib al-jidhū*) from three other tribes in *yamānī* Rāziḥ (al-Shawāriq, al-Izid, and Birkān) to force their submission. The rebels consequently renewed their allegiance to their shaykh, and pledged terraces as tokens of their adherence to the agreement.[12]

FIGURE 4.5.
Drawing up a defection contract, 1979. The *ḥākim,* Sayyid Muḥsin Aḥmad Abū Ṭālib, is far right, with the Birkānī defector next to him. Far left is Shaykh ʿAwaḍ Manṣūr.

Inter-tribal defections are legalized ceremonially and by written contract. In February 1980 a Birkānī man and his sons, who wanted to defect to al-Naẓīr, arrived in the market early one morning, where they were welcomed by Shaykh ʿAwaḍ. They brought a sheep, which was slaughtered before a small audience to gunfire accompaniment, symbolizing the defector's appeal to be accepted by al-Naẓīr. Then the leading defector and Shaykh ʿAwaḍ made brief, formulaic speeches of welcome and acceptance, the shaykh extolling tribal values, and they repaired to the shaykh's *dīwān*. There they drew up the defection contract, literally "a pact of severance and entering" (*qāʿidat al-inqitāʿ wa al-dukhūl*), with the help of the judge of Rāziḥ, Sayyid Muḥsin Abū Ṭālib, who endorsed and stamped it on behalf of the government. After midday prayers the defectors then consolidated their new relationship by sharing a celebratory meal of the meat of the slaughtered sheep, and chewing qāt with the shaykhs and elders of al-Naẓīr.

Defection contracts must justify the action, and record the defector's pledge of allegiance to his new shaykh and tribe, and the shaykh's reciprocal pledge to solve his problems and protect his rights. For example, the contract drawn up when another Birkānī man and his sons defected to al-Naẓīr in 1979 (see page 115) begins by asserting that their shaykh

> fails to enforce tribal or religious law. When he and his colleagues encounter problems, he is notoriously incapable of putting them right. And he is conspicuously letting someone else usurp his position. (D1979b)

The "someone else" was the shaykh of Munabbih, whom they believed to be exerting undue influence over their tribe. The document then affirms that they henceforth

> belong with the people of al-Naẓīr in everything, major and minor . . . heart and soul, and support the tribe and its members whatever is required . . . Their houses and land are now [politically] among those of al-Naẓīr . . . They will pay taxes to the government representative (*al-mutawallī*), or to any other party, with the rest of the tribe of al-Naẓīr (*bayn qabīlat ahl al-Naẓīr*). They will subscribe to their collective payments (*fī farq-wa-ṭarq*) whatever liabilities they incur . . . They also accept responsibility for any expenses they cause if they are disobedient or abandon Naẓīrī ranks, even to the extent of [sacrificing] their houses, land, or any other property.

A reciprocal pledge follows from the leaders of al-Naẓīr, in which they take pains to affirm that they have carefully considered the legal justification for the defection as required in tribal law:

> Once the shaykhs and elders (*aʿyān*) of al-Naẓīr understood why [the defector] was seeking refuge, they welcomed him and it was ratified, and he was accepted in their tribe with the [customary] rights and duties [of a tribesman]. For their part, they undertake to support him in every way, whether in tribal or governmental affairs, and to defend him and promptly sort out any of his problems . . . This agreement is endorsed by the shaykhs and elders of al-Naẓīr who append their names below. [The defector] and his sons now belong to the tribe of al-Naẓīr . . . according to the terms of former inter-tribal agreements on defections . . . unless their behavior flouts the conditions mentioned . . . For the aggressor is responsible for [the consequences and expenses of] his aggression if it is unjustified.

Defectors obviously enhance the prestige of receiving shaykhs, and swell their tribes' numbers; they are trophies in the perennial shaykhly competition for influence and wealth. Naẓīrīs, for example, who regard their tribe as the best in Rāziḥ, boasted that few of them ever defected: "Most people defect to *us*." Shaykhs must be wary, however, of embracing defectors too readily or jubilantly. As always in intertribal affairs, there is a tension between competition and cooperation. Shaykhs must be careful to observe the proper procedures so as to avoid accusations of inciting defections from other tribes, interfering in their affairs, or subverting the authority of their shaykhs. And it is particularly important that they avoid alienating close allies. This was a crucial factor in a failed defection attempt at the beginning of the Civil War.

In 1963 Ibn Sarīʿ, the shaykh of al-Izid, tried to rally men and collect money to support the republicans. But his aforementioned rival feared he would "eat" the money, refused to pay, and appealed with his supporters to join al-Naẓīr. The Naẓīrīs then invited Ibn Sarīʿ to submit his case to their arbitration so that "the grievances, extortions, and unfair judgments" could be investigated (D1963). If the shaykh admitted and "honorably" righted the alleged wrongs, they would reject the defectors' application. But if he failed to attend the hearing, or made no attempt to retrieve his tribesmen "according to tribal regulations," they would accept them and take up their case against their shaykh. As always, costs were a major preoccupation. If the complaints were upheld, the expenses of the litigation (*shijār*) would be charged to their shaykh, but if not, the aspiring defectors would have to pay the costs of their dissension. Ibn Sarīʿ must have failed to make his case, because the legitimizing ritual sacrifice took place. However, the attempted defection petered out through inaction. "The aspiring defectors slaughtered two sheep and so did we," a Naẓīrī explained, "but we failed to support them against their shaykh. So it came to nothing, and they still pay (*yifruqū*) with al-Izid, not al-Naẓīr."

It was probably inevitable that the attempted defection would be overwhelmed by the long-term importance of the close "brotherly" alliance between al-Izid and al-Naẓīr, to be described in the following chapter. Although shaykhs compete for the prestige and material rewards of receiving defectors, as already stressed, they ultimately share an overriding "establishment" interest in maintaining structural stability and preserving key alliances. As one Naẓīrī put it: "No shaykh can accept other tribesmen without careful consideration; otherwise there would be chaos, with people changing tribes back and forth all the time."

A rejected shaykh suffers public humiliation and loss of prestige. He also reduces his constituents and subscriptions. The mere threat of defection can therefore pressure him to mend his ways, and this is often the main aim. Defectors do not necessarily want to repudiate their shaykhs and tribes forever, but often (like "fleeing" women) just want their grievances addressed. This is illustrated by a rare instance of an attempt to switch clan allegiance. In the late 1970s two members of Ilt Ibrāhīm in al-Naẓīr applied to join Ilt al-Ḥājj, which was then dominated by a cohort of tough brothers. Their grievance was that their own elders had failed to support them in a quarrel with their shaykh. A defection contract was drawn up in which they pledged their allegiance to Ilt al-Ḥājj and its leading light, and this was witnessed by several Naẓīrī *aʿyān,* and endorsed and stamped by the judge of Rāziḥ (D1978/9). This had the desired effect. Their clan elders persuaded them back into the fold by reminding them of their indissoluble blood ties to their natal clan, and by promising to support them in the future. As a result, "they still pay with Ilt Ibrāhīm." Shaykh ʿAwaḍ Manṣūr, who had contributed to this crisis, vehemently denied that it was possible to change clan membership: "People cannot repudiate their *descent!*" But this clan-swapping case is not unique.

If an unpopular shaykh refuses to stand down, his internal opponents—elders and constituents—can pressure him to change, or even try to depose him. They typically do this by calling meetings and writing pacts identifying themselves and proclaiming their grievances. Sometimes—perhaps usually—copies of these documents are forwarded to al-Qalʿah in the hope of discrediting the shaykh and convincing the governor to deal with his rival. This does not, of course, mean that tribal elders cede their jealously guarded power of appointment to the state. Since it generally serves government interests that the most effective shaykh should emerge by the customary selection process, it anyhow tends to bounce the problem back to the tribe.

This happened during a power struggle in one tribe in 1972, soon after Rāziḥ joined the Republic, when its "elders, *amīn*s, and certain individuals" denounced their shaykh, in writing, for the "huge penalties (*gharāmāt*)" he had incurred trying to wrest the shaykhship from a rival, accused him in extremely florid terms of being a national traitor, and denied his moral right to retain office or even membership in his tribe.

> He is without ethics or humanity. He has no concern for anyone's honor (*ʿarḍ*), nor for the rights of the inhabitants of his tribe or Rāziḥ. He seems to have a different religion from others, as all Rāziḥīs acknowledge whatever their station . . . everyone knows about his innumerable crimes. He has perpetrated something which no honorable or considerate *qabīlī* would ever do by libeling his rival . . . and the elders of his tribe to government officials *in writing* . . . This was perjury . . . yet he still signed [his statement] with his own pen. We refute all [his allegations], public and secret, and cast him out from our midst, never to take him back. The claims against him . . . will emerge in time, as will his emnity, now disguised as friendship, to our well-guided government . . . Can such a man be counted as a comrade (*ṣāḥib*), friend, or brother? Indeed not! He is an enemy. They therefore repudiate his claim to the shaykhship, strip him of his position, and renounce responsibility for him forever. He will no longer remain a member of their tribe, even as a layman. (D1972b)

The shaykh's rival sent this document to the governor of Qaḍā Rāziḥ, who added his confirmation that this was the tribe's decision, and forwarded it to a higher official. But the latter returned it to him, directing him to resolve the dispute. Perhaps he did, or the tribe did themselves, for decades later the shaykh concerned was still in power. Once appointed, shaykhs are not easily ousted, and the longer they retain office, the greater their chances of remaining shaykh until senility or death. But it would be a foolhardy shaykh who failed to modify his behavior and repair relationships after such a powerful expression of public opinion.

The strong language of the above denunciation should not be taken at face value. Political competition is customarily waged in a style of hyperbolic rhetoric which would be deeply offensive in normal circumstances, or between strangers. The insults traded by political opponents are comparable to the scathing jibes of joking relationships, which similarly reflect closeness and permanence. Furthermore, the verbal abuse expressed and disseminated in oppositional documents, or hurled by political antagonists in face-to-face confrontations, is not necessarily as terminally destructive of their relationship as one might suppose. After the resolution of their immediate differences, erstwhile opponents are obliged to mix socially and cooperate in tribal governance, albeit with gritted teeth. The ritualized denigration of unpopular shaykhs by their constituents and rivals is also symptomatic of the democratic aspects of tribal politics. Men dare speak (often highly exaggerated) truth to power because it is they who appoint shaykhs and uphold their authority, and because they have the backing of their clans.

Grassroots pressure through institutionalized modes of complaint and opposition provides an important curb on shaykhly excess and abuse of position. If shaykhs are irremediably weak or corrupt, however, they can be usurped by clan rivals. The fact that there is always an alternative, potentially better, leader waiting in the wings helps protect the institution of hereditary leadership from self-destructive damage by an inadequate incumbent who fails to improve his performance. While individual shaykhs might lose prestige or position, therefore, the notion of tribal leadership being rightfully monopolized by certain clans has endured, contributing to the stability of tribes as structures of governance.

CHAPTER FIVE

Wider Structures and Relations

We have seen that Rāziḥ is a zone of intensive trade, that each tribe is embedded in a matrix of other tribes, and that its people are interconnected by countless ties of friendship, marriage, and economic interdependence which necessitate their constantly crossing tribal borders to shop, work, or fulfill their social obligations. Local fortunes also depend on the free flow of trade within the whole of northwest Yemen. Rāziḥīs therefore need order and safety to be maintained over a much larger area than the territories controlled by individual tribes. These realities are reflected in centuries of formal agreements and alliances among the tribes of Rāziḥ and with their neighbors, and in an overarching judicial structure which encompasses the whole of Khawlān ibn ʿĀmir.

The Regions of Khawlān ibn ʿĀmir

Rāziḥīs conceptualize the identities and interrelations of the four major tribal regions which, in their view, comprise Khawlān ibn ʿĀmir in an idiom of patrilineal kinship and descent. The regional eponyms Rāziḥ, Ṣaḥār, Jumāʿah, and Khawlān are thus vaguely imagined to have been the "sons" (sing. *akh*) of Khawlān ibn ʿĀmir. As Sayyid Zayd Abū Ṭālib explained:

> The whole region (*manṭaqah*) is named after Khawlān ibn ʿĀmir just as Washington was named after the liberator [*sic*] of

> America, George Washington. And Rāziḥ, Ṣaḥār, Jumāʿah, and Khawlān are all sons of Khawlān ibn ʿĀmir.

By this agnatic symbolism, he was expressing his perception of Khawlān ibn ʿĀmir as a distinct geo-political entity, the constituent regions of which are interrelated and structurally equivalent.[1] Some Rāziḥīs additionally volunteer that Khawlān ibn ʿĀmir was the son or grandson of Quḍāʿah, the eponym of "Bilād Quḍāʿah"—the alternative name for the entire region. Quḍāʿah is regarded as an ancient personage, "from the days of Maʿīn [a pre-Islamic kingdom]," as Shaykh ʿAwaḍ put it. Sayyid Zayd Abū Ṭālib summarized the alternative historical opinions regarding Quḍāʿah as follows:

> There are two accounts of the origins of Quḍāʿah in the old histories . . . Some say he was ʿAdnānī and originated from the north. Others say that he was from Kahlān—that is, of Himyarī stock—and that the southern tribes are descended from him. And that is the truth. This story is from the time before our Prophet Muḥammad.

Variations on the above constructions are mostly elaborated by literate Rāziḥīs, partly to parade their learning, partly to extol the great age of their groups, and owe much to the famous tenth-century Yemeni geographer, al-Hamdāni, who lived in Ṣaʿdah and tried (with difficulty and inevitable inconsistencies) to fit the Yemeni tribal groups of his time into comprehensive genealogical frameworks.[2] Al-Hamdāni's efforts conformed with the state-inspired custom, dating back to the early Islamic period, of constructing all-encompassing genealogical schemes to conceptualize and unify the expanding Muslim empire (see Dresch 1988), and classify and hierarchize its tribal structures for administrative purposes. We can therefore deduce from the fact that al-Hamdānī describes Rāziḥ and Ṣaḥār as being "sons of" Khawlān ibn ʿAmrū (as he wrote it) that these regions were already equivalent and interrelated geo-political entities a thousand years ago.[3] More interestingly, al-Hamdānī describes Rāziḥ as "the most numerous of Khawlān [ibn ʿAmrū] today," and as representing two-fifths of the region. This suggests that then, as later, it was a lucrative tax domain which provided a large fraction of Khawlān ibn ʿĀmir's state revenues.[4]

Rāziḥīs did not usually spontaneously mention ʿUqārib in their scheme. When I asked where ʿUqārib fitted, they either said that it was another "son" of Khawlān ibn ʿĀmir, or that it was a "son" of Rāziḥ. These statements reflect co-existing conceptions shared by the people of both regions.

The former acknowledges that ʿUqārib is considered an equivalent tribal region to Rāziḥ; the latter that ʿUqārib is part of the state sub-province of Qaḍā Rāziḥ. This close geo-political connection also goes back a millennium (al-Hamdāni 1963:350). Rāziḥīs considered the tribal region of Munabbih al-Shām north of Rāziḥ to be part of Jumāʿah—presumably because it is part of that sub-province—and never spontaneously described it as a fifth tribal region separate from, and equivalent to, Jumāʿah, Ṣaḥār, Rāziḥ, and Khawlān, although it is regarded as such by its own people (Gingrich 1989a, 1993), and once was by rulers.

Inter-tribal Relations in Rāziḥ

The tribes of Rāziḥ are bound by numerous pacts and treaties intended to prevent or defuse problems or promote common interests. These cover a wide range of issues including law-and-order, defense, and relations with the state. The following agreement (D1863a) between the neighboring tribes of Banī Rabīʿah, al-Naẓīr, al-Izid, and Birkān provides a simple example. This follows the customary structure. It starts by naming the representatives (*muqaddamīn*) who are entering this pact on behalf of their tribes. Then follows the subject of the agreement, which is here about harboring criminals. The pact then concludes with the names of the guarantors (here all from the same tribes as the representatives), the scribe, and three witnesses, including a *sayyid* from Āl Muṭahhar. There are presumably no secondary guarantors, in this instance, because it is a general agreement without specific or difficult undertakings to be enforced.

> Attending (*ḥaḍar*) were those mentioned from the tribes (*qubul*) of Rāziḥ: Muḥsin Sulaymān Ḥayyān and Aḥmad Ṣāliḥ ibn ʿAlāwī representing (*qaṭaʿū wa taqaddamū*) all the men of Banī Rabīʿah, present and absent; Jubrān Qāsim ʿAlī Faraḥ representing all the people of al-Naẓīr and its Thirds, present and absent; Aḥmad Ḥasan Sarīʿ, Shāʿib ʿAlī al-Maʿnaqqī, and Ḥasan Ṣāliḥ ibn Katībah representing all the men of al-Izid, present and absent; and Aḥmad ʿAlī al-ʿAfrīt representing all the men of Birkān, present and absent.
>
> The above-mentioned met and agreed that each should protect his own domain (*bilād*) against aggressors, fugitives [from justice], and thieves from outside their region, from wherever they hail—the east, the north, the south, the west, or the coastal plain, or from near or far. If any fugitive is given sanctuary he, or anyone who harbors him, will suffer

> reprisals (*naqā*) subject to the approved arrangements of the signatories. They are united against any tribesman who threatens (*shawwaf*) their honor, or wrongs or harms anyone; he will receive no sanctuary (*wazā*) in any of their domains . . .
>
> Guaranteeing (*ḍummanū*) from Banī Rabīʿah are [four names]; from al-Izid [three names]; from the people of al-Naẓīr [three names]; and from the people of Birkān [four names].
>
> Whoever is co-opted [as guarantor] should be recorded (*man nuṭī kān ruqim*), and whoever mentioned causes problems shall bear all the consequences and expenses as recorded.
>
> Those whose names are recorded witness (*ashhadū*) [this agreement], and God, praise be upon Him, bless the witnesses. The month of *muḥarram,* 1280 [in numbers and words]
>
> Witnessed and written by Yaḥyā Ḥasan Shitwī
> Witnessed by al-Ḥājj Aḥmad, who lives in al-Naẓīr
> Witnessed by [*sayyid*] Aḥmad ibn ʿAlī ibn al-Qāsim Muṭahhar

Each tribe sits at the hub of a small, constantly activated political network created by such agreements, and each network overlaps with other tribe-centered networks. These span the whole of Rāziḥ, and interconnect at their edges with the networks of neighboring regions. Tribes in close proximity have the most intensive politico-legal relations; almost all the inter-tribal pacts and treaties I copied are between two, three, or four bordering tribes. However, the generally limited compass of bilateral or multi-lateral agreements by no means represents the maximum range of each tribe's formal relations because the meetings at which they are compiled are invariably attended by prominent men from other tribes acting as arbitrators, supporters, guarantors, or witnesses. The tribal leaders of Rāziḥ are therefore constantly involved in each others' affairs in various capacities, and are consequently intimately familiar with each others' leading personages, internal structures, key alliances, and current political conditions—especially those of their neighbors. This interconnectedness and mutual understanding are significant factors in inter-tribal politics.

Differences in the size and wealth of tribes, their variable positions and topographies, and the resources they possess and control, especially markets, can all have temporary or permanent political significance. Tribal leaders are, of course, acutely aware of the significance of these factors. As

Shaykh Nāṣir spontaneously remarked during the dispute between Birkān and al-Naẓīr to be described in Chapter Eight:

> Birkān has only about three hundred men altogether, including their shaykhs, but they are wealthy. They have a lot of good agricultural land, and their territory is wide and lower-lying than ours [i.e., warmer and more productive]. Our land is less extensive [other Naẓīrīs disagreed with this] and very mountainous. But we have *barakah*—it is very productive.

SW: How many Naẓīrī men are there?

> *Shaykh Nāṣir* [instantly]: A thousand and a quarter . . . And al-Izid has only three or four hundred; it has lots of land, but few men . . . Banalqām has a large territory, and maybe the best land of all of us, but only about four hundred men . . . Banī Rabīʿah has only three hundred and fifty to four hundred men, but they also have lots of land with good deep earth.

Inequalities between tribes create particular needs and dependencies, and temporary or permanent inequalities in power, and these in turn provoke cooperation, compromise, or friction in different circumstances. Al-Naẓīr and Munabbih, for example, are large, wealthy tribes, with a consequent tendency to dominate others. Small, weak tribes offset this pressure, and strive to preserve their autonomy and maintain the inter-tribal balance of power, by making defensive alliances with other tribes. They can also influence or restrain more powerful neighbors by allowing or preventing access to resources in their territories. This applies, for example, to Banī ʿAbīd and Banī Ṣafwān on Jabal Ḥijlah, whose territories contain plentiful *qafarah* land on which Naẓīrīs depend for firewood, and to Banī Rabīʿah, on whose wells in Wādī al-Muʿayan many Rāziḥīs depend during water shortages.

When supplies are plentiful, people cross tribal boundaries to exploit such resources, and often reward those living near them with gifts. But when tribes are at odds or during shortages, such cooperative, reciprocal relations become strained or arrangements are temporarily suspended. This happened during a drought period in 1980 when relations between Birkān and al-Naẓīr were politically tense. When their own springs dried up, Naẓīrī men drove their women to the "Well of Birkān" to collect water, and Birkānī men tried to prevent them. The situation was successfully resolved by negotiation, but it contained inflammable ingredients—competition for scarce and vital resources, and threats to women—which have precipitated major inter-tribal conflicts in the past.

The different positions of tribes in relation to trade routes and markets have particularly important implications for inter-tribal relations. Ghamar, Banī Rabīʿah, al-Naẓīr, and al-Waqir are all on the main route through Qaḍā Rāziḥ, and have major markets in their territories, while other tribes are off the beaten track, and have smaller markets or none at all. The leaders of the former tribes are therefore permanently advantaged by controlling trade, by having generally wealthier constituents, and by receiving more important visitors. They can also impose a powerful economic sanction on an enemy tribe by banning its members from their markets. The shaykh of al-Waqir, Ibn Ghalfān, who controlled al-Ḍayʿah, was particularly powerful in this respect, which led to frequent problems, historically, between al-Waqir and Rāziḥ. Tribes which control major markets are, however, especially vulnerable to boycotts and blockades by neighboring tribes.

As we will see in Part III, position and resources also variably affected each tribe's historical experience of encroaching or occupying states. The tribes of ʿUqārib, whose hills could easily be taken from the coast, were sometimes tempted or forced to submit to Tihāmah-based powers—to the consternation of highland tribes, whose trade was often affected. Similarly, Banī Maʿīn and Munabbih, which control the northern gateway into Rāziḥ along the flank of Jabal Ḥurum, could resist incursions by unwanted Ṣaʿdah-based states, when other Rāziḥ tribes praised them for their bravery; or, as repeatedly happened, they could submit to fear or inducements and "open up" (*fataḥ*) to states, provoking accusations from other tribes of "treachery" and being "bought." As cynics say, "Wherever the wind blows, we winnow," meaning people succumb to bribes. Strategically situated tribes where rulers made their seats and built their forts were also obviously subject to greater state control than more peripheral tribes. The different positions, populations, and productivity of tribes also variably affected shaykhs, for states rewarded them for their allegiance and cooperation in proportion to the military and fiscal importance of their domains.

Inter-tribal Alliances

Because inter-tribal agreements are always drawn up for contingent legal or political reasons, the formal relationships they create and govern are of variable stability and duration—notwithstanding the rhetoric of everlasting "brotherhood" (*makhuwwah*) in which they are invariably couched. Pacts necessitated by transient situations or temporary crises tend to create short-lived coalitions, while those based on constant conditions and interests create more enduring relationships which are reaffirmed by successive generations of leaders. Assertions by local people that such-and-such tribes are "allies" (*aṣḥāb* or *ahl al-ṣaḥab*) or "brothers" (*akhwāh*) should never, therefore, be assumed to indicate primordial or immutable bonds based on kinship or descent, but should always invite the questions "Since when?" and "Why?"

Among the most durable inter-tribal alliances are those between certain pairs of neighboring tribes. An example is that between al-Izid and al-Naẓīr, which can be dated back at least two centuries (D1801) but is probably much older. The other examples are the alliances between Banī ʿAbīd and Banī Ṣafwān, Banī Maʿīn and Banī Asad, and al-Waqir and al-Wuqaysh, which are also of great long standing. These twinned tribes are referred to, like all allies, as "brothers" or "one hand" (*yid wāhidah*)—the local idiom for tribal solidarity—but more emphatically so as to convey the strength and permanence of their relationships. They are also routinely mentioned in tandem—for example Izdī-*wa* (and)-Naẓīrī—and rhetorically described as "one tribe" (*qabīlah wāḥidah*) to emphasize their closeness. But according to the crucial criterion of political sovereignty they are separate tribes. Each has its own discrete territory with political borders, and is represented and administered by its own hereditary shaykh and elders, who have exclusive jurisdiction within their respective tribal domains and the right to act unilaterally in external affairs.

The principal constant condition which underlies these stable alliances is that each set of twinned tribes shares a mountain, creating a strong common interest in defense and security. Their territories are, furthermore, at different altitudes, so that the higher tribe, in each case, must keep on good terms with its twin lower down in order to maintain right of way through its territory. Three sets of twinned tribes are also jointly responsible for the safety and security of a market, which they loudly proclaim at appropriate moments. Thus the leaders of al-Naẓīr, who share protection of their market with al-Izid (which has none), invariably preface their public announcements (sing. *ẓāhirah*) with the following formulaic preamble:

> The market is safe and secure under God's protection, and the protection of its Naẓīrī and Izdī guarantors (*ḍumanā*).[5]

TABLE 5.1. THE "BROTHER" TRIBES OF QAḌĀ RĀZIḤ

TRIBES (and 1975 pop)	*JOINT NAME*	*SHARED TERRITORY*	*SITE OF SHARED MARKET*	*SENIOR SHAYKH*
al-Izid (2500) al-Naẓīr (4000)	Izdī-wa-Naẓīrī	Jabal al-Izid rises above Jabal al-Naẓīr	al-Naẓīr	Ibn Faraḥ of al-Naẓīr
Banī Maʿīn (3000) Banī Asad (750)	Maʿīnī-wa-Asadī	Jabal Ḥurum	Banī Maʿīn	Abū ʿAwthah of Banī Maʿīn
Banī ʿAbīd (700) Banī Ṣafwān (900)	ʿAbīdī-wa-Ṣafwānī	Jabal Ḥijlah	none	Ibn Farwān of Banī ʿAbīd
al-Waqir (1250) al-Wuqaysh (2750)	Waqrī-wa-Wuqayshī	Jabal Shidā and hinterland	al-Waqir	Ibn Ghalfān of al-Waqir

Banī ʿAbīd and Banī Ṣafwān (ʿAbīdī-wa-Ṣafwānī) do not, however, share a market, and Banī Rabīʿah shares the protection of its market at Shaʿārah with the Munabbihī ward of Ghumār without Banī Rabīʿah and Munabbih being twinned in people's consciousness. Variable numbers of tribes also historically made temporary pacts to safeguard markets—especially Sūq al-Ḍayʿah—when they were threatened by inter-tribal, tribe-state, or inter-state conflicts.[6] But such alliances did not outlast the exigency which provoked them; once it passed, they lapsed. The market-protection agreements of twinned tribes, by contrast, are generations or centuries old, and are perceived as a central component of permanent relationships.

Twinned tribes are economically inter-dependent. Most obviously, the ally without a market depends on access to that of the other. Those with markets, on the other hand, need the products of their twins, which differ from their own because their territories are at different altitudes. Al-Izid, for example, which occupies the cool heights above al-Naẓīr, mainly produces grain which must be marketed and exchanged for other food and commodities. Because al-Izid has no market, its people mainly depend on the large biweekly market of al-Naẓīr for customers (the markets of al-Shawāriq and Banalqām are as close, but much smaller). Because of its intensive production of cash crops, al-Naẓīr, for its part, historically needed

Izdī grain. Al-Izid and al-Naẓīr therefore share an interest in protecting the Naẓīrī market, as well as the trans-Rāziḥ trade route which crosses the long and vulnerable border between their two tribes. Members of both tribes also cite as a further reason for their special "brotherhood" the fact that "their houses and land are all mixed up at the borders," meaning that some border hamlets contain members of both tribes. The example Naẓīrīs most often mention is a hamlet called ʿĀs al-Qirn, which lies just inside the Izdī border on the high saddle which joins al-Izid to eastern al-Naẓīr, and which is said to have been "half Naẓīrī and half Izdī" in population since a defection long ago. The fact that such commingling of members of neighboring tribes is cited as a cause or evidence of their closeness is another example of the dominance of place in imagining political identities.

The longevity and inequality of the relationships between twinned tribes is reflected in the fact that their respective shaykhs are permanently ranked, one being the "senior shaykh" (*shaykh al-shamil*). In the case of those which share market protection, this is always the shaykh with the market in his territory — reflecting the key importance of trade in their alliances.[7] It should be stressed that this does not imply any diminution of the junior shaykh's jurisdiction within his own tribe, nor dilution of its political sovereignty. It just means that one shaykh has formal seniority when making joint representations to other tribes or government, or implementing the terms of their bilateral agreements. Thus when al-Naẓīr was at odds with Banī Asad in 1980 over tit-for-tat impounding of cars, the shaykh of Banī Maʿīn, the senior shaykh of the Maʿīnī-and-Asadī "brotherhood," negotiated the solution. "He is close to [Banī Asad]," a Naẓīrī explained. "They are brothers like Izdī-and-Naẓīrī."

The bilateral pacts between twinned tribes contain more precise and permanent terms than other inter-tribal agreements. Maʿīnī-and-Asadī, for example, divide responsibility for the Wednesday market in Banī Maʿīn between three sets of *ḍumanā* represented by three stones in the marketplace. If anyone is attacked in the market, he stands on one of the stones to announce his predicament, and the *ḍumanā* for that stone are obliged to help him. In another fractional arrangement typical of tribal affairs, Izdī-wa-Naẓīrī divide responsibility for Sūq al-Naẓīr on a one-third/two-thirds basis, with al-Naẓīr having the heavier responsibility. Thus when anyone violates the sanctity of the market, al-Naẓīr is obliged to provide two-thirds of the guarantors to deal with the offense and al-Izid one-third. When both tribes are involved in unlawful incidents they also pay the associated fines and expenses on a similar fractional basis. However, as Shaykh ʿAwaḍ was keen to emphasize, each tribe otherwise manages its own internal affairs: "Whatever misfortune an individual or his tribe suffers which doesn't affect us collectively, then al-Izid and al-Naẓīr deal with it separately, for example with regard to subscriptions and penalties."

Twinned tribes have comparably precise agreements concerning their external relations. Izdī-and-Naẓīrī, for example, are permanently pledged to support one another through the whole gamut of inter-tribal and tribe-state encounters—peaceful negotiations, litigation, or hostile engagements. And if their alliance is activated for defense or war, they allocate guard duties, damages, and expenses on a fractional basis according to the border on which hostilities occur (see Chapter Eight; D1891a). In the context of outside threats, therefore, their joint territories become one defense zone, but only for the duration of the emergency.[8]

It is easy to see how twinned tribes could amalgamate. The border between them could be permanently dissolved, and their senior shaykh could be accorded sole jurisdiction over their combined territories. However, I found no evidence of such an occurrence. Tribes must have adjusted to their optimum territories long ago.

Moieties: Jihwazī and Ḥilfī

The tribes of Qaḍā Rāziḥ are permanently aligned in two conceptually and sometimes politically opposed moieties or leagues named Jihwazī (pl. Jihwaz) and Ḥilfī (pl. Aḥlāf).[9] People describe these large, invisible structures and their interrelations, as they do others, using idioms of kinship and descent:

> The tribes of Rāziḥ are divided into two parts (*fakhadhayn*) called Jihwazī and Ḥilfī which are named after their ancestors (sing. *jidd*). And the ancestor of both was Rāziḥ.
>
> Jihwazī and Ḥilfī were brothers. They had the same father, Rāziḥ, but they quarreled—maybe because they had different mothers [a common cause of fraternal dissension].

No attempt is made to extend this model downward to include tribes, their clans, or their individual members in one all-encompassing genealogical scheme, nor to elaborate any human historical reality for Jihwazī and Ḥilfī. People do not believe that they are literally descended from these "ances-

TABLE 5.2. THE MOIETY AFFILIATIONS OF THE TRIBES OF QAḌĀ RĀZIḤ

Tribal region	*Jihwazī tribes*	*Ḥilfī tribes*
RĀZIḤ	Banalqām Birkān Ghamar Munabbih	Banī Asad Banī Maʿīn Banī Rabīʿah al-Izid al-Naẓīr al-Shawāriq
ʿUQĀRIB	Banī ʿAbīd Banī Ṣafwān al-Waqir	Ālat al-ʿUṭayf Banī Ṣayāh al-Wuqaysh

tors"; neither do they celebrate them in rituals or personify them in legends. "These names are just a traditional way of identifying themselves," Sayyid Zayd Abū Ṭālib explained. "They don't have meanings which can be analyzed."[10] As an official of the imāmate and then of the republic, Zayd had a lifetime's experience of tribal politics. When he spontaneously wrote the moiety affiliation of each tribe of Qaḍā Rāziḥ on a map I asked him to draw, therefore, it was clear that these alignments were significant.

An important aspect of moieties is that the territories of their constituent tribes are discontinuous; each tribe therefore borders tribes from both the same *and* opposing moieties (see Figure 3.3). Al-Naẓīr, for example, borders two fellow Ḥilfī tribes (al-Izid and al-Shawāriq), and two Jihwazī tribes (Birkān and al-Waqir). This interspersal is crucially important for preventing the escalation of inter-tribal conflicts.

Within the Jabal Rāziḥ massif the major Jihwazī tribes are situated in the north (*al-shawāmī*), and the major Ḥilfī tribes in the south (*al-yamāniyah*), so that moieties are often assimilated to *shawāmī* and *yamānī* Rāziḥ in political discourse. This reflects the pervasive tendency for politico-legal structures to be imagined as places, *and* to be symbolized by their shaykhs. Each moiety has a "senior shaykh" (*shaykh al-shamil*) or "shaykh of shaykhs" (*shaykh al-mashāyikh*), who embodies its identity and permanence, and these positions are permanently vested in the shaykhly dynasties of specific tribes in northern and southern Rāziḥ: Munabbih (in *shawāmī* Rāziḥ), whose shaykh (Ibn Sālim) is always, ex officio, the senior

FIGURE 5.1.
The *maradd* of Rāziḥ, ʿAlī Aḥmad al-ʿAzzām (*left*), 1979

shaykh of the Jihwazī tribes; and al-Shawāriq (in *yamānī* Rāziḥ) whose shaykh (Ibn al-ʿAzzām) is always senior shaykh of the Ḥilfī tribes. These moiety shaykhs are, furthermore, ranked. The senior shaykh of the Ḥilfī moiety (the shaykh of al-Shawāriq) is simultaneously the *shaykh al-shamil* for the whole of Rāziḥ, and is therefore structurally superior to the senior shaykh of the Jihwazī moiety. So these senior shaykhs wear more than one turban, so to speak. In their primary capacity they are the leaders of their own tribes, which gives them the status and power base to perform their wider functions; and in their secondary capacity they have supra-tribal roles. These are mainly judicial, but can also become political.[11]

Senior shaykhs mainly function as supra-tribal arbitrators and courts. This is reflected in the more specific title of their judicial office, *maradd* (or sometimes *marjiʿ*), meaning someone to whom one resorts for solutions and judgments—in other words, a shaykh of appeal.[12] Jihwazī and Ḥilfī, which I call moieties simply to mean two parts of a whole, are therefore jural domains; and they together comprise the larger jural domain of Rāziḥ. This system works roughly as follows. When disputing tribes are from the same moiety, shaykhs tend to appeal to the *maradd* of that moiety, and if they are from different moieties, to the senior *maradd* of all Rāziḥ. But this is not prescribed; either *maradd* can be approached. Like other prominent men, *maradds* are also expected to intervene between disputing tribes; and they commonly guarantee inter-tribal agreements. In the past they also played important roles as mediators and guarantors of pacts between local *dawlahs* (see Chapter Nine).

Maradds derive their authority from other tribal leaders, who can choose whether to invite or accept their help; shaykhs therefore invariably described their relationship with their *maradds* as activated from below, not above. They say, for example, "We called in Ibn so-and-so." *Maradds* cannot insist on being consulted, nor can they exert authority over tribes other than their own. As I have stressed, each shaykh jealously guards his own jurisdiction, and no tribesman owes allegiance or obedience to any shaykh other than the leader of his own tribe. In other words, *maradds* have no permanent, institutionalized executive power or political authority congruent with their jural domains; they do not *govern* them. Appeal to a *maradd* does not therefore imply any diminution or sacrifice of any tribe's sovereignty.

In addition to their jural roles, *maradds* can also represent their moieties or all the tribes of Rāziḥ—typically when it is necessary to negotiate with tribes in other regions or with the state. But again they can only perform this role with the agreement of their fellow shaykhs, and for the particular contingency; after it ends, their ad hoc role and authority lapse. And if a *maradd* is unsuitable, the task can be delegated to any other shaykh. Although Jihwazī and Ḥilfī, and even the whole of Rāziḥ, are sometimes rhetorically referred to as *qabīlahs*, therefore, there is no permanent *political* office over these structures, and they are not sovereign domains with defined borders. In other words, they are not by my definition "tribes."

While the positions of *maradds* are permanently sustained from below, they also have the potential to be strengthened and changed from above. This has happened historically in Rāziḥ, as will be described, and occurred elsewhere in highland Yemen during and after the 1960s Civil War when Yemeni and Saudi states created or boosted certain "paramount shaykhs."[13] Consistent state patronage over a long period could therefore theoretically transform the office of *maradd* into a politically more powerful institution. But in Rāziḥ other shaykhs would certainly resist any *maradd*'s attempt to encroach on their sovereign powers or amalgamate their domains into one large polity. In the present political environment, therefore, the constitutional powers of the *maradds* of Rāziḥ are limited.

The moiety system is also important in containing inter-tribal conflicts.

When two tribes of different moieties are seriously at odds, people say, "There is Jihwazī and Ḥilfī between them," which is a figure of speech for "enmity." The conflict is then usually solved by third-party intervention followed by negotiations or litigation, with each side supported and advised by one or two moiety allies—typically the shaykhs or elders of neighboring tribes—and perhaps their *maradd*. If these conciliation procedures fail, however, and hostilities look imminent, other tribes not involved in the dispute are expected, according to tribal ideals, to declare their neutrality, and prevent the conflict escalating by ordering the "closure" (*taghlīq*) of their borders. The interspersal of Jihwazī and Ḥilfī tribes then operates to maintain order over wide areas; for if a Ḥilfī tribe threatens a neighboring Jihwazī tribe, other strategically situated Jihwazī tribes can act as neutral buffer zones, and prevent other Ḥilfī tribes from gaining access to their ally. As a Naẓīrī *sayyid* explained:

> The Jihwazīs prevent the Ḥilfīs from going to war, and the Ḥilfīs prevent the Jihwazīs. But the Ḥilfīs shouldn't join in with their Ḥilfī ally, nor the Jihwazīs with their Jihwazī ally—that would be "ganging up" (*aṣabiyyah*) [an offense in tribal law].

The bipartite division of the Rāziḥ tribes into "naturally" opposed "sides" is at the forefront of everyone's political consciousness. When a Birkānī woman learned I was "from al-Naẓīr," she spontaneously informed me: "*We* are Jihwazī and the *Naẓīrīs* are Ḥilfī." As Shaykh ʿAwaḍ put it: "Jihwaz and Aḥlāf are natural opponents (*ʿadāwah tabiʿiyyah*), like Zaydīs and Shāfiʿīs." Such oppositional values are inculcated from childhood and constantly stressed. "When I attended qāt parties as a boy," a Naẓīrī told me, "men constantly admonished me to beware of Jihwazīs because they are treacherous (*ghaddārīn*). Now I can't think about Jihwazīs without that word ringing in my ears." And whenever Naẓīrīs mentioned Birkānīs to me, they invariably tossed off deprecating remarks, such as, "They are Jihwazī, they have sweet tongues but break their word"—a violation of the tribal ideal of reliability and trustworthiness. And the Jihwazī tribes no doubt mirror such sentiments when talking about the Aḥlāf. Tribal leaders deliberately foster such disparaging images. When I asked Shaykh Nāṣir the difference between Jihwazī and Ḥilfī, for example, he played down the size of the Jihwazī moiety to exaggerate its weakness, then painted a picture of Jihwazīs as nevertheless dangerous because of their poor ethical standards:

> Jihwazīs are few in numbers, not like Aḥlāf. But they are treacherous. They make promises but don't keep them. And they are oppressors. Ḥilfīs are honest. Once a Ḥilfī gives his word it would be easier for him to cut off his own head than go back on it. A Ḥilfī would *never* tarnish his own reputation, whereas Jihwazīs break their promises.

Shaykh ʿAwaḍ independently expressed a similar sentiment:

> The Aḥlāf tribes are more numerous and wealthy and powerful, but the seven Jihwazī tribes can overcome them by treachery. They are dishonest and two-faced. But Aḥlāf are reliable, and "honesty overcomes perfidy" (*al-ṣidiq ghalab al-khiḍaʿ*).

Such propaganda keeps the notion that moieties are justifiably opposed simmering, and when disputes escalate into direct action leaders bring it to the boil with rhetorical invective in order to rally their followers and allies. When such crises are channeled (as they always are) into negotiations and litigation, moieties revert to their judicial mode.

The alternate modes in which moieties and *maradds* function are a paradigm of the tribal political process generally. The dominant ideology and associated practice are firmly oriented toward peaceful reconciliation. At every level of the tribal system, the ideal is to defuse and contain inflammatory disputes as quickly as possible. In reality, however, leaders sometimes activate the adversarial potential of tribal structures to defend or promote their tribe's or group's interests to the detriment of others, or to expand their personal influence, score over rivals, and reap financial rewards. Rāziḥīs are well aware of these perennial dangers, and alert for shaykhs or *maradds* who might be exacerbating disputes for their own ends instead of solving them.

The Moieties of Khawlān ibn ʿĀmir

The moiety structure of Rāziḥ, described above, is paralleled in each tribal region of Khawlān ibn ʿĀmir (Fig. 5.2). That is, the tribes in Khawlān, Jumāʿah, and Ṣaḥār are similarly aligned in moieties, which (on the evidence of Ṣaḥār) are likewise territorially discontinuous.[14] Their moieties are also headed by ranked *maradds* who are drawn from the shaykhly clans of specific tribes, and who perform similar roles as mediators, courts of appeal, and supreme guarantors within their moieties and regions to the *maradds* of Rāziḥ. In the eighteenth century, the junior and senior *maradds* of Ṣaḥār

KHAWLĀN IBN ʿĀMIR
(Ibn Miqīt)

RĀZIḤ (Ibn al-ʿAzzām)		KHAWLĀN (Ibn Rawkān)		JUMĀʿAH (Ibn Miqīt)		ṢAḤĀR (Ibn Jaʿfar)
Jihwazī (Ibn Sālim)	=	Jihwazī (Ibn Bishir)	=	Nāṣrī (Ibn Miqīt)	=	Mālikī (Ibn Jaʿfar)
Ḥilfī (Ibn al-ʿAzzām)	=	Ḥilfī (Ibn Rawkān)	=	Ḥilfī (Ibn Ḥadabah)	=	Kulaybī (Ibn Kubās)

FIGURE 5.2.
The moieties and *maradds* of Khawlān ibn ʿĀmir

were particularly active in mediating and guaranteeing pacts between and among the rival *dawlahs* of Rāziḥ and Khawlān Saʿdah (see Chapter Nine).

The structures of the four tribal regions are, furthermore, linked at a higher structural level by a *maradd* at the apex of the system, who functions as a kind of supreme court of appeal for the whole of Khawlān ibn ʿĀmir. This supreme *maradd* is invariably from a shaykhly dynasty called Bayt Miqīt in the tribal region of Jumāʿah. Ibn Miqīt, as the incumbent is usually called, is simultaneously the shaykh of his own tribe, the *maradd* of his moiety (called Nāṣrī), the *maradd* of Jumāʿah, and the *maradd* for the whole of Khawlān ibn ʿĀmir. The superior position of Jumāʿah appears to be of extremely long standing; a thousand years ago al-Hamdānī described Jumāʿah as a "great tribe" led by the Banū Nāṣir, and said that it collected tribute from other tribes in Khawlān [ibn ʿĀmir] (al-Hamdānī 1963:322). One of the present-day moieties of Ṣaḥār, Kulaybi, could also have a political antecedent in al-Hamdāni's time, for he mentions the "Banū Kulayb" as being owners of a fertile valley near Ṣaʿdah (which is in present-day Ṣaḥār) (Heiss 1987).

In addition to their "domestic" judicial roles within their own tribal moieties and tribal regions, *maradds* are expected and invited to provide similar services in other jural domains. When the *maradds* of one tribal region, such as Rāziḥ, cannot settle an internal inter-tribal dispute, or when the dispute involves tribes of two different tribal regions, the *maradd* of a third region is likely to be invited to arbitrate. This happened, for example, in a mid-nineteenth century dispute (D1846a) between tribes in Rāziḥ and Jumāʿah which was adjudicated by Ibn Rawkān, the *maradd* of Khawlān.

Alternatively, tribes at odds can appeal to the supreme *maradd* of Khawlān ibn ʿĀmir, Ibn Miqīt. Looking wistfully back to a golden age when he imagined shaykhs were stronger, Shaykh Nāṣir of al-Naẓīr explained:

> They went to Ibn Miqīt for decisions about disputes when the smaller shaykhs couldn't settle them. He was above the other shaykhs, and he had to be obeyed (*muṭīʿ*) when they had no government (*ḥukūmah*). People submitted to his judgments like sheep lying down for slaughter. He adjudicated and they paid up (*yiḥkum wa yisūqū*).

Shaykh Nāṣir was, of course, exaggerating Ibn Miqīt's power. *Maradds* are only arbitrators, and cannot enforce their judgments. Neither is there an obligatory route of appeal up the judicial hierarchy; the system is flexible in the interests of defusing and resolving crises. The formal judicial structure of appeal is rather the framework within which everyone accepts that inter-tribal problems should ideally be settled. That acceptance, and the corresponding practice, reinforce the fundamental notions that tribal legal authority is legitimately vested in a hierarchy of hereditary shaykhly clans, and that tribes should appeal to *some* institutionalized higher authority or notable third party in order to solve their problems instead of allowing them to escalate.

When *maradds* are personally implicated in disputes, compromising their neutrality, or when a crisis is especially grave, such as when it involves tribes from different regions, or when specialized knowledge of sharīʿah law is required, a respected *sayyid* is more likely to play a mediatory role. The judge, Muḥsin Abū Ṭālib, described the idealized *sayyid* vision of such situations with reference to the roles played by *sayyids* who live in *hijrah* communities:

> If a sacrosanct *sayyid* (*muhajjar*) leaves his *hijrah* to mediate (*tawassaṭ*) between two warring tribes, they cease fire as soon as they see his *imāmah* (turban) out of respect (*iḥtirām*) [for his status] . . . Then he reconciles them, or says he's done his best and leaves. [Whatever the outcome] he leaves safely. No one would insult him or shoot him.

The most effective *sayyid* mediators have the same political know-how as successful shaykhs and *maradds*: they are impartial and wise, well informed about tribal politics, and know how to negotiate face-saving compromises which leave everyone's dignity intact. However, contrary to the *sayyid* perspective on tribal politics (see Serjeant 1977), the tribes of Rāziḥ did not invariably, or even usually, need members of the religious elite to mediate their disputes or solve their conflicts. As documents, oral history, and current practice all show, most inter-tribal problems were and are solved by shaykhs. Furthermore, when Rāziḥ had an independent *dawlah, maradds* and other shaykhs constantly mediated in inter-*sayyid* disputes (Chapter Nine).

Despite differences in nomenclature, the moieties of the different tribal regions of Khawlān ibn ʿĀmir are equated (see Figure 5.2). For example, Rāziḥīs say of the Ṣaḥār moieties: "Mālikī is the same as Jihwazī, and Kulaybī is the same as Ḥilfī."[15] It should be stressed that this perceived correspondence does not reflect the potential for tribes of equivalent moieties in different regions—for example a Ḥilfī tribe in Rāziḥ, and a Kulaybī tribe in Ṣaḥār—to support one another militarily. I heard of no such obligation, and found no such pact. Individual tribes rarely if ever have such long-distance commitments. The significance of moieties being equated cross-regionally rather reflects the potential, I suggest, for mutual support when disputes take place between tribes *at the peripheries* of different tribal regions. This is also primarily geared toward the containment, not the propagation, of conflicts. Shaykh ʿAwaḍ of al-Naẓīr explained the ideal situation, emphasizing the essentially defensive functions of moiety alliances:

> Jihwazīs support Jihwazīs, and Ḥilfīs support Ḥilfīs. No one reneges on their alliance *ever*. A Ḥilfī [tribe] of Rāziḥ will support a Ḥilfī [tribe] of Khawlān . . . They try their hardest to resolve the dispute, and if negotiations fail, each supports its ally.

SW: How is that? The divisions are not all called Jihwazī and Ḥilfī. For example, they have different names in Jumāʿah.

> Yes, Jumāʿah has Ḥilfī and Nāṣrī, and the Nāṣrīs support the Jihwazīs. And in Ṣaḥār they have Kulaybī and Mālikī, and the Kulaybīs support the Ḥilfīs, and the Mālikīs support the Jihwazīs. This is our traditional defense system (*al-ḥamiyyat al-jāhiliyyah*)—everyone supporting his ally (*kull wāḥid yaqūm maʿṣāḥibōh*).

The significance of this model should be understood in the context of the usually narrow compass of inter-tribal relations, and the overwhelming emphasis on the prevention rather than the promotion of conflict. Although most inter-tribal interaction takes place between neighboring or closely situated tribes, it is obviously not confined within tribal regions such as Rāziḥ. Tribes at the edges of tribal regions interact just as intensively with neighboring tribes in adjacent regions as they do with neighboring tribes within the same region. Al-Naẓīr, for example, in southwest Rāziḥ, is constantly engaged with the neighboring ʿUqārib tribe of al-Waqir in the Tihāmah foothills below. According to Shaykh ʿAwaḍ's model, when al-Naẓīr (which is Ḥilfī) falls out with al-Waqir (which is Jihwazī), al-Naẓīr should expect defensive support from the Ḥilfī tribes of ʿUqārib as well as those of Rāziḥ, and al-Waqir could likewise expect support from the Jihwazī tribes of Rāziḥ, and in the only inter-regional dispute for which I have detailed evidence (described in Chapter Eight), this is just what occurred. However, it should be stressed that these inter-regional alignments are neither prescriptive nor accurately predictive. They are rather ideologies for the recruitment of allies which tribal leaders stress and manipulate, and can follow or forsake, according to the contingent circumstances of particular disputes.

What I have tried to emphasize is that political action in Rāziḥ, like political action between states, is governed by interests, events, and geographical position, and by the terms of the pacts and treaties which reflect those realities, not by notional kinship (which is an idiom for *describing* major political relationships, not their cause). It is therefore impossible to elicit an abstract description of ideal patterns of alliance which is not tautological. When I asked questions such as, "If tribe X had a dispute with tribe Y, who would support whom?" for example, people would reply: "Each tribe would be supported by its allies/brothers," or, more informatively, "Who would support them? It depends on their *qawāʿid*." Only when discussing the collective interests of the whole of Rāziḥ would people generalize their commitments, and agree that, were Rāziḥ threatened, all its tribes would ideally stand together regardless of their moiety affiliations. But this is no more than saying, "We would all defend our territory." And as we shall see, the tribes of Rāziḥ were as often divided as united by outside forces.

View from al-Naẓīr east toward Banalqām and al-Shawāriq, 1979
Center is the house of a former coffee merchant.

View of *madīnat* al-Naẓīr, 1977

Ploughing a large terrace in al-Naẓīr, early 1977

Men doing a dagger dance during a circumcision ceremony, *madīnat* al-Naẓīr, 1979

A circumcision ceremony, *madīnat* al-Naẓīr, 1979

Quran teacher, Ḍayf Allāh Manṣūr, dressed up for ʿĪd Ramaḍān, 1979

Shaykh Nāṣir Manṣūr of al-Naẓīr and sons Ṣāliḥ (left) and ʿAbdallāh (right), 1979

A neighborhood mosque surrounded by sorghum terraces, 1977.
Note the men studying in the courtyard.

The *ḥākim* of Rāziḥ, Muḥsin Aḥmad Abū Ṭālib (*left*),
doing a property division in his sitting room, 1977

Man begging for help with a blood debt, Sūq al-Naẓīr, 1980

Money changer with Maria Theresa dollars in the market of al-Naẓīr, 1977

The peace ceremony after the War of al-Ḍayʿah, 1985. The shaykh of al-Wuqaysh, Ibn Salāmah, has just laid his turban on the slaughtered animals as an apology on behalf of al-Waqir, and an entreaty for peace. (Photo: Aḥmad Muḥammad Jubrān)

Shaykh Ḥasan Muḥammad of Munabbih making his opening speech at the start of the Qullat Ḥajar case, November 1979

Sūq al-Naẓīr in 1993. On the right is the new mosque, built in 1985, and at the far end the government telephone exchange. The new trans-Rāziḥ highway can be seen on the opposite mountainside.

PART II

Tribal Governance

CHAPTER SIX

Principles, Rules, and Sanctions

The high population density of Rāziḥ, the consequent pressure on resources, the high value of crops, and the constant human traffic between tribes create a favorable environment for disputes and crimes. But their destructive potential is offset by a countervailing drive for order fueled by religious and secular ideals, and by a vivid awareness that everyone's livelihood is intensely vulnerable to major disorder (*ghāghah*) when people dare not leave home, and work and trade are paralyzed. Most therefore respect "the law" as an abstract ideal, and yearn for order and security (*imin-wa-amān*)—both within their own mountains, and throughout their entire geographical sphere of activity. "Law and order" thus has wide, grassroots support, and does not solely serve the interests of the rich and powerful, though they are its prime movers and beneficiaries. Out of these realizations and interests was born a remarkably legalistic "customary law" (*ʿurf*) in which tribal leaders implement a wealth of rules and sanctions using formal, institutionalized procedures; in this culture we indeed find Malinowski's "codes, constables and courts."[1]

Order-maintenance in Rāziḥ has marked voluntaristic and collective features, and there is a perpetual tension between the impulse to support family and clan, and the requirement to comply with the law. But contrary to the segmentary model of tribal societies, unauthorized unilateral action by individuals or groups within tribes is generally frowned upon—especially if it causes other people problems. Order is rather ideally maintained through the permanent structures of governance described in previous chapters; shaykhs and elders enforce "the law" within their tribes through their internal administrative divisions (wards, fractions, and clans), and with the help (when necessary) of the leaders of allied tribes. "The law" is not, however, a dictatorial imposition by an elite few on a powerless and unwilling majority. It is rather an ideal system which people charge their leaders with administering on their behalf, and for their benefit, under pain of damaging their reputations and authority, or inciting dissidence or defection, if they do so inadequately or pursue their own interests to the detriment of those of their constituents.

This second part of the book will describe this indigenous legal system, paying particular attention to how leaders manipulate its rules, symbols, procedures, and dramas not only to maintain law and order, but also to reinforce the key structures of tribal governance and their own positions and power. As Caton (1991) has notably stressed, with special reference to tribal poetry, in order to understand the perpetuation of authority, it is essential to examine how political ideologies are mediated in "concrete acts of communication." In this I would include the dictation, writing and reading out of documents, and rituals of law enforcement.

ʿUrf and Sharīʿah Law

If Rāziḥ was inhabited and politically organized before Islam, which seems probable, then some form of indigenous law, adapted to its time and circumstances, must have pre-dated religious law (*sharīʿah*). Since the advent of Islam and the Arabic language in Yemen in the seventh century, however, tribal and religious law have co-existed, and have inevitably exerted a reciprocal influence. Just as sharīʿah law was partially based on the pre-existing south Arabian law (Serjeant 1962; Schacht 1964:12, 62), so *ʿurf* has undoubtedly absorbed many terms, principles, and practices from the sharīʿah.

Rāziḥīs regard themselves first and foremost as Muslims striving for piety. Whether they be of *sayyid, qabīlī,* or butcher status, their Muslim identity is a fundamental part of their self-conception, religious notions permeate their thinking, and their daily lives are saturated with Islamic practices.[2] They punctuate their speech with imprecations to Allāh, and feel that all their concerns are subject to his blessing or displeasure. Their customs and laws are often, and self-consciously, couched in similar lan-

FIGURE 6.1.
A neighborhood mosque surrounded by sorghum terraces, 1977.
Note the men studying in the courtyard.

guage to that of the Quran and other religious texts, or quote them. Most conspicuously endeavor to fulfill their religious obligations by performing their daily prayers, paying their *zakāt,* giving alms (*ṣadaqah*) to the poor, providing religious endowments (sing. *waqf*) for the common good, fasting during Ramaḍān, and slaughtering an animal at the annual Feast of Sacrifice (*ʿīd al-aḍḥā*); and they historically supported rulers in conflicts defined as "holy war" (*jihād*). They also proclaim their adherence to the worldly injunctions of sharīʿah law with regard to theft, violence, adultery, inheritance, rights of preemption (*shufʿah*), marriage payments, and penalties for crimes, although—as elsewhere in Yemen and the Muslim world—local practices can diverge from the strict letter of Holy Law as interpreted by jurists (see Mundy 1995; Donaldson 2000).

Sharīʿah law is silent or unspecific, however, on numerous issues of prime local concern, such as the rights and responsibilities of the owners of terraces, houses, and animals, and the protection of markets, springs, pastures, and pathways, on which *ʿurf* has a plethora of rules. Neither does sharīʿah doctrine take account of the legal status and collective obligations of corporate groups (al-Abdin 1975:198), whereas an important feature of *ʿurf* is its recognition of tribes and their sub-groups, as well as individuals, as legal entities. The sharīʿah, furthermore, lacks procedures for reconciling adversaries, resolving conflicts, or conducting inter-tribal relations. It therefore leaves wide scope and need for *ʿurf*.

Like other Yemenis (Obermeyer 1981a), Rāziḥīs regard *ʿurf* as compatible with sharīʿah law, and repeatedly assert their adherence to both "God's law and tribal law" (*sharaʿ Allāh wa sharaʿ al-qubul*) in their speeches and documents. They also vehemently reject the notion that *ʿurf* is synonymous with heathen *ṭāghūt*—the powerful Quranic epithet with which certain Zaydī rulers and *ʿulamā* vilified the tribes for allegedly flouting Islamic ideals—especially by depriving women of their rightful inheritance.[3] This public stance did not, however, reflect any state's intention of eradicating *all* tribal law. On the contrary, even the relatively strong regimes of the seventeenth-century Qāsimīs and twentieth-century Ḥamīd al-Dīns tolerated *ʿurf* in practice despite their fierce anti-*ʿurf* rhetoric.[4] They could hardly do otherwise because they depended on tribal leaders, employing *ʿurf*, to help them maintain order and fulfill their political agendas. The intermittently hostile public stance of states toward tribal law should therefore rather be seen as providing a religious pretext for encroaching on certain tribal sovereignties and crushing dissidence.

All schools (sing. *madhhab*) of Islamic law recognize the legitimacy of *ʿurf* provided that it does not contravene the sharīʿah,[5] and the pragmatic Hādawī *madhhab* of the Zaydīs—named after Imām al-Hādī (d. 298/911), the founder of the first Zaydī state in Yemen—is especially tolerant of *ʿurf*. Judges and governors in Rāziḥ therefore routinely took its rules and procedures into consideration when dealing with cases. Furthermore, everyone observed *ʿurf* whatever their role or status category—up to and including *sayyid* rulers. Tribal law in Rāziḥ has therefore always been a truly *common* law.[6] Behind intermittent, state-inspired propaganda implying that *ʿurf* is antithetical to the sharīʿah, therefore, lies a complex historical relationship of substantial mutual accommodation and integration.[7] Whatever the rhetoric, *ʿurf* and sharīʿah law have in practice always comprised a composite system for solving problems and ordering relations. Cooperation between tribal leaders and state officials was also facilitated by the fact that they share the same cultural assumptions and values, and employ similar symbols and rituals of enforcement. This legally dualistic environment is therefore very different from that in European colonies, where the ideologically subordinate system articulated with the superior system only at the highest judicial levels, and practice was inevitably riddled with linguistic and cultural misunderstandings (Bohannan 1967:52).

Concepts and Scope

Rāziḥīs objectify their common or customary law as a collection of precepts, rules, and procedures inherited from the past, and embodied and transmitted in local documents and in the memories of shaykhs and elders. Rāziḥīs refer to their law as "the laws and traditions of the tribes" (*shurū ͑ al-qubul* or *aslāf wa a ͑rāf al-qubul*). The term *shurū ͑* (sing. *shara ͑*) connotes "the correct way" like the cognate term *sharī ͑ah* for Islamic law; the term *a ͑rāf* (the plural of *͑urf*), from the root "to know," suggests a body of specialized knowledge; and *aslāf* (sing. *silf*), meaning "ancestral traditions," reflects the belief and fact that similar laws have been practiced for generations.[8] These notions resemble those of sharī͑ah law, which is likewise inherited from the past and embodied in texts and memories, and is also intended to regulate human affairs through the expert interpretation and application of specialized "knowledge" (*͑ilm*) (Messick 1993). Both systems of law are also rhetorically opposed to the state of chaotic "ignorance" (*jāhiliyyah*) which Muslims believe existed before the enlightenment of Islam, and Rāziḥīs imagine existed before the advent of tribalism. The sharī͑ah is, of course, ideologically superior to *͑urf* because of its divine origin and purpose, its universalistic aim to be the law of the entire Islamic community (*ummah*), and its transmission by a distinguished chain of named religious scholars (*͑ulamā*). The origins of *͑urf*, by contrast, are secular and anonymous, its aims are worldly and geographically limited, and its transmitters are varied and diffused. Nevertheless, Rāziḥīs have immense respect for their legal traditions and the papers which enshrine them, which have often been preserved for centuries. This parallels the respect for prestigious human descent and hereditary leadership. Great value is placed both on the continuity of politico-legal authority in the same dominant clans *and* on the perceived continuity of the rules and procedures which leaders implement (Pospisil 1971:35; Messick 1993:217). As Shaykh ͑Awaḍ explained: "As the Quran says, 'We found our forefathers (*ajdād*) behaving this way, and we followed them.' So we follow ancestral tradition (*aslāf*)."

͑Urf embraces a wide range of activities and situations, some of which have already been described: rules and procedures, penalties and modes of enforcement, the conduct of political relations, constitutional events

such as accession to shaykhly office and political defection, and the rights and responsibilities of individuals and groups. Essentially similar rules and procedures are also invoked and implemented in *ʿurf* regardless of the scale of a dispute or the social distance between protagonists; the same rules apply whether a problem is defined as between individuals, clans, or tribes, or between tribes and the state. Tribal law is not, therefore, merely concerned with offenses and disputes; it is also a medium for conducting the full spectrum of politico-legal relationships. A more appropriate rendering of *ʿurf*, in many contexts, is therefore "tribal governance"—a concept expressed in the phrase *ḥukum ʿurfī*. This conceptual and practical comprehensiveness reflects the absence of any clear separation of executive, legal, and political powers among tribal leaders; as we have seen, the same men perform different roles in different contexts. Law is therefore inextricably bound up with politics, and every legal problem has potential political implications, and vice versa. Leaders routinely pursue their personal ambitions by judicial means; and their constituents use legal procedures to further *their* interests, and to oppose or protest against leaders.

The Wider Jural Context

Rāziḥīs consider their *ʿurf* to be part of, and essentially similar to, the "common traditions" of all Khawlān ibn ʿĀmir. A 1930s document, for example, stipulates that crimes in the marketplace of al-Naẓīr should be dealt with "according to the sūq regulations of Khawlān ibn ʿĀmir" (D1936a:32). The dilemma local variations in rules could cause in inter-tribal disputes is resolved by the custom, as elsewhere in Yemen, of adjudicating and making awards according to the rules of the plaintiff's tribe (Dresch 1989:107; Donaldson 2000:163, 212).

The relative legal homogeneity within Khawlān ibn ʿĀmir reflects a major socio-economic field; it is a direct consequence of constant interaction across the borders of tribes, and along the trading networks which span the entire region. Human agency must be recognized here. Rules and procedures have not been passively or automatically replicated, but actively maintained and modified by generations of Rāziḥī leaders. The evident similarity of tribal law throughout the northern highlands of Yemen is likewise the product of constant interaction between the leaders and inhabitants of tribes linked mainly by trade. This legal convergence over a vast region derives from the fact that *ʿurf* is as much about permanent relationships as about disputes and offenses; it is the medium by which scores of tribes articulate with one another "horizontally," and are "vertically" integrated into supra-tribal structures and states.

Acquisition and Transmission

Underlying the rules and practices of *ʿurf* are fundamental assumptions about the rights of individuals and groups to dignity, autonomy, security, justice, compensation, retribution, and apology. An important strength of *ʿurf* is that these principles and their related procedures are rooted in the values and norms of ordinary relationships and therefore widely understood. The language of *ʿurf* is demotic. Information about problems or disputes is rapidly disseminated in mosques, markets, and everyday social gatherings. Tribal law is easily observed in practice. And there is a high level of participation in its procedures because of collective responsibility and corporate subscription; many men also become *amīns* or elders when they mature. There is therefore little mystification about tribal law.

Tribal law is a hereditary specialism like other professions, and is considered the province, if not the monopoly, of shaykhs and elders—a notion which the latter of course foster. The boys of leading families are, as mentioned, advantageously situated for learning the rules and honing the performative skills needed to operate effectively in the politico-legal domain. They witness countless meetings in their homes, and accompany their fathers and uncles on business around their tribes, eventually acting as their scribes and deputies. They constantly hear and absorb the special words and succinct phrases which encapsulate the central tenets of tribal law, and become adept at reproducing them. They also have easy access to the documents in which tribal law and agreements are enshrined. As Shaykh Nāṣir explained:

> I learned about *ʿurf* from the agreements of our forebears (*qawāʿid al-awwalīn*). And we rule as they did (*naḥkum ʿalā mā ḥakamū ʿalayh*).

Another time I pressed him for details of blood-money compensation (*diyah*), and he replied: "It's all in the *qawāʿid*—I meant to refer to them before you came." He then spontaneously recited a formulaic statement of tribal collective responsibility:

> The tribe is united whatever expenses, misfortunes, deaths, or retribution might afflict it, except that anyone who commits adultery, or breaks sharīʿah law, or kills someone with hostile intent, forfeits the support of his fellow tribesmen [literally, will have no brother nor cousin].

I later read many variations on these words in tribal documents, and heard them reproduced in shaykhly speeches. "*That,*" he concluded, "is what they decreed at the time of the ancestors."

By constant exposure, the boys of leading families develop the vital ability to couch speeches and dictate documents in the correct forms of words, and to conduct tribal meetings and rituals with the appropriate blend of showmanship and political cunning. In quiet, lamp-lit evenings they are also the rapt audience (as I was) for the exemplary and cautionary tales of older men. Shaykh Nāṣir, for example, would typically respond to my queries about tribal law not by abstract theorizing, but by plunging into a gripping account of some famous case in which he, his father, or his grandfather had been personally involved, and which illustrated that legal point in action. He was a consummate storyteller, combining gestures, sound effects, word pictures, and often poetic neologisms to startling effect. Such theatrical performances, both entertaining and didactic, probably instilled the fundamentals of *ʿurf* into impressionable minds more effectively than would more formal instruction.

The relatively wide diffusion of *ʿurf* and its methods of transmission contrast with the much more restricted understanding of Islamic jurisprudence (*fiqh*), and its more formal, institutionalized, and prolonged pedagogy (see Messick 1993:108). Sharīʿah law, like *ʿurf,* is a mainly hereditary specialism. The sons of Islamic judges (sing. *ḥākim*), jurist-administrators (sing. *qāḍī*), and jurists (sing. *faqīh*) are also advantaged, like the sons of tribal notables, by their exposure to knowledge and practice, and are similarly encouraged and instructed by the older generation. In the 1970s, for example, the *ḥākim* of Rāziḥ, Sayyid Muḥsin Abū Ṭālib, gave his sons and nephews weekly lessons in *fiqh* and *ʿilm* in the hope of perpetuating his family's scholarly tradition. But the acquisition of sharīʿah knowledge depends on becoming literate in Classical Arabic, which is like learning another language. This not only requires intellectual ability, but also freedom from subsistence tasks for years of study—economically impossible for most. Before the expansion of state education during the late 1970s, therefore, most Rāziḥīs were illiterate, and although many acquired a smattering of Classical Arabic during Friday sermons, only a minority of *sayyids* and members of other status categories acquired any expertise in religious law. Its high language, rigorous training methods, and associations with religious status and the state therefore distanced sharīʿah law from ordinary

FIGURE 6.2.
Shaykh ʿAwaḍ (right) drawing up papers in his *dīwān,* 1979

people, most of whom felt ignorant and in awe of its legal intricacies and sacred knowledge, and admired and deferred to those who devoted years to attaining it. This still applies today, despite the recent expansion of literacy. Tribal law, by contrast, is neither mysterious nor awe-inspiring; it is comprehensible and accessible to ordinary people—more their own.

Contracts

The Rāziḥī desire for order and regulation is manifest in the remarkable degree to which relationships are mediated by written agreements. Even at the interpersonal level, most important economic and social transactions are accompanied by contracts (sing. *ʿaqd*) defining the rights and responsibilities of the parties, the terms and conditions of their agreement, and the associated material exchanges. To take a few examples: sharecropping agreements on land specify the division of harvests, and on cows divide responsibility for collecting fodder and caring for the animal, and rights to its calves, milk, and dung; sale contracts for houses and other buildings record associated properties such as yards, pathways, dung heaps, and wood piles to which the purchaser acquires rights; land-sale contracts record the owners of the land bordering the terrace or *qafarah* parcel being transferred, and any attached rights to runoff or spring water; and marriage contracts record, among other terms, the brideprice, and the amounts and due dates of installments.

This high level of contractual activity reflects the potential for contention inherent in particular inter-personal relationships—especially those involving the protection and transfer of wealth. At the same time, it shows the choice and control which people exercise over their social relations, their respect for the law as an ideal system, and their preference for exerting rights through formal judicial mechanisms. Routine, intensive contract-making presupposes a realistic hope that rights might be upheld by due processes. It is also a response to the fact that both tribal and state authorities have always required documentary evidence of agreements and claims and their terms in order to deal with disputes and deliver judgments.

Law-making

The variety of documents written at the behest of tribal authorities fall into several categories, some already encountered: records of litigation proceedings (*daʿwā wa ijābah*) and arbitrated settlements (sing. *ṣulḥ*); judgments (sing. *ḥukum* or *faṣal*); defection contracts (*waraqāt al-qiṭāʿ wa al-dukhūl*); shaykhship contracts (*waraqāt al-mashīkh*); and agreements within and between tribes, between tribes and states, or between rulers (*qawāʿid;* also *ẓunnāt, mawāḍīn*). Of these documents, *qawāʿid* are (as mentioned) the key instruments of tribal governance. They record decisions and agreements made by the representatives of the main administrative structures of the tribal system (clans, wards, or tribes). They cover the full range of their legal and political concerns, including law enforcement, personal security, territorial defense, and the protection of markets and trade. Rules surface in them in the breach. And they explicitly formulate or reiterate laws with the "intention of universal application" vis-à-vis the parties in future similar cases (Bohannan 1967: 45; Pospisil 1971: 79).

In *qawāʿid* tribal leaders pledge their adherence to specific rules or procedures, occasionally agree on or "enact" new rules in response to changing circumstances (though legal innovation may be disguised as reiteration), and sometimes set out the terms and conditions of their relationships. The rules or terms invariably need reaffirming (or modifying) either because they have just been criminally flouted, or because current events, such as impending hostilities, have enhanced their importance. Sometimes *qawāʿid* allude briefly to the background problem, but it can usually only be deduced from the rules mentioned or agreements reached. Since *qawāʿid* are virtually simultaneous records of the words spoken during meetings, they often reproduce the colloquial, condensed style of politico-legal discourse. Because scribes record the interjections of participants as they are made, the sequence of topics can also be illogical or repetitive.

Whether or not they actually reiterate earlier decisions, *qawāʿid* are often wrapped in a legitimizing aura of ancestral tradition (*aslāf*). Some explicitly invoke precedent by stating that decisions are "according to previous agreements" (*ḥasb al-qawāʿid al-sābiqah*), or by alluding to the agreements of a named deceased shaykh to which leaders still feel bound, or wish others to be bound.[9] When Shaykh Jubrān Qāsim was struggling to establish his authority at the beginning of his regime, for example, he issued an edict (D1853b) in which he meted out (*taṣāwab*) penalties to offenders and a rival for the shaykhship

> according to all the old and recent agreements (*mawāḍīn*), binding on the tribe, which are in his possession (*iladhī bi yideh ʿala al-qabīlah*), [dating] from the lifetime of Shaykh Nāṣir [his brother and predecessor].

He also affirmed:

> The agreements and settlements in the shaykh's possession, old and recent, and their calculations, terms, and guarantees, are valid.[10] . . . The above decisions should be enforced by the internal and external guarantors (*razz wa jidhū*), according to the agreements (*ẓunnāt*) made by former and recent shaykhs.

Some documents even cite earlier documents by date, stating that they confirm or do not contravene their terms (D1939a). Conversely, they sometimes explicitly "renounce and relinquish" (*ṣadar-wa-ṣaddar*) prior agreements or commitments which they now wish annulled (D1891e).

The respect for former commitments is often more than a salute to the ancestors, for their terms can remain relevant, and be invoked, long after they were written. This is clear, for example, from the fact that leaders sometimes submit, or refer to, old papers in order to substantiate their claims and decisions. Sometimes papers are hand-copied in such situations. In 1921, for example, the Naẓīrīs copied a fifty-year-old inter-tribal agreement (D1870a) which affirms regulations for avoiding future conflict. At the end of the copy is written:

> This is a word-for-word reproduction of the original document made in the presence of [two named shaykhs] in the month of Shawwāl, 1339. Scribe (*kātib*): ʿAlī ʿĪsā Faraḥ.

Qawāʿid are powerful cognitive instruments. Writing has tremendous prestige and significance in Rāziḥī and Yemeni culture because of its central importance in the transmission and propagation of religion and holy law, and even humble tribal documents share this aura. The special words of *qawāʿid* and other local documents also have strong local resonance because they reproduce the mantric repetitions of formal speeches and everyday political discourse—the pithy, coded expressions which crystallize and imprint the centrally important values and concepts of the tribal politico-legal order. This is strikingly similar to the way pious texts condense religious precepts into mnemonic phrases with immense cognitive and pedagogical power, as Messick (1993) has vividly described.

If all the meetings at which Rāziḥīs agree and ratify their laws and enshrine them in *qawāʿid* are considered collectively, and as connected processes, they can be regarded as functionally equivalent to the legislative assemblies of states. Moore's "sites of reglementation," which she rightly stresses should always be identified, are in this society scattered and peripatetic (Moore 1978:27). Legislation does not, however, need to be centralized in a building in order to affect a wide area if legislators attend each other's meetings. This happens in Rāziḥ. Even when agreements are internal to one tribe, the web of commitment and knowledge has a wider span because (as mentioned) witnesses and guarantors are often from neighboring tribes. And when agreements are inter-tribal, leaders of several Rāziḥ tribes are involved, and sometimes even *maradd*s or prominent *sayyid*s from other parts of Khawlān ibn ʿĀmir or beyond. No tribe therefore makes or modifies *ʿurf* in isolation; it always does so with the knowledge, approval, and support of others. It is this diffused and overlapping legislative activity, I argue, which creates the "jural region" of Rāziḥ, and the others of Khawlān ibn ʿĀmir, without prejudicing tribal judicial sovereignty. While agreeing on a common law, tribal leaders retain the exclusive right to administer it within their own tribes, while depending on one another for help in enforcement according to the terms of guarantee of their many bi-lateral and multi-lateral *qawāʿid*.

In piecemeal and cumulative fashion, the *qawāʿid* of Rāziḥ form a kind of tribal constitution. But they are nowhere aggregated for reference or comparison; neither are learned commentaries produced on them, or their essentials distilled in secondary writings (*sharḥ*) as in the sharīʿah tradition. This allows a degree of operational and constitutional flexibility. As Maine (1986) realized, once laws are codified in writing the authorities must maintain an illusion of continuity while making adjustments to fit changing circumstances. This problem is magnified when law is sacred and theoretically immutable, as well as silent or ambivalent on many issues. These dilemmas have generated centuries of doctrinal disputes and interpretive endeavors (*ijtihād*) in sharīʿah law, but not in tribal law because of the absence of binding divine authority, and its dispersed and informal method of document preservation. While promoting a conservative ideology, tribal leaders can therefore manipulate documents and innovate as circumstances warrant. They can invoke the weighty authority of *qawāʿid* in their possession, and cite the great shaykhs of old who dictated or penned them, while plucking papers from their collections which pertain to current situations, and ignoring others which are irrelevant, inconvenient, or contradictory. Thus, through time, do laws which cease to serve current purposes and interests become obsolete, or lapsed laws get resuscitated. These processes are flexibly responsive to changing conditions. The constant production of new documents means that leaders can easily absorb and legalize new norms and penalties, and can also adapt to alterations in groups and leaders, and adjust to the changing demands of states. The tribal evocation of precedent does not, therefore, necessarily imply conservatism as Schacht (1964:17) suggested, because assertions of precedent can mask innovation.

The relatively stable but occasionally changing precepts of Rāziḥī law and governance are therefore permanently inscribed in thousands of scrolls stored in baskets, chests, and cubbyholes in hundreds of houses—a scattered repository corresponding to the distribution of tribal authority in space and through time. This documentary abundance contrasts with the situation among the Ḥāshid and Bakīl tribes, where document production appears to be less prolific, and documents are centralized, and jealously guarded, by shaykhs, arbitrators, or "heralds" (sing. *dawshān*) who restrict access to them.[11] Attempts have also been made to codify the laws of the plateau tribes, presumably by governors or judges, despite reported state antagonism to *ʿurf*.[12] The comparative profusion, diffusion, and accessibility of the tribal documents of Rāziḥ reflects, I suggest, its highly participatory and devolved system of tribal governance; and the apparent absence of attempts to centralize or codify its law the determination of the Rāziḥ tribes to safeguard their autonomy.

Protection

Certain scholars have exoticized Yemeni tribal or "customary" law by focusing on the special protection it gives to particular categories of person or place defined as "inviolable" (*muḥarram*) (Rathjens 1951; Rossi 1948; Chelhod 1985). It therefore needs emphasizing that Rāziḥī law protects the full range of people, property, resources, and basic rights, *all* of which are considered perpetually "inviolable." At the same time, tribal law accords *extra* legal protection to categories of special value or vulnerability which, especially during conflicts, are collectively referred to as *bawāyis* (sing. *bāyis*). Human *bawāyis* include people defined by the *qabīlī* majority as either "weak" or "defective" (*ḍaʿīf, nāqiṣ*)—women, small children, "butchers," new immigrants (*jīrān*), "foreign" travelers, political refugees (*hāribīn*), and *sayyid*s. Non-human *bawāyis* named in documents include money, terraces, crops, *qafarah* land, mines, livestock, houses, *kufalah* zones, and watchtowers. Any damage *bawāyis* suffer attracts excess penalties above the norm. Tribal law decrees, for example, that *sayyid*s and *sharīfah*s should be compensated elevenfold for any deliberate insult, injury, or loss, and that owners should receive compensation of double the value of their property if it is stolen or willfully damaged (D1867c; D1870a).

The terms of such superior legal cover, like normal protection, tend to be committed to paper only when rules or rights are flouted, and to be generalized to the entire category. *Hijrah* protection, by contrast, is awarded to, or won by, specific families, referred to as *muhajjarīn,* and its conditions are enshrined in contracts (sing. *qāʿidat* or *waraqat al-tahjīr*) with the leaders of specific tribes—those they live in, and sometimes others.[13] These papers were drawn up or renewed in particular circumstances, such as when a family was threatened or its head died. In D1855b, for example, after the death of a senior member of the *qāḍī* family, Ilt al-Judhaynah, the shaykh of al-Naẓīr and representatives of its Thirds confirmed their protection of his sons and grandchildren, and their "guests, workers, property, and journeys," the penalty for harming which should be double the norm. They also exempted the family from the obligation to pay tribal subscriptions (sing. *farq*) or "anything else," meaning mobilizing militarily for the tribe. It was also forbidden to wage war against *muhajjarīn,* in return for which they were supposed to remain neutral during inter-tribal hostilities.

Together with extra legal protection, these military and fiscal concessions are the main privileges of *hijrah* status.

The religious elite grasped chances to negotiate favorable *hijrah* terms. During a conflict between al-Naẓīr and Munabbih in 1893, for example, Munabbihīs stole or destroyed a valuable amount of coffee belonging to Ilt al-Judhaynah, and the latter reduced the compensation for which Munabbih was liable in return for a *qāʿidat al-tahjīr* containing terms similar to their earlier protection contracts. They also reciprocally promised never to participate in hostilities against Munabbih unless ordered to by the imām. These undertakings were guaranteed by the leaders of eight Rāziḥ tribes including Munabbih (D1893a).

Some *sayyid* families also have *tahjīr* papers, although Bayt Abū Ṭālib (formerly Āl Muṭahhar) claimed they did not need them because they were once the *dawlah* of Rāziḥ—in other words, too powerful to need tribal patronage. But there *were* times when they felt vulnerable and negotiated special protection from al-Naẓīr—notably when their position was threatened by imāms or other rulers. In D1880b, for example, when the main Zaydī imām regained control of Rāziḥ and Āl Muṭahhar presumably felt threatened, the leaders of al-Naẓīr affirmed all previous protection pacts with "their *dawlah* Āl Muṭahhar," and promised to exact severe penalties from anyone who harmed them or plotted against them. The 1960s Civil War, when *sayyids* again felt threatened, likewise provoked a rash of protection pacts between their clans and the tribes in which they lived. Such agreements also needed renewing when people died, as Shaykh ʿAwaḍ emphasized: "We affirm the authenticity of the original (*nishhid bi ṣaḥḥat al-awwalah*). It's essential to renew them every generation . . . For example, there are agreements between our grandfathers and theirs and our fathers and theirs." As this implies, the terms of *hijrah* protection can lapse. This has happened to Ilt al-Judhaynah, who (as mentioned) failed to maintain their family tradition of learning, no longer perform specialized services for the tribes, and are no longer considered *muhajjarīn*.

Extra penalties are also due when people or their property are harmed in places where they have a particular right to feel "secure" (*āmin*), or where they are exposed to increased risks. Houses, for example, are considered especially inviolable, and malevolent intrusion is deemed a grave insult to male honor. Such enhanced legal protection linked to place often needs to be understood with reference to tribal sovereignty, specifically the responsibility of each tribe for the safety of people "from abroad" (*min khārij*), who have the right to safe passage through the territories of other tribes. Such "foreigners" are referred to as classificatory "affines" (*aḥsāb*), or as "protégés" (*munūʿ*, sing. *manaʿ*), and their protection operates like travel insurance. As a Naẓīrī explained:

> Your *manaʿ* is more important than your brother. Everyone should cultivate *munūʿ* in other tribes. A *manaʿ* can be anyone you lend to, or help when you are traveling, or who arrives asking for help—for example if their harvest has failed and they need grain. If I'm stuck far from home, my *manaʿ* will protect me and feed me, and get me out safely—if there's a war or a standoff, for example. If a stranger arrives and says he's a friend of my *manaʿ*, I will also help him for the sake of my *manaʿ*.

Men are obliged to provide visiting *munūʿ* with shelter and food. Another Naẓīrī told me: "My mother used to shout to my father, 'Your *manaʿ* is here,' then she would rush to prepare a meal for our guest." This host-guest bond is sometimes described as a relationship of "bread and salt" (*ʿaysh-wa-milḥ*) (see Gingrich 1989b). The obligation to protect and help *munūʿ* is also generalized to tribes, which should, if necessary, provide them with guardians or traveling companions (sing. *rafīq, sāyir*) to conduct them safely (*āmin*) to the border. Similarly, the extra legal protection women are permanently afforded by reason of their "weak" gender is even greater when they visit other tribes for work or social reasons, or if they are *ḥamīlah*s married "abroad," where they are beyond the physical protection of their own tribesmen.

The protection of markets and trade routes, the focus of much attention in the Yemeni literature, is one of the most important examples of the extra legal protection of especially valuable or vulnerable places. This phenomenon must also be understood in relation to tribal sovereignty. Each Rāziḥ tribe imposes extra penalties if anyone is harmed while visiting its weekly market, or traveling through its territory to reach it, and the penalties increase if the victims are "foreigners." In the case of entrepôt markets, this enhanced protection extends over three days (market day and the days before and after) to cover long-distance traders staying overnight. People visiting the main Sunday market of al-Naẓīr, for example, are specially protected on Saturday, Sunday, and Monday "until dusk." Once a person crosses the Naẓīrī border into a neighboring tribe, however, that tribe (or twinned tribes with bi-lateral market-protection pacts) becomes accountable for their safety, and for dealing with offenses against them.

Other places specially protected by special rules and extra penalties are the *kufalah* zones along certain tribal borders, where (as mentioned) potentially dangerous inter-tribal disputes are more likely to occur, and have historically occurred, because of their settlement patterns and topography. Within these areas it is forbidden to fire guns, "to wage war from them or upon them," or to engage in any behavior which could threaten the neighboring tribe and provoke inter-tribal conflict. Each *kufalah* zone also has its own specific prohibitions to which neighboring tribes agreed after violent incidents. Those governing the Naẓīrī-Birkānī *kufalah,* for example, forbid the building of houses over two storeys high, or the investment of existing houses or watchtowers during inter-tribal hostilities. Such rules can become dormant during peaceful periods, and be reaffirmed or modified when they become relevant again. This happened in the 1990s when a Naẓīrī built a house in the *kufalah* zone near the border with Birkān described in Chapter Three. The Birkānīs objected on the grounds that it was against the regulations, but eventually allowed it on condition that its entrance faced toward them so they could monitor comings and goings. One can imagine this becoming a "rule" if further building takes place.

Each sovereign tribe is therefore a clearly defined space within which *everyone's* personal and property rights are protected by rules and penalties. And its borders enclose other spaces (houses, markets, trade routes, and security zones), and certain temporarily or permanently "weak" social categories and properties, which are more heavily protected by multiples of the normal penalties. The honor of each tribe depends on its leaders' ability to maintain law and order within their sovereign domain, and especially on their ability to protect their *bawāyis,* and when they succeed, people feel proud. One market day in al-Naẓīr, firecrackers were let off to get everyone's attention, the crowd fell silent, and a Naẓīrī elder announced (*aẓhar*) from the roof of the mosque that a Birkānī shopper had dropped some money, and offered a reward for its return. A Naẓīrī immediately held up his hand to say he had found it, and refused the reward. A bystander beamed at me: "You see how honorable we are, and how safe our market is!" Conversely, people feel ashamed, dishonored, and defiled if their specially protected categories are harmed or desecrated. It is in these circumstances that they are most likely to goad their leaders into taking legal or military action in order to restore their collective honor; flagrant abuses demand proportionate responses. All these notions of protection and honor are applied to, and help define, structures at each level of tribal society. As a Naẓīrī idealistically explained, "My first responsibility is to protect my home, then Ilt Ibrāhīm [his clan], then al-Naẓīr [his tribe], then all of Rāziḥ."

Compensation and Fines

The detailed prohibitions and prescriptions of *ʿurf* are matched by equally detailed penalties for infringements, which are explicitly intended as deterrents. "People consider the consequences, and it makes them more careful," Shaykh ʿAwaḍ explained. Penalties are scaled according to the presence or absence of intent, the severity of the offense, the damage inflicted, and other considerations. In contrast to sharīʿah law, which institutionalizes corporal punishment for several crimes as well as murder, tribal law exacts mainly material penalties. Were tribal leaders to beat an offender, for example, they would be transgressing the boundaries of their powers and grossly insulting his "honor" (though they might get away with it if their positions are strong, and their victim is socially *ḍaʿīf*). So even a criminal is ideally physically inviolable unless he commits culpable homicide.

Two distinct categories of material penalties or amends can be due following a crime: *compensation payments,* which must invariably be paid to the victim or his immediate family; and *fines,* which must be paid, in addition, to the leaders of the tribe in which the crime was committed.[14] Either type of payment can be increased when a specially protected category is harmed or violated. Compensation payments and fines are easily confused because they tend to be assimilated to one another in speech and practice; for example, fines are typically calculated as a fraction of the compensation payment. And they can also take the same material forms—food, money, or animals. It is important to distinguish between these penalties, however, and also to define who pays and who receives them, in order to understand how tribal law sustains tribal structures.

A fundamental precept of tribal law is that whoever does wrong should put it right, expressed in the Rāziḥī saying: "Whoever tears with his hand must patch with his skin (*man razaq bi yideh raqaʿ min jildeh*)" (D1939a). Things can only be "put right," however, and justice served if victims are compensated in a manner commensurate with the gravity of the offense. This is illustrated by a case of minor defamation. A Birkānī visited a fellow tribesman, and was so disgusted by his broken-down tobacco pipe (*madāʿah*) and poor-quality charcoal that he ridiculed his host's hospitality in a poem. The latter complained about this public insult to their shaykh, and he instructed him to fix his equipment and invite his guest back. This he did, and the latter composed another poem praising his hospitality. This also fixed the relationship, and put things right. Putting right is often described in the idiom of "black and white." A wrong or shameful deed "blackens" (*sawwad*) the "face," "honor," or "authority" (*wajh,* pl. *wujūh*) of one's clan, tribe, shaykh, or guarantors, and the gestures made and penalties paid to redress the wrong "whitens" (*bayyaḍ*) them.

In more serious offenses, moral as well as material criteria are employed in deciding compensation, and whether fines are also due. A major consideration in making these assessments, as in sharīʿah law, is whether an act was "deliberate" (*ʿamd*) or "mistaken" (*khaṭā'*)—often phrased as "one of God's accidents" (*ghāribah min ghawārib Allāh*). In either case, accounts must be justly and legally settled before the matter can be closed.

The compensation to the victim for theft or property damage is usually a return in kind or cash to the value of the loss, and a multiple of that value for repeat offenses. Those who suffer non-fatal injuries, for example, were formerly entitled to "sustenance" (*maraq*), literally "meat broth"—a prestigious and nutritious food like meat, but which means, in the legal context, all the food a victim needs to restore his health and enable him to work. Later, compensation was more often paid in cash, the amount being influenced by the personal injury rules (*arsh*) of sharīʿah law, which specify damages according to precise criteria such as type of bruising and depth of wound (D1918). Reparations can also combine *maraq* with cash, as in a bilateral agreement between al-Izid and al-Naẓīr following a wounding in Sūq al-Naẓīr, the protection of which they share. The "sixths" mentioned are the three wards of both tribes.

> If someone is injured in a fight in the sūq or elsewhere, [it should be dealt with] according to the regulations (*qawāʿid*) for non-fatal injuries (*faʿl al-salāmah*). Two assessors should observe [the victim] every ten days, and his sustenance (*maraq*) and attendant expenses should be provided until he is cured and recovers. The administrative fees (*ijrah*) of this should be charged to the offender (*faʿʿāl*). This [support and compensation] should include wheat, soup, water, sorghum, and firewood, plus half the sharīʿah *arsh,* reduced (*tusqaṭ*) on account of the rights and duties of the close treaty relationship (*ṣaḥab*) between their sixths [i.e., the two tribes]. (D1919)

After a homicide the bereaved family (*ahl al-naqṣ*) has the right to choose between taking revenge (to be discussed in Chapter Eight) or accepting blood-money (*diyah*), which people are said to prefer unless it was a particularly heinous crime. The *diyah* is paid to the deceased's heirs, who ideally divide it between them according to Islamic inheritance law.[15] Either it is or was paid entirely in cash, or wholly or partly in kind (land, houses, or guns) (D1833c; D1860a; D1879e). Rāziḥīs distinguish between sharīʿah *diyah,* which is fixed and non-negotiable, and tribal *diyah,* which is substantially less, is subject to inflation and deflation, and *is* negotiable. It also varied between tribes according to their size and wealth, the *diyah* current in the *victim's* tribe at the time of the killing being payable. In the nineteenth and twentieth centuries the sharīʿah *diyah* for a man was 800 *qirsh* or *riyāl faranṣī* (Maria Theresa dollars)—equivalent to two to four times the fluctuating tribal *diyah* for unintentional homicide. Women's *diyah* was up to half that of men.[16]

The tribal *diyah* is adjusted according to several criteria. A normal or reduced *diyah* is paid for a homicide deemed accidental or mistaken, if there are extenuating circumstances like extreme provocation, or if it is intra-tribal or happens during war, when killing is legitimate. However, the "maximum diyah" (*ʿaẓam al-diyah*), meaning the sharīʿah *diyah* or more, is likely to be offered or demanded if the killing was deliberate, disproportionate to the provocation, or perpetrated in a cowardly way—for example, anonymously, or by shooting or stabbing someone in the back. Multiples of the normal *diyah* are also due if a homicide violates a specially protected category. For example, as mentioned, eleven *diyah*s are due to the bereaved family if a *sayyid* with *hijrah* protection is killed. Such extra payments acknowledge and expiate a gross moral breach, and recognize that the bereaved have waived their right to revenge, or to demand capital punishment under the sharīʿah. Whatever adjustments are made, the *diyah* has always been a massive sum in relation to income or to the other major expenditures of life—equivalent in value to a laborer's annual earnings, several brideprices, a large terrace, or a house. The *diyah* is a weighty deterrent to murder because the offender's tribe can reject collective responsibility for his crime and insist he pay it alone; as the saying goes: "Those who remember the *diyah* don't kill." It also offers bereaved families a strong incentive to forgo revenge, and helps push dangerous crises along the path of peaceful resolution by litigation, and away from the riskier route of reciprocal violence.

A fundamentally important aspect of compensation payments is that they are conceived as healing wounded relationships. This is most obvious with *arsh, maraq,* and *diyah* payments, which are negotiable, and are routinely reduced (*saqaṭ*) as a gesture of forgiveness and reconciliation—particularly when the injury or homicide was accidental.[17] After a *sayyid* from the ruling family of Rāziḥ killed a fellow *sayyid* at the end of the eighteenth century, for example, the bereaved family accepted "half the *diyah* which obtained in the lifetime of [the victim]," reducing their demands "to promote the well-being" of the offender's family and "to restore good relations" (D1793). The fact that *diyah* payments are conceived as binding parties to a relationship is also shown by the fact that they are customarily paid, like brideprices, in two or three annual installments (*aḥlāl*). The bonds between the parties are thus renewed in stages, allowing time for relations to mend under the watchful eyes of the guarantors of the settlement.

Fines (*ṣawāyib*), the other main category of penalty, differ from compensation payments in being conceived as amends or reparations "to the tribe" for the violation of its "honor"—meaning its politico-legal integrity, and the capacity of its leaders to maintain law and order within their sovereign domains. Fines are therefore the political equivalent of compensation payments. They repair the damage done to the relationship between the offender and his leaders, or between different tribes; and, more profoundly, they recognize that offenses also injure "society," manifested as tribes, by flouting its ideals and defying its authorities.

As in modern states, fines are instrumental in maintaining the structures by which they are exacted, though without any bureaucratic detour; they are paid directly to the leaders (shaykh and *aʿyān*) of the tribe in which the crime is committed, and are regarded as fees or awards (sing. *ijrah, thawb*) for their services. Leaders or arbitrators agree on the fees and decide how to apportion them. Fines in homicide cases are often expressed as a multiple or fraction of the *diyah*. If a "foreigner" killed someone in Sūq al-Naẓīr during its three sacrosanct days, for example, he or his tribe had to pay the equivalent of a half or a whole *diyah* (at different times) "to al-Naẓīr" in addition to the *diyah* due to the bereaved family. Similarly, if a specially protected *jār* is killed, the perpetrator must pay a *diyah* to his family, and an equivalent fine (*ʿayb*) to his shaykh and elders. Fines are also distributed among any tribal officials involved in resolving or enforcing criminal settlements. After a murder in the market of Banalqām, for example, the arbitrator (probably the shaykh of al-Naẓīr) decreed that, in addition to paying a 400 *qirsh diyah* to the bereaved family, the murderer should pay a 250 *qirsh* fine to the tribal authorities to be divided as follows: 60 to be divided among the external guarantors, 20 among the internal, Yalqamī, guarantors, 20 to the arbitrator (himself), and the remainder to the victim's family and ward (i.e., its elders) (D1880d).

Fines for smaller offenses commonly take the form of animals, referred to as *ḥukum,* the number, value, and kind depending on the severity of the crime. The value of the *ḥukum* is sometimes specified in settlements. In D1867d, for example, representatives of several Yalqamī clans agree that anyone who gangs up in a fight (an offense in tribal law) should pay an animal fine (*ḥukum*) worth two *qirsh* to their *ḍumanā*. More often animal fines are just referred to as "expenses" (sing. *gharāmah*), "food," or "sheep," or an animal and its "trimmings" (*ʿalf-eh*) (meaning fenugreek broth, *ḥilbah,* and clarified butter, *saman*). It is implicitly understood, and sometimes stated, that these are intended for the tribal leaders, and that they will make a meal of them. Often the authorities share the food and animals, which are usually slaughtered at the crime scene, with the victim and the offender—one of many examples of food combining punitive and conciliatory functions.

Fines also depend on moral evaluation of the offense, and are multiplied accordingly. Crimes are usually referred to in documents as (sing.) *ʿayb.* This common Arabic term, usually translated as "shame" or "disgrace," is best rendered as "wrong," for Rāziḥīs apply it to the full spectrum of misbehavior, from children's naughtiness to grave crimes.[18] The term *ʿayb* is similarly applied to a range of legal misdemeanors. These are divided into two main categories: *ʿayb aswad,* literally "black wrong," and *ʿayb sālim,* meaning "breach of the peace," which is more serious.[19] These are chiefly differentiated according to the presence or absence of intent to cause physical harm, as Shaykh Nāṣir Manṣūr explained with reference to the regulations governing *kufalah* zones:

> Shooting in the *kufalah* zone without harmful intent is subject to an *ʿayb aswad* fine, but if the shot is intended to kill, *ʿayb sālim* is due. This is because *ʿayb aswad* [only] wrongs (*ʿayyab*) the guarantors (*ḍumanā*) and the people at the border and us [the shaykhs]. It tramples on their authority (*daʿʿas wujīh-him*). *ʿAyb sālim* is more serious than *ʿayb aswad* because [the offender] meant to wipe someone out, to murder him, even though he missed, whereas *ʿayb aswad* just shatters security (*akhrab al-amin*).

Shaykh Nāṣir's distinction is upheld by the documentary evidence. Most of the offenses classified as *ʿayb aswad* in the *qawāʿid* are acts of constitutional impropriety or civil disobedience, while *ʿayb sālim* offenses invariably involve intent to harm. Fines reflect these distinctions. Animal fines vary through time and between tribes, but for *ʿayb aswad* offenses a bull and four sheep were often due, and for an *ʿayb sālim,* two bulls and four sheep. In 1980, MT$75 was also payable for an unlawful shot, plus "half a *diyah*" of MT$100 if the shooting was intended to harm.

Compensation payments and fines are often mentioned together in documents, as in the following agreement (D1834a) between two clans of the Izdī ward of al-Jabal following a fight over animal trespass:

> Any clan member who clubs someone in a fight (*khuṣmah*) shall pay a penalty of five *qurūsh,* half for the food [for the officials] and half [compensation] for the injured person . . . Anyone who gangs up in a fight shall be subject to a fine (*ʿayb sālim*) in accordance with tribal law (*ʿala shurūʿ al-qubul*) . . . Thieves must buy food for five people [i.e., tribal officials], and repay their theft [to their victim] twofold in five installments.
>
> If animals trespass and damage crops, on the first occasion the animal owner must give the landowner the equivalent in crops to those he lost; on a second occasion he must reimburse him for double their value as estimated by a crop assessor (*mufaqqil*); and on a third occasion he must provide food (*taʿām*) for five people [tribal officials], including a goat worth a qirsh (*jalabat qirsh*) . . . Any woman who collects fodder or grazes her animals on someone else's pasture must also compensate the owner for his loss, and pay an animal worth a *qirsh* [to the authorities].

Liability

The distinction between unintentional (*khaṭā*) or accidental (*ghāribah*) offenses, on the one hand, and deliberate or unjustified offenses (*ʿamd*), on the other, is crucial in deciding liability for compensation payments and fines. A fundamental principle of tribal law is that the offender's clan, ward, or tribe is collectively liable in the former case. Each tribe has its own "domestic" agreements about allocating such liabilities. In al-Naẓīr, for example, the sustenance (*maraq*) of men injured in inter-tribal hostilities was and remains the responsibility of their wards (Thirds) (D1879a). But all tribes hold the entire tribe responsible for accidental or justifiable homicides which occur in its own territory—regardless of the identities of the perpetrator or victim. When my landlord was a boy he accidentally shot dead a fellow Naẓīrī, and the whole of al-Naẓīr contributed to the *diyah*. This was reduced to MT$300 because it was an internal matter, and the perpetrator's wealthy paternal uncle contributed most (MT$50) to express his regret for the tragedy. Tribes are even responsible for self-inflicted deaths within their borders. In 1980, for example, a Naẓīrī scribe accidentally shot himself in the head while on official duties in Ghumār, and the latter allegedly paid the *diyah*. (Perhaps the whole tribe of Munabbih contributed, but the status of Ghumār is ambiguous, as mentioned, and it sometimes acts like an independent tribe.)

In contrast to the above, when an offense is deliberate (*ʿamd*) and unjustified, the offender is held personally responsible for the compensation payment and the fine, and for the expenses of the enforcement and settlement procedures. This cardinal rule of *ʿurf* is encapsulated in the constantly reiterated maxims "Whoever transgresses must bear all the damages (*man khalaf ḥamal al-takālīf*)," and "has neither brother nor cousin (*mā lahōh akh walā ibn ʿamm*)." This is the opposite of the indiscriminate support of fellow tribesmen reported from elsewhere in the Middle East, and expressed in the saying "My brother right or wrong." It also contrasts with the moral relativism Dresch (1989:151) reports from the Ḥāshid and Bakīl tribes, where "right and wrong are always questions of us and them."

We have seen that all offenses and disputes generate expenses, the distribution of which simultaneously restores order and supports tribal structures and governance. Compensation payments appease victims and mend personal relationships. Fines appease leaders and tribes, mend political relationships, and also reward leaders and support their offices. Both categories of penalty activate and affirm the politico-jural identities of tribes, and reinforce the ideal of a just and orderly society. And when they fail to deter offenders, they punish them, and restore them to the fold of the law-abiding. These order-maintaining functions and effects co-exist with competition for the rewards of office, and (as mentioned) sometimes tempt the very officials who should solve problems into exacerbating them for their own greedy ends. These themes will be explored further in the following chapters on politico-legal practice.

CHAPTER SEVEN

Enforcing the Law

Legal Choices

Within the sanctity of the home, where outside interference would insult patriarchal "honor," offenses are routinely dealt with, as elsewhere in Yemen, by members of the extended family (see Mundy 1995:56). People can also order another family to "deal with your offender!" (*liff khāmilak*), on the understanding that families are responsible for the reckless behavior of their members, and best positioned to restrain them; "only the bark can enclose the stick," as they say. But tribal or state authorities invariably become involved, and demand to be, when people cannot solve their own problems and endanger public order and security. Usually "the law" is activated at grassroots initiative; people notify the authorities about incidents, or request their help when rights or safety are threatened. Otherwise, the latter intervene.

Rāziḥīs have a choice of law-enforcement systems. They usually appeal to *ḥākim*s or other sharīʿah specialists (including government officials and independent experts) to resolve property and marriage disputes, and occasionally to demand sharīʿah penalties for culpable injury or homicide. But in the case of most crimes and disputes, they resort to *ʿurf*—a preference expressed in the saying, "Rather a tortuous tribal solution than straightforward sharīʿah" (*ṣulḥ aʿwaj wa lā sharīʿah muṣīb*).[1] It is not that *ʿurf* is considered more likely to deliver justice; people know that any authority can make biased or mistaken judgments, and that justice is an abstract ideal which must often be compromised for the sake of a resolution. It is rather that sharīʿah law is perceived as delivering and imposing immutable verdicts (*ḥukm,* pl. *aḥkām*) based on divinely ordained laws and penalties (*ḥudūd*), and as being slow and ineffective in resolving problems—largely because it lacks the reconciliation procedures and rituals of *ʿurf.* This view derives from observing the more unyielding government officials in action. Tribal law, on the other hand, is seen as more flexible and palliative. It solves (*ḥall, sadd*) problems and achieves solutions (sing. *ṣulḥ*) by negotiation, arbitration, and compromise; appeals can be made against the arbitrator's decision; and, most important, it has procedures for what Meissner calls "healing the social breach"—a fundamental concern shared by leaders and constituents (Meissner 1987:271; Messick 1993:184–185). Its practitioners are also well known, and more amenable to being approached and influenced.

There is considerable overlap and integration between the practice of *ʿurf* and that of sharīʿah. Tribal leaders sometimes deal with matters within the sphere of sharīʿah law: they solve property and marital disputes, write marriage contracts, and even sometimes divide land between heirs—especially for those who want to sidestep Islamic prescriptions (see Mundy 1995:161). Although they express adherence to the sharīʿah, however, they cannot be said to implement it, since they lack the necessary specialized knowledge—not least of the immensely complex Islamic rules of inheritance. *Qāḍīs* and *ḥākims*, on the other hand, are extremely knowledgeable about *ʿurf* from living cheek by jowl with tribesmen, participating in their meetings, and constantly dealing with their claims, and they have always implemented its rules and relied on its procedures.[2] Thus the nineteenth-century *ʿālim* and *ḥākim,* Sayyid ʿAlī Ḥusayn al-Ḥūthī, repeatedly judged cases and mediated settlements according to tribal law, and affirmed the validity of tribal pacts (*qawāʿid al-ṣaḥab*) in his judgments, often quoting the rules of *ʿurf* verbatim as they appear in the documents (D1879e; D1892a; D1893c; D1900b).

The above options give individuals room for maneuver, enabling them to choose which legal specialist might best deliver justice or a solution to their liking, and reducing the danger of the legal process being dominated by unsatisfactory or corrupt men. Client choice therefore creates a perennially competitive tension between (and within) the two imbricated systems which generally benefits appellants, but which can also annoy tribal leaders if their authority is undermined. This was perhaps the situation in 1859 when, prior to meting out penalties to Naẓīrī offenders, Shaykh Jubrān Qāsim asserted:

> No *ḥākim* nor *ʿālim* can annul [the shaykh's pronouncements], which are the last word on the subject (*qawleh qāṭṭaʿ kull qawl*). (D1859)

Access and Visibility

The reputations and livings of tribal leaders depend on being invited to implement *ʿurf*, and on being perceived to do so fairly and effectively. It is also the medium in which leaders compete with one another for prestige, followers, and the material rewards of law enforcement and litigation. They therefore demand to be consulted whenever crimes or disputes take place within their sovereign domains, and constantly remind their constituents of the dire consequences of taking the law into their own hands—that they must bear all the expenses alone (*man khalaf ḥamal al-takālīf*). Tribal leaders therefore make themselves accessible, and people have no compunction about approaching them, wherever they are, to request their help; they consider it their right to do so, and their leader's duty to respond, and if he is persistently unavailable they approach a rival.

A strength of *ʿurf* is that its practice is familiar and visible. Most problems are dealt with in a routine, informal way, and in the idioms of ordinary human relationships. Shaykhs can be found most days holding court in their *dīwāns* facing men arguing vociferously and flourishing documents in support of their claims. It is also common to see shaykhs and elders squatting outside their houses, or in the shade of a tree, earnestly conferring with a constituent or writing him a paper, or out and about in markets or settlements dealing with common problems such as fights, theft, crop damage, animal trespass, or disputes over marriage payments, water, or land.

Ḥākims likewise make themselves available for consultations in their houses or public places, especially the main markets, where people converge from wide catchment areas to get their problems solved while doing their shopping.[3] During fieldwork the *ḥākims* of Rāziḥ invariably attended the main weekly market in al-Naẓīr, gliding in their white robes among the motley crowds, and inviting petitioners to their homes in the afternoon.

FIGURE 7.1.
Jubrān Yaḥyā of Ilt Faraḥ (*center*) discussing a problem with some of his constituents, 1979

FIGURE 7.2.
The *ḥākim* of Rāziḥ, Muḥsin Aḥmad Abū Ṭālib (*left*), doing a property division in his sitting room, 1977

During the pre-republican era major markets even had special *ḥākims* allotted to them; they were centers of law as well as commerce. However, the state also distanced sharīʿah activity from everyday life, and put supplicants in their subordinate places, by locating government courts (sing. *maḥkamah*) in intimidating buildings such as the massive fortress at al-Qalʿah. Before motor transport, the senior *ḥākim* of Rāziḥ, Sayyid Muḥsin Abū Ṭālib, used to ride once a week on a striking white mule from his home in al-Naẓīr to al-Qalʿah to hear cases. But the rest of the week he received plaintiffs in the comfort of his home, elevated on a bed at the head of his *dīwān*, and writing papers on his knee in the age-old fashion.

In 1979 the government sent their senior officials large gray desks and swivel chairs, but Sayyid Muḥsin rejected this culturally alien furniture in favor of his more comfortable and traditional way of working. By the 1990s, however, these symbols of growing state bureaucracy were firmly installed in a new concrete extension to the fortress at al-Qalʿah, and plaintiffs sat on mattresses round the walls of a waiting room—another cultural innovation for people who had formerly been free to drop in on proceedings and witness each other's cases.[4]

Submission to Law: Sureties

Tribal leaders employ a repertoire of customary legal procedures with both instrumental and ideological effects: they solve problems, uphold structures of authority, and by the force of their symbols and dramas, affirm the desirability of order and governance. Each stage in the transition from disorder to order is marked by powerful symbolic gestures. These gain power from being legalized versions of everyday practices and discourses; they are not an esoteric mystery like legal procedures in complex modern states. They also chime with ideals of personhood and piety which Rāziḥīs respect and cherish.

A plaintiff or culprit formally submits to the law by submitting (*aqdeh, arbakh*) a surety (sing. *rabākh, qādī*)—usually a dagger or gun—to an elder or shaykh (or government official, if he wants a sharīʿah solution).[5] This act of capitulation breaks the tension, averts disorder, and initiates the legal process by empowering a leader to arbitrate or adjudicate; and he responds, "You have our promise" (*maʿak wujīhnā*), meaning to deal with the matter fairly. If the offender fails to submit a *rabākh*, his kinsman often pacifies the injured party by doing so on his behalf (*yirbakh ʿannōh*), or if the offender is obstinately resisting the law, the shaykh issues an order (*amr*) to a *ḍamīn* of his clan to seize a surety from him and deliver him up. This coercive aspect is suggested by the term *qādi,* which means "leading" or "pulling." As one man explained, "A *qādī* pulls someone to justice, like leading a camel." If the offense was committed in another tribe ("abroad"), its leaders grant the offender a courtesy day, called "a white day (*yawm abiyaḍ*)," to return to his own tribe safely pending legal proceedings or vengeance.[6] They then petition his shaykh to submit a surety on his behalf, and the problem is either solved by the two shaykhs agreeing on appropriate penalties, and the offender's shaykh extracting them and paying them over; or (if the facts are contested) the case goes to inter-tribal litigation.

A man's submission of one of his most valuable portable possessions represents a substantial commitment to the legal outcome because he forfeits it if he rejects the legal judgment or defaults on penalties or expenses. Since a cash surety would theoretically serve the same purpose, the persistence of sureties in kind, especially in a cash-rich period, points to a symbolic element. Because daggers and guns symbolize male "honor"—their ideal ability to defend their personal, family, or group interests—handing them over to the authorities is a (literally) "disarming" and conformist gesture which signals rejection of socially dangerous self-help, and voluntary submission to "the law" administered by tribal officials. Although it is normally shameful to lose one's dagger or even have it stolen, therefore, no shame attaches to submitting it as a *rabākh*. On the contrary, it is an esteemed gesture which demonstrates that the person is an admirably law-abiding citizen. When a Naẓīrī man was quarreling with his affines over his divorce arrangements, his shaykh heard that trouble was brewing and summoned him. He complied and submitted a *rabākh,* and the shaykh mediated. "When I did that," he told me, "people said '*Aqdēh!*' meaning 'He has behaved properly'!"

Tendering a *rabākh* is equally admirable when it implies guilt. Corresponding to the Islamic doctrine of mercy and forgiveness for human fallibility, people accept that anyone can "stray (*yimīl*) from the right path"; the important thing is to admit one's wrongs, put them right, and correct one's ways (*yirtudd*). It is a fundamental imperative in tribal law "to proclaim the white and bury the black" (*aẓhar al-bayḍā wa dafan al-sūdā*) (D1793). It is honorable, therefore, to confess fault and demonstrate preparedness to pay the penalty and make amends, which puts things right ("proclaims the white"). People are also motivated to volunteer their *rabākhs*, especially if they are guilty, in the hope of gaining credit and tilting the outcome in their own favor. "The first to hand over a *rabākh* should be the wrongdoer," explained a Naẓīrī, "to show that he submits to whatever solution his shaykh or the sharīʿah metes out. Then the shaykh tells the injured party, 'We will seek redress for all your gains or losses,' and they hand the solution over to him." This man later put this ideal into practice when a fellow tribesman threatened to go to the sharīʿah court in al-Qalʿah to recover a debt from him. He quickly lodged his gun with their shaykh, and explained to me that this gesture would reflect well on him, and force his adversary (*gharīm*) to accept the shaykh's arbitration (which it did). Whether men tender sureties voluntarily or under coercion, therefore, they do not see themselves as passively or impotently submitting to judicial authority, but as actively cooperating in the maintenance of law and order, and influencing the outcome of their predicament. The *rabākh* is therefore both an instrument of social control manipulated by the authorities, and an instrument of persuasion manipulated by offenders and victims.

The act of submitting a surety gains force from being a formal, legalized version of a commonplace mode of appeal. When a man wants someone's forgiveness, instead of sitting beside him as in normal socializing, he squats facing him, and places his turban, dagger, or gun on the floor before him, uttering the formula "I place my honor in your hands in order to put things right with you."[7] This act is part of the rich body language of Rāziḥ; in the heat of argument, men often instinctively slam down any object to hand, such as a stick, in front of their adversary. In its most insistent and irresistible form this gesture is called a *maqṣad,* a term best rendered as "entreaty." When men submit *rabākhs*, therefore, they are engaging in a symbolically coercive act like presenting a gift or offering hospitality. Just as prestations and meals demand both a relationship and reciprocation, so sureties demand legal action to mend a relationship damaged by misbehavior, and goad officials into performing their duty. The giver and the receiver of a *rabākh* are therefore bound by mutual expectations and obligations; while one side submits to the law, the other must implement it. The act therefore initiates a contractual bond.

Leaders cajole those who resist their authority by reiterating the formal obligations of tribesmen, reciting the hallowed maxims of *ʿurf,* and reminding them of the severe penalties for refusing to comply—especially the strongly deterrent rule that "he who offends must shoulder all the expenses." A tribal official might also place his turban (*shāl*) on the ground before or between them, saying, "My honor is in your hands (*jāhī naḥkum*)"—a powerful *maqṣad* which mirrors the tendering of sureties, and similarly upholds the moral imperative of respecting and submitting to the law. Anyone can use his turban thus, but the doffing and depositing of the distinctively colorful and bulky turbans which shaykhs and elders wear is especially difficult to resist. The most powerful *maqṣad* by turban in the past was when *sayyid*s removed their smooth white *imāmah*s—headwear redolent of their superior religious status and their close connection with the imāmic state. *Sayyids* tell how when their ancestors placed their turbans on the ground between warring tribes, "they immediately stopped fighting out of respect for the *imāmah*." When shaykhs or *sayyid*s make these gestures, therefore, the formula *jāhī naḥkum* can be understood to mean, "I entreat you to desist from violence out of respect for my political (or religious) authority."

Judicial Animal-Slaughter

Sometimes seizure of a *rabākh* is insufficient to impose order, and more serious measures are needed. When the law is flagrantly or repeatedly broken, when specially protected categories of person or place are violated, when tribal authorities are flouted, or after inter-tribal hostilities, sheep or bulls must be slaughtered. The general term for slaughter-beasts (to borrow Dresch's term) is *ʿaqāyir* (sing. *ʿaqīrah*), and for those slaughtered for legal reasons, *hajar* or *ḥukum*. And the person ordering judicial slaughter is referred to as the *muhajjir* or *muḥakkim*.

Just as a *rabākh* can either be volunteered by an offender or seized by the authorities, so ritual slaughter can be initiated by the offender (or a member of his family or clan on his behalf), or imposed by tribal authorities as part of their law-enforcement duties. In both instances, the animal or animals should ideally be slaughtered at the scene of the offense—for example at the house, in the market, or on the path where the theft or fight took place. For example, if a thief's relatives discover that he has robbed a house, they should rush to slaughter an animal at its threshold, and say to the victim, "Open your house so we can slaughter for you (*iftaḥ baytak w-anḥā niḥakkimak*)." This is called "slaughtering for the house" (*hajar lil-bayt*), by which is included "for the head of the house" (*li-ṣāḥib al-bayt*). Or if a man clubs another in the market, he or his relatives should slaughter there (*hajar lil-sūq*), and so on. The same terminology is used if the shaykh or elders do the slaughtering.

Judicial slaughter has various meanings depending on the key actors and contexts.[8] When it is initiated by the offender or his representatives, it is a powerful "entreaty" (*maqṣad*) to the victim to refrain from retaliation and settle the problem peacefully. If a Naẓīrī kills someone in another tribe's sūq, for example, his shaykh and elders, acting as *ḍumanā,* should immediately take animals and slaughter them at the scene of the crime. Shaykh ʿAwaḍ explained:

> We go there to settle the matter where the crime took place. We satisfy the bereaved family (*ahl al-naqṣ*) with entreaties (*maqāṣid*)—slaughterings and money, and whatever's necessary. And that's it—we leave as "brothers" again (*narūḥ akhwān*). Then we write a paper confirming that the termination of aggression and restoration of honor are guaranteed by the guarantors.

As with the speedy submission of a *rabākh,* the aim of such quick preemptive slaughtering is to curtail the problem, put oneself in a good light, force a peaceful settlement, and restore good relations. It derives persuasive force from its virtuous intent—to admit wrongdoing, and demonstrate eagerness to put things right and make amends, the animal itself being often sufficient. If the entreaty is accepted, as is usual, the two parties share a meal of meat from the slaughtered animal, by which commensality they repair their damaged relationship, then negotiate any further compensation. Voluntary animal sacrifice therefore signifies contrition, but in contrast to western notions of apology, it is (like tendering a *rabākh*) an assertively proud act, not an abject gesture of humility. As I have stressed, whatever the crime, admitting guilt and beseeching the victim to accept amends are always admirable and honorable because they put things right, prevent the problem escalating, and spare the offender's clan or tribe the burdensome expenses of investigation and litigation—the unavoidable consequences of denying blame.

"Domestic" animal slaughter by tribal leaders is similarly intended to halt disorder quickly and decisively. When they are breaking up a fight leaders sometimes even use their *jambiyyah*s to kill the animal instead of an ordinary knife. This saves time, and increases the pressure on the combatants to submit to the law by showing them that they are prepared to soil their precious daggers. Such official slaughter is potentially more punitive and coercive than slaughter by an offender, as the following account of a fight in al-Naẓīr illustrates:

> There was recently a fight (*khuṣmah*) between Ilt al-Ḥājj [of the Middle Third] and Ilt Rāshid [of the Upper Third]. Three men on each side were hitting each other with umbrellas in the marketplace. People were scared it would become serious, and tried to separate them. Then the shaykh and the *aʿyān* of their Thirds intervened, saying: "We must stop this brawl," and they slaughtered five sheep on the spot—it must always be where the fight is. So they had to cease fighting and pay for the sheep. If they hadn't stopped, the leaders would have kept on slaughtering more and more sheep until it became too expensive for them to continue. Both sides shared the cost of the sheep.

Because all the combatants must contribute to the cost of the animals slaughtered, the longer they persist in fighting, the more they all suffer financially. Slaughtering is seen as an instant penalty; they say "costs were incurred" (*waqaʿ al-kalaf*), meaning "judicial animal slaughter took place" (D1949). Those fighting or otherwise transgressing are therefore forced to obey the law by the escalating cost of resisting. Tribal officials also demand that animals be slaughtered following other serious, though not necessarily violent, transgressions. These are the animal fines (*ʿayb sālim, ʿayb aswad*) usually shared between the shaykh and *ḍumanā* as their fees, and are sometimes also shared with the offenders. Where voluntary animal slaughter admits wrongdoing and readiness to make amends, punitive slaughter by the authorities *asserts* wrongdoing, and coerces the offender to accept responsibility for his transgression and put it right. In either case, once the crisis is defused, slaughter is transformed, through commensality, from a symbol of entreaty, apology, and coercion into a symbol of reconciliation—a transformation for which animals are uniquely well qualified because meat is the supreme food.

Rāziḥīs take the legal significance of slaughtering for granted, and often concluded their descriptions of fights with the offhand remark, "Then the shaykh intervened and slaughtered." Sometimes they dispensed with words, and just made a swift cutting gesture across their throats to demonstrate the finality of judicial slaughter. When I asked Shaykh ʿAwaḍ how shaykhs solved problems, he also automatically conflated the notion of imposing order with slaughtering, and emphasized how it materially punishes the offender.

> If an incident occurs, they come to me and I call up the appropriate guarantor (*ḍamīn*) and the culprit (*gharīm*), and if the latter complies with the law and admits the truth and puts things right, then everything's fine. But if he doesn't, then we take a bull or a sheep and slaughter against him (*nadhhab ʿalayh*) at his expense, even if he has to forfeit his property to pay for it, until he puts things right and discharges whatever the *ḍamīn* fines him.

Ritual slaughter thus marks the decisive conclusion of criminal or violent acts, and the onset of problem resolution by the peaceful application of tribal law. The oft-repeated statement, "They intervened and slaughtered," therefore has profound moral and legal significance, referring to nothing less than the victory of right over wrong, order over chaos, and governance over anarchy. Rāziḥī linguistic usage supports this interpretation. *Ḥukum* means "judgment" or "ruling," as well as "judicial slaughter," and *muḥakkim* means "arbitrator" or "adjudicator," as well as "the person who orders the slaughtering."

The dramatic bloodletting of judicial slaughter is powerful propaganda for tribal government. Men sacrifice animals on diverse occasions to secure God's blessings, celebrate joyous events, and strengthen human relationships, and judicial slaughter partakes of all these positive meanings. More specifically, it reminds people that each tribe constitutes an inviolable, sovereign domain, and publicizes its ability to police its territory and its most valuable and vulnerable places—its houses, terraces, paths, marketplaces, and security zones. This was spontaneously stressed by informants. One said, "Slaughtering shows people from other tribes that it's safe to visit your tribe and your sūq. It's an important sign that you can maintain order." And another explained, "The *hajar* is sacrificed in the sūq to demonstrate to people that it's wrong to violate it [by offending] . . . they can also slaughter a *hajar,* that is a *ḥukum,* at the threshold of a house if someone enters it and commits a crime there, because a house is inviolable (*muḥtaram*) like the sūq." The spectacle of judicial slaughter thus enhances the reputations of tribes and their leaders, and stamps visions of the latter's power and authority into people's imaginations.

FIGURE 7.3.
Animals in Sūq al-Naẓīr, 1977

Attribution and Intention: The Oath

Problems involving offenses cannot be resolved until the culprit is identified, and the offense is classified as deliberate (*ʿamd*) or unintentional or justified (*khaṭā, ghāribah*), on which depend the attribution of liability and assessment of penalties. If the suspect confesses, or there are reliable witnesses, the case can be quickly solved. But settlement is obstructed if the culprit is unknown or he denies or justifies his deed. Lacking the investigative techniques of modern states, tribal authorities resort to demanding that oaths be sworn (*yiḥlifū yamīn*). Like the oath (*qasāmah*) in sharīʿah law (Schacht 1964:181), the *yamīn* of tribal law harnesses divine sanctions to secular aims, providing a way to overcome the logjam of ignorance and propel the legal process toward settlement. As one man put it: "The victim has no more claims once the oath has been taken." The procedure may not always elicit the truth or deliver justice, but it *is* decisive and irrevocable.

Either the victim and his supporters swear to the identity of the culprit, or, more commonly, they or an arbitrator demand a defensive oath-taking from the suspect and possible accessories in his clan, hamlet, or tribe, the collective responsibility of corporate groups being taken for granted. Shaykh ʿAwaḍ explained:

> They choose men who might be harboring the truth (*lihim sirr*), or who have some idea (*lihim khibrah*), or whom they suspect (*lihim shakk*), or who have been accused (*mutahhamīn*), or those likely to have secret information such as a shaykh.

The number of oath-takers depends on the severity of the problem and the size of the groups involved. Oath-taking is not invariably collective; individuals can also be asked to swear their innocence of crimes, or of corrupt or illegal political actions. The procedure can therefore be used to investigate and control leaders as well as ordinary people. A strange feature of collective oaths is that the number of oath-takers above five is always a multiple of ten or eleven: ten, eleven, twenty, twenty-two, forty, or forty-four (I found no examples of thirty or thirty-three). The documents show that up to five oath-takers were historically required for fraud, theft, property damage, infringements of *kufalah* regulations, and non-violent offenses against specially protected categories of people; ten or eleven for grave crimes against women, *qāḍīs*, or *sayyids*; and twenty-two after intertribal homicides.[9] The only documentary example I found of more oaths being required was after an important "foreigner" was found dead in a Naẓīrī *madfan,* when forty-four oath-takers from al-Naẓīr had to swear that he had not been murdered, but had suffocated while stealing grain. This huge number was evidently needed in order to defuse a major crisis, for (most unusually) all the shaykhs of Rāziḥ attested to the oath's validity (D1863b). The number of oath-takers which can be demanded is obviously limited by the size of co-liable groups, which presumably explains why more are required for equivalent offenses among the much larger Ḥāshid and Bakīl tribes (Dresch 1989:111n7).

The responsibility for summoning the oath-takers (sing. *ḥallāf*) and organizing the procedure (*ḥallaf*) rests with an elder of the suspect's clan or his shaykh, and the oath-taking is administered in any public place in his tribe such as a mosque or market, or even in a house, in the presence of witnesses and the shaykh or arbitrator dealing with the case. I did not witness an oath-taking, but was told that the oath-takers stand in line, and swear (*yiḥlifū*) in turn on the Quran "the gravest oath" (*al-yamīn al-mughallaḍah*) before God that they themselves are innocent, and do not know or suspect who the culprit is; or if he is identified, that his deed was unintentional or justified. These oaths are called "the oath of innocence or absence of intention" (*yamīn jīd*), "the oath of suspicion" (*yamīn al-tuhmah*), and "the oath of ignorance or justification" (*yamīn ʿilm*). Shaykh ʿAwaḍ recited the following example:

> Before Almighty God, the Violent One and Avenger, who can destroy property and progeny, I swear I have no secret knowledge about this killing nor have I been told anything whatsoever. I am as innocent of this deed as of such-and-such [sexual relations] with my mother.

Individual perjurers are subject to divine punishment, but not their entire communities as in the Moroccan Atlas (Gellner 1969:112). As Shaykh ʿAwaḍ explained:

> If someone commits perjury (*ḥalaf fajarah*), it's on his own head. God would know and *he* would punish him (*Allāh dhī bā yi ʿāqibeh*) . . . [Similarly] anyone who kills another human being will meet a bad, unnatural death. As [the Prophet] Muḥammad said, "Tell the killers they will be killed, and the spendthrifts they will get their deserts."

Leaders constantly stress that "God destroys (*ankal*) perjurers," and there is a widespread belief that they are punished by infertility, disease, death, or loss of land. If oath-takers later suffer personal misfortune, people say, "It was *him*!" meaning *now* the perjurer is revealed. A childless *sayyid,* a tribal leader who died prematurely, and a money changer who was murdered were all pointed out to me as perjurers who got their deserts. The fact that criminals sometimes perjure themselves is expressed in the saying: "He who steals swears [his innocence]" (*man siriq ḥalaf*). Another saying justifies lying under oath to protect a fellow group member and retain his friendship and support: "Don't swear against a friend or a path" (*lā tiḥlif lā min ṣadīq walā min ṭarīq*), meaning one day you might need them. One man told me, "People would never admit someone from their own clan did it. Instead they threaten the culprit that he will be severely punished if he offends again." However, contrary to this idealistic assertion, I heard of many examples of people refusing to take the oath or making excuses to avoid it, presumably for fear of divine punishment. Perjury to protect a fellow group member is also conditional on their "returning to the right path"; a persistent recidivist, whose crimes are a constant charge on his clan, would tend to be identified or disowned.

The oath is backed by secular as well as supernatural sanctions. If any of the selected oath-takers fails to take the oath (*ʿathar min al-yamīn*) he is assumed to be guilty, or to know or suspect who is. If he then insists that he is personally innocent, he must either identify the culprit, or personally bear all the penalties and expenses of the crime. Furthermore, the whole tribe has to "shoulder the expenses" if a crime is committed in its territory, and the criminal is not identified. As Shaykh ʿAwaḍ explained in relation to homicide:

> If one of them knows who did it, he should say, "It was so-and-so," then that man must take the consequences of his crime (*taḥammal bil-jarīmah ṣāḥibeh*) . . . But if someone lies under oath, he makes his whole tribe liable for the penalty. So those who know who is guilty *must* speak out . . . Then the killer takes responsibility for the expenses (*gharāmah*), the *diyah* and everything.

Oath-taking therefore encourages people to seek out and "shop" offenders from their groups in order to avoid having to subscribe to the penalties for their crimes. The operating principle of collective oath-taking is not, therefore, invariably "My clan right or wrong" as Gellner (1969 : 114) argues for the Moroccan Atlas. Overall the institution of the oath is a force for order, in Rāziḥ, because it motivates men to control or expose their unruly fellows.

Subscription

Once criminal settlements are reached, tribal leaders are responsible for assessing, collecting, and distributing the compensation payments and other expenses (*gharāmah* or *takālīf*) for which their tribe or its groups are liable. These administrative procedures (*ṭarq*) are among the most important executive functions of shaykhs and elders. Once all the money is collected, the leaders of the liable group hand over the amends to the victim's representative (his elder or shaykh), who passes it on to them or their family. Leaders also distribute fees among themselves, and to the arbitrators and scribes who provided services during any litigation; and they reimburse the butchers who provided and slaughtered the animals, and the households whose women cooked the food for the feast of reconciliation. These costs can be considerable, so the constantly reiterated rule that "whoever transgresses must bear all the expenses" is a potent threat.

Subscriptions (sing. *farq*) toward collective liabilities are calculated by dividing the total due by the number of subscribers in the liable group. If the whole tribe is liable, this is done ward by ward (if a tribe has them), then by clans and households. In D1847b, for example, the leaders of al-Izid agree that each of its three wards (Banī Mālik, al-Jabal, and al-Gharbī) should pay a third of a *diyah* for which their tribe is liable. Contributions are also graded according to means into three or so tiers, with nothing required from the poor. All this is worked out with the help of *amīn*s who know the number of men in each household, clan, and hamlet, and their current financial situations. Defaulters are dealt with (as for other repeated misdemeanors) by doubling the sum demanded, and escalating it further if they continue to resist paying (D1879a).

As mentioned in Chapter Four, the apportioning process (*mafraq*) lends itself well to patronage, since leaders can easily find reasons to exempt individuals or groups. Certain social categories are also permanently exempted from the duty of corporate subscription—women, the poor, and *sayyid*s and *qāḍī*s with *hijrah* status.

Shaykhs delegate the thorny task of extracting (*naza*ʿ) subscriptions to the *aʿyān* (or *ḍumanā* in this capacity). This is administratively necessary, but also shifts men's resentment at large expenses, or suspicion of unfairness or corruption, onto lower-level officials. From the perspective of the *ḍumanā,* on the other hand, it keeps the shaykh at bay, and helps them preserve some local autonomy. This concern can be discerned in the following mid-nineteenth century agreement (D1852) between the elders of al-Naẓīr, to which the shaykh of the time, Nāṣir Qāsim, is conspicuously neither a signatory nor a witness. The agreement is repeated in triplicate, more or less verbatim, for each of the tribe's Thirds (which were then divided into "fifths").

> Present from the Middle Third were the following [five named elders], each representing his "fifth" (*khamīs*), including dissenters and compliers (*shādhdh-wa-bādhdh*), and those present or absent (*ḥāẓir-wa-ghāyib*). All the above-mentioned, representing the whole Middle Third, held a meeting and reached a true lawful decision: that each "fifth" should be responsible for its offenders (*khāmil*) and fugitives from justice (*shārid*), and for pursuing them (*ṭarad*) for whatever expenses they have incurred or been allocated by Shaykh Nāṣir Qāsim, according to the terms of the agreements incumbent on the tribe in his possession and his verdicts (*fuṣūl*). It is not the shaykh's responsibility to pay whatever liabilities they incur such as subscriptions, but that of the guarantors (*ḍumanā*), each of whom is responsible for his fifth. The apprehending of criminals and fugitives is likewise [each fifth's] responsibility, whatever the size [of the offense]. (D1852)

A Naẓīrī spontaneously interpreted this passage as an assertion of autonomy by the *ḍumanā* rather than a reluctant acceptance of responsibilities:

> By offering to catch their offenders and collect their subscriptions, the *ḍumanā* were trying to prevent the shaykh interfering in their affairs. They were tying his hands so that he could not take too much, or take more from one than another. All this is disguised as honoring him and relieving him of work!

Once it is established (usually by oath) that an offense was accidental and unintended, the clan, ward, or tribe of the perpetrator has collective responsibility for paying the compensation and associated legal expenses. In the case of minor transgressions, the offender's clan or ward is responsible. In D1853b, for example, Shaykh Jubrān Qāsim decrees that the losses a member of the Middle Third caused an outsider should be reckoned up, and levied from the entire ward, and affirmed that "each Third is responsible for its offenders (sing. *khāmil*) according to the [written] agreements (*mawāḍīn*)." When someone commits unintentional homicide, however, his whole tribe is liable for the *diyah;* and if the perpetrator is unknown, the tribe in which the killing took place is responsible. After certain men resisted contributing toward the *diyah* for such a death, Shaykh Jubrān Qāsim and sixteen elders representing the Thirds of al-Naẓīr and their fifths reiterated this rule:

> Should anyone suffer an accidental (*ghāribah*) killing, whether within or between Thirds, the whole tribe (*al-qabīlah jār-wa-qarār*) is liable provided the perpetrator (*fa"āl*) [and members of his clan or Third] swear twenty-two oaths to God Almighty that it was one of God's accidents (*ghāribah min ghawārib Allāh*) and neither intended nor planned (*lā ʿamad walā ṣamad*). Then a *diyah* of 260 *qirsh* should be paid for the victim in three installments (*aḥlāl*). The *ḥukum* [slaughter-beast] for the bereaved family (*mawlā al-qatl*) is the killer's responsibility, but everyone in the tribe, including *jīrān,* must contribute to the *diyah* according to tribal regulations, except for up to ten men (*gharrāmah*) from the deceased's clan . . . No one else is exempted unless he emigrated from the area (*bilād*) with all his effects before the offense occurred. (D1884a)

The institution of corporate subscription is a powerful mechanism for promoting law and order and conformity. Men are encouraged to observe the law and bound to their groups by the threat of having to pay all the damages and expenses themselves if they willfully transgress or refuse to pay their dues. Their group membership is also their insurance policy, and their record of law-abiding behavior is their credit rating, should they get entangled in a dispute or accidentally kill someone. This harsh fact of life is reinforced by regular encounters with unfortunate men from other regions who have, for example, killed someone in a car crash, and must pay the whole *diyah* themselves because they do not belong to a tribe, or have lost its support. Such a man came to al-Naẓīr in 1980 to seek help with paying a *diyah.* He announced his predicament in the sūq, brandished a paper in which reputable men attested to the truth of his situation, and several Naẓīrīs made contributions (Figure 7.4).

Corporate subscription also has profound implications for tribal and state governance, because—in principle and practice—it defines and sustains tribal structures. A group which is not collectively liable for *diyah,* for example, cannot be considered a tribe. This was illustrated during my fieldwork when a leading elder of Ghumār was lobbying for it to be considered an autonomous tribe rather than a ward of Munabbih, and a Naẓīrī

FIGURE 7.4.
Man begging for contributions to a *diyah* payment, Sūq al-Naẓīr, 1980

unsure of its status commented: "Perhaps they *are* an independent tribe; it depends whether they pay *diyah* with Munabbih." The structural statuses of clans and wards are similarly defined and consolidated by their financial and legal responsibility for the actions of their members in different circumstances.

The practice of corporate subscription is a particularly potent social mechanism because it frequently activates the structures which maintain order. Co-liable groups, to borrow E. Marx's (1967: 63ff) useful term, are visibly inscribed in lists of subscribers' names, and their members are regularly goaded into action—paying up, or (more rarely) physically mobilizing. At the same time, those who belong to social categories which are permanently or temporarily exempted from subscribing (women, the poor, and *qāḍīs* and *sayyids* of *hijrah* status) are reminded of their subordinate or outsider status in relation to this central tribal process. When shaykhs and elders appear in sūqs compiling lists, or sit in their *dīwāns* working out the amounts due according to group, wealth, and status, therefore, they are helping to maintain the social order on which their positions and order-maintenance alike depend. Leaders are also strengthened, or have their weaknesses exposed, by the recurrent necessity to collect subscriptions.

FIGURE 7.5.
Money changer with Maria Theresa dollars, Sūq al-Naẓīr, 1977

Their power and prestige are bolstered if they do so successfully, but their standing is diminished, and doubt is cast on the strength, wealth, and cohesion of their tribes, if they encounter resistance or provoke defections.

As we shall see in Part III, the principles and practices of collective liability and corporate subscription also lent themselves well to the fiscal and hegemonic aims of states. The requisite ideology existed—that groups have collective material liabilities, and that each adult male or household is obliged to contribute his or its share. And the necessary organization was in place for the assessment, allocation, collection, and disbursement of money and grain. Only minor adaptations were therefore needed for these mechanisms to be harnessed to state purposes.

Enforcing Penalties and Dues

As the above agreement shows, primary responsibility for extracting penalties and costs from reluctant criminals or subscribers falls on the *ḍumanā* of their clans and wards. They are contractually bound to enforce the legal agreements which they or their predecessors have guaranteed, and those under them are legally bound to comply with their demands. If *ḍumanā* cannot persuade an offender to pay up, they resort to summoning external guarantors from their own or another tribe—according to the severity of the problem and the relevant pacts (D1862). As one agreement states: "If anyone rejects a guarantor's authority, then external guarantors (*ahl al-ṣaḥab*) will be united against him" (D1891a). In order to persuade the offender to fulfill his financial or other obligations, the *ḍumanā* descend on him at his home, and he is legally obliged to "open his house" to his uninvited "guests" and provide them with meals and qāt until he pays up, when they leave. He is thus coerced into complying with the law by the hospitality expenses (*gharāmah*), and these escalate the longer he resists. If this pressure fails, then the guarantor responsible for him (the head of his clan, fraction, or ward) has to fork out the payment himself, and try to retrieve it from him later. In Shaykh Jubrān Qāsim's time the heads of "fifths" who were unwilling or unable to make those under them pay their subscriptions or penalties had to pay double the amount owed (D1874b). Similar arrangements apply to ordinary debts, which are always underwritten by guarantors; if the debtor defaults on a loan, his guarantor is obliged to repay it.

Shaykhs also used the above method against *ḍumanā* who failed to fulfill their official obligations. Just after Shaykh Jubrān Qāsim succeeded his brother Nāṣir Qāsim in 1853, some *ḍumanā* in the Middle Third of al-Naẓīr boycotted meetings and failed to extract subscriptions from their "fifths"—perhaps in resistance to Shaykh Jubrān's promotion. The shaykh therefore summoned secondary guarantors (*ṣaḥāyib al-jidhū*) from the other Thirds, and they enforced his demands by taking bonds "according to the terms of prior agreements." Shaykh Jubrān then meted out penalties to those who had defaulted on their duties, reminding the recalcitrant *ḍumanā*:

> If any [primary guarantor] from the "fifths" fails to attend a meeting or to submit subscriptions (*furūq*) or anything else, then the head (*kabīr*) of that "fifth" must open his house to [i.e., feed] the [secondary] guarantors . . . and bear the expenses and penalties levied by Shaykh Jubrān. (D1853b)

This coercive manipulation of the hospitality code parallels the *kafāl* custom at circumcision ceremonies when a man's affines descend on his house and oblige him to feed them in order to punish him for his failure to observe the proper social courtesies. It also resembles the state law-enforcement method called *tanfīdh,* best translated as "coercive billeting," whereby armed police descend on the home of a miscreant, at his expense, until he complies with the law (see Chapters Eight and Ten). As we will see, tribal leaders also recruit this state procedure to help them enforce the law.

There is no provision in *ʿurf,* to my knowledge, for tribal leaders to take men into custody, and I encountered only one example during fieldwork—when a shaykh detained an alleged thief in his house overnight until he could deal with him in the morning. Imprisonment is a state procedure, and is used mainly as an instrument of law enforcement, not punishment. In this respect it resembles the tribal custom of lodging sureties. It is commonplace for the local Head of Security to keep men in the prison at al-Qalʿah for a few days in order to persuade them to comply with their legal obligations, such as paying their taxes or tribal subscriptions, or to get them to admit their guilt or identify an offender. Provided this is done respectfully, there is no more stigma attached than to submitting a *rabākh*—for it equally demonstrates praiseworthy compliance with the law. It can even enhance men's tough-guy images as they nonchalantly swagger back to their tribes after "doing time" in the fortress. But it would be a foolhardy official who imprisoned a man without his shaykh's permission. Tribal leaders cooperate with government to maintain law and order, but on their own terms. If men are summoned into government custody, therefore, they either make their own way, or shaykhs *deliver* them. For a man to be publicly escorted from his home to prison by government police would be a humiliating loss of face for his tribe and its leaders, especially if he is himself a leader.

If all the above pressures failed to persuade offenders to comply with the law and fulfill their liabilities, tribal leaders could, in the past, confiscate their houses or land, somewhat like bailiffs, or sell or destroy them (D1880b; D1892a; D1905b). The ultimate punishment for a serious criminal or persistent recidivist is to pronounce him worthless, as having "the blood of a snake" (*damm ḥanash*) in the local idiom (D1949). A Naẓīrī explained:

> If someone commits a terrible crime, or keeps on offending, his clan or his tribe can say, "Your blood is worthless" (*ahdar dammak*). That means they take no more responsibility for him, and he loses all right to their protection and support. He becomes worthless (*hadar*), he has no value (*mā lōh qīmah*). This means anyone can kill or wound him without having to pay *diyah* or *arsh*.

The safety net of mutual support and collective responsibility is wrenched away, and the criminal must meet all his own expenses if he is harmed or harms others. This is tantamount to banishment from the tribe, and the only recourse for such outlaws is to emigrate to a distant tribe with which their tribe has no extradition treaties and where they are unknown, and try to reconstitute themselves as men with full social and legal value.[10] As we have seen, this scenario of an outlaw making good in a new *bilād* is a common trope in tales of ancestral origins.

CHAPTER EIGHT

Conflict and Violence

The *shibāb* of Rāziḥ strut and swagger, projecting a short-fused, uncompromising, tough-guy image. Men have boisterous public arguments. Leaders hurl abuse at their adversaries during confrontational meetings. Every market sells daggers, guns, and ammunition. Men wear daggers, and sometimes carry guns. There is much dagger-waving and celebratory gunfire at weddings, circumcision ceremonies, and religious celebrations. And men march in processions and attend meetings festooned with weapons. These displays of symbolic violence do not, however, usually signal imminent hostilities. They are rather intended to proclaim individual and group strength, deter insults, and publicize the ability to defend interests by peaceful legal means as much as by force. Far from being the militaristic hot-heads of urban nightmares and certain scholarly imaginings, the tribesmen of Rāziḥ dread bloodshed because it causes major disruption and expense, and they do not idealize physical violence. It has a legitimate place in human relations, but should be curbed and regulated. Every effort should be made to prevent conflicts escalating, and to channel them into peaceful negotiations. As the saying goes: "Settlements are desirable (*al-ṣulḥ khayr*)!"

Rules of Affray

The above ideals are articulated in two strict rules of affray:

> Noone must gang up, not even with his son or his father's brother.
>
> If two men fight, any third person present must separate them.[1]

As Naẓīrīs pointed out, these rules echo the Quranic injunctions to intervene in fights, support the oppressed against the oppressor until he returns to God, and effect reconciliation. One commented: "It is against Islam to let a fight grow, that would be ganging up (*aṣabiyyah*)!" (This term has a negative value in Rāziḥ, in contrast to the Khaldunian usage.) In the case of a brawl (*khuṣmah*) between two men, therefore, onlookers are not only forbidden to gang up (*ʿaṣab*), but are legally and morally obliged to separate (*faraʿ*) the combatants in order to prevent harm to the weaker man, then to persuade the adversaries to resolve their differences peacefully.[2]

These rules apply, like other tribal laws, whatever the status of the transgressor—though ignorance of the law can be a mitigating factor. After a *sayyid* was accused of joining in a fight, Sayyid ʿAlī Ḥusayn al-Ḥūthī exonerated him on the grounds that he must have been "unaware of the tribal law on ganging up" (D1900b).

Disputes (sing. *khilāf*) therefore invariably generate a tripartite structure comprising the parties at odds and someone who intervenes to separate them. Any bystander might deal with a minor skirmish, but the shaykh or elders of the tribe should be summoned to deal with more serious fights, which they typically do by slaughtering and seizing *rabākh*s.

The above rules of affray are centrally important principles of everyday life and tribal governance—the shared imperatives which determine expectations and motivate countless interactions. Such is their power that men who witness a "scene" feel compelled to wade in, and those embroiled in conflict await and crave intervention. This is why quarrels and fights are often melodramatic, and tend to erupt in public—especially in the sacrosanct sūq. As a jokey saying goes: "Heroes in the market are drums" (*shājaʿ issūq madhrabah*). The main aim is not to harm or overpower an adversary, but to restore wounded honor by publicizing a grievance in a manly way, and to thrust the issue into the legal domain and force a mediated settlement. Men therefore often choreograph their fights to ensure the maximum attention with the minimum of harm. As in the "umbrella fight" described in the previous chapter, they choose an important "stage" with an assured "audience," some of whom will be sure to intervene; they attack each other with roughly equal numbers; and they arm themselves with token "weapons" unlikely to inflict serious injury. A fight between Naẓīrī *sayyids* during the Civil War contained all these elements of honor slighted, theatrical bravado, and guaranteed damage limitation. A *sayyid* merchant suspected some *shibāb* from another *sayyid* family of peeping at his wife and ridiculing him. As one of the latter told it:

> Next day he went to his mother's [neighboring] hamlet and recruited four of his [*qabīlī*] affines, and they attacked us with sticks in the sūq. One of us bled quite badly from the head. People separated us, and the shaykhs slaughtered a bull and two sheep. Both sides paid toward the animals, but the other side paid more because they started the fight. Then Shaykh Nāṣir wrote a paper forbidding us to fight ever again. He was very strong then when there was no government.

The rules of affray also govern disputes defined as being between clans or hamlets. Before I understood this I tried to discover whether, in a dispute between clans from different Naẓīrī wards, for example, each clan would be supported by other clans in its ward—in other words, would they behave in a "segmentary" manner? Shaykh Nāṣir decisively quashed my expectation with a forceful expression of the Rāziḥī ideal of order-maintenance:

> *SW*: If there was a fight between Ilt Rāshid [of the Upper Third] and Ilt Faraḥ [of the Middle Third], would the other *bayt*s of the Upper Third support Ilt Rāshid?
> *Shaykh Nāṣir*: *Certainly not!* They must *not* rise and support one another! If they did, then the shaykh and the elders would come and separate the wrongdoers. Elders not involved in the dispute should intervene and resolve the problem, and return those who have strayed to the right path (*innahum ghāwū raddūhum*). And if they resist, then they seize *rabākh*s from them—a gun or a *jambiyyah*. Then they take [i.e., slaughter] a sheep and make a settlement (*sulḥ*), and quickly solve the problem (*yiḥillū al-mushkilah*). Everyone supports his *bayt* to prevent the problem growing.
> *SW*: Tribal governance (*ḥukum qabalī*) is good!
> *Shaykh Nāṣir's daughter-in-law*: What do *you* have?
> *SW*: We have a strong government.
> *Shaykh Nāṣir*: *We* don't!

SW: [The hamlet of] al-Farq contains about seven *bayts*. If there's a dispute, which *bayt* supports which?
Shaykh Nāṣir: If they have an internal dispute in al-Farq, everyone supports his *own bayt*. Then the elders intervene and crush it by slaughtering, and force them to make it up and return to the right path (*yiruddūhim*). There must be *no* ganging up! It should only be one on one.

Inter-tribal Disputes

The above rules and practices also apply in inter-tribal disputes. Two tribes at odds might typically recruit diplomatic or military support from a close ally according to the terms of their bilateral *qawāʿid* in order to even the balance of power between often unequal opponents. But other tribes are forbidden to stoke the conflict by "ganging up" aggressively with either side, and should instead intervene, or invite intervention, to prevent the conflict widening and escalating. These principles are sometimes reiterated in inter-tribal treaties. In 1814, for example, at a time of unrest on the coast, the representatives of al-Naẓīr, al-Izid, Banī Rabīʿah, and "the people of al-Bār" agreed that "should any two of the three tribes and the people of al-Bār fight one another, then a third must intervene, and none must side with another except to separate them" (D1814b).[3] Inter-tribal conflicts require intervention by one or more men who are respected by both sides, and perceived as politically neutral with regard to the specific case. Often a fellow shaykh or *maradd* will intervene spontaneously to curtail a crisis, or be invited to do so by deadlocked tribes. *Sayyids* can also step in or be asked for help, especially when problems are severe or affect a wide area. In order to succeed, arbitrators must dispense fair judgments based on sound knowledge of "the laws of Khawlān ibn ʿĀmir" and their local variants, and persuade the opponents to compromise while helping them save face. Since good arbitrators are highly esteemed, and also profit materially from disputes, inter-tribal conflicts create opportunity niches for men ambitious for prestige and influence, or fired by moral or religious principles to restore peace. Mediation is therefore inevitably competitive, creating tensions among and between prominent shaykhs and the religious elite.

Inter-tribal disputes can have a variety of causes, including honor crimes, broken agreements, failure to admit collective blame or fulfill liabilities, competition over resources, or collaboration with unpopular government officials or rulers. Tribes do not pursue every issue, however, because the procedures for doing so cost money or involve mobilizing men. Contrary to the headstrong stereotype of tribesmen as ready to spring into action at the slightest provocation or shaykhly summons, the financial and martial support of Rāziḥī men is contingent on economic and political circumstances. They are loath to subscribe to expensive litigation during hard times, or when they distrust their leaders or the cause; and they cannot mobilize when they are absorbed in agriculture. Since leaders have no means of mass coercion, they therefore have to persuade their followers that their interests are threatened in order to galvanize their support. Strong, honest, and politically astute shaykhs with a good case and wealthy tribes are therefore better able to pursue inter-tribal disputes than shaykhs with poor, weak tribes and shaky pretexts. For every grievance pursued, therefore, many are ignored.

Rāziḥīs are well aware of the above realities, and have a good idea of the strength and "domestic" standing of shaykhs in other tribes. This knowledge is especially important for tribal leaders contemplating action. They must judge whether the opposing tribe is united, or there are internal rifts they can exploit; take account of its defense pacts; and consider its size and financial resources.

Inter-tribal conflicts, like smaller confrontations, are filled with dramatically aggressive words and gestures, the meanings of which are well understood because the tribes all follow the same "rules of engagement," and draw from the same repertoire of formulaic expressions and symbolic gestures. As Caton (1987; 1990) notably realized, despite their often alarming appearance, tribal confrontations are essentially exercises in communication and persuasion, not attempts to overcome adversaries by brute force. Their aim is to restore damaged honor as a basis for making the compromises necessary for achieving the ultimate goal of settlement and reconciliation. Even when in the wrong, tribes must look strong.

Inter-tribal Litigation: The Qullat Ḥajar Dispute

Inter-tribal disputes are often resolved by litigation (*muwājahah, mushājarah*). One such case took place at the beginning of my second fieldwork in 1979, and is worth describing in some detail because it shows how tribal law and politics are routinely practiced.[4] It also exposes the perennial tension between shaykhly ambition and the ideals of good governance; while following proper procedures, leaders were simultaneously manipulating them for their own political ends. The case also reveals the central importance of wealth and numbers in the politico-legal process. The financial burden of litigation creates an uneven playing field. From the point of view of order-maintenance, however, it diverts potentially dangerous crises into battles of words, money, and food.

On the evening of ʿĪd al-Aḍḥā, 31 October 1979, after a day of circumcision ceremonies, a youth called Ḍayf went out at dusk from the Naẓīrī hamlet of Qullat Ḥajar to guard his neighbor's qāt. The qāt terrace adjoined one owned by the shaykh of Birkān, Ibn al-ʿAfrīt, and both were in the *kufalah* zone on the Naẓīrī side of the border.

According to the Birkānī version of what happened that night, al-ʿAfrīt's sons discovered Ḍayf stealing their qāt and passing it to accomplices in a truck, and restrained him. Ḍayf's cronies in Qullat Ḥajar then set upon them, firing their guns. According to the Naẓīrīs, Ḍayf was innocently on guard when the Birkānīs fired warning shots at him without reason, then beat him up, snatched his dagger, and kept it. His friends in Qullat Ḥajar intervened only in order to break up the fight, and fired no guns.

Realizing this was serious, Ibn al-ʿAfrīt immediately sent for his closest ally, Shaykh Ḥasan Muḥammad of Munabbih, the *maradd* of the Jihwazī tribes, who rushed through the mountains that very night, and (the Naẓīrīs alleged) stationed his henchmen on the summit of Birkān with their guns trained on al-Naẓīr. Shaykh Ḥasan represented Birkān throughout the ensuing dispute. Al-ʿAfrīt could not do so himself because his sons were centrally implicated in the case.

This matter could not be dealt with by quiet, bilateral diplomacy like lesser incidents. Violations of honor and the sacrosanct *kufalah* zone had allegedly occurred involving important men. The economic situation also favored action. Qat prices were soaring, so action against theft was a popular cause. Leaders were also confident, in this affluent period, that they could raise the funds for litigation. There were also political incentives for pursuing the case. The shaykhs of al-Naẓīr and Munabbih, the most powerful tribes in Rāziḥ, were long-standing rivals—not least for influence over Birkān. And in a context of weak but growing state control, it was a chance to demonstrate to the government their loyalty and desire for order.

Next morning, Shaykh Ḥasan of Munabbih wrote to Shaykh ʿAwaḍ of al-Naẓīr requesting a meeting. But the latter had preempted him by reporting the incident to the Director of Security (*mudīr al-amn*) at al-Qalʿah. The latter responded by sending a *tanfīdh* of six policemen to Birkān, who billeted themselves on Ibn al-ʿAfrīt for three days while they "conducted investigations." This cost SR10,600 (about $3,000) in fees, food, and qāt which Ibn al-ʿAfrīt levied from his tribesmen at roughly SR40 ($11) per head—equivalent to a half day's wage. In one fell swoop Shaykh ʿAwaḍ thus managed to penalize the whole tribe of Birkān as well as its shaykh, define the Naẓīrīs as the victims by making the first move, and ingratiate himself with the Director of Security, who granted the tribes a week to solve their dispute themselves.

Then followed several days of tit-for-tat gamesmanship. Meetings were arranged and boycotted, and oath-takings were demanded and vetoed. Thus expired the week of grace, and the Director of Security tried to move things on by demanding that al-ʿAfrīt's three sons and Ḍayf be imprisoned in the fortress at al-Qalʿah. Shaykh Ḥasan agreed, but only on condition that three matching Naẓīrīs also be imprisoned. He duly delivered the Birkānīs on the appointed day, but Shaykh ʿAwaḍ ignored the Director's request. Instead he ordered a second *tanfīdh* against al-ʿAfrīt from the provincial capital, Ṣaʿdah, levying SR50 ($14) a head from his tribe to pay his envoys' costs. This *tanfīdh* cost Birkān a further YR$15,000 ($3,300).

Shaykh ʿAwaḍ then upped the ante. On Thursday 8 November, in Sūq al-Naẓīr, he announced a travel ban against Birkān for the following day, and stationed armed men at the border to enforce it (this customary procedure is described in more detail below). This move was perfectly timed to prevent Birkānī traders passing through al-Naẓīr to market their perishable qāt, which they had already picked, in the Friday market of al-Ḍayʿah. That same Friday, a member of Ilt Faraḥ went down to Birkān with the *ḥākim* of Rāziḥ, Sayyid Muḥsin Abū Ṭālib, and Sayyid Zayd Abū Ṭālib, to collect testimony from disaffected Birkānīs who had witnessed the incident. Early next morning a furious al-ʿAfrīt rushed up to the *madīnah* of al-Naẓīr to complain to the *sayyid*s about the travel ban and seek their help. "He was looking for a sharīʿah solution," a Naẓīrī told me later, "but nothing came of it. It takes too long to settle things by sharīʿah." The *sayyid*s played no further formal role in solving the dispute, though they tried to help behind the scenes.

Having pounded the Birkānīs with two *tanfīdh*s and a travel ban, Shaykh ʿAwaḍ now prepared to clobber them with litigation expenses. Both sides agreed to go to court, appointed Ibn al-ʿAzzām, the shaykh of al-Shawāriq and senior *maradd* of Rāziḥ, as arbitrator, and submitted five gun *rabākh*s to him as pledges of submission to his judgment. He then wrote to the Gov-

FIGURE 8.1.
Shaykhs and *sayyids* discussing the Qullat Ḥajar case

ernor of the Province of Ṣaʿdah that he was dealing with the dispute, and would resort to him "for a sharīʿah solution" if he failed. This courtesy tactfully acknowledged government supremacy, while avoiding its interference. Each side also wrote to its respective Ḥilfī and Jihwazī allies, requesting their support. Al-Naẓīr's closest ally, the shaykh of al-Izid, immediately responded with a note saying: "I'm ready to help with arms, money, and men."

To enable each side to prepare its case and collect testimonies, the first hearing was set for twelve days later in Qullat Ḥajar. Meanwhile, a Birkānī family fed up with the expenses the dispute had already caused them, and Shaykh Ḥasan's influence over their shaykh, defected to al-Naẓīr.[5] This was the first concrete prize in the shaykhly competition for prestige and influence.

On the appointed date the Naẓīrī representatives huddled under a spreading ficus tree in Qullat Ḥajar, a traditional meeting-place, to await the arbitrator and his advisors from al-Shawāriq. Eventually they arrived, but no Birkānīs turned up. They thus intentionally burdened Shaykh ʿAwaḍ with providing the visiting dignitaries with lunch, qāt, and overnight accommodation in Naẓīrī homes.

The following day (23 November) the main participants and their supporters, most carrying guns, finally gathered on an uncultivated terrace near Qullat Ḥajar and squatted in a circle. At one side stood Shaykh ʿAwaḍ, the advocate for al-Naẓīr, leaning on a stick because of an arthritic knee. He cut an imposing figure, with his handsome face, pure white beard, long robe covering an unusually ample belly, and bulky turban of red and white silk. Facing him across the circle sat his younger opponent, Shaykh Ḥasan Muḥammad of Munabbih, a small, lean, intense man with an equally charismatic presence. He was advocate for the shaykh of Birkān, Ibn al-ʿAfrīt, who squatted beside him looking subdued. Midway between the adversaries, flanked by advisors from his tribe, sat the arbitrator, Ibn al-ʿAzzām, a dapper young man in a spotless white Saudi-style robe.

Ibn al-ʿAzzām opened the proceedings by reminding the Birkānīs and Naẓīrīs of their close relationship "as neighbors and affines," and assuring them that he had come to settle their dispute, not for personal reward. The advocates then made brief opening statements, respectfully acknowledging al-ʿAzzām's judicial authority as the *maradd* of Rāziḥ, and inviting fair judgment under God's watchful eye. Shaykh Ḥasan began by picturing himself as a perpetual victim of Naẓīrī slurs:

> I swear to God, I always speak well of the people of al-Naẓīr, though they speak ill of me. But I'm big enough to take it, even though I'm small . . . Everyone must account to God for his deeds [on judgment day]. Meanwhile we must put each other to the test . . . and the culprit will be revealed.

Shaykh ʿAwaḍ declared that al-Naẓīr had no quarrel with "Birkānīs in general, who are our brothers and affines," only with "those people who live on the summit of Birkān"—meaning Ibn al-ʿAfrīt and his sons. By drawing this distinction, he hoped to further undermine al-ʿAfrīt's domestic support. He then turned his attention to his great rival, Shaykh Ḥasan, and accused him of cowardly and illegal behavior: "You, O shaykh, came all that distance to attack us! And you mobilized your men against us *at night,* and stationed them with guns!" As all present knew, such threatening action should be taken in daylight, and be preceded by a proper public warning. It also constituted "ganging up" with al-ʿAfrīt instead of intervening to defuse the crisis as incumbent on a shaykh—especially a *maradd*. Finally, Shaykh ʿAwaḍ accused his opponent of sabotaging the peace process by boycotting the previous day's meeting: "We invited you to bring as many men as you

FIGURE 8.2.
The first meeting of the Qullat Ḥajar case, November 1979.
Shaykh ʿAwaḍ is standing far right.

FIGURE 8.3.
Shaykh Ḥasan Muḥammad of Munabbih (*seated center*) making his opening speech at the start of the Qullat Ḥajar case, November 1979.

wanted to negotiate a solution, and we would reciprocate with the same number whether it was one or ten or twenty or a hundred."

Having summarized his case, and boasted of his (political and financial) ability to entertain and field large delegations, Shaykh ʿAwaḍ claimed a pressing business appointment and ostentatiously bustled off, reassuring al-ʿAzzām that his opponents would feed him and his retinue, and that they would all reconvene next morning. This parting gesture retaliated for the previous day's hospitality expenses which his opponents had heaped on *him*. "What a crafty devil Shaykh ʿAwaḍ is!" a Naẓīrī commented. "He's so politically astute! He didn't say, 'Lunch is on the *people of Birkān*.' He said, 'Lunch today is on *you*, our opponents'—meaning the shaykhs of Birkān and Munabbih. This will be expensive for them. They must slaughter sheep and buy lots of qāt. We'll hear more of this when al-ʿAfrīt tries to collect subscriptions to the meal from his tribesmen!"

Early next morning the participants squeezed into a small shack in Qullat Ḥajar, and the proceedings continued in a more moderate vein. Despite the humble setting, this was the tribal court. Al-ʿAzzām, the arbitrator, sat in the middle, flanked by a senior advisor from his tribe and the clerk (*kātib*), the *faqīh* Ḍayf Allāh Manṣūr, who took notes and read out depositions. On one side sat Shaykh Ḥasan and his client, al-ʿAfrīt, who remained silent. And facing them sat Shaykh ʿAwaḍ and his nephew (BS), Ṣāliḥ Nāṣir, who was aspiring to succeed his father as shaykh, and seized every chance to show off his knowledge of legal terminology and procedure. Each side was supported by moiety allies: the Birkānīs (Jihwazī) by the leading elder of the Munabbihī ward of Ghumār, and the Naẓīrīs (Ḥilfī) by a leading elder from al-Izid, and the shaykh of Banī Rabīʿah. Other supporters dropped in at intervals to observe progress, and nosy passersby were told "important matters are being settled" and shooed away.

The judicial hearings—called "claim and response" (*daʿwā wa ijābah*)—followed a customary framework.[6] Having established themselves as the main plaintiffs, the Naẓīrīs presented their claims (*daʿwā*) first; then Shaykh Ḥasan presented his "response" (*ijābah*) to the accusations on behalf of the Birkānīs, and made counter-accusations; then the Naẓīrīs responded and reiterated their case. After each side made its presentations, the other left the meeting to compose its responses in private huddles with allies and advisors.

The Naẓīrī case was that while Ḍayf was innocently guarding qāt, al-ʿAfrīt's sons had violated his honor by attacking him unjustifiably and snatching his dagger; Shaykh Ḥasan and his Munabbihīs had then illegally "ganged up" with their Birkānī allies and violated the *kufalah* zone by firing shots and stationing armed men, and subsequently obstructed a government solution. For these alleged offenses they claimed various *ʿayb* fines of specified amounts of money "according to the tribal regulations" (*ḥasb al-qawāʿid*), and a collective oath from eleven Birkānīs denying the charges. They concluded their presentation by railing against the shaykh of Munabbih, revealing their resentment of his ambition and jealousy of his power:

> Shaykh Ḥasan has committed numerous previous offenses against al-Naẓīr in those areas with armed men, despite there being a government in power! He constantly foments discord between the tribes of Rāziḥ. He claims to be shaykh of all the Jihwazī tribes from Ghamar as far as the *ʿabīd* of Ibn Ghalfān [al-Waqir]. Yet despite this [responsible position], he persistently offends by stationing armed men on the summit of Birkān! . . . And because the *markaz* is in his territory [i.e., Ghumār], he deludes himself that government officials are under his control!

Shaykh Ḥasan then presented his "response" (*ijābah*) to these accusations on behalf of the Birkānīs. He repudiated all the Naẓīrī claims, including that he had stationed men on the summit of Birkān "in the name of Ḥilfī and Jihwazī" (a figure of speech here for escalation), and counter-claimed that Ḍayf *had* been stealing qāt, that the Qullat Ḥajar men *had* fired shots and attacked al-ʿAfrīt's sons, and that al-Naẓīr had imposed the travel ban without justification. For his part, he had come to Birkān only to solve the problem "like I do most of the problems in Rāziḥ and elsewhere." He respectfully assured Shaykh ʿAwaḍ that he "regarded him like a father, and Rāziḥ as like a single tribe," but the Naẓīrīs he was accusing were a different matter.

> They showed no respect for our close affinal relationships or shared borders. While the Birkānīs were [virtuously] visiting their *ḥamīlahs* [because of the religious feast], *they* were stationed at Qullat Ḥajar with guns!

He concluded by claiming damages and expenses from the Naẓīrīs, "according to tribal law" (*ḥasb aslāf wa aʿrāf al-qubul*), for their various alleged breaches of law and procedure, and the costs of the two *tanfīdhs,* which he condemned as a ridiculous over-reaction. "If we took this lying down it could get out of hand, and even *women* would start demanding *tanfīdhs* when they quarreled!"

The Naẓīrīs responded by repeating and elaborating their accusations and denials, and accusing Shaykh Ḥasan of hostility and bias toward al-Naẓīr. They then exaggerated their closeness to Birkān in the rhetoric of twinned tribes and geo-political position, and denied the closeness of Munabbih and Birkān, implying that Shaykh Ḥasan had been quite unjustified in rushing to Birkān's defense:

> Al-Naẓīr and Birkān share borders and [their people and land] are all intermixed. Also, Birkān's allegiance (*dāʿī*) is "Naẓīrī-and-Birkānī" not "Birkānī-and-Munabbihī." Birkānīs and Naẓīrīs are also southern Rāziḥīs (*ahl al-yamāniyah*), whereas Munabbihīs are northerners (*ahl al-shawāmī*). Al-ʿAfrīt is *our* ally; we have previous treaties with him.

After these oral presentations, both sides presented written testimonies to support their cases. The *ḥākim* had collected most of these, and they included his endorsements of the credibility and honesty of the witnesses he had interviewed.

All morning, while this was going on, the meat of two sheep stewed in the ovens of Qullat Ḥajar, and women labored in their smoke-filled kitchens baking huge stacks of bread. At midday the proceedings were adjourned for prayers; then all the participants, including the opponents, shared a lavish meal, relaxed and friendly despite their vehement exchanges and ignorance of the outcome. Afterward, while al-ʿAzzām deliberated, they chewed qāt together. By this commensality they began to mend their relationship.

That evening al-ʿAzzām delivered his judgment (*ṣulḥ*). He dismissed the Naẓīrī claims against Shaykh Ḥasan of Munabbih as outside the purview of this case, but he upheld some of their claims against the Birkānīs. For "ganging up" against Ḍayf, and "confiscating his *jambiyyah* until now," he fined the sons of al-ʿAfrīt a *ḥukum* of four sheep "to wipe out the disgrace and restore honor," plus MT$75 compensation payment. Since "only God knows" what really happened, these awards were conditional on Ḍayf taking an oath confirming that he was assaulted. Al-ʿAzzām dismissed police testimony which the Birkānīs had submitted as untrustworthy "because of their close friendship with them" (the police hailed from Ghumār). However, he would accept the testimony of Naẓīrī witnesses that al-ʿAfrīt's sons had fired three shots at Ḍayf on condition five Naẓīrīs swore oaths to its veracity. If they did, the Birkānīs must pay MT$75 compensation per shot, "according to tribal law" (*ḥasb al-ʿurf*). But if any of the Naẓīrīs failed the oath (an admission of guilt), then al-ʿAfrīt and sons must swear five oaths that they did not fire their guns nor intend Ḍayf harm. "The penalty for taking the *jambiyyah* was more than for firing each shot," a Naẓīrī explained, "because it is a much greater wrong (*ʿayb*). It is like reducing a man to a woman—saying he is not a proper man."

Regarding the reciprocal accusations of stationing armed men in the *kufalah* zone, al-ʿAzzām ruled:

> Eleven oath-takers (*ḥallāf*) from each side must swear that they did not station a single armed person against the other side . . . and if either side fails the oath, then they must give a bull and three sheep to wipe out the disgrace and restore honor according to customary law.

And regarding the Birkānī claim that al-Naẓīr unjustifiably imposed a travel ban against their whole tribe:

> The shaykh of al-Naẓīr must swear that the blockade was only against the sons of al-ʿAfrīt in order to compel them to behave correctly. If he fails the oath, he should be fined a *ḥukum* of two sheep.

Al-ʿAzzām also ruled that al-ʿAfrīt and his sons were liable for the expenses of the first *tanfīdh* from al-Qalʿah, and that the two sides should share the expenses of the second from Ṣaʿdah.

The Naẓīrīs immediately accepted al-ʿAzzām's rulings, but Shaykh Ḥasan and the Birkānīs vehemently rejected them despite the arbitrators' removing their turbans in entreaty (*maqṣad*). Both parties therefore decided to submit the case to Ibn Miqīt, the supreme *maradd* of Khawlān ibn ʿĀmir, who agreed to hold court at his home in Bāqim in Jumāʿah on 10 December.

In the interim the Naẓīrī leaders calculated their financial damages. These included fees (for the arbitrators, the scribe, and the envoys), *tanfīdh* expenses, and the costs of providing hospitality—every last item of which was detailed, including qāt, animals, flour, salt, fenugreek (*ḥilbah*), clarified butter, and even the ginger and cumin seasonings. The total came to SR44,775 (about $1,600). They then discussed how to levy this from their tribe. First, they decided to exempt Wadī Dahwān in the Upper Third of al-Naẓīr, where, as mentioned, Ilt Faraḥ has land and close relationships. Shaykh ʿAwaḍ rationalized this favoritism: "The people of Dahwān aren't expected to pay because they are distant from the problem. If there was a

FIGURE 8.4.
Shaykhs and elders discussing how to allocate the costs of the Qullat Ḥajar case, 1979.

similar problem near *their* border, only that side of the tribe would be expected to pay the expenses." They then decided to collect subscriptions of SR75 ($16) from a proportion of the remaining adult men, as follows:

> The money will be collected from 640 men, which is two-thirds of the men in the tribe excluding Dahwān. This means only two-thirds of the men in each household must contribute. For example, if they have nine men, six will pay and three won't. There are also about fifty poor men, without land or work, who are exempted from paying.

They presumably shared the remainder (about SR4,250) as their fees for conducting the litigation. As often happens, the leaders of al-Naẓīr were later accused of "eating" more than their fair share of the subscriptions to the Qullat Ḥajar case, and their constituents held a series of meetings to try and modify the tribe's administrative arrangements so as to avoid future problems.

The *amīn* of Qullat Ḥajar was delegated to represent al-Naẓīr at the appeal court in Jumāʿah, and he gathered all the relevant papers: the record of the hearings, which al-ʿAzzām had had copied for each side to make an immensely long scroll; and some local *qawāʿid,* one a century old, which Ibn Miqīt had asked to consult on Rāziḥī law.

FIGURE 8.5.
The *amīn* of Qullat Ḥajar with the scroll of the litigation proceedings, 1979

To the consternation of the Naẓīrīs, Ibn Miqīt rejected al-ʿAzzām's judgment on the original offense on the grounds that Ḍayf's oath of innocence could not be trusted because "he who steals swears" (*man siriq ḥalaf*). He also noted a procedural omission:

> The traditions (*aslāf*) of the tribes of Khawlān ibn ʿĀmir require that whenever the devil tempts someone to steal—whether qāt or anything else—after the crime is revealed the amount taken should be specified.

Adducing "current tribal law" (*al-ʿurf al-jārī*), Ibn Miqīt made several rulings, some upholding Naẓīrī claims, but most favoring Birkān. The Naẓīrīs therefore rejected them, and two days later the parties trekked off through the mountains to appeal to the senior *maradd* of Khawlān, Ibn Rawkān. He upheld al-ʿAzzām's original judgment in favor of al-Naẓīr, and there the case petered out.

I do not know which judgment was implemented, but assume that both sides reduced (*saqaṭ*) their demands in the cause of restoring good relations, as is customary in tribal settlements. The Naẓīrī leaders collected subscriptions from their tribe to meet their financial liabilities, and on 30 January 1980, al-ʿAzzām confirmed in writing that they had paid them. The Birkānīs presumably did the same. A few days later (4 February), a second Birkānī family defected to al-Naẓīr for similar reasons to the first. It is their ceremony which is described in Chapter Four.

Demonstrations

If their adversaries refuse to submit to negotiations or litigation, shaykhs can resort to various kinds of direct action to pressure them. One procedure is to muster an armed demonstration, called a *wijhah,* against the opposing tribe (or the local governor). This requires any intervening tribes agreeing to "open up (*fataḥ*)," so if they disapprove they can prevent it. This happened when al-Naẓīr mounted a *wijhah* against the governor in al-Qalʿah, in Ghumār, to protest against his incarceration of one of their men. Ghumār (with whom the governor undoubtedly has pacts of protection) wrote to the intervening tribe, Banī Rabīʿah, requesting them to "close their borders" (*taghlīq*); they agreed, and the Naẓīrīs had to turn back. On another occasion, however, when the protest was against the high cost of *tanfīdhs*, Banī Rabīʿah allowed the Naẓīrīs through because they sympathized with their cause.

Shaykhs should send the other tribe prior warning that they plan to mount a *wijhah*. They then arrive with their men early in the morning, obliging their adversary to give them a midday meal or lose face. As so often, the instrument of persuasion is food. Despite men bristling with weapons, no physical harm is intended: "A *wijhah* is supposed to cause the offending tribe expense, and avoid violence," a Naẓīrī explained. It also enables a shaykh to parade his following. The implicit message might be paraphrased as: "We are united behind our shaykh, we are many, and we can afford to take you on." The aim is to flaunt unity and numbers, and the capacity to finance litigation, while conjuring up the specter of more serious confrontation. Just the threat of a *wijhah* can achieve the desired end. A Munabbihī trader defaulted on his debts to a Naẓīrī trader. The latter complained to Shaykh Nāṣir; he wrote to the shaykh of Munabbih, saying, "If our man isn't paid, we'll mount a *wijhah* against you"; and the debtor paid up.

Like all forms of direct action, *wijhah*s are powerful statements of popular will; busy men do not drop their work and march through the mountains without good cause. Refusal to mobilize is equally significant. This happened in a scandalous case just after the Civil War. A man from tribe A was murdered in Banī Rabīʿah territory on his way home from Sūq al-Naẓīr, and Shaykh Nāṣir suspected the victim's own shaykh (X) of having ordered the crime:

> So we asked tribe A, "Where are your elders (*kubār*)? Bring Shaykh X to justice!" But nothing happened. So I summoned our *ḍumanā*, and we entered into litigation (*tashājarnā*) [with tribe A]. We appealed for justice (*ṭālabnā*), and held meetings (*taqābalnā*), and judgments (*aḥkām*) were made.

But Shaykh X ignored the judgments. Shaykh Nāṣir therefore appealed to the highest tribal authority in Yemen, Shaykh ʿAbdallāh al-Aḥmar of Hāshid, and he referred the case to a leading shaykh in Ṣaḥār, who ordered Shaykh X to pay amends (*ʿayb-wa-hajar*) to al-Naẓīr. He refused, and the case was finally referred back to Rāziḥ, where it was heard by Ibn ʿAwfān, the shaykh of Banī Asad on Jabal Ḥurum. Shaykh Nāṣir:

> We held meetings, and Ibn ʿAwfān confirmed that tribe A should pay *ʿayb-wa-hajar* to Sūq al-Naẓīr and its people . . . he throttled them with his penalties! But Shaykh X *still* refused to pay. I called in the *ḍumanā,*

> but there was no government, and we couldn't make him comply with the law—he just refused.
>
> So I cried, "Fellow men!" (*khubrah*), and they answered, "What?" I replied, "We should ask Banī Rabīʿah to supply twenty men, and we can muster fifty; then we can spring a *wijhah* on Shaykh X. Then either he will comply with the law, or war will break out, and then the [other] tribes of Rāziḥ (*ahl* Rāziḥ) will intercede." But they were deaf as peaches, absolutely useless! And I couldn't do anything alone. So our judgment against Shaykh X was demolished. Sharīʿah died when the republic arrived, and so did tribal laws and traditions (*al-aʿrāf wa al-aslāf*).

Tribal leaders often blame weak government for failures in tribal law enforcement, and (had there been any police) a *tanfīdh* might have helped. But there are perfectly good "tribal" explanations for Shaykh Nāṣir's failure to mobilize a *wijhah*. First, according to the rules of tribal sovereignty, a tribe is not responsible for a crime committed beyond its borders by a member of another tribe—even if the victim is returning home from its market. Shaykh Nāṣir and the appeal shaykhs were therefore stretching the law by claiming that al-Naẓīr was due amends for a crime committed in Banī Rabīʿah when both the alleged offender and the victim were members of a third tribe (A). Second, the prolonged litigation had already cost the Naẓīrīs dearly, and they had probably had enough. Furthermore, Shaykh Nāṣir's constituents suspected that he was pursuing this case so assiduously because of his political rivalry with Shaykh X. Though this crime was immoral and disgraceful, therefore, al-Naẓīr was not legally responsible for dealing with it, and its men were presumably unprepared to escalate the situation at their own expense to serve their shaykh's ambition. This case therefore illustrates one shaykh abusing his power with apparent impunity, and another's power being curbed by popular will.

Bans and Boycotts

A stronger form of inter-tribal coercion is for shaykhs to impose a travel ban (*qiṭāʿ*) on members of an offending tribe, preventing access to their territory or market—the method Shaykh ʿAwaḍ employed against Birkān during the Qullat Ḥajar dispute. The ban is enforced by "cutting the route" (*yiqṭaʿū al-ṭarīq*), which involves stationing armed guards (*murattibīn*) at checkpoints (sing. *nuqṭah*) where paths and tracks cross their borders. Leaders should initiate a ban by making the following formulaic announcement (*ẓāhirah*): "We ban you, and renounce responsibility for the safety of whoever comes here."[7] This formal declaration suspends the law of "foreigner" protection toward their opponents, and temporarily legitimizes violence against them. If any are injured while flouting the ban, they are due only *diyah* or *arsh* compensation, which are never waived, but not *ʿayb* amends because they were not wronged. Once the dispute is channeled into inter-tribal negotiations or litigation, as it invariably is, the tribe which imposed the ban must justify its action in law, or if it cannot, must apologize to the other tribe by slaughtering and paying amends.

An alternative sanction is to boycott the opposing tribe's market. However, this is effective only if all the surrounding tribes block their paths and roads and guard their borders, or "open up" (*fataḥ*) to enable other tribes to do so. This is when the targeted tribe is likely to activate its Jihwazī or Ḥilfī allies, or other alliances, in order to keep corridors open and breach the blockade. Since all tribes are bordered by several others, each with its own alliances and interests, a total blockade is hard to impose unless a tribe's policies are so threatening that all its neighbors perceive a common interest in uniting to force them to change. Boycotts are obviously most effective against tribes with important markets, such as al-Ḍayʿah, which are the very tribes with the power to impose effective bans and disrupt trade for others.

Vengeance

Rāziḥīs recognize two categories of legitimate, organized physical violence—vengeance and war—each of which has its own rules of procedure. As mentioned in Chapter Six, when someone is killed, the bereaved family (*ahl al-naqṣ*) has the right, in tribal law, to choose between revenge in kind (talion) (*naqā, jizā, thār*) or being paid (*wadā*) blood-money (*diyah*), and their leaders are obliged to support them "until everyone is compensated for their losses and is satisfied."[8] Thus when an Izdī was killed in a Ḥāshid tribe in 1970, the leaders of al-Izid agreed in writing to back the bereaved family

> in the pursuit of vengeance (*thār*) and restoration of honor (*ʿār*), and to meet all the expenses until the killer is revealed, and the bereaved family is avenged or compensated for its loss according to the terms of the old *qawāʿid*. (D1970a)

Revenge proved unnecessary, however. Letters were exchanged between tribal leaders; then a retinue of Ḥāshidīs traveled through Rāziḥ to al-Izid with escorts (sing. *rafīq*) from each tribe they traversed to guarantee their safe conduct. In al-Izid they slaughtered animals for the bereaved family to apologize for the death, and *diyah* was negotiated and accepted.

They say of a killer "there is a blood debt against him" (*ʿalayhōh dayn damm*), and there is great tension and insecurity until it is paid. Murder is a collective responsibility in tribal law, so it is legitimate for any member of the offender's clan (in internal killings) or tribe (in inter-tribal killings) to be killed in retaliation.[9] Deliberate killings therefore severely jeopardize the peace. Revenge should also equal and not exceed the original crime, but things can easily go wrong. The clan or tribe of the alleged killer might insist he was innocent, and retaliate; or more than one person might be killed in retaliation, provoking another revenge killing. In many Middle Eastern and Mediterranean societies, such situations lead to "feuds"—best characterized as a chain reaction of reciprocal homicides between groups which can span generations, and which (crucially) knows no end, nor means to an end. By this definition, however, as should already be clear, Rāziḥ does not have feuds.[10] On the contrary, after murders or other serious crimes, tribal leaders, employing *ʿurf* methods of conflict resolution, strive to achieve decisive closure.

After a homicide, the killer's family or the leaders of his tribe typically try to defuse the crisis by immediately slaughtering animals for the bereaved family to admit their responsibility, and to entreat them to accept *diyah* and waive their right to revenge. The representatives and friends of the bereaved also pressure them to be merciful, and accept money instead of blood. The high *diyah* is explicitly intended as an inducement to waive vengeance, and most bereaved families are said to settle for compensation when deaths are accidental, for example when they are caused by stray bullets or car crashes, or are crimes of passion (*qatl khimrah*) committed under extreme provocation. Vengeance is not, therefore, necessarily considered more honorable than accepting compensation for homicide, as elsewhere in Yemen and the Middle East.[11] It depends on how the act is morally evaluated. The bereaved are more likely to insist that only a life for a life can restore their honor and achieve justice when the killing is deliberate, unjustified, or disgraceful, or the victim is from a "weak" (*ḍaʿīf*) social category or was killed in a specially protected place. Then the leaders of the murderer's tribe might try to stave off reprisals by offering a greatly inflated *diyah*. This happened when an ʿAbīdī woman was killed in the 1830s. In order to avert retribution from Banī ʿAbīd, Izdī-and-Naẓīrī jointly offered her family a *diyah* of fifty *qirsh*—"five times the Banī ʿAbīd *diyah*"—plus an extra twenty *qirsh* to be divided between her family and the ʿAbīdī leaders as "a reward for wisdom and acceptance" (*thawb ʿaql wa thawb qublān*) (D1836a).

If the bereaved family rejects compensation and demands revenge, leaders strive to control the situation. They insist on authorizing any action, and try to deter the bereaved from freelance revenge by reminding them that men must bear the expenses of their unsanctioned actions. This is spelled out in internal tribal agreements such as the following:

> Should any Naẓīrī be killed or wounded, or anyone else living among them whoever they are, and retribution is to be exacted in kind, then the head of the bereaved family (*ṣāḥib al-naqṣ*) must seek permission to inflict an injury for an injury and a death for a death. If he refuses, the tribe will be united against him until he acknowledges the authority of the guarantors (*wujīh al-ḍumanā*). [Subject to these conditions] the tribe of al-Naẓīr is united behind anyone who [decides to] take revenge (*majāzāh*). (D1921b)

If the bereaved family persists in seeking vengeance, their shaykh must secure formal agreements from the killer's shaykh and the shaykhs of any intervening tribes to their "opening up" (*fatḥ*), and not "closing" (*taghlīq*), their borders, so that avengers can enter or traverse their territories. In D1829b, for example, the shaykhs of four tribes of *yamānī* Rāziḥ agree to open their borders so that an Izdī can take revenge on an unidentified party. "This is like giving a visa," a Naẓīrī explained. "There would be terrible trouble if avengers entered without permission." In these tense situations, the shaykhs involved also try to limit the fallout by creating or reaffirming the regulations on vengeance-taking. Only adult males or "avengers" (sing. *al-rajul al-jāzī*) are legitimate targets (*mubāḥ*), and specially protected persons and properties (*bawāyis*) are exempt from vengeful action under pain of severe penalties. Sometimes leaders also specified when revenge must be taken:

> If there is a killing [in Sūq al-Bār], it should be avenged on a particular day, or within the following week before the next sūq day. (D1801)

Once a homicide crisis is resolved, leaders strive to close the matter forever. After the bereaved family has taken revenge or accepted *diyah* it must relinquish (*yuṣaddir*) all further claims, and if it resuscitates the matter it could be liable for severe sanctions, such as the destruction of houses or its members being killed (D1880a). Leaders also sometimes decreed that they should erect a stone pillar (*naṣībah*) over their victim's grave after they had taken their revenge (D1879a). "This was like a flag," a Naẓīrī explained. "It was to show that the original murder was wiped out, and order and safety restored."

The Rules of War

Wars (sing. *ḥarb*) are the prerogative of tribes (and states); clans and wards cannot "wage war," they can only have "brawls" (sing. *khuṣmah*). Wars were caused by grave honor crimes, especially against women, or by competition for vital resources, as in the war of 1985 described below. States also historically provoked wars by encroaching on tribal sovereignties, "buying" leaders, and pitting tribe against tribe. Vengeance could also become a casus belli, blurring the distinction between vengeance and war. Inter-tribal homicides did not, however, invariably trigger wars, as has often been assumed in the literature on Middle Eastern tribal politics.

During the strong state rule of the Ḥamīd al-Dīn imāms in the twentieth century, inter-tribal wars were suppressed, so none had taken place within human memory before that of 1985. It is therefore difficult to assess how frequent or violent they were historically, or how widespread, because people describing past conflicts can rarely date them, and invariably generalize them to entire regions; a war between a tribe in Rāziḥ and a tribe in Khawlān, for example, will be typically described as "between Rāziḥ and Khawlān," giving a false impression of its scale. However, the evidence from war stories and relevant documents suggests that, consistent with the prohibition on "ganging up," only one or two tribes usually engaged in hostilities on each side, that the periods of armed combat were brief, and that only a minority of men from each tribe mobilized.

There is no evidence that inter-tribal wars were invasive or attritional. Leaders had no "imperialistic" intention of conquering, colonizing, or annexing enemy territory, nor of vanquishing or slaughtering its inhabitants. Like other forms of direct action, wars took place between autonomous tribes in mutual respect of each other's political and territorial integrity, and with a shared concern to minimize casualties and achieve a speedy conclusion. These ideals are reflected in exemplary or cautionary tales of legendary wars. These strikingly do *not* extol military heroes or glorify victories, but rather eulogize men who successfully intervened to stop hostilities, or they describe the dire consequences when customary methods of containment and resolution were flouted.

There are stories of how, when tribes were suddenly threatened by states, people rushed to their markets to cry for help (*ghārah! ghārah!*), and men were mobilized (*nakkaf bil-qabāʿil*) by *dawshāns* beating drums and announcing (*bawwaqū*) the crisis through cowskin megaphones (sing. *bōq*). Beacons were also lit on mountain summits to alert other tribes and summon allies. Inter-tribal wars, by contrast, are ideally initiated in a more planned and regulated manner. Before declaring war, an offended tribe should demand of its enemy, "Whiten your faces" (*bayyaḍ wujūhkum*), meaning "Reverse the shame you have brought on yourselves by your actions"; or they fly a white banner (*tarjīyyah*) to convey the same message. "This gives the enemy a week to negotiate and put things right," an Izdī elder claimed. "But if they don't, their enemy flies a black one (*malāmah*)." War is formally declared by letter, or by proclaiming in the market or other public place: "We renounce responsibility and guilt toward you" (*nakhlā wa nibrā minnakum*) and "Our faces are white" (*wujīhnā bayḍ*). These obligatory formulaic statements suspend normal relations until peace is made, and legitimize intentional killing or wounding during the day or days of battle (called *yawm shāhir* or *yawm abiyaḍ*).

It appears from old men's tales that "wars" mostly involved protracted periods of unsuccessful negotiations and symbolic violence, culminating in pitched battles at pre-arranged dates, usually at tribal borders. Even these had their elements of display; one Naẓīrī tellingly claimed that they would look to see how many were mustering on the other side, and try to mobilize the same number. If the adversaries were not neighboring tribes, these staged confrontations obviously could be achieved only if the intervening tribes allowed access. The latter could therefore protect their allies by "closing" (*taghlīq*) their borders. This is when Jihwazī and Ḥilfī alignments were activated to contain conflicts and prevent them escalating.

As mentioned, it is one of a tribesman's main obligations to muster for direct action, including "going to war" (*saraḥ*). In addition to engaging in combat, war duties include doing a shift (*dawl*) of guard duty (*ritib*, pl. *artāb*) at borders, and contributing toward the fees and support of guards. Each tribe's leaders decide how many men to mobilize and how to deploy them according to the size and direction of the threat. Shaykh ʿAwaḍ explained:

> The shaykh calls up those responsible [the *aʿyān*], and they instruct their men [of their respective wards] to meet on an appointed day. Then they discuss and examine the situation, and select who should go to the front, and who should stay behind, and they make all the arrangements. If it lasts two or three days, we replace the men at the front with others.

The Naẓīrīs organized guard duty, like other tasks of governance, by wards. D1876b records, for example, that each Third of al-Naẓīr had guarded a border for a month. All such defense plans were subject to internal agreements such as the following:

> Wherever they are attacked from, the numbers required for border duty (*ritib*) should be assessed by three [elders], one from among those living on the [threatened] border, and two from each of the other two Thirds, together with the shaykh. (D1879a:34–35)

When hostilities were imminent, leaders motivated their followers with rousing speeches, persuading them that the war was just and vilifying their opponents. And men sang *maghrad*s "to give the enemy a picture of unity, aggression, and power," as one Naẓīrī put it. Leaders also made or confirmed defense pacts with their allies, agreeing how their joint operations should be organized and financed. In 1891, for example, during a conflict between Izdī-and-Naẓīrī on one side, and Birkān and Munabbih on the other, the former agreed to divide responsibilities and losses fractionally, just as they do policing and sūq protection:

> . . . regarding territorial defense procedures (*fī ṭarīqāt al-ḥudūd wa-al-sudūd wa al-artāb*), al-Naẓīr should be responsible for two-thirds [of the costs] of guards (*artāb*) or casualties (*naqṣ*) on their borders, and al-Izid one-third. And al-Izid should be responsible for two-thirds [of the costs] on their borders, and al-Naẓīr one-third. And liability for retribution or compensation payments (*jizā wa ilā wadā*) which they incur on their borders should be similarly allocated. (D1891a)

In the nineteenth century, those who refused to do guard duty were fined the cost of a half or whole animal and its trimmings, so their leaders shared a meal at their expense—the familiar punishment by food.[12] Defaulters were also liable for double what other tribesmen subscribed toward the costs of the war, including compensation payments (*maraq, diyah*) for enemies wounded or killed. The Naẓīrīs organized this, like peacetime injuries, by wards (D1874a; D1879a; D1887).

Prior to hostilities leaders tried to limit the potential damage. They made or reaffirmed agreements about the "security zones" (sing. *kufalah*) along their shared borders, and confirmed the categories of persons and property (*bawāyis*) which should be specially protected, and the excess penalties for harming them—including people living "abroad" in the enemy tribe when war broke out, who were granted non-combatant immunity.[13] About three months after the 1891 Izdī-Naẓīrī defense pact quoted above, for example, the crisis evidently worsened, endangering security throughout greater Rāziḥ. A major inter-tribal conference was held, and the unusually large number of eight shaykhs from Rāziḥ and ʿUqārib acted as secondary guarantors (*jidhū*) of a pact in which the adversaries agreed

> to protect children, women, animals, crops, and watch-towers. If anyone from Izdī-and-Naẓīrī or Birkān kills someone [from the opposing tribe], he must not steal his weapon . . . No one must enter watchtowers, which are included in this *bāyis* protection, nor shoot from them or destroy them . . . Traders and travelers through their territories also come under Jihwazī-and-Ḥilfī protection. (D1891b)

"Jihwazi-and-Ḥilfī protection" is a formula, here, for the neutral tribes whose shaykhs guaranteed the agreement. They were clearly concerned to safeguard trade during the emergency, and presumably blocked access to the war zone to prevent escalation.

Hostilities were ideally curtailed by the rapid intervention of one or more neutral notables, who entreated the two sides to stop fighting by customary symbolic gestures. As mentioned, it is such men, not warriors, who are invariably the heroes of war stories. An example is the infamous "ʿAlwah Incident" (*Ḥijjat* ʿAlwah) of around 1870. This was triggered by a disgraceful crime involving a woman (ʿAlwah) from Ghamar and a man from a tribe in Jumāʿah. A major battle took place in Sūq Badr in which "Rāziḥ sided with Ghamar, and Khawlān and Ṣaḥār with Jumāʿah," meaning that some tribesmen from each region mobilized. There are two versions of how this dangerous crisis was curtailed. According to Bayt Abū

Ṭālib, their ancestor, Sayyid Muḥammad Qāsim, "placed his *imāmah* (turban) between the two sides to entreat them to stop fighting," and advanced the *diyahs* of the thirteen excess dead on one side to secure the peace, for which the tribes reimbursed him. "That's what always happens," Zayd Abū Ṭālib explained. "People choose a learned, wise man (*ʿālim wa ʿāqil*) to deal with crises." The other version emphasizes the role of a *qabīlī* poet, Abū Ḥāmid, who allegedly reconciled the adversaries with the following verses still remembered today:

> Abū Ḥāmid's had a sleepless night about the war in Khawlān ibn ʿĀmir
> Over ʿAlwah's infamous behavior
> But everyone knows that's women's nature, whether hidden or disclosed
> Sharp men should be vigilant over their homes!

Abū Ḥāmid's second verse encapsulated a profound truth (for men): women are untrustworthy, so men must watch them or trouble is inevitable. With marvelous economy, his words shifted the blame from the warring parties onto female nature and a negligent husband, providing a focus for peaceful settlement.[14]

Once hostilities are halted, the two sides appoint the intervener or another man to negotiate a settlement (*ṣulḥ*), and he assesses each side's claims for the deaths, injuries, and damage to crops, animals, and other property. If losses are equal, they cancel each other out; otherwise the tribe with fewer losses must even the balance by paying *diyah, arsh,* or other compensation to the one which suffered more. These payments are therefore a significant deterrent against inflicting casualties. *ʿAyb* payments can be claimed only if the war rules are breached. This happened after a conflict in 1875 between Izdī-and-Naẓīrī on one side, and Banalqām and al-Shawāriq on the other. After it was over the two sides went to litigation before the shaykh of al-Waqir. Al-Naẓīr accused Banalqām of flouting war rules and inter-tribal agreements, and of "ganging up" with al-Shawāriq, and Banalqām counterclaimed that they had declared war properly, and had pacts which obliged them to support al-Shawāriq (D1875).

After all claims and calculations are agreed to and recorded in writing, the conflict is decisively concluded by ritual slaughterings and shared banquets. Each side then sets about collecting subscriptions toward its expenses and liabilities.

The War of al-Ḍay ͑ah, 1985

In 1985 a war broke out between al-Naẓīr and al-Waqir which I was able to reconstruct retrospectively from interviews, tape recordings, photographs, and documents.[15] Like the Qullat Ḥajar litigation, this real case shows the remarkable extent to which the tribes adhere to their rules and principles in practice, while revealing aspects of inter-tribal conflict which are usually skated over or absent in documents and oral histories, including the background causes and the wider political and economic context.

The general background to this conflict was the perennial tension between the neighboring tribes of al-Naẓīr and al-Waqir over control of Sūq al-Ḍayʿah and its exactions. This was exacerbated toward the end of the Civil War, when Rāziḥ was virtually stateless, when the son of Ibn Ghalfān, the shaykh of al-Waqir, started collecting rents and customs dues — ostensibly to pay his black henchmen (*ʿabīd*) to patrol it and guard its stores. This annoyed all Rāziḥī traders, and particularly aggravated the Naẓīrīs, who depend so heavily on trade, and their shaykhs, Ilt Faraḥ, who were jealous of Ibn Ghalfān's power and wealth. "We asked him to desist," Shaykh ʿAwaḍ told me. "After all, he's our nephew (*bazī*); our cousin (FBD) is married to his father, Ibn Ghalfān senior. So they are all our relatives." But Ibn Ghalfān junior ignored their appeals to affinal values, allegedly proclaiming, "*I'm* paramount shaykh (*shaykh al-shamil*) of all ʿUqārib from Ḥamāṭah to am-Maḥāṭah [its southern and northern limits], and *you* aren't paramount shaykh of *anywhere*!" Some Rāziḥ tribes mounted a *wijhah* against him, and when this failed to budge him, they stationed armed men at his border and blockaded his market. War loomed, but several Rāziḥī shaykhs and Sayyid Zayd Abū Ṭālib intervened, and negotiated a settlement in which Ibn Ghalfān agreed to cease his exactions, and the Rāziḥīs agreed to lift their blockade.

After the Civil War the republican government established a customs post (*jumruk*) at Sūq al-Ḍayʿah, and appointed a Naẓīrī as its head (*mudīr al-jumruk*). He was lenient, but many still resented paying dues, trouble erupted, and he was replaced by a "Yemeni." Then during the economic boom in the early 1980s, when al-Ḍayʿah swelled into a major transit station between Saudi Arabia and Yemen, the government put Ibn Ghalfān junior in charge, gave him an official title, arms, and "a uniform with pips," and authorized him to collect the dues.

Ibn Ghalfān's *ʿabīd* and allies he recruited from other ʿUqārib tribes manned a road barrier, and were allegedly officious and greedy—insisting drivers wait for their papers to be checked so their cargos spoiled, and collecting heavy dues on every truck so that "oil barrels by the roadside overflowed with money." "And if people refused to pay," a Naẓīrī explained, "his *ʿabīd* beat them up. And we couldn't retaliate because they are *ḍaʿīf*, it would have been shameful. So he became like a prince or a king." Many also resented being excluded from a share in this windfall: "He kept too much for himself and his cronies in Sanaa." Others, however, considered that the shaykh did a good job of maintaining security at his busy and expanding entrepôt, and was generous with the proceeds.

This situation simmered for two years, with repeated increases in customs dues, and humiliating searches and holdups. As tension mounted, delegations of tribal leaders from al-Naẓīr, al-Izid, and other Rāziḥ tribes went down to al-Ḍayʿah to try and persuade Ibn Ghalfān junior to curb his activities, or (according to more cynical accounts) to try and corner a share of his wealth, but all to no avail. Later some leading Naẓīrīs, including members of Ilt Faraḥ, refused to pay his customs dues, and he imprisoned them in a hut, "fed them fodder like animals," and blocked the motor track, forcing them to climb back up the mountain ignominiously on foot.

Incensed by this flagrant contempt for their honor, the Naẓīrī leaders decided to build a motor track bypassing al-Ḍayʿah, and establish a rival entrepôt nearby. They hired a bulldozer and driver, raised subscriptions toward the costs, and began work. Predictably, the track and the bulldozer were sabotaged; Naẓīrī goods were also stolen from stores in al-Ḍayʿah. Ibn Ghalfān junior was obviously the prime suspect, but he denied responsibility and refused compensation. This was the final straw. The Naẓīrīs pressured Ilt Faraḥ to defend their interests by force, and old women shamed them into action, yelling: "If you can't behave like men, give us your weapons and *we'll* go to war!" So in early April Ilt Faraḥ declared war with the ritual statement *nabrā wa nakhlā minnakum,* and designated the period of combat (*yawm shāhir*) for early May. During the intervening month, normal travel and trade throughout Qaḍā Rāziḥ was suspended because of the insecurity.

As *yawm shāhir* approached, the Naẓīrī leaders waged a virulent propaganda offensive against Ibn Ghalfān junior and his Jihwazī tribe, al-Waqir:

> They stoked people up for the war. They exhorted us to be courageous, and threatened those who might abscond. They told us, "This is a holy

> war (*jihād*)," and, "Ibn Ghalfān drinks and doesn't pray," to stimulate aggression and justify fighting him. They warned us that Jihwazīs are excellent shots, and kept repeating, "Jihwazīs are treacherous (*ghaddārīn*)." During that time "Jihwaz-and-Aḥlāf" was on everyone's lips.

Both sides also summoned allies according to their treaty obligations, and their moiety and regional affiliations. Al-Naẓīr called in its closest Ḥilfī ally, al-Izid, and al-Waqir recruited fellow ʿUqārib and Jihwazī tribes—ʿAbīdī-wa-Ṣafwānī, and the Munabbihī ward of al-Uzhūr, which is also Jihwazī and was once part of ʿUqārib. Despite the conflict being rhetorically described as being between "ʿUqārib and Rāziḥ" or between "Jihwazī and Ḥilfī," however, it did *not* widen to include all the tribes of each tribal region or moiety. Al-Waqir and its allies were evidently perceived as balancing the formidable Izdī-and-Naẓīrī alliance, and no other tribes joined in as combatants. Furthermore, Birkān (which is Jihwazī) and Banī Ṣayāḥ (Hilfī), which border al-Naẓīr and al-Waqir, formally declared their territories neutral zones (*kufalah*), and banned either side from passing through or stationing themselves there. The conflict was thus contained by tribal rules and mechanisms. As a Naẓīrī youth commented: "During *Ḥarb* al-Ḍayʿah I realized how important tribal agreements are. Men kept saying that things must be done according to the *qawāʿid,* and took it very seriously. People really respect their forefathers' customs." He also recalled the start of the war:

> The muezzin proclaimed from the mosque loudspeaker that hostilities had commenced, and made rousing speeches urging men to fight bravely, and women to bake bread. I remember being surprised that as soon as hostilities began my mother started baking!

The front was the border between al-Naẓīr and al-Waqir in the foothills. Naẓīrīs of all statuses, including *sayyid* youths, went to the front, where the Izdī-and-Naẓīrī contingent trained their guns on al-Ḍayʿah from their side of the border, and the Waqrīs did the same from theirs. Other Naẓīrīs stayed behind to guard the settlements at the top of the mountain, and youths climbed up and down supplying the fighters with food and drink and changes of clothing. At one point a crowd of Naẓīrīs carried a cannon (*madfaʿ*) down the mountain, scaring off the traders in Sūq al-Ḍayʿah.

The hostilities lasted two or three days. Two men were killed by ricocheting bullets, including a "Yemeni." And seven others were slightly injured—all on the Naẓīrī side. No Waqrīs were harmed. "All we killed was a donkey," a Naẓīrī wryly observed. At this point the hostilities were halted by the shaykhs of Ghamar, who learned of the bloodshed and sent urgent messages requesting a cease-fire and offering to mediate. "We were waiting for someone to intervene," said one Naẓīrī, "but they were late." Another commented, "It helped that they were distant from the conflict, and not involved. We were expecting Jumāʿah or Ṣaḥār to step in, but Ghamar did. This was their duty." And Shaykh ʿAwaḍ explained, "If there's a problem between two tribes, a third *must* step in. We observe tribal traditions (*sawālif*)!"

Each side sent ten guns as *rabākh*s to the Deputy Governor of the Province of Saʿdah in order to reassure the government that they were submitting to due process and had things in hand. Then they appointed four Ghamarī shaykhs and Abū ʿAwthah, the shaykh of Banī Maʿīn in northern Rāziḥ, to arbitrate the peace process and draft the settlement. A round of meetings and meals ensued, in al-Naẓīr and al-Waqir, and each tribe collected subscriptions to meet the expenses. Meanwhile, government officials arrived on the scene from Ṣaʿdah and al-Qalʿah, and were tactfully included in the proceedings. This enabled the tribes to demonstrate that they were loyal, law-abiding citizens, while showing off their ability to resolve their own conflicts. The officials were only *observers,* Naẓīrīs stressed, and played no substantive role in the proceedings: "They knew they couldn't solve the problem themselves because they didn't understand tribal laws and traditions. They were just there for their fees."

The peace settlement (*ḥukum*) included the following terms. The arbitrators should supervise the construction of the Naẓīrī motor track. Al-Waqir should pay *diyah* and wound compensation (*arsh*) "according to tribal traditions" (*ḥasb al-aslāf*), and reduced as the Naẓīrīs think fit. Such reductions (as mentioned) are customarily made in order to help mend wounded political relationships. Twenty-two Naẓīrīs and twenty-two ʿUqāribīs should swear oaths before God that they did not steal goods from the sūq, or sabotage the bulldozer, and if the Naẓīrīs succeed, ʿUqārib must get the bulldozer mended or pay for a new one. Each side must bear all its own war expenses, meaning the costs of its ammunition, its supplies, and the fees and hospitality of the arbitrators and government observers. The settlement also recorded that no "disgrace" fines (*ʿayūb*) had been incurred because the war was announced and organized according to tribal tradition (*sālif al-qubul*) and the rules of war (*ʿādāt al-ḥarb*) (1985a).

FIGURE 8.6.
The shaykh of al-Waqir, Ibn Ghalfān senior (*center*), arriving in al-Naẓīr with his henchmen and Ibn Salāmah of al-Wuqaysh (*left*) for the peace ceremony after the War of al-Ḍayʿah, 1985. (Photo: Aḥmad Muḥammad Jubrān)

The settlement subtly indicated that Ibn Ghalfān junior carried most blame for the conflict. It could not therefore be signed, and normal relations restored, without a peace ceremony in which the Waqrīs publicly admitted wrongdoing and readiness to make amends by *maghrad*s and ritual slaughter. Naẓīrīs told me how vital it was that the ʿUqāribīs conduct themselves at this ceremony in a convincingly apologetic manner, and how they were all on tenterhooks in case it went wrong.

The ceremony was scheduled for a few days after the drafting of the settlement "to allow al-Waqir time to get the slaughter-beasts." On the appointed day, a crowd of ʿUqāribīs drove up the mountain, and left their vehicles on the outskirts of *madīnat* al-Naẓīr. Bristling with guns, they then processed toward the marketplace chorusing, in high-pitched voices, a *maghrad* by Ibn Ghubays, the famous poet (*shāʿir*) of al-Uzhūr. The tone and content of his song, and of all the words uttered in the following minutes, were vitally important, Naẓīrīs stressed, to the ritual's success. The procession was headed by Ibn Ghalfān senior (his son prudently stayed home), shaykhs from other ʿUqārib tribes, and the Ghamarī arbitrators.

Awaiting them tensely in the marketplace were the shaykhs of Ilt Faraḥ, and a crowd of Naẓīrīs, Izdīs, other Rāziḥīs, and government officials—all straining to catch the words of their *maghrad* as its rhythmic falsetto soared above the excited clamor of the waiting crowd:

> Greetings from my wondrous tongue to everyone present and absent
> We come from ʿUqārib to put things right [with] the best of men [the mediators]
> We willingly come, harboring no grudge, nor wanting to prolong this disaster
> Resolution and settlement are vital, so let's call a halt to the harm!

To everyone's relief the *maghrad* encapsulated the essential elements for peace-making—goodwill, contrition ,and the desire for resolution. Key figures then made brief shouted speeches expressing brotherly conciliation; relief and pride at resolving the conflict; loyalty to Islam, tribal traditions, and the government; and rueful acknowledgments that "these things happen." The chief Ghamarī arbitrator then yelled:

> All these tribes have come, and the government, the shaykhs, one and all want peace. So here are two cows and twenty sheep to apologize to you, leaders and followers, and those from far and near, to put things right with you, O Izdī-and-Naẓīrī. We are all at the point of no return, the solution is upon us. Peace be on you all.

His final words were drowned by a crescendo of shouts: "Where are the butchers! Slaughter the *ʿaqāyir!* Hurry! Hurry!" The shaykhs of Ghamar started slashing the animals' throats and others rushed to help. The ʿUqāribīs and the Ghamarī mediators laid their guns on the heap of bleeding carcasses. And "to strengthen and enforce the apology," Ibn Salāmah, the shaykh of al-Wuqaysh, placed his turban on the guns as an entreaty (*maqṣad*) for reconciliation (Figure 8.7). As the blood of the *ʿaqāyir* was spilled, the high-pitched voices of the Naẓīrīs and Izdīs soared above the commotion singing their *maghrad* of acceptance composed by their own *shāʿir,* Muḥammad Yaḥyā Ibrāhīm:

> Welcome with a necessary welcome! To everyone present and absent,
> To shaykh and Deputy [Governor], greetings to our guests!
>
> O our brothers of ʿUqārib, fate brings amazing outcomes!
> Everyone fights for his honor, but we are all [still] brothers!

FIGURE 8.7.
The peace ceremony after the War of al-Ḍayʿah, 1985. The shaykh of al-Wuqaysh, Ibn Salāmah (*second left*), has just laid his turban on the slaughtered animals as an apology on behalf of al-Waqir, and an entreaty for peace. (Photo: Aḥmad Muḥammad Jubrān)

The punch line—"short but with big meaning," as one Naẓīrī put it—condensed the eternal verities of tribal relations, and clinched the peace-making. The ʿUqāribīs and Naẓīrīs formed two facing lines and sang their *maghrads* in turn, the tension lifted, and there was an atmosphere of joyful celebration. Women, meanwhile, set to work cooking the meat of the slaughtered animals and baking bread so their men could cement the peace with a feast.

After the peace ceremony, the settlement was signed and guaranteed by shaykhs and elders from several tribes of ʿUqārib and Rāziḥ in front of the arbitrators and government officials (D1985b, D1985c). Ten days later, the parties met again to promise the bereaved they would discharge their obligations (D1985d). Three months later, the Governorate of Ṣaʿdah asked the courts (i.e., *ḥākims*) of Shidā (ʿUqārib) and Rāziḥ to administer the collective oaths, which they did (D1985e). And several months later, al-Waqir and their ʿUqārib allies delivered the compensation payments, fines, and expenses for which they were liable to the Naẓīrī leaders, who distributed them.

Soon after, certain Naẓīrīs accused Ilt Faraḥ of having "eaten" money they had collected toward the war and the peace-making, and demanded twenty-two oaths that it had been properly disbursed. This failed because one oath-taker refused to swear, suggesting guilt. However, the accusation forced Ilt Faraḥ to convene a meeting of leading Naẓīrīs, and draw up an agreement to improve their administrative methods, which was sent for endorsement to government officials in Ṣaʿdah and al-Qalʿah. After the customary sentiments of religious piety, loyalty to the government, and tribal unity, this promised that

> the *amīns* and *aʿyān* of al-Naẓīr will compile lists of the tribesmen under them, and the shaykhs will amalgamate these to make a list for the whole tribe. This will enable [more accurate] estimates to be made when subscriptions (*furūq*) are to be paid according to means. (D1985f)

This was clearly to avoid accusations that the number of subscribers had been understated, so that more money had been collected than required. The shaykhs also agreed that the *amīns* would return any excess to subscribers.

The case of the war of al-Ḍayʿah shows that, despite plentiful motives and means for escalating the conflict, it was limited, resolved, and decisively concluded by the application of tribal ideals and practices. Circumstances also favored this outcome: no one in Rāziḥ or ʿUqārib wanted prolonged disruption of trade, especially during a boom period. State power was also still locally weak, but growing. The tribes were therefore compelled and enabled to defuse their crisis by their own methods. In the hope of deterring future interference, they therefore seized the chance to flaunt their problem-solving ability in front of government officials, while simultaneously deferring to their formal authority, demonstrating their willingness to cooperate with them in the restoration of order, and (not least) rewarding them generously for their token roles in the peace process. These are perennial themes of the tribe-state relationship, and will be explored further in the final part of this book.

The traders never returned to Sūq al-Ḍayʿah, and it died. Naẓīrīs blame the war, but the market had survived much worse insecurity in the past, as we shall see. What really doomed it was the development and improvement of motor transport during the 1980s, after which al-Malāḥīṭ became the main entrepôt for the northern Tihāmah.

PART III

The State-Tribe Relationship

CHAPTER NINE

The Qāsimī Period

The Zaydī State

For most of the four centuries considered in this final part of the book, Rāziḥ was "ruled" by Zaydī *dawlahs*. Before considering the effect on its tribes of constant state governance, it is necessary to summarize key features of Zaydism and the Zaydī state, with particular reference to the long period of Qāsimī rule which followed the first Ottoman occupation of Yemen between the sixteenth and seventeenth centuries.[1]

The first Zaydī state in Yemen was founded over a thousand years ago by Yaḥyā b. Ḥūsayn (d. 298/911), a Hijazi *sharīf* and scholar (*ʿālim*) of great learning and vaunting political ambition. According to his biography, which echoes key images of the foundation of Islam, and implicitly contrasts religious-based order with the alleged disorder of tribalism, warring tribes in the Ṣaʿdah area invited him to mediate between them. After making peace, Yaḥyā proclaimed himself head (*imām*) of the Zaydī *dawlah,* adopting the honorific "al-Hādī ilā al-Ḥaqq" ("the guide to what is right"), and with the military support of allied tribes, defeated others which opposed him. Tribal strife provided fertile ground for state-building by a member of the religious elite; and state-building exacerbated tribal strife. These are perennial themes of Yemeni and Rāziḥī history, though the former is stressed and the latter is downplayed in Zaydī historiography.

Imām al-Hādī's voluminous theological and legal writings formed the basis of the Hādawī *madhhab* of Zaydī North Yemen. It is a central tenet of Hādawī-Zaydism that the spiritual leader of the Muslim community should also be supreme ruler (*imām*) of the Muslim state.[2] The doctrine also extols the transmission of politico-legal authority through "the people of the (Prophet's) house (*ahl al-bayt*)." This is the basis for the *sayyid* belief that it was their sacred duty to study and promote *ʿilm*, and their exclusive birthright to establish government based on the *sharīʿah*—"to command the good and forbid the reprehensible," in the Quranic formulation of every Muslim's duty. Hādawī doctrine therefore upholds the principle of hereditary rule which also underpins Rāziḥī tribal leadership, and likewise abjures automatic father-to-son succession, prescribing a merit-based selection process within a restricted field. Thus any male descendant of Ḥasan or Ḥusayn (the sons of the Prophet's daughter Fāṭimah and son-in-law ʿAlī) was deemed eligible for the imāmate on condition he fulfill a demanding list of personal qualifications including soundness of mind and body, deep religious and legal knowledge (*ʿilm*), and the political and military ability to enforce "just rule" (Serjeant 1983a:77). The ideal imām, epitomized by al-Hādī, was both a warrior (*mujāhid*) and an expert legal interpreter (*mujtahid*), ready and able to wield sword as well as pen.

Ruling families were adorned with impressive religious titles expressing entitlement and status. Imāms were conventionally referred to and addressed as "Our Lord" (*mawlānā*) and "Commander of the Faithful" (*amīr al-mu'minīn*), their sons and brothers as "Sword of Islam" (*sayf al-islām*), and their relatives as "glory of Islām" (*ʿizz al-islām*) or "son" or "descendant" of an imām (*ibn al-imām*). Imāms also assumed personal pious honorifics (sing. *laqab*), the short forms of which were prefixed to their given names—for example, "Imām al-Hādī Yaḥyā." These titles and nicknames, which were inscribed on documents, tombstones, and coins to assert authority, and recited in mosques to express allegiance, reflected and enhanced the immense prestige which the majority accorded religious pedigree (*nasab*) and learning (*ʿilm*), and reinforced the *sayyid* claim to the divine right to rule. The aura of supernatural sanction and "awe" (*haybah*) enveloping imāms was further intensified by the popular belief that they could effect miracles, even from their graves—despite official Zaydī disapproval of the veneration of "saints" or their tombs—and that spirits (sing. *jinn*) advised them. Their remotest subjects therefore felt under surveillance by an invisible ruler, as they now feel observed by the anonymous agents of the republican state.

The primary coalition of Zaydī states was between the imām and leading *ʿulamā*. Imāms rose to power by making a public "claim" (*daʿwah*) to the imāmate in a widely disseminated written manifesto, and by winning the support of a kind of electoral college of prominent *sayyids* and *qāḍīs* called "the people who loosen and bind" (*ahl al-ḥall wa al-ʿaqd*) (Meissner 1987:89; Eagle 1994). This crème de la crème of the educated, religious elite assessed the contender's qualifications, then (if they favored him) legitimated his claim by swearing their allegiance (*bayʿah*) in written responses—a profound moral, religious, and political commitment. Imāms subsequently chose officials from among the ranks of such men, some to serve at the center, some in the provinces.

Each North Yemeni *dawlah* was constituted by the superimposition of this small ruling clique onto a broad base of largely self-governing tribes whose leaders also solemnly pledged their allegiance in written pacts. This was the second fundamental coalition of Zaydī states. It provided them with grassroots legitimation. It helped create their states as *places* without erasing tribal boundaries—for state domains were aggregations of tribal domains, plus whatever non-tribal areas could be dominated with the help of loyal tribes. And it completed states as structures of control and governance, for all ruled through the tribes.

Imāms based themselves in various strongholds on the plateau or nearby mountains, and recruited tribal support by "buying" their leaders with money or land, by playing on fears of a worse alternative, or by force of arms—pitting tribe against tribe as al-Hādī had done. Tribes around these power centers, particularly certain Ḥāshid and Bakīl tribes, formed the "core" of Zaydī imāmates, as Meissner (1987) puts it, because of their accessibility, their strategic positions on trade routes, and their marginal agriculture and frequent economic desperation; needy men make good mercenaries. Some more prosperous, distant, or defensible tribal regions, including Rāziḥ, spent long periods as independent or semi-independent domains under rival *dawlahs*.[3] And other regions too unproductive or inaccessible to attract state rule experienced long "stateless" periods beyond the pale of any Zaydī (or colonial) ruler.[4] Two or more rival Zaydī *dawlahs* therefore sometimes co-existed; and there could be *dawlahs* within *dawlahs*, as when a subsidiary *dawlah* gave tribute and formal allegiance to another by which it was loosely governed. Like the term *qabīlah*, therefore, the term *dawlah* was historically applied to equivalent or nested entities of different sizes, statuses, and powers—the referent being understood from the context of any statement, and a geographical or nominal qualifier.

Tribal allegiance implied several fundamental undertakings: to submit to sharīʿah law as dispensed by state judges; to collaborate in the maintenance of order; to protect and support rulers administratively and militarily; and to pay the canonical taxes (*zakāt*) to the imām's treasury (*bayt al-māl*). Taxes were mostly levied on crops and herds above a certain size, and paid in kind.[5] Agricultural taxes were paid at harvest times, which varied regionally. Rāziḥīs paid theirs twice a year: on wheat, barley, and coffee at the spring (*rabīʿ*) grain harvest in February or March; and on sorghum, fruits, and vegetables after the main winter (*shitā*) grain harvest in October, when a wind blows which helps winnowing. Installments of brideprice, blood money, and trading debts are also customarily paid at this key date in the agricultural calendar, creditors being begged to "wait till the harvest wind." This seasonal association between religious and secular obligations helped normalize and legitimize the "political technology" of surplus appropriation, and imposed regular deadlines which recurrently pressured and subjectivized taxpayers. Taxation is also strongly backed by supernatural sanction. Rāziḥīs believe that if some default on their obligatory dues (*wājibāt*), God will withhold his *barakah* (rain), and the whole community will suffer drought and famine. As an elderly Naẓīrī explained about the last major famine in 1943: "Certain people didn't pay their *zakāt* for nine harvests, so God sent us the year of hunger (*sanat al-jōʿ*)."

Taxes were the prime symbol of the state-tribe relationship. They not only signified that the constituents of tribes were good Muslims and loyal subjects (*raʿiyyah*) of the religious state, but also had profound secular significance. Just as each Rāziḥī's promise to contribute to corporate subscriptions (sing. *farq*) bonded him to his shaykh and fellow tribesmen, and helped define his tribe, so the commitment to pay taxes bound tribes to their chosen rulers, and helped define and constitute the domains of states.

In return for pledging their allegiance and taxes, Rāziḥīs and others required their rulers to administer sharīʿah law justly; to collect and distribute taxes equitably and according to religious prescriptions; to pay stipends to their leaders for their support and services; to respect tribal pacts and honor state-tribe agreements; and to respect tribal law and allow it to be

FIGURE 9.1
Men praying for rain, al-Naẓīr, early 1980

practiced unhindered, provided it did not contravene the sharīʿah. Their compact was therefore conditional, and if imāms or their officials violated their ideals of good governance or threatened their interests, tribes withheld their taxes and support, switched allegiance to a rival, or rebelled (see al-Abdin 1975:46; al-ʿAmrī 1985:11,37).

The most important agricultural taxes in highland Yemen were those levied on sorghum and coffee. Sorghum could, as mentioned, be preserved for two or more years in *madfans*, and coffee had a longer storage life. Because of transportation costs, the sorghum tax was mostly disbursed in kind within the regions of production as salaries and welfare payments (*ṣadaqah*), whereas coffee was disbursed more widely because of its higher value by weight, and its important role in prestige consumption and formal prestations. The other major sources of revenue were customs dues collected at the Red Sea ports and major internal markets, including—importantly—the chain of entrepôts, such as al-Ḍayʿah, which nestle in the foothills of the western mountains the length of the Tihāmah. These imposts had the advantage that they could be more easily converted to money, facilitating the state's centralization and dispersal of its wealth. But market taxes (*mukūs*) are technically unlawful in Islam, so were a recurrent source of resentment and dissension. Other taxes, called "aid" (*maʿūnah*), which were collected on an ad hoc basis, could be argued to be religiously legitimate because they financed "righteous" *jihāds* against rebels and rivals (necessarily) defined as "irreligious."[6] None of these taxes was assured. Adverse climatic, economic, and political conditions took a regular toll. People resisted paying during hard times or in protest. It was difficult to centralize the grain tax or convert it to cash. And provincial governors sometimes withheld dues.

According to Hādawī doctrine, it was the imām's prerogative to receive the *zakāt* revenues, and to distribute them however he wished among the eight categories of "rightful recipient" (*ahl al-ḥuqūq*) stipulated in the Quran. These categories include the poor, the needy, slaves, debtors, travelers, and "tax officials" (*al-ʿāmilīn ʿalayhā*).[7] Since everyone involved in tax collection—governors, supervisors, organizers, and enforcers—could be defined as *ʿāmilīn ʿalayhā,* the doctrine provided religious sanction for channeling taxes into the administration and maintenance of the Zaydī state. The remainder was ideally disbursed as charity (*ṣadaqah*) as prescribed in the Quran. Hādawī law forbids *sayyids* to be supported by the *zakāt,* on the model of Imām al-Hādī, who conspicuously denied himself a share. But when they were state officials, or their relations, or were themselves hard up, the line could be, and was, blurred.[8] This was the case in Rāziḥ. "The *wājibāt* were like the salaries (*maʿsh*) of our forefathers," one *sayyid* told me. "They lived off them, and distributed the rest to the poor, and to visitors from outside the tribe, and toward rooms in the mosque where they stayed." The distribution of charity could also diverge from the religious ideal, especially during shortages, when some unscrupulously profited from poverty instead of alleviating it.

Taxation was therefore a perennial cause of friction between imāms, the *ʿulamā,* and tribal leaders. When tribes refused to pay the *zakāt* to the imām's local representative in protest at bad governance or extortionate demands, or governors withheld the imām's portion, the latter condemned them in religious rhetoric which masked and denied the grounds for their grievances, and provided him with justification for waging *jihād* against them.[9] Taxes therefore flowed upward into state coffers, and downward as payoffs and stipends, and every link in this chain of appropriation and disbursement provided ample scope for ideological contention and greedy conflict. The taxation system funded Zaydī *dawlahs*, but also destabilized them.

Because of their limited and unreliable resources, pre–twentieth century Zaydī *dawlahs* were perforce minimalist states with restricted objectives:

manifestly implementing sharīʿah law, which was vital to their legitimacy as Muslim rulers; collecting taxes; maintaining and expanding their domains; and fending off internal and external rivals. Even in the early eighteenth century, therefore, when imāms were enriched by revenues from trade, and pomp and ceremony burgeoned around their courts, state governance was still small-scale and personalized. Their "governments" or *dīwāns*, based in their highland fortresses or palaces, comprised a coterie of *sayyid* and *qāḍī* officials, supported by secretaries and storekeepers, who had charge of judicial, military, and fiscal matters, religious endowments (*waqf*), and "tribal affairs." And a similar, smaller contingent, headed by a governor (*ʿāmil*), was based in each province and in major towns and ports.[10]

Imāms usually appointed governors and judges outside their native *bilād*s, and moved them if they were corrupt or ineffective, or built threatening local power bases (see Messick 1993:193). These key officials were often their brothers or cousins who had gained administrative and military experience during campaigns against the Ottomans or rivals for the imāmate, or had themselves been rivals and been awarded compensatory positions. Imāms also recruited provincial *sayyids* and *qāḍīs* as judges and administrators, many of whom were "naturalized" descendants of earlier officials who had stayed in post. These local officials, who were thoroughly integrated into their communities by marriage and other ties, and intimately conversant with their dialects, customs, and politics, were crucial agents of state power, providing a vital "intelligence" and administrative link between the state and the tribes, as well as continuity between regimes. But they were also politically dangerous as the potential nuclei of breakaway *dawlahs*.

Zaydī regimes had limited military capacity. The wealthier imāms maintained small armed forces commanded by a close relative or a foreigner (whose loyalty was more assured); and provincial governors had garrisons of often locally recruited armed police (*ʿaskar*).[11] But no imām could support a standing army sufficiently large to subdue or defend his entire domain. All therefore relied on tribal mercenaries for major campaigns. The problem of control was, of course, massively exacerbated by the difficult terrain. It was hard enough for imāms to maintain their hegemony over the vast plateaux of the northern and central highlands, and a major struggle to do so over the more fertile and tax-productive regions some also aspired to dominate—the western mountains, the Tihāmah, Lower Yemen, and South Yemen.

Instability was inherent in Hādawī-Zaydism and its often flawed practice. In contrast to Sunnīsm, which requires unconditional "obedience" (*ṭāʿah*) to Muslim rulers, regardless of their behavior, Hādawī doctrine enjoins violent "uprising" (*khurūj*) against those deemed unjust or illegitimate. Since imāms often flouted Hādawī ideals, especially from the eighteenth century (Haykel 2003), they provided abundant pretexts for domestic opposition and dissension from rival *sayyids* (who were often close relatives) and their tribal allies. Imāms were also challenged by a succession of foreign powers (during the period considered here the Ottomans, the Wahhabis, the British, and the Idrīsī of ʿAsīr), though this also strengthened them. They could more easily rally tribal supporters against enemies defined as "infidels," and during and after inter-state conflicts they (or their rivals) were able to consolidate their power within the Zaydī heartlands of highland North Yemen. Some were also able to expand their domains beyond, and incorporate the Shāfiʿī (Sunnī) territories of Lower Yemen, the richest agricultural region of Yemen, and the Tihāmah with its important revenue-yielding entrepôts and ports. This happened, most notably, following the two century-long Ottoman occupations of Yemen.

The Early Qāsimī State

Because of their dependence on trade, Rāziḥīs have always had to capitulate to any power which controlled both the coast to their west and the plateau to their east. We can therefore assume that the Ottomans occupied Rāziḥ and ʿUqārib, and crowned their summits with forts, during the 1540s—soon after they captured ʿAsīr and Ṣaʿdah.[12] Like all subsequent (and presumably earlier) rulers, the Ottomans governed Khawlān ibn ʿĀmir from Ṣaʿdah, and Rāziḥ from Ghumār, which was well-protected by Jabal Ḥurum. By 1560 Rāziḥ was one of the most lucrative tax districts in "*vilayet* Ṣaʿdah," and its fiscal importance can only have increased as the coffee trade developed during subsequent decades.[13]

Following earlier Zaydī uprisings, in 1598 Imām al-Manṣūr al-Qāsim launched a *jihād* against the Ottomans.[14] After prolonged campaigns his tribal forces captured Ṣaʿdah, and in 1613 he expelled the Ottoman garrison from Rāziḥ, where he installed his own governor.[15] It was not until 1635, however, after al-Qāsim's death, that the occupiers were finally driven from all Yemen by his son and successor, Imām al-Mu'ayyad Muḥammad (Tritton 1925:110; Blackburn 1980).

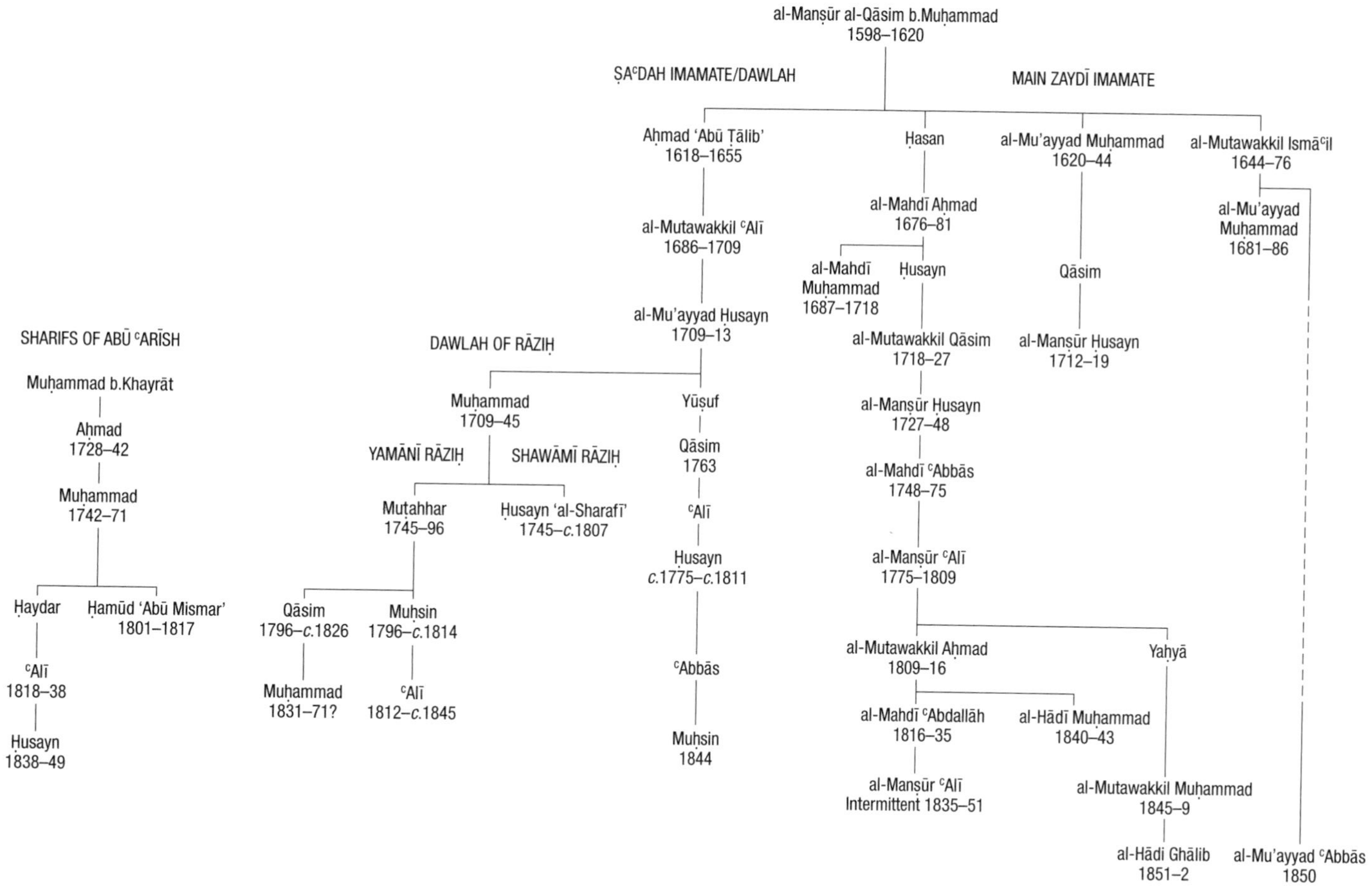

FIGURE 9.2
Seventeenth- to nineteenth-century rulers of Yemen and ʿAsīr. Dates indicate regimes, or periods when politically active

The Ottoman occupation and economic conditions in the seventeenth century laid the foundations for centuries of dynastic rule in Yemen and Rāziḥ by members of Bayt al-Qāsim. The early Qāsimīs had gained useful military and administrative experience under the Ottomans, when Zaydī resistance alternated with periods of collaboration. They also inherited a valuable legacy of fortresses, arms, and taxation methods from the Ottomans, some of whom remained in Yemen to help them run their state (Serjeant 1983a:80). The major factor in the establishment of Qāsimī rule, however, was undoubtedly the growth of the Yemeni coffee trade during the seventeenth and early eighteenth centuries, and the associated efflorescence of commerce with Europe, Persia, India, and China. Goods and currency poured into Yemen, and state revenues were massively augmented by dues collected at ports and markets.[16]

This unprecedented wealth stimulated and funded imperialist ambition. When Imām al-Mu'ayyad Muḥammad died in 1644, his brother Imām al-Mutawakkil Ismāʿil (1644–76) rose to power, and, flush with revenues and religious and military zeal, violently expanded the Zaydī state to its greatest ever extent to include ʿAsīr and Najrān in the north, the Tihāmah in the west, and Jabal Yāfiʿ, Hadramaut, and Ḍufār in the south. However, this vast domain was administratively unviable and soon disintegrated. Imām Ismāʿil's regime was also riven and undermined by controversies over taxation and doctrine, corruption and dissension among officials, and fierce competition for power and revenues within Bayt al-Qāsim, whose scholarship and legitimacy waned.[17]

Imām Ismāʿil established his seat south of Sanaa, the better to control his most lucrative tax bases in Lower Yemen and the Tihāmah.[18] This inevitably weakened his hold over the north. Imām Ismāʿil had appointed his brother and erstwhile rival, Aḥmad b. al-Qāsim, nicknamed "Abū Ṭālib," as governor (*ʿāmil*) of Khawlān Ṣaʿdah.[19] When Aḥmad died in 1655, his son ʿAlī b. Aḥmad succeeded him as governor, and opposed Imām Ismāʿil's supremacy over Khawlān Ṣaʿdah (Klaric 2000:61). ʿAlī remained governor of the province under the following imām, but in 1686 he proclaimed his own independent imāmate in Ṣaʿdah in opposition to the corrupt and ill-qualified Imām al-Mahdi Muḥammad, who was based south of Sanaa, titling himself al-Mutawakkil ʿalā Allāh, and (following family custom) sent his son Ḥusayn to govern Rāziḥ.[20] According to his descendants, Ḥusayn b. ʿAlī entered Rāziḥ with soldiers from Banī ʿAwf in Bakīl who intermarried with the Banī Asad tribe on Jabal Ḥurum. This is said to be why Banī

Asad is nicknamed "Bakīl," and its dialect contains what Rāziḥīs regard as "Yemeni" features. It could also be why the shaykhly clan of Banī Asad is named ʿAwfān. The soldiers were perhaps to defend Rāziḥ against Imām al-Mahdi's governor in ʿAsīr, who invaded the massif and was defeated.[21]

Rāziḥī documents show that the early Qāsimīs administered Rāziḥ as two sub-districts—the *shawāmī* and the *yamāniyah*—which are still important divisions, as we have seen, though now with mainly "tribal" connotations. The documents also show that they defined the tribes as "tax-paying units" (*makātib*, sing. *maktab*), and charged their leaders with paying large monthly sums to the *dawlah* in Ghumār, suggesting a tax-farming arrangement.[22] The Tihāmah entrepôt was then at the ancient site of al-Bār in the foothills of Jabal al-Naẓīr, and must have been a large and bustling settlement at that economically vibrant time, for it was then known as "*madīnat* al-Bār." Dues (*majbā*) were levied at al-Bār on a variety of imports and exports, including coffee (D1654). State officials also collaborated with tribal leaders to maintain law and order, and accepted tribal law in conflict resolution (D1667; D1668). We can assume that, as later, shaykhs and elders were rewarded for their services in taxation and law enforcement according to the importance of their markets, revenues, and political clout. The wealth of the coffee boom must therefore have helped shaykhly clans to consolidate *their* dynastic monopolies in parallel with those of the Qāsimīs, and have created or reinforced the inequalities between shaykhs and tribes which can still be discerned today.

The Dawlahs *of Rāziḥ and Ṣaʿdah*

Ḥusayn b. ʿAlī succeeded to the imāmate of Ṣaʿdah when his father died in 1709, taking the title al-Mu'ayyad (Zabārah 1957, I:572–573). Following Qāsimī custom, he appointed his son, Muḥammad b. Ḥusayn (1709–45), as governor of Rāziḥ. In contrast to his predecessors, however, when Muḥammad's father died (in 1714) he remained in Rāziḥ, and the imāmate of Ṣaʿdah passed to his brother Yūṣuf.[23] Muḥammad Ḥusayn can therefore be considered the true founder of Rāziḥ's semi-independent *dawlah*. Coffee prices reached their peak during the first decade of Muḥammad's regime, and despite the tribute he was obliged to send to Ṣaʿdah, he must have accumulated substantial wealth from taxes on agriculture and trade, which undoubtedly helped him consolidate his rule over his little domain. His descendants credit him, for example, with building a fort beside an old Ottoman one on the summit of Jabal Ḥurum.

A vivid glimpse of the way Muḥammad Ḥusayn strengthened key relationships by dispensing lavish hospitality and gifts is provided by a contemporary chronicler, who describes how, in 1745, he entertained the Sharīf of Abū ʿArīsh, now independent of Sanaa, "in a sumptuous fashion impossible to describe" (Tuchscherer 1992:84). The *sharīfs* were important allies of the *dawlah* of Rāziḥ because they controlled the trade routes through the ʿAsīr Tihāmah (historically known as Mikhlāf al-Sulaymānī), and the major port of Jīzān. At the same time, Rāziḥī products—especially coffee—were vital to the *sharīfs*, whose power depended on taxing goods in transit through their towns and ports.

Soon after the *sharīf's* visit, Muḥammad Ḥusayn died and was succeeded by his son, Ḥusayn b. Muḥammad (1745–c. 1807), who took the title Sharaf al-Dīn and was nicknamed "al-Sharafī." Al-Sharafī based himself in Ghumār in *shawāmī* Rāziḥ, and, according to his descendants, built the eponymous fortress at al-Qalʿah. His younger brother, Muṭahhar b. Muḥammad (1745–96), settled in al-Naẓīr, where his house still stands, and had jurisdiction under him for the *yamānīyah*. Muṭahhar Muḥammad organized tax collection in the *yamānīyah* and adjacent areas of the Tihāmah then under Rāziḥī control, and forwarded a proportion to al-Sharafī in the *shawāmī;* and the latter collected the taxes of the *shawāmī* and adjacent areas, and forwarded a proportion of all Rāziḥ's taxes to the *dawlah* of Ṣaʿdah. The two brothers also shared responsibility for paying stipends to all those employed in tax collection and state business (the *ahl al-ḥuqūq*) within their joint domain.

After Yemen lost its monopoly of the international coffee trade during the 1720s, prices slumped, inevitably damaging commerce and revenues. This downturn in fortunes undoubtedly contributed to the deterioration of relations between the *dawlah* of Rāziḥ and the *dawlah* of Ṣaʿdah, and to the latter's demise as an independent imāmate (as described below). These northern *dawlahs* must also have been affected by the conflicts over doctrine, taxation, and the Qāsimī monopolization of power, which embroiled the main Zaydī imāmate, by then based in Sanaa, from the mid-eighteenth century.[24]

Throughout his long regime of about fifty years, al-Sharafī was repeatedly at odds with his cousins and overlords in Ṣaʿdah over the collection and disbursement of taxes. He regularly defaulted on his tributary obligations, spurning their authority and undermining their power and resources. He also constantly quarreled with his brother, Muṭahhar, who

FIGURE 9.3
Fortress on the summit of Jabal Ḥurum, 1977

stayed loyal to Ṣa ʿdah, over their joint and separate rights and responsibilities within greater Rāziḥ. This protracted and sometimes violent dance of power and appropriation between and within the *dawlahs* of Ṣaʿdah and Rāziḥ, which continued into the nineteenth century, repeatedly implicated a wide supporting cast of shaykhs and their followers. Tribal leaders not only defended their overlords' domains (which were, of course, aggregations of tribal domains), but also mediated and judged their disputes (for which they were handsomely rewarded), and guaranteed and witnessed their agreements and settlements.

It is striking that the politico-legal relations of *dawlah-wa-qabīlah,* and also inter-*dawlah* relations, were conducted just like tribal relations, employing the same structures and practices. Documents emanating from ruling *sayyids*, furthermore, are formulated in closely similar ways to many tribal documents, are based on the same underlying assumptions about proper conduct, and even contain many of the same special terms and formulaic expressions. In other words, although the ruling elite were differentiated from the tribes by religious descent, legitimation, and learning, they shared the same political culture.

By the time of Niebuhr's travels in Yemen in 1763, the domain of the imāmate of Ṣaʿdah had shrunk to part of Ṣaḥār and the town of Ṣaʿdah, where the imām collected revenues on goods in transit from Sanaa; and he was having to defend even this reduced territory "against the shaykhs of the surrounding mountains." He had apparently lost Khawlān (south of Rāziḥ), which Niebuhr describes as under an independent shaykh.[25] He was also, it seems, trying to depose al-Sharafī as governor of Rāziḥ—probably because he was defaulting on his tributary obligations to Ṣaʿdah, and failing to meet his stipendiary obligations within Rāziḥ.

In 1764, in an apparent effort to regulate Rāziḥ's fiscal affairs, Muṭahhar Muḥammad—perhaps on instructions from the imām of Ṣaʿdah—compiled a "blessed register" (*daftar*) setting out Rāziḥ's tax obligations to Ṣaʿdah, and the stipends due (or disbursed) to his and his brother's officials (*ahl al-ḥuqūq*). This document (D1764) shows that the domain of the *dawlah* of Rāziḥ then included ʿUqārib, Jabal Rāziḥ, and Jabal Ghamar and adjacent areas of the Tihāmah; that Muṭahhar and al-Sharafī divided their respective rights and responsibilities by tribe and market; and that they depended on tribal as well as religious elites to run their statelet, for which they rewarded them with products of the *bilād* as well as money and other gifts—all undoubtedly derived from local taxes. Most of the stipendiaries named in the *shawāmī* and *yamānīyah* sections of the *daftar* can be identified as shaykhs and elders from their titles or clan names, which are the same as those of today's tribal leaders. Shaykhly stipends were not merely rewards for loyalty, but were also the equivalent of salaries for services in tax collection, law enforcement, and defense. Furthermore, as will be described, these stipendiary rights were conceived as vested in shaykhly clans. This hereditary prerogative is centrally important for understanding how religious dynasties helped sustain tribal dynasties.

Shaykhs therefore benefited both ideologically and materially from accepting Zaydī rule. Not only did their right to lead their tribes receive impeccable religious legitimation, but also their right to receive a fraction of the taxes (see below)—and the two notions were conflated. This obviously gave shaykhs and leading elders, who shared these stipends, a vested interest in helping solve inter-*dawlah* tax disputes, apart from the generous fees they received for doing so. In the context of the inter-*dawlah* conflicts which rent Khawlān Ṣaʿdah as the Qāsimī empire declined, the shaykhs of strategically situated tribes were especially enriched and empowered because *dawlah*s repeatedly needed their military support. Notable examples are the Ibn Jaʿfar shaykhs, the senior *maradd*s of Ṣaḥār, who control a major trade route from Ṣaʿdah to Rāziḥ and Khawlān which passes through their tribe (Banī Muʿādh).[26] In the early eighteenth century, presumably to guarantee access to his western province, Imām al-Mu'ayyad Ḥusayn of Ṣaʿdah awarded them hereditary tax-collecting (or tax-farming) rights over Sawād, which is now a ward of Ghamar.[27] And three succeeding generations of Ibn Jaʿfar shaykhs allied alternately with the *dawlahs* in the *mashriq* and the *maghrib,* for which they received substantial annual payments in cash and kind (mainly coffee and grain).[28] After the decline of the *dawlah* of Ṣaʿdah in the 1770s, however, they lost their strategic influence and presumably their privileges.

Whatever problems the 1764 *daftar* was supposed to solve, it clearly failed, for in 1765–66, there was a major "tax revolt" in Rāziḥ which al-Sharafī ruthlessly crushed with the help of his father's old friend, Sharīf Muḥammad b. Aḥmad of Abu ʿArīsh. According to the chronicler, al-Bahkalī, the sharīf's Bakīlī mercenaries invaded Rāziḥ and killed and looted its inhabitants—a gross violation of tribal sovereignty and values which understandably "sowed hostility and hatred" toward al-Sharafī (Tuchscherer 1992:177–178). Al-Sharafī left for Ṣaʿdah "hoping his ancestral rights to the revenues of Jabal Rāziḥ would be restored to him." They evidently were, and al-Sharafī and Muṭahhar made (temporary) peace (D1768).

By the mid-1770s the *dawlah* of Ṣaʿdah had suffered a drop in status. Although the name of its new head, Ḥusayn ʿAlī Qāsim (c. 1775–c. 1809), is ornamented with religious honorifics in the documents, and he has his own official stamp, he entitles himself only "son of the imām," not "imām" (D1775). This presumably means that he had formally submitted to the main Zaydī imāmate in Sanaa, although the relationship remained fraught and hostile (al-ʿAmrī 1985:37–38). Ḥusayn ʿAlī Qāsim's turbulent thirty-year "rule" over Khawlān Ṣaʿdah was bedeviled, like his predecessor's, by conflicts with the senior *dawlah* of Rāziḥ, al-Sharafī, who either withheld revenues or had difficulty collecting them. He also appears to have lost control of parts of the Tihāmah, from which he had previously collected taxes (Tuchscherer 1992:73; D1776b). Throughout these disputes his brother, Muṭahhar Muḥammad, of *yamānī* Rāziḥ consistently backed his Ṣaʿdah overlord against him, for which he was rewarded with a share of Rāziḥ's taxes. This provoked repeated conflicts between the *dawlahs* of *shawāmī* and *yamānī* Rāziḥ in which each side recruited the support of the tribes. Between the 1770s and the 1790s the shaykhs of greater Rāziḥ repeatedly opened or blocked their territories in support of one or the other *dawlah;* and shaykhs and *maradd*s from the whole of Khawlān ibn ʿĀmir intervened in their overlords' sometimes murderous conflicts, and mediated, guaranteed, and witnessed their settlements.[29]

A particularly serious inter-*dawlah* conflict broke out after Muṭahhar's death in 1796 between his son and successor, Muḥsin Muṭahhar, and al-Sharafī over the revenues of Sūq al-Bār, just inside Naẓīrī territory, which Muḥsin controlled, and al-Sharafī's failure to honor either his tax-sharing agreements with Muḥsin, or his tributary commitments to Ṣaʿdah (D1798b). Muḥsin secured the support of al-Naẓīr, and of the gatekeeping tribes Munabbih, Banī Maʿīn, and Banī Asad in al-Sharafī's *shawāmī* domain. These crucial defections enabled Ḥusayn ʿAlī Qāsim to enter the massif with his men in order to force al-Sharafī to discharge his obligations (D1796a; D1796b). Shortly after, the shaykh of al-Waqir also rejected al-Sharafī's authority and pledged support for Muḥsin (D1797). And a year later al-Shawāriq, Banalqām, and Banī Rabīʿah joined the alliance with Muḥsin Muṭahhar and Ḥusayn ʿAlī Qāsim. Evidently wanting to avoid the conflicts between their overlords wrecking their own relations, however, they would not, they assert, fight any *shawāmī* tribes (D1798a).

This crisis must have jeopardized peace throughout the far north of Yemen, for the defense pact (D1798a) between Ḥusayn ʿAlī Qāsim of Ṣaʿdah and Muḥsin Muṭahhar of *yamānī* Rāziḥ is guaranteed by an extraordinarily wide range of senior shaykhs: the junior and senior *maradd*s of Khawlān and Ṣaḥār (Ibn Rawkān, Ibn Bishir, Ibn Jaʿfar, and Ibn Kubās), and shaykhs from Jumāʿah, Hamdān Ṣaʿdah, and even Jabal Baraṭ. This weighty tribal intervention appears to have forced a resolution, for a year later the *dawlah*s of *shawāmī* and *yamānī* Rāziḥ made a pact (D1798b), witnessed by several shaykhs. In this they agreed to share the revenues (*mawājīb* and *makhārij*) of Sūq al-Bār half each; that Muḥsin Muṭahhar and his officials should have jurisdiction over the market; that both he and al-Sharafī should be able to visit it safely; and that the entrepôt and its trade routes should be specially protected for four days each week (Thursday to Sunday)—a clause closely echoing purely inter-tribal pacts, and which Muḥsin Muṭahhar of course depended on tribal leaders to implement (D1801).

Al-Sharafī died in 1807, sparking another dispute between Āl al-Sharafī and Āl Muṭahhar (as their clans were by now called) over the fiscal obligations of the *dawlah* of the *yamānīyah* to the *dawlah* of the *shawāmī.* This quarrel was resolved by Āl Muṭahhar's confirming that they would pay Āl

FIGURE 9.4
Bayt al-Dawlah in *madīnat* al-Naẓīr, 1977, said to have been built by Muḥsin Muṭahhar, the then *dawlah* of *yamānī* Rāziḥ, in the late eighteenth century.

al-Sharafī, biannually, fixed amounts of grain from specific tribes and areas (*makātib*) in the *yamānīyah* and ʿUqārib, and half the revenues of al-Bār. This settlement (which smacks of a tax-farming arrangement) was mediated and guaranteed by the leaders of several tribes of Rāziḥ and ʿUqārib, and endorsed by leading *sayyids* including (presumably) the *dawlah* in Ṣaʿdah (D1807a). Soon after, Muḥsin Muṭahhar and his two brothers agreed to split the taxes of the *yamānīyah* three ways after paying their officials, and that Muḥsin's share should be extended (by the addition of part of Banī Ṣayāḥ to his tax domain) in recognition of "his superior authority and responsibility over *ahl al-ḥuqūq*." The brothers also agreed that the grain remaining in the *dawlah*'s silos (*madāfin*) should be divided equally between them after the discharge of debts (presumably meaning the stipends outstanding to their tribal and other officials). For mediating and guaranteeing this contract, the shaykh of al-Naẓīr received a substantial fee of forty *qirsh*, and his associates ten (D1807b).

The *dawlah* of *yamānī* Rāziḥ continued to be inherited and divided patrilineally, in this way, for most of the nineteenth century (as presumably was that of the *shawāmī*). The size and number of Rāziḥ's little tax domains therefore depended on the numbers of senior men in each generation, but they continued to be congruent with one or more tribes or wards, as they had to be; tax collection and law enforcement absolutely depended on tribal structures and practices.

Conflict in the Tihāmah

From the beginning of the nineteenth century, Rāziḥ was again troubled by inter-state conflict—this time on the coast. A major new politico-religious force—Wahhabism—was burgeoning, and there was fierce competition for control of the Tihāmah and its trade routes and ports between the pro-Wahhabi *amīr* of ʿAsīr, the *sharīfs* of Abu ʿArīsh, and the weakened imāms of Sanaa.[30] In 1809, perhaps triggered by these unsettling events, a major shift took place in Rāziḥ's relationship with Ṣaʿdah. Notwithstanding the long-standing alliance between the *dawlah* of the *mashriq* and the *dawlah* of *yamānī* Rāziḥ, and for reasons the documents fail to reveal, Ḥusayn ʿAlī Qāsim of Ṣaʿdah threatened *both* Rāziḥ's *dawlahs*. In response, the latter made a defense pact (D1809), guaranteed by leaders of Banī Maʿīn, al-Izid, and al-Naẓīr, which is strikingly similar, in wording and content, to tribal agreements. In a fractional arrangement also typical of tribal pacts, for example, representatives of the *shawāmī* and *yamānī dawlahs* agree to halve between them the costs of any losses or injuries they might sustain should hostilities break out. This crisis was curtailed, however, by Ḥusayn ʿAlī Qāsim's death around 1811. Shortly afterward his brother and successor sent the *dawlah*s of Rāziḥ a pledge of friendship, reassuring them that he would take no action concerning their joint domain without their agreement (D1811a). This concession was symptomatic of an enfeebled *dawlah* in the *mashriq*.

In 1811, Egyptian forces invaded the ʿAsīr Tihāmah, and were defeated by the *amīr* of highland ʿAsīr allied with the *sharīf* of Abū ʿArīsh (al-Zulfa 1987:32). Presumably in response to this nearby, threatening conflict, the tribes of *yamānī* Rāziḥ reaffirmed that they were under the rule (*ṭāʿah*) of their *dawlah,* Muḥsin Muṭahhar, and his son ʿAlī Muḥsin, and pledged to defend his domain and Sūq al-Bār if he required them to mobilize for war.[31] In 1815, the Egyptians invaded again, this time defeating the ʿAsīrīs.[32] The same year the *dawlah* of the *yamānīyah* ordered the Tihāmah entrepôt to be shifted from al-Bār a kilometer or two north to al-Ḍayʿah in al-Waqir, and in an apparent effort to assert his authority and keep the market alive, appointed a *ḥākim* to the sūq "to deal with sharīʿah problems," and pledged to protect its patrons—named as Sharīf Ḥāmūd of Abu ʿArīsh, and "the people of Jabal Rāziḥ, Jabal Shidā, and Jabal Ḥamāṭah" (D1815). This was a major coup for al-Waqir's shaykhly clan, Ilt Ghalfān, whose enrichment and empowerment had long-lasting repercussions on tribal politics.

State-provoked insecurity continued on the coast into the 1820s, inevitably damaging Rāziḥ's trade and revenues, and further aggravating the problems within and between the weakened and fragmented *dawlah*s of Rāziḥ and Ṣaʿdah, whose disputes continued to involve, and benefit, tribal leaders (D1821a; D1821b). In a defense pact of 1822, for example, Ilt Faraḥ and Ilt Ibrāhīm of al-Naẓīr "and their allies and relatives" agree to be "their *dawlah*'s soldiers" and bear half the military costs, provided the *dawlah* does not interfere in their leadership. In return, Āl Muṭahhar agree to pay them twenty *qirsh* if they mobilize their men (D1822a). Āl Muṭahhar divided the costs of such operations between them in a typically fractional manner, and defrayed them from "off the top of the taxes" (*min ra's al-zakāt*), inevitably reducing the tribute sent to Ṣaʿdah (D1825). The *dawlah* in the *mashriq* always suffered from trouble in the *maghrib*.

During the mid-1820s Rāziḥ's control over its Tihāmah entrepôt, now at al-Ḍayʿah, was again threatened by inter-state competition on the coast, which was captured by the Egyptians.[33] Soon after, Sayyid ʿAlī Muḥsin and his brothers of *yamānī* Rāziḥ sent an open letter (D1829a) to the Āl Ḥurrāth, Ibn Ghalfān of al-Waqir, and "all Muslims whether leaders or subjects," proclaiming: "If we are asked to mobilize our men for war against the infidels, we will respond immediately." "Our men" were, of course, the tribes of Rāziḥ. In January 1830, the *dawlah*s of *shawāmī* and *yamānī* Rāziḥ endeavored to secure control over their vital entrepôt by obtaining a pledge of allegiance from "all Banī ʿUqārib," who acknowledged ʿAlī Muḥsin's authority over al-Ḍayʿah, and affirmed its special days of protection (D1830).[34] Although al-Waqir is represented in this pact, however, the name of its shaykh, Ibn Ghalfān, is conspicuously absent from the signatories. A major pan-Rāziḥ defense pact shortly after reveals why (D1831a). This shows that Ibn Ghalfān was failing to maintain the security of his market, and prejudicing Rāziḥī trade. In reaction (and most unusually) the shaykhs of *all* the tribes of Jabal Rāziḥ arrogated to themselves responsibility for protecting al-Ḍayʿah and the trade routes which traversed Waqrī territory, which they clearly define:

> The market and its trade routes shall be protected by the above-mentioned [shaykhs] from *ahl al-shawāmī* and *ahl al-yamānīyah* for three days—Thursday, Friday, and Saturday until Sunday morning. This [protection] includes the well-known hinterland of the *sūq* from al-Muhaymilah to al-Ḥashaw to al-Ḥaswah to al-Mashshāf, according to tribal custom on territorial [responsibilities] (*ʿalā aslāf-him min al-ḥudūd*). (D1831a)[35]

Ibn Ghalfān was evidently withholding the revenues of Sūq al-Ḍayʿah, and the signatories pledge that they will mobilize militarily in order to "extract their *dawlah*'s rightful dues from markets and territories." Ibn Ghalfān had perhaps switched his allegiance to the future Sharīf of Abū ʿArīsh, Ḥusayn ʿAlī Ḥaydar, who later sided with the Egyptians during their renewed campaigns to control the Tihāmah, and was rewarded in 1836 with a high post in Mokha. Sharīf Ḥusayn's Egyptian-fueled ambitions certainly included Sūq al-Ḍayʿah, for in 1838, the year he succeeded to Abū ʿArīsh, he wrote to the *dawlah* of *yamānī* Rāziḥ, Sayyid Muḥammad Qāsim of Āl Muṭahhar, asserting jurisdiction over al-Waqir, and challenging him to contest his claim in the sharīʿah court (D1838b). It is doubtful the latter rose to this challenge, given the *sharīf*'s powerful patron. By 1845, however, al-Waqir and al-Ḍayʿah were back under Rāziḥī control (D1845d).

In 1840 the Egyptians abruptly withdrew from the Tihāmah, making their client, Sharīf Ḥusayn ʿAlī Ḥaydar, its nominal ruler, and two years later the Ottoman Sultan recognized his overlordship of the Tihāmah in return for annual tribute of coffee and money.[36] Sharīf Ḥusayn aspired to control the whole of Yemen, and subsequently conquered the Tihāmah as far as Mokha, and even attacked Taʿizz, while alternately opposing and supporting the rival imāms of Sanaa.[37]

Throughout these upheavals on the coast, the *dawlah*s of Rāziḥ remained formally subordinate to the *dawlah* in Ṣaʿdah, which was still demanding a quarter of the taxes of the *yamānīyah* (and presumably also of the *shawāmī*), less local administrative expenses (D1844a). However, both highland *dawlah*s must have been greatly debilitated by the disruptions to trade, and by losing the revenues from al-Ḍayʿah for several years, and by the late 1840s the Qāsimī *dawlah* of Ṣaʿdah appears to have become defunct after a hundred and thirty years of relative independence. The main Zaydī imāmate in Sanaa was also undermined by the dire economic and political situation on the coast, and the consequent drop in revenues, and from the 1840s to the 1870s it was ravaged by bitter in-fighting between a series of rival contenders, none of whom succeeded in maintaining power or viable domains for more than a few years.[38]

At the beginning of this "period of disorder" (*ayyām al-fasād*), as Yemeni historians call it, a *sayyid* from Khawlān (south of Rāziḥ), Aḥmad b. Ḥāshim al-Waysī (1848–50), proclaimed himself imām in opposition to the imām of Sanaa, taking the title "al-Manṣūr billāh," and Sayyid Muḥammad Qāsim of Āl Muṭahhar journeyed to Sāqayn to pledge him Rāziḥ's allegiance.[39] This action ensured that the *dawlah* of Rāziḥ continued to be religiously legitimated by an imām, while retaining its relative autonomy. It also revealed its preference, which was shown repeatedly, for an imām based in Khawlān Ṣaʿdah instead of distant Sanaa.

The fact that a member of Āl Muṭahhar represented Rāziḥ to this short-lived claimant to the imāmate shows that they had, by then, gained supremacy over their erstwhile overlords and cousins, Āl al-Sharafī, in the *shawāmī*. This had perhaps been achieved after a violent power struggle, for that same year (1848), someone from Āl Muṭahhar killed someone from Āl al-Sharafī. This major inter-*dawlah* crisis, which must again have threatened security over a wide region, was defused and mediated by shaykhs and *sayyid*s from *shawāmī* Rāziḥ for a tenth of the *diyah;* and the peace agreement (D1848a) was guaranteed by an extraordinary number and range of shaykhs and *maradd*s from Rāziḥ, ʿUqārib, Ṣaḥār, and Khawlān.

This settlement is notable for its use and abuse of tribal law. Āl Muṭahhar were outraged that Āl al-Sharafī had demanded the maximum, sharīʿah, *diyah* instead of a lower tribal *diyah,* and in reaction insisted on flagrantly disproportionate penalties should Āl al-Sharafī flout the settlement and threaten or harm Āl Muṭahhar in even minor ways. The document specifically states, for example, that if any member of Āl al-Sharafī so much as fires a gun or brandishes a dagger, his clan will be liable for an *ʿayb aswad* equivalent to the sharīʿah *diyah* (800 *qirsh*) "because [Āl al-Sharafī] would not accept a tribal diyah (*diyah shurūʿ al-qubul*)," and if anyone from Āl al-Sharafī merely wounds a member of Āl Muṭahhar, he will be executed, his house and land will be destroyed, and the taxes of his domain will be paid to Āl Muṭahhar. And all this would be enforced, if necessary, by the guarantors' tribes waging war against al-Sharafī. These terms appalled an untutored *qabīlī* from al-Naẓīr: "It's not sharīʿah law to demand more than an eye for an eye!" Nor, it should be added, does it conform with the conciliatory evenhandedness of *ʿurf.*

However gross the crime to which the victims, Āl Muṭahhar, were reacting, the fact that they could impose such punitive conditions on Āl al-Sharafī provides further evidence that they were now dominating them. This is confirmed by an imāmic edict a decade later in which another short-lived imām delegates jurisdiction over "Jabal Rāziḥ" to Muḥammad Qāsim of Āl Muṭahhar, who is instructed "to refer any problems he cannot solve" to the imām's representative in Ṣaʿdah. He affirms, however, that Āl al-Sharafī and Āl Muṭahhar should remain in joint charge of tax collection, and should "keep what they need" (meaning for their own subsistence, and for paying shaykhs and officials), and remit any surplus to the treasury (*bayt al-māl*) (D1858). This document is redolent of imāmic weakness. Neither this pretender to the imāmate, nor any other who announced his *daʿwah* and struggled for power during the turbulent 1850s–1870s, was in any position to demand stringent conditions from friendly *dawlah*s such as those of Rāziḥ.

With the demise of the *dawlah* of Ṣaʿdah, and the enfeeblement, fragmentation, and in-fighting of the Zaydī imāmate, the *dawlah*s of Rāziḥ gained greater political and fiscal autonomy than they had enjoyed during previous generations. In addition, the Ottomans did not take Jabal Rāziḥ during their second occupation from the early 1870s, as they did other highland regions. The *dawlah* of Rāziḥ was therefore able to enjoy a few years of independence from any overlord during a period of national instability and foreign domination, and to continue their symbiotic tax relationship with the leaders of Rāziḥ's tribes.

The Tax Relationship in the Nineteenth Century

Nineteenth-century documents from *yamānī* Rāziḥ reveal something of the tax relationship between *dawlah-wa-qabīlah,* and of how tribal leaders benefited materially from their cooperative relationship with their religious rulers. As we have seen, after the leading *sayyids* of the *dawlahs* of Rāziḥ died, their local tax domains and privileges were inherited by their sons and successors like other property, often provoking disputes. After any adjustments of domains between heirs, tribal leaders pledged their allegiance and taxes to their new overlord or one of his brothers in writing, sometimes seizing the opportunity to renegotiate their terms. (*Sayyid* families similarly pledged their taxes to the *dawlahs* of their parts of Rāziḥ [see D1873c].) These contracts show how religious and secular leaders upheld each other's positions, symbolically and materially, through the medium of taxation.

When tribal leaders made their pledges on behalf of their tribes (or sometimes wards), they were clearly conscious that they, together with other tribal groups, were constituting the domain of a particular *dawlah,* or one of its administrative divisions. For example, those in the south explicitly define themselves in tax pledges as "among the tribes of southern Rāziḥ" (*min jumlah ahl al-yamāniyah*), or as part of "the southern tax domain" (*maktab al-yamāniyah*) (D1821b; D1827c). Tax pledges also show that tribal leaders saw themselves as appointing and empowering their overlords, and dictating the terms of the relationship. This markedly unsubservient stance reflects the weakness of *dawlahs* during this period, and the realization of tribal leaders that they depended on them to collect taxes and enforce the law against defaulters. Furthermore, since statements of allegiance usually embrace the families, forebears, and descendants of the ruling *sayyid,* tribes upheld dynasties as well as individual rulers. Tax pledges often state, for example, that the tribe will pay its overlord and "whoever succeeds him, always and forever" (*man yukhallif ba'deh dā'iman mustamirr*) (D1827a)—meaning his heirs and descendants. The important point with regard to the tribal system is that, by supporting religious hereditary rule and the right of local *dawlahs* to be paid the *zakāt,* tribal leaders were simultaneously upholding the principles and practices which sustained their *own* inherited positions and tax privileges. This is evident in a pledge of allegiance and taxes by the leaders of Banī Ṣayāḥ to Muḥsin ʿAlī when he succeeded his father, ʿAlī Muḥsin, as *dawlah* of *yamānī* Rāziḥ in 1845:

> [The shaykh and *aʿyān* of Banī Ṣayāḥ], representing their tribesmen, have appointed (*wallū*) Sayyid Muḥsin b. ʿAlī al-Muṭahhar and his successors (*man warāhu*) over their land and the *zakāt* on all the fruits of the earth, and with regard to all fines and punishments. They [remain] within the domain (*maqām*) of his father, Sayyid ʿAlī b. Muḥsin b. al-Muṭahhar, and his predecessors, regarding the payment and delivery of their canonical taxes (*wājibāt*). They will discharge their taxes [only] to them [i.e., their clan], and comply with their orders.
>
> Their shaykhs require only a tenth [of the *zakāt*] plus *muwāsah* [travel and administrative expenses] . . . And this should go only to whomever his constituents (*raʿiyyah*) make shaykh, and who is [consequently] responsible for exercising authority and dispensing official hospitality (*ʿalayhi al-wajāh wa al-ḍayfah*). And he must take nothing from the people's *zakāt* without the *dawlah*'s permission. If he does, the *ẓumanā* [of the tribe] guarantee to return it and [to implement] whatever the *dawlah* rules against him . . .
>
> Sayyid Muḥsin ʿAlī and his successors shall be revered like their forefathers and predecessors, and their dependents, officials, tax collectors, associates, and guests; whoever they offer sanctuary to and his nephew shall be respected on the road and in the *bilād* [i.e., in Banī Ṣayāḥ]. Anyone who threatens them must bear whatever penalty the *dawlah* decrees according to their ancestral custom, and to the original agreements and regulations in Sayyid Muḥsin's possession . . . which they affirm. (1845c)

As this extract shows, shaykhly stipends (sing. *taqrīr*)—also called the "return" (*marjūʿ*)—were calculated, at this time, as a fraction of the *zakāt* from each shaykh's tribe. At other times, as in the 1764 register mentioned above, the *taqrīr* appears to have been a fixed sum, and to have included other gifts as well as money. In D1826, for example, the shaykh of al-Shawāriq sells a member of Āl Muṭahhar two-thirds of the *taqrīr* "which [the shaykh] and his forefathers got" to defray a debt of MT$60, and this two-thirds consisted of six *zabadī*s of grain, six *qadaḥ*s of coffee, and "all the other things connected with feasts and clothing (*kiswah*)."[40] As this shows, the shaykhly right to stipends was also conceived of as hereditary.

When stipends were paid as a "return" (*marjūʿ*) or fraction of the taxes, they generally amounted to a tenth of the *zakāt* of the tribe, as in the above agreement, but powerful shaykhs got more (D1808; D1845c). To secure support during crises, the *dawlah* could also top up the basic *marjūʿ*, or cede shaykhs extra taxes from specified areas within their domains. In 1850, for example, Muḥsin ʿAlī agreed to pay Ilt Ghalfān of al-Waqir a quarter of the *zakāt* of Sūq al-Ḍayʿah "because they are the shaykhs of the area," and an extra quarter for their support in a dispute he was having with the tribes of Jabal Rāziḥ until it was resolved (1850a). And in 1873 the same Muḥsin ʿAlī awarded Ibn al-ʿAzzām of al-Shawāriq (the senior *maradd* of Rāziḥ) three quarters of the *zakāt* of al-Juwwah, a fertile coffee-growing area in the lower reaches of his tribe, "for the duration of his lifetime" (D1873a). The *muwāsah* payments for expenses associated with tax collection also undoubtedly provided shaykhs with leeway to negotiate extras beyond their contractual allowances.

In return for their stipends and expenses, and in order to safeguard these lucrative rights, tribal leaders supported the taxation system administratively, legally, and militarily. While each taxpayer appears to have had to deliver (*waddā*) his own grain tax to the *dawlah*'s stores (sing. *makhzān*), for which the *dawlah* normally paid the transportation fees (*kirā*) (D1833a; D1881b), tribal leaders were responsible for organizing assessments and helping to record payments (D1846d). They also enforced the law against tax defaulters in their own tribes or groups, and sometimes even united against fellow leaders who opposed their *dawlah* over taxation matters. After a tax dispute in 1821, for example, elders from the three Thirds of al-Naẓīr guaranteed to prevent a rebellious member of Ilt Faraḥ from harming their *dawlah,* and shaykhs of four other Rāziḥ tribes acted as secondary guarantors (*jidhū*) of their pact (D1821b). Tribal leaders also supported their *dawlah* when the latter's share of the taxes was challenged or withheld by their overlords in the *mashriq* (which obviously also threatened the shaykhly *marjūʿ*) (D1844a). And as we have seen, they sometimes mobilized their tribes to protect key markets, such as al-Bār or al-Ḍayʿah, when their revenues were threatened by encroaching enemy states.

Tribal leaders strove to maintain their exclusive grip on tax collection, both to safeguard their generous stipends and to minimize state interference. In their pledges, therefore, as well as promising to be honest, they often assert that *they* will be the tax assessors, and *they* will monitor assessments, guarantee payments, and deal with tax defaulters, using the same customary procedures as for enforcing other legal liabilities—chiefly the oath. In the early nineteenth century, for example, when the tax domains of Rāziḥ were already fragmented between heirs to the *dawlah,* three representatives of al-ʿArḍ in lower al-Shawāriq affirm on behalf of "their fellow men and protegés" that

> they will pay all the winter, coffee, and spring taxes, and take responsibility for discharging whatever the tax assessors (*ṭawaf*) put down, provided they are from al-ʿArḍ . . . Anyone who claims he was wrongly assessed should swear an oath to God to that effect, and if he fails to do so, the guarantor (*ḍamīn*) [of his clan] will make him discharge his debts. The above-named three from Ahl al-ʿArḍ shall be the tax assessors, responsible to God. They will neither cheat the farmer nor deprive the *bayt al-māl* of God's dues. (1827b)

Their followers expected tribal leaders to spend their government stipends, like their tribal fees, on official duties, and to share them with other members of their clans who had responsibilities. This sharing was also subject to contractual agreement. In D1838a, for example, the shaykh of al-Naẓīr and his nephew agree to split in half the stipend (*taqrīr*) from the *dawlah* and the *zakāt* from al-Muhaymilah (which the *dawlah* must have ceded them). They also agree to share the expenses of collecting the tax, and of other official duties such as entertaining guests, "for whom they are obliged to slaughter and provide hospitality," and add that they will halve between them any leftover meat or clarified butter. When shaykhs failed to disburse their tax shares as agreed, or otherwise abused their privileges, it appears that clans and wards could sidestep them and pay the *dawlah* directly. This situation seems to underlie an early nineteenth-century tax pledge by two Birkānī clans (D1833a), in which they rather defiantly assert that they will deliver their taxes to named members of Āl Muṭahhar "despite any objection from Birkān," and another fifty years later (D1878a), in which groups in the *shawāmī* assert that they will no longer pay taxes through Ibn ʿAwfān (the shaykh of Banī Asad), but will henceforth pay with *maktab al-yamānīyah,* suggesting that they were also switching their allegiance between *dawlahs*.

Tribal leaders were clearly concerned that their *dawlah*s should use their taxes for proper governmental purposes: for entertaining important visitors, for the welfare of the people, for paying stipends, and for defense. In D1822b, for example, when the two ruling *sayyid*s of *yamānī* Rāziḥ decided to earmark the revenues from a specified area toward hospitality expenses, their agreement was witnessed, guaranteed, and no doubt mediated by Naẓīrī elders—including a member of the shaykhly family, Ilt Faraḥ. The interesting point to note is that such matters were the subject of agreement between *dawlah-wa-qabīlah,* as well as between the ruling *sayyid*s. The tribes were partners in state governance, and seen as such by both parties. This continued to be the case during the resurgence of the Zaydī imāmate in the late nineteenth century, and the consolidation of its power in the twentieth.

CHAPTER TEN

The Ḥamīd al-Dīn Period

Rāziḥ Reincorporated into the Main Zaydī Imāmate

In the early 1870s the Ottomans again occupied ʿAsīr and parts of highland Yemen (though not this time Rāziḥ), and again stimulated a resurgence and expansion of the Zaydī state. In 1879 a non-Qāsimī *sayyid,* al-Hādī Sharaf al-Dīn (1879–90), announced his claim (*daʿwah*) to the imāmate, seized Ṣaʿdah from a rival, and from there launched an anti-Ottoman *jihād*. Soon after, the leaders of "the whole tribe of al-Naẓīr" agreed:

> Should God send them a true imām, and all Rāziḥ accepts his rule . . . then the shaykhs and *dawlah* of al-Naẓīr should treat with him, and will comply with whatever the rest of Rāziḥ agrees . . . They are united with whoever "commands the good and forbids the reprehensible" [the imām], and affirm that they uphold the *sharīʿah* of [the Prophet] Muḥammad b. ʿAbdallāh . . . and reject the accursed *ṭāghūt* which God rejects as unadulterated paganism. (D1879a)

Rāziḥīs still wanted to maintain their long-standing symbiotic relationship with their local overlords, however. Thus the Naẓīrīs renewed a defense pact with "their *dawlah*" Āl Muṭahhar (D1880b); and the Yalqamīs confirmed how their taxes should be divided between "our *sayyids*" (two members of Āl Muṭahhar), their shaykh, and the poor "until we get an imām" (D1880d).

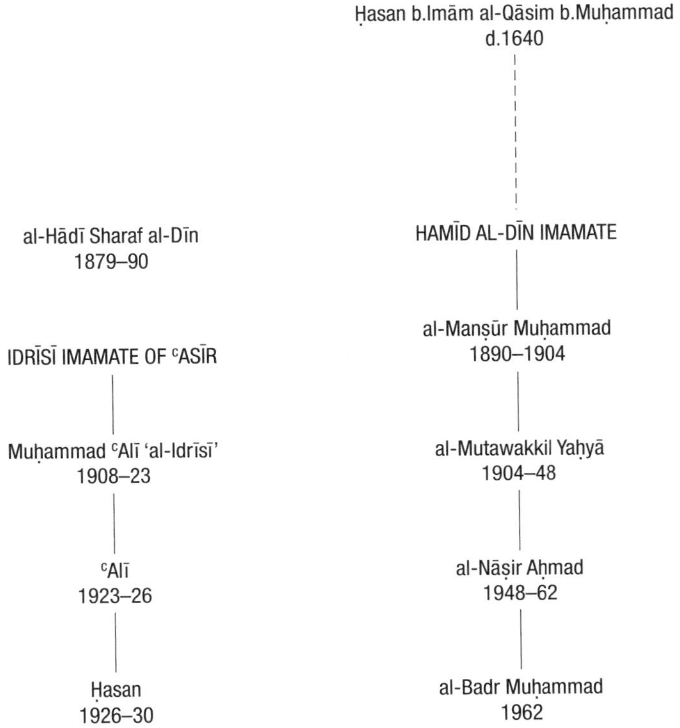

FIGURE 10.1
Late-nineteenth- to twentieth-century rulers of Yemen and ʿAsīr. Dates indicate regimes

Imām al-Hādī obtained the allegiance of Khawlān, Rāziḥ, and Jumāʿah apparently peacefully, but was opposed by a powerful shaykh in ʿUqārib (probably of al-Wuqaysh). This border region between the highlands and the coast, with its lucrative entrepôt, was of great strategic and economic importance to any imām trying to create and defend a northern domain, and fund resistance to the Ottomans. It was therefore a significant coup when the shaykh of al-Waqir, who still controlled Sūq al-Ḍayʿah, pledged his support and sent him two cannons, then—allied with the shaykh of Banī Ṣafwān—forced the defiant shaykh to capitulate.[1]

So important was Rāziḥ to the new imām that he spent four months there in 1882 "in order to rebuild its administration," and probably also to recruit fighters. During his sojourn, al-Naẓīr and al-Izid (and presumably other Rāziḥ tribes) declared themselves as among the *ahl al-ṭāʿah*—literally "the obedient ones"—meaning those who have submitted to imāmic rule (D1882).

Imām al-Hādī Sharaf al-Dīn died in 1890, and was succeeded by Imām al-Manṣūr Muḥammad (1890–1904)—the first imām from Bayt Ḥamīd al-Dīn, and from a Qāsimī line which had not previously held the imāmate (al-Wāsiʿī 1947:268). Al-Manṣūr, who was based in Shahārah, immediately launched his own anti-Ottoman *jihād,* and took firm control of Rāziḥ through his commander (*qāʾid*), Sayf al-Islam Muḥammad "Abu Nayb" (a son of Imām al-Hādī).

Both Imām al-Hādī and Imām al-Manṣūr had limited resources, and were preoccupied with their enemies, so they did the minimum required to impose their rule. They secured their hold over greater Rāziḥ by taking hostages (sing. *rahīnah*) from each tribe as bonds of their submission and obedience, an old method of state control in South Arabia (see below).[2] And they imported governors (sing. *nāẓirah*) and *ḥākims,* and superimposed this thin top layer of "foreign" officials onto the existing tribal and religious hierarchy, which functioned much as before. The *dawlah*s of Rāziḥ continued to receive the *zakāt,* though they were now in a tributary relationship with the imāms and had to cede them half (D1889; D1890a; 1907b). Local scholars, including Sayyid ʿAlī Ḥusayn al-Ḥūthī, who arrived in Rāziḥ as a *muhājir* around the 1870s, continued to dispense sharīʿah and tribal law, and to mediate in inter-tribal disputes and witness tribal agreements. And tribal leaders, who started being referred to as "trusted officials" (*ahl al-ʿahidah*), continued running their tribes, and protecting trade routes and markets, while collaborating with their new rulers.

The imāms secured the loyalty and services of key local figures by the usual favors and dispensations. Imām al-Hādī, for example, rewarded Shaykh Ghalfān of al-Waqir for his military support by placing him in charge of revenue collection at Sūq al-Ḍayʿah, though during inter-state strife in the Tihāmah in 1888 Shaykh Jubrān Qāsim of al-Naẓīr took charge of the entrepôt with the agreement of the *nāẓirah* of Rāziḥ, and of tribes in ʿUqārib and *yamānī* Rāziḥ defined as *ahl al-ṭāʿah.*[3] And in the same month that he proclaimed his *daʿwah,* Imām al-Manṣūr informed the *qāḍīs* of Ilt al-Judhaynah that he would preserve their protected (*hijrah*) status, and exempt them from giving hostages, contributing to tribal subscriptions (*farq*), or having tax collectors imposed on them; instead they could pay their taxes directly to him, implying they could self-assess (1890b). Āl Muṭahhar and Āl al-Sharafī must have obtained similar contracts guaranteeing their protected positions, and confirming their fiscal roles and privileges, because the shaykhs of Rāziḥ continued to refer to them as their *dawlahs* and to cooperate with them in tax-collection. As before, shaykhs were allocated fractions of the taxes of their tribes (D1891d; D1891e).

Soon after Imām al-Manṣūr took power in Rāziḥ, war broke out between Birkān and Munabbih on one side and Izdī-and-Naẓīrī on the other, perhaps provoked by resentment of hostage charges and hikes in taxation. Afterward the imām extracted a punitive MT$600 from Izdī-and-Naẓīrī toward *diyahs* and other compensation payments (D1891a, D1892a); and when their *aʿyān* quarreled over their war and hostage expenses, he authorized Sayyid ʿAlī al-Ḥūthī "to intercede, and sort out their obligations and claims." In so doing, the latter honored the terms of the tribes' bilateral *qawāʿid,* including their agreements to divide their joint liabilities on a one-third/two-thirds basis as described in Chapter Five (D1892b).

Imām al-Manṣūr divided the canonical taxes (*wājibāt* or *ḥuqūq Illāh*) into two categories: "for the treasury (*bayt al-māl*)," and "specially for the imām" (D1897). The former was the *zakāt* on agriculture and animals, and the latter "aid taxes (*maʿūnah*)" for the war chest. Most *maʿūnah* was probably collected at major markets as rents on traders' pitches (*ḥaqq al-qāʿ* or *ḥaqq al-mafrash*) and imposts on goods in transit, especially through Sūq al-Ḍayʿah. With the Ottomans striving to control ʿAsīr, however, the entrepôt had become a vulnerable frontier post, and so was also a financial drain. This is shown by a letter which Imām al-Manṣūr sent to Shaykh Jubrān Qāsim of al-Naẓīr in the mid-1890s instructing him to use the revenues of al-Ḍayʿah of MT$80 a week (and no more implied) to pay the monthly wages of the market's guards. This arrangement was subject, he added, to the agreement of his *nāẓirah,* and of the leaders of al-Izid, Banī Rabīʿah, Banalqām, and Birkān (who were perhaps supplying the guards). The imām also thanked Shaykh Jubrān for his news about Khawlān and the "insane and fiendish activities" of Ibn Rawkān (its senior *maradd*).[4]

In 1896 anti-Ottoman insurrections in the Tihāmah so threatened the security of al-Ḍayʿah that Imām al-Manṣūr ordered the establishment and fortification of an alternative entrepôt "within his domain" (*bilād ahl al-ṭāʿah*). However, the traders and transporters found the new site inconvenient. Naẓīrī leaders "responsible for opening and protecting the new route" therefore petitioned the imām, through the *ḥākim* Sayyid ʿAlī Ḥusayn al-Ḥūthī, for permission to establish an alternative warehousing and staging post (*malqā li baẓāyiʿ wa makhraṭ*) at al-Muhaymilah, southeast of al-Ḍayʿah, which they undertook to "protect."[5] The market thus returned to Naẓīrī territory after seventy years in al-Waqir. The leaders of al-Naẓīr requested permission to collect the *maʿūnah,* specifying the sums they would levy on camel-loads of different commodities. They proposed that the *amīn*s who collected the taxes, under government inspectors (sing. *kāshif*), should be "respected local merchants"—namely six *aʿyān* from major Naẓīrī clans, including the coffee merchant ʿAbdallāh ʿAlī. Al-Ḥūthī confirmed their sacred vows to God to "keep honest records and not cheat," and would supervise, and the imām agreed (D1896b). Thus did the tribal elite exploit state neediness to their own benefit; no tax collector impoverishes himself.

Rebellion

Shortly afterward a major rebellion erupted in Rāziḥ. This crisis illustrates the tensions in the state-tribe relationship at that time, and how the state recruited tribal structures and practices to quash dissension. The story goes that there was a fight in Sūq Shaʿārah (in Banī Rabīʿah) between a *sayyid* (perhaps an official) from al-Qalʿah, and Ibn Karāmah, a high-ranking *qabīlī* from al-Izid. The *sayyid* allegedly slapped Ibn Karāmah's face in public (a disgraceful insult to male honor), and Ibn Karāmah ambushed him in al-Izid (to ensure his own tribe would deal with the crisis) and shot him dead. The *nāẓirah* imprisoned Ibn Karāmah at al-Qalʿah, and al-Izid accepted responsibility and pleaded to pay *diyah* as allowed in tribal law. But the *sayyid*'s family demanded execution, the sharīʿah punishment for intentional homicide, and the *nāẓirah* had Ibn Karāmah beheaded.

Distraught at the *nāẓirah*'s lack of mercy, Ibn Karāmah's brother tried to activate the Izdī-and-Naẓīrī alliance for revenge. But they refused, proclaiming: "Like for like is God's law. He killed a *sayyid,* so they killed him." Ibn Karāmah could not accept this, and donning female dress to shame his fellow tribesmen, announced in Sūq al-Naẓīr: "Are there any men left in Izdī-wa-Naẓīrī, or shall we call up *women*?" But still they did nothing. So Ibn Karāmah went to al-Qalʿah and, while the *nāẓirah* was bending over in prayer, shot him dead from behind. Whatever retribution the state then took for this scandalous and cowardly crime precipitated a rebellion.

Between 1897 and 1900 al-Izid, al-Naẓīr, Birkān, and "most" of al-Shawāriq built an anti-government coalition which the state scornfully dubbed "the allies (*ahl al-ḥizām wa al-lizām*)" and "the people of the treaty (*ahl al-qāʿidah*)," ridiculing their tribal pacts. Opposing them were tribes which remained loyal to the imām (*ahl al-ṭāʿah*)—Munabbih, ʿAbīdī-wa-Ṣafwānī, Banalqām, Banī Rabīʿah, Banī Ṣayāḥ, and the rest of al-Shawāriq. It will be noted that this lineup reflected resentments, interests, and treaty obligations, and cross-cut moiety affiliations and Rāziḥī and ʿUqāribī alignments.

In their defense treaties, written partly for government eyes, "the allies" took pains to affirm their adherence to sharīʿah law and their allegiance to the imām, while reminding him of his contractual agreements with them on which he had evidently reneged:

> They agree that Imām al-Manṣūr, God protect him, is their imām, and that they will pay their *wājibāt* like the rest of *ahl* Rāziḥ to his *nāẓirah* on the mountain [here meaning Jabal Rāziḥ] . . . They are responsible for ensuring that God's dues are paid . . . [But while] that which belongs to the imām and the treasury is his, that due to his officials (*ahl al-ʿahidah*) is *theirs*. [Because] contracts local *sayyids* (*sādāt al-bilād*), shaykhs, or anyone else in authority possess from Imām al-Manṣūr or previous imāms are [still] valid. They submitted to the Imām's rule only upon his affirmation of [these] agreements (*qawāʿid*). (D1900e)

The rebellion was not therefore against the imāmate, nor (initially) the imām, but against specific policies and actions, of which the *nāẓirah*'s merciless execution of Ibn Karāmah was probably the final straw. The treaties hint at several substantive grievances: government failure to respect tribal customs and pacts, including the right to take vengeance; the location of hostages and *rabākh*s, which the tribes insist should stay in Rāziḥ, but which the imām wanted to send outside; the costs of supporting hostages (see below); other tribes (presumably Munabbih) "opening up" (*fataḥ*) their territories to the state; Munabbihī hostility toward southern Rāziḥīs; legal appeals being heard outside their *bilād;* "oppressive verdicts" against them at al-Qalʿah; and the failure to honor tax-sharing contracts with shaykhs and *sayyid*s (D1897; D1900e). The overall picture which emerges from these fragmentary allusions is of the state trying to maximize its revenues from Rāziḥ, and erode the prerogatives of the local tribal and religious elite.

In their 1900 treaty, "the allies" also agree to boycott the court at al-Qalʿah until the imām honors his agreements "with *dawlah*s, judges, and shaykhs." Instead they will settle their internal problems by tribal-style negotiation (*ṣulḥ marḍī*), which (they defensively assert) is Islamically respectable, or they will take sharīʿah cases to Sayyid ʿAlī Ḥusayn al-Ḥūthī in the *yamāniyah*. Furthermore, they will pay the imām (only) half their *zakāt* (the other half presumably going to shaykhs and Āl Muṭahhar). And they forbid government officials (*ṣāḥib al-amr*) to erect buildings in their territory—an expression, perhaps, of their resentment of projected new forts (D1900e).

This defiance triggered "the war of Ibn Karāmah." Hostilities lasted months, and ended only after the imām dispatched forces to Rāziḥ under his commander, Abū Nayb (D1901). "The allies" were then judged in the sharīʿah court, where the imām's *ḥākim* condemned them in absolutist religious rhetoric which discounted the validity of tribal pacts or the existence of legitimate grievances:

> They refused God's law and wrote their own agreements, repudiating it and facilitating evil. And this opposition took place while the imām was preoccupied with his bigger *jihād* against the foreigners [the Turks]. They were cowards because they knew he was vulnerable; it is not brave to rise against a weak and solitary enemy. So al-Izid, al-Naẓīr, Birkān, and al-Shawāriq made an alliance to pursue pagan things and reject the sharīʿah and its judgments . . . They escalated the hostilities, but God was with *ahl al-ṭāʿah*. There were many deaths, and those on one side went to heaven and on the other to hell. (D1901)

The imām's officials calculated every detail of the damages the treasury (*bayt al-māl*) and loyal tribes (*ahl al-ṭāʿah*) had suffered during the rebellion: hostage expenses; soldiers' fees and ammunition, down to the last bullet; and compensation for the dead and injured, and for harm to land, crops, trees, and animals. All this came to a massive MT$20,000—a figure seared into the memories of older Rāziḥīs. The imām's *ḥākim* deemed "the allies" liable for the entire amount, and disallowed any reduction for the latter's own losses on the grounds that "whoever rebels against the rule of God (*amr* Allāh), the imām or the sharīʿah, must bear all the costs." The imām subtracted a third of the damages from the current year's taxes, and decreed that rebels should pay the remainder in three annual installments (D1901). Pleas for clemency were refused (D1902), but the rebels were saved from paying the final installment by Imām al-Manṣūr's death in 1904.

It is notable that, throughout the Ibn Karāmah crisis, the imām took the tribes for granted as the key local polities. Not only did he recruit his allies on a tribal basis, but his judge also listed the compensation due to the *ahl al-ṭāʿah* tribe by tribe, and implicitly assumed that the shaykh of each rebel tribe would use the method of corporate subscription to extract contributions toward these penalties from his constituents (D1901). Even in punitive mode, therefore, the state acknowledged, depended upon, and reinforced tribal structures and practices.

The Idrīsī Period

Imām al-Manṣūr was succeeded by his son, al-Mutawakkil Yaḥyā Ḥamīd al-Dīn (1904–48), the imām who laid the foundations of "modern Yemen" (Peterson 1982). It was not until the 1930s, however, after years of struggle against competing powers, that Imām Yaḥyā consolidated his rule. He was opposed from the start by a rival in the Ṣaʿdah area, to whom some or all Rāziḥī leaders gave their allegiance for several years, ensuring the continuation of their stipends (*marjūʿ*).[6] During this unstable period of competition for the imāmate and resistance to the Ottomans, Āl Muṭahhar renewed their pacts of mutual support, and obtained reaffirmations of their tax privileges from the tribes. And tribal leaders similarly asserted their age-old rights, including over tax collection and to tribal sovereignty (D1906a; D1907b).

In addition to his Zaydī rival and the Ottomans, Imām Yaḥyā also had to contend with a religious leader in coastal ʿAsīr—Muḥammad b. ʿAlī al-Idrīs of Ṣabyā, who had his own state-building ambitions.[7] The Idrīsī formally proclaimed his anti-Ottoman *daʿwah* in 1908, and during 1909 gained the allegiance of regions which Imām Yaḥyā also claimed—the Yemeni Tihāmah, and adjacent mountains including those of ʿUqārib, Jabal Rāziḥ, and most of the rest of Khawlān ibn ʿĀmir.[8] The following year the Idrīsī visited Rāziḥ for a week, where he was welcomed by exuberant crowds beating drums and shooting guns (al-ʿAqīlī 1982: 660–661), and ordered fortifications to be strengthened on the summits of ʿUqārib and Rāziḥ. Like previous rulers, he also dispatched a governor and a *ḥākim* to Rāziḥ, both of whom lived in the tribe of al-Naẓīr and intermarried with Āl Muṭahhar; and he employed Sayyid ʿAlī Ḥusayn al-Ḥūthī as his secretary (*kātib*).

The Idrīsī controlled the coast, including Jīzān, and was flush with arms and money from port and market revenues and foreign patrons (Baldry 1973: 11). He was therefore able to cede Āl Muṭahhar and shaykhs a half-share of the *zakāt*, and pay tribal mercenaries well. His Sunnī affiliation was no obstacle to his acceptance, even to the Zaydī *ʿulamā*. He upheld their positions and privileges, and they regarded him as of comparable noble birth: "The Idrīsī was a Ḥāshimī, like Imām Yaḥyā." He was also considered a strong, wise, and generous ruler who had introduced desirable administrative reforms and infrastructural development in ʿAsīr. Imām Yaḥyā, by contrast, had a reputation for being mean and ruthless, unconcerned for his subjects' welfare, and for wanting to undermine local power holders. When he tried to impose his rule in Rāziḥ, therefore, he met violent resistance fueled by Idrīsī money and arms.

The Restoration of Ḥamīd al-Dīn Rule in Rāziḥ

In the 1911 Treaty of Daʿʿān the Turks recognized Imām Yaḥyā's jurisdiction over the Zaydī highlands, and substantially increased his monetary and military resources.[9] Muḥsin Abū Ṭālib: "They gave him arms and ammunition and cannons, and their commander in Ṣaʿdah, ʿAlī Rūḥī." Disgust at this accommodation with the foreign occupier caused many Yemeni tribes to switch sides to the Idrīsī.[10] Much of Khawlān ibn ʿĀmir also still supported him, but during 1913, with Turkish help and the support of tribes loyal to the imāmate, Imām Yaḥyā conquered most of the region. In December that year his forces invaded Rāziḥ through its northern gateway, and there pro-Idrīsī tribesmen famously ambushed them in Wadī ʿAmiq, a gorge below Jabal Ḥurum which must be skirted to take al-Qalʿah. There was a fierce battle in which the imām's side suffered heavy casualties—Rāziḥīs still intone "the wādī flowed with blood"—and the survivors were "chased out to Sāqayn." A few weeks later, however, Imām Yaḥyā's northern commander, the aforementioned Abū Nayb, allegedly bribed the northern gatekeeping shaykhs to "open up" to his soldiers, which enabled him to take *shawāmī* Rāziḥ (al-ʿAqīlī 1982: 661–662). Then Abū Nayb purportedly announced: "O men of Rāziḥ. We have established security in the rest of Yemen, which just leaves you." But the *yamānī* tribes resisted. "We said we would never let him in or submit to his rule," Shaykh Nāṣir explained, "because Munabbih had opened up to him. So we distributed lookouts along our borders, and wherever an attack came from, there we massed." This continued for a year until, with the help of the *shawāmī* tribes, Abū Nayb blockaded the *yamāniyah* from the north. He then besieged the massif from the coast, preventing the importation of essential foods and Idrīsī arms. The *yamānī* tribes were thus forced to capitulate. Then, Shaykh Nāṣir explained: "We demanded treaties (*qawāʿid*). Our conditions were that the imām could take hostages from leading families, but he must withdraw the Turks [soldiers] from our *bilād,* and we should not have to go to war outside. Then we submitted." Inter-state competition had, as usual, divided the tribes of greater Rāziḥ, and their perceived betrayal by the *shawāmi* tribes still rankled among the old men of the *yamāniyah* in 1980. Rifts were also created *within* tribes. Shaykh Jubrān b. Jubrān Qāsim of al-Naẓīr, for example, was famously betrayed to the Idrīsī by members of his own tribe for "plotting to sell out to Imām Yaḥyā," and was imprisoned in Ṣabyā for thirteen years.

By late 1914, therefore, Imām Yaḥyā had taken all Jabal Rāziḥ, "partly by bribes, partly by force," as one man put it. Soon after, he ordered Abū Nayb to build a fort on the summit of al-Jabal in al-Izid, where it overlooked all southern Rāziḥ and even Sāqayn in Khawlān. In 1980, older Rāziḥis still associated this sturdy panoptic structure with its famous builder and with a major turning point in their history—the inauguration of strong Ḥamīd al-Dīn rule.

The state-tribe relationship was, as usual, reconstructed by contracts—referred to as "treaties of state rule" (*qawāʿid al-amr* or *qawāʿid al-ṭāʿah*). The Naẓīrīs, for example, pledged their loyalty to "the learned ruler (*al-malik al-ʿallāmah*) Imām al-Mutawakkil ʿalā Allāh" and his *nāẓirah* for Rāziḥ, Sayyid Muḥsin al-ʿAwāmī, promising to adhere to their *qawāʿid* with Abū Nayb, and to cooperate in tax collection, hostage arrangements, law enforcement, and if necessary *jihād* (D1914; D1915). Imām Yaḥyā kept some hostages at al-Qalʿah, and others in Sāqayn, where his *nāẓirah* for "Qaḍā Khawlān ibn ʿĀmir" was then based, and in al-Sinnārah, a fortress near Ṣaʿdah (D1915). Tribal pacts from those early years of Yaḥyā's rule show Rāziḥī leaders trying to persuade the new regime, as it flexed its muscles and asserted divine authority, that tribal governance was effective, and that they were loyal, God-fearing subjects (D1917; D1918; D1919; D1921b).

With the end of the First World War and the Ottoman occupation, state fortunes were transformed. Imām Yaḥyā received administrative and military aid from the Turks—some of whom stayed in Yemen to help him build his state. (A significant new benefit was the Turkish telegraph system, which, with radio, revolutionized communications with distant provinces.) As the imām's power waxed, the Idrīsī's waned. The massive British aid Muḥammad ʿAlī al-Idrīsī had received during the First World War collapsed; and after his death in 1923 his polity was further weakened by disunited leadership (Bang 1996: 115).

Following the historical pattern whereby Zaydī states were forged in "righteous" wars, in the early 1920s Imām Yaḥyā launched an anti-Idrīsī *jihād* aiming to regain territories which his Qāsimī ancestors had ruled

FIGURE 10.2
The fort of al-Dāmagh in southern Rāziḥ, 1980

in the seventeenth century. Much of the Tihāmah, including Hodeidah, was still under Idrīsī control, as were the Banī al-Ḥurrāth and most of ʿUqārib—although Banī Ṣayāḥ had sided with the imām. To ensure its security, Rāziḥ's Tihāmah entrepôt was again shifted to al-Muhaymilah in Naẓīrī territory, and the *nāẓirah* decreed that it should be jointly administered by the *ḥākim* and the shaykh of al-Naẓīr supported by named guarantors (*ḍumanā*) from each loyal tribe in Rāziḥ and ʿUqārib.[11] Then between 1925 and 1927, the forces of the imām's fearsome son, Aḥmad, including some Rāziḥīs, captured the rest of ʿUqārib (Jabal Shidā, Jabal Ḥijlah, and Jabal Ḥibrah) from the Idrīsī.[12] After this victory, Shaykh Jubrān Jubrān Qāsim was released from the Idrīsī prison in Ṣabyā and welcomed home to al-Naẓīr by an excited crowd firing guns, and chanting the following famous *maghrad*:

> Our warmest greetings to our Shaykh Jubrān
> With our long tresses and herbal wreaths
> He's spent thirteen years on the foreign coast!

During the battles for ʿUqārib some Rāziḥīs had sided with the Idrīsī, and Imām Yaḥyā took ruthless revenge on these rebels (*ahl al-fasād*), incarcerating them in al-Sinnārah and Sāqayn. They included two brothers from Ilt Shārah of al-Naẓīr who eventually died in prison "from broken hearts." In 1927 Ilt Shārah sued their tribe before the *nāẓirah* of Rāziḥ and leading local *sayyids* (including from Āl Muṭahhar) for the fines and expenses they had incurred while their men were imprisoned, claiming that the whole tribe of al-Naẓīr had sided with the Idrīsī, so should be collectively liable. The Naẓīrī leaders counter-pleaded that Ilt Shārah were liable because they had acted unilaterally, without their authority, and: "Everyone is responsible for the consequences of his own actions under God's law and according to government regulations (*qawāʿid al-amr*)." Ilt Shārah pursued their claims with the *nāẓirah* of Khawlān ibn ʿĀmir then in Sāqayn, then appealed to the *nāẓirah* of Rāziḥ, but all to no avail (D1930b).

Imām Yaḥyā also incarcerated Sayyid ʿAlī Ḥusayn al-Ḥūthī in Sāqayn, from whence he emerged years later a broken man. This was his punishment for serving the Idrīsī, and for his popularity; Rāziḥīs say, "We thought of him as like an imām." Such revered local scholars were a threat to Imām Yaḥyā, and their influence had to be reduced (see Haykel 2003:200). Presumably to this end, he dispatched *ʿulamā* from Zaydī centers on the plateau to teach *ʿilm* in Rāziḥ, some of whom stayed and intermarried with the local elites, including Āl Muṭahhar.

Naẓīrīs who had sided *with* the imām in the Idrīsī war, including its shaykh, sued their tribes for the expenses, injuries, and losses they had sustained "according to [the terms of] tribal agreements and collective responsibility, and agreements relating to state rule (*ḥasb ṣaḥab wa mukāfāh wa qawāʿid amr*)." Their petition was heard by the *nāẓirah* of Rāziḥ and a leading *sayyid* from Āl Muṭahhar, who upheld some of their claims (D1931b, D1933b). The long "claim and response" document (D1931a), which is endorsed by the *nāẓirah,* clearly shows that Imām Yaḥyā's officials fully accepted the legitimacy of *ʿurf* rules and practices, including the collective rights and responsibilities of tribes and wards. The adjudicators, for example, reject claims that the whole tribe of al-Naẓīr should contribute to the sustenance (*maraq*) of its injured men because, according to tribal law, this is the responsibility of their respective Thirds.

Strong Ḥamīd al-Dīn Rule

Imām Yaḥyā's hostilities with the Idrīsī ended when he abdicated sovereignty of ʿAsīr to Ibn Saʿūd in 1930 (Baldry 1973:281–283; Bang 1996:127), but they rumbled on with the latter, culminating in the Saudi-Yemeni war of 1934. Rāziḥīs were unavoidably involved in this conflict because of their proximity to the front. Members of Āl Muṭahhar and other local *sayyids* were among the imām's commanders, and some Rāziḥī *qabīlīs* fought for him under ungenerous conditions. Rāziḥīs also had to support mercenaries from Khawlān and ʿAmrān who were billeted on them; in al-Naẓīr these "hospitality expenses" (*ḍayfah*) were paid by its Thirds (D1934c).

After the war, the Treaty of Ta'if defined Yemen's border with Saudi Arabia, and in the northwest it skirted the ʿUqārib hills which remained in Yemen (Philby 1952). Jabal Shidā and Jabal Ḥijlah thus became frontier mountains, and the imām built or rebuilt forts on their summits, as he also did on Jabal Ḥurum. He also strengthened the fortress at al-Qalʿah, and enlarged the garrison by importing "Yemenis," thus reducing his dependence on local soldier-police (mainly Ghumārīs) whose loyalties to tribe and states had often conflicted. Yemen's southern border with the British Aden Protectorates had been delineated in 1905, and recognized de facto in 1934. Yemen thus acquired defined (if partially contested) international borders for the first time in history.

Having dealt with external threats and installed his officials in well-fortified buildings, Imām Yaḥyā set about consolidating his internal hegemony "less in the manner of the traditional imāmate than in that of an absolutist monarchy" (Peterson 1982:15)—he even named his domain "The Mutawakkilite Kingdom (*mamlakah*) of Yemen." Under this new rubric, which displeased Zaydī traditionalists (Haykel 2003:211–212), Imām Yaḥyā developed the strongest and most centralized state Yemen had hitherto known. He created a regular army, embryonic ministries, and an institutionalized judicial hierarchy. He tightened his personal control over *waqf* endowments, taxation, trade and commerce, land transfers, education, and

FIGURE 10.3
The fortress of al-Qalʿah in Ghumār, looking toward al-Naẓīr, 1980. The fort of al-Dāmagh can just be seen on the far horizon.

law enforcement. And he increased the state's grip on the legal system and sharīʿah pedagogy by formalizing and publishing Hādawī law, and developing colleges of religious and legal education to train his administrators.[13] Āl Muṭahhar sent their sons to some of these colleges, where they gained qualifications which ensured their continued government employment, and also built nationwide networks, including by marriage, with other prominent religious families—all of which reinforced their status and influence within Rāziḥ. Yaḥyā's "security" measures were harsh, but Rāziḥīs (like other Yemenis) admit they created nationwide order—"You could go anywhere in safety." While building state institutions, Yaḥyā continued the personalized, hands-on style of dynastic governance of his predecessors, receiving streams of daily petitioners.[14] He was also renowned, as was his son and successor Aḥmad, for his grasp of tribal organization throughout his domain, and for remaining *au fait* with the shifting power plays and alliances of even the remotest tribes.

Imām Yaḥyā adopted Ottoman administrative divisions and nomenclature nationwide, and adapted them to embrace Rāziḥ. Though renamed and slightly reconfigured, state structures therefore remained essentially based on tribal geo-political structures. Khawlān ibn ʿĀmir became "The

Province (*liwā*) of Ṣaʿdah," and a governor (*ʿāmil*), treasury officials, and a supreme court were installed in the provincial capital.[15] Greater Rāziḥ became a "sub-province (*qaḍā*)," and continued to be presided over by a *nāẓirah* based at the *markaz* in al-Qalʿah. And *qaḍā* Rāziḥ was subdivided into two districts (sing. *nāḥiyah*) corresponding to ʿUqārib, which was administered from Jabal Shidā, and Rāziḥ (which included Jabal Rāziḥ and Jabal Ghamar) administered as always from al-Qalʿah.[16] *Nāẓirah*s were, as before, prominent *sayyid*s or *qāḍī*s from outside, as were certain other officials such as *waqf* supervisors and treasurers. But like his predecessors, Imām Yaḥyā also recruited prominent and well-educated local *sayyid*s as judges, administrators, and taxation officials. He also upheld the tribal method of selecting their leaders, and continued to depend on shaykhs, *aʿyān,* and hamlet *amīn*s for lower-level administrative services.

Imām Yaḥyā took a tighter administrative grip on Rāziḥ by requiring that the names of shaykhs and elders (*aʿyān*) be registered with the *nāẓirah,* commissioning censuses of each tribe which were compiled by shaykhs and authenticated by local *sayyid*s, and insisting that his officials ratify tribal agreements including shaykhship contracts (D1936a; D1938b; D1955). Appended to the contract of Shaykh ʿAlī ʿAlī ʿĪsa Faraḥ quoted in Chapter Four, for example, are notes from the *ḥākim* (a senior member of Āl Muṭahhar) confirming that he has seen and approved it, and from the *nāẓirah* at al-Qalʿah attesting that the signatories of the contract are good and reliable men (D1936a). This illustrates, in microcosm, the structure of local governance in Rāziḥ under the imāmate: elders representing their tribes appointed their shaykhs; and the appointments were approved in turn by a *sayyid* official of Rāziḥī origin, then by the governor of Rāziḥ, who was always an outsider. Local *sayyid*s thus continued to be a crucial link between the state and the tribes.

While Imām Yaḥyā sought to dominate other *sayyid* clans, especially those whose learning and reputations threatened his ascendance, he also needed their cooperation. He therefore seems to have adopted a kind of divide-and-rule policy of favoring Qāsimī *sayyid*s over others, simultaneously defusing the former's potential rivalry while exploiting their valuable local experience, knowledge, and connections. To this end, around 1937 his officials ordered Sayyid Muḥsin ʿAlī Yaḥyā of Āl Muṭahhar to list all the *sayyid bayt*s of Rāziḥ and confirm their pedigrees (*ansāb*) and therefore status credentials.[17] It is striking that Muḥsin ʿAlī organized his report (D1937a) geo-politically. He starts with *yamānī* Rāziḥ, then taking each family in turn (beginning, of course, with his own), first states the hamlet or area in which its members live, then traces their pedigrees back to Imām al-Qāsim and (when possible) to the Prophet's son-in-law, ʿAlī ibn Abī Ṭālib, citing books, family papers, and tombstone inscriptions in evidence. He then does the same for *shawāmī* Rāziḥ. This shows that the religious elite conceptualized their social identities spatially as well as genealogically, and identified their clans with specific settlements and tribes, just like other status categories whose culture they shared.

Muḥsin ʿAlī died the following year (1938), and his tombstone, carved with his pedigree back through Imām al-Qāsim to ʿAlī b. Abī Ṭālib, stands in the graveyard in front of his former home, Bayt al-Dawlah—testifying to the enhanced importance of proving *sayyid* and Qāsimī status at that period. Shortly afterward his collateral, Muḥsin Aḥmad (later *ḥākim* of Rāziḥ under the republicans), decided to rename his clan "Bayt Abu Ṭālib" after its prestigious apical ancestor, Aḥmad "Abū Ṭālib," b. al-Imām al-Qāsim. This, he told me, was in order to link his family with the better-known Abū Ṭālib clan near Sanaa. Despite their former support for the Idrisi, members of Āl Muṭahhar/Bayt Abū Ṭālib were the main Rāziḥī *sayyids* to whom Imām Yaḥyā awarded posts in Rāziḥ and other parts of the Province of Ṣaʿdah. By this patronage he ensured their dependence on, and support for, his regime, and helped maintain his supply lines of local information.

On 17 February 1948 Imām Yaḥyā was assassinated by order of a coalition of traditionalists and modernists who wanted a new style of Zaydī government. The former resented, among other breaches of Hādawī ideals, Yaḥyā's illegitimate designation of his son Aḥmad as his heir apparent (*walī al-ʿahd*) (Haykel 2003:211); the latter were disaffected by his isolationist policies, which were retarding Yemen's economic and social development. Aḥmad nevertheless gained power, dispatched his rivals by execution or imprisonment, proclaimed himself imām, and continued and intensified his father's policies from his capital in Taʿizz.

Only days after the failed coup the *nāẓirah* of Rāziḥ gathered "all its people and social classes (*tabaqāt*)"—defined as "*sayyids* and commoners, shaykhs, elders, and ordinary people (*sādāt-wa-ʿarab mashāyikh-wa-aʿyān wa afrād jār-wa-qarār*)"—to request their allegiance (D1948). This was quickly given; Ḥamīd al-Dīn rule was firmly established, and there was now no tempting rival. By 26 February the tribe of al-Naẓīr, represented by Shaykh Nāṣir Manṣūr, had drawn up their pledge of loyalty and taxes (*wājibāt*) to Imām Aḥmad, couched in the customary hyperbolic religious

FIGURE 10.4
Tombstone of Muḥsin ʿAlī Yaḥyā of Āl Muṭahhar (died 1938), with his inscribed pedigree, 1977

rhetoric, and compiled their optimistic conditions of allegiance. These are redolent of respect for the contractual relations and commitments on which their system is built: existing tribal and tribe-state agreements (*qawāʿid al-ṣaḥab bayn al-qabāʾil wa qawāʿid al-ṭāʿah*) should be upheld "because they reduce problems and ensure peace"; shaykhship contracts and sūq treaties should be observed; "shaykhs should get a fifth of the *zakāt* [i.e., twice their previous stipend], as agreed for the shaykhs of ʿUqārib, because they accepted the imām's rule willingly and without trouble"; the state treasury (*bayt al-māl*) should pay for the upkeep (*maṣrūf*) of hostages; heirs should control the proceeds of family *waqf*s; and shaykhs, not government police, should be responsible for delivering up criminals (D1948). Despite the state's increased strength, tribal leaders evidently felt empowered to try to negotiate terms which would safeguard their structures and practices. This confidence stemmed from knowing that they had the backing of their tribes, and that their system was still administratively indispensable to the state. This is strikingly exemplified by the hostage system—ironically, the very mechanism which enforced tribal subordination.

The Hostage System

There are interesting parallels between the state practice of demanding boys as hostages (*rahāyin,* sing. *rahīnah*) and the tribal procedure of taking sureties (sing. *rabākh*). In both cases something cherished is placed in hock to express submission to politico-legal authority, and that authority is or was supposed to reciprocate with fair governance. Tribal leaders therefore obstructed the process and demanded changes when rulers broke their side of the bargain—including with regard to where hostages were kept, which was a repeated source of dissension (D1897; 1904b). Most of the time, however, the submission and support of hostages was an orderly, regulated procedure, like the submission of *rabākh*s, with terms and conditions which were clearly understood by both sides.

Hostages were selected according to tribal structures, and supported using tribal practices. "The government asked each tribe how many divisions it had," a Naẓīrī elder explained, "and demanded *rahāyin* from a leading *bayt* in each." So al-Naẓīr, for example, submitted four hostages, one from Ilt Faraḥ (the shaykh's son or another boy), and one from a leading clan in each of the Upper, Middle, and Lower Thirds. Smaller tribes submitted only two hostages. Each hostage did a stint, then was replaced by another from the same leading clan or another. Imām Yaḥyā kept his first hostages for two years. "Our families did not dare try to retrieve us," explained one ex-hostage, "because they were so afraid of the imām." Tribal leaders then pressured the imām to "rotate" (*dāwal*) the hostages every three to five months, to which he agreed. The state supported the hostages, though frugally, with food and pocket money. Eventually it also contributed half of the generous monthly stipend (*ijrah* or *rahn*) with which the hostage's family was compensated for the loss of his labor—the other half being paid by their tribe. Some families lived off this money, while wealthy leaders used it to "hire" the sons of poorer families as proxy hostages to avoid sending their own. These stipends can be considered a form of political bribery by which the state rewarded tribal leaders for their loyalty; and this was cleverly achieved partly at the expense of their tribes.

Contributions to hostage stipends were collected by the same methods as other corporate subscriptions; hamlet *amīns* listed names and adjusted contributions according to means (D1937b; D1947). As the hostage system became routinized and institutionalized, it had a reciprocal effect on tribal structures and methods. As a Naẓīrī observed: "The division of our tribe into Thirds became more important, because they were responsible for sending hostages and paying their stipends." The fact that *ijrahs* were a regular, predictable expense also led to adjustments in tribal administration; special posts were created and groups were redefined. In al-Naẓīr, for example, an elder in each Third was designated its "hostage agent" (*walī al-rahan*) and charged with collecting hostage subscriptions (sing. *farq al-rahīnah*) from its members. The tribe was also subdivided, for the purposes of collecting *ijrahs*, into "fifths" (*akhmās*)—two each in the Upper and Middle Thirds, and one in the less populous Lower Third. This sometimes necessitated adjustments to ensure the equitable distribution of subscriptions to hostage dues. Thus in 1933, the Naẓīrī leaders did a "census of subscribers" (*ḥisāb al-gharrāmah*) and redistributed (*tardīd*) some *jīrān* (butchers and poor recent immigrants) in the Middle Third to the single "fifth" of the Lower Third (only on paper, of course). They also confirmed the concentric rings of responsibility for law enforcement, and (specifically) the extraction of hostage dues:

> Each Third is responsible for its offenders (*khāmil*) and those closest to them (*qarīb*). And those nearest [meaning the clan or "fifth"] have primary responsibility (*al-aqrab fī al-aqrab*) for delivering them up or arresting them (*fī taqrīb wa ḍābiṭ*). (D1933b)

In his endorsement at the head of the paper, the *nāẓirah* adds that *jīrān* should pay only half what others pay, and invokes the tribal rule that subscriptions should be graded according to means, adding that the poor should not be overburdened.[18] In a system obviously susceptible to corruption, he was defending tribesmen against the potentially extortionate demands of their leaders.

The hostage system shows how easily the tribal structures of Rāziḥ could be harnessed to new administrative purposes. It also demonstrates how social systems can be created and re-created in the collective consciousness. In time people internalize and reify new structures, and start thinking of them as "natural" entities with obvious significance. Older Naẓīrīs, looking back on this period, clearly thought of themselves then as "members" of "fifths," as well as of clans, Thirds, and tribes. Hostage agents (*awliyā al-rahan*) also joined the ranks of tribal leaders, and began to be mentioned as representing their tribes—together with *aʿyān* and *mashāyikh*—at the head of agreements (D1936a). The hegemonic tool or "technology" for this restructuring and rethinking was the centrally important tribal institution of corporate subscription, adapted, in this instance, to state purposes.

Law Enforcement

The tribal system also remained vital to Imāms Yaḥyā and Aḥmad for law enforcement. Despite the state's increased powers of coercion, its officials continued to depend on coordinating with tribal leaders, and held them responsible for dealing with transgressions within their domains or by their constituents according to tribal law. They also required them to allow government police into their territories, or to deliver up their offenders for trial or imprisonment in al-Qalʿah. Tribal leaders, for their part, strived to protect their roles and positions by embellishing their pacts with florid assurances of their loyalty and obedience to imām, governors, and *hākims*, and acknowledging that sharīʿah law must be obeyed. At the same time, they repeatedly asserted their adherence to tribal agreements and the validity of their terms, and their determination to deal with "their" offenders in accordance with *both* tribal and government regulations (*qawāʿid*). This dual concern of placating a more powerful *dawlah,* and upholding the cherished principles and practices of tribal law, can be discerned in pacts from this period which were partially written for the eyes of the *nāẓirah,* who usually endorsed them. The modes of tribal governance and conflict resolution did nevertheless change. More disputes appear to have been submitted to *ḥākims* rather than to shaykhs or *maradds*. And inter-tribal demonstrations and wars were apparently banned and ceased.

Changes also took place in law enforcement. The main instrument of coercion of the Ḥamīd al-Dīn imāms was the *tanfīdh,* literally "execution [of duties]," which I translate as "coercive billeting"—a method which goes back to at least the eighteenth century (Serjeant 1983a:85), and has survived (as we have seen) into the republican era. The essential feature of *tanfīdhs*, then as now, is that the police billeted themselves on the alleged offender, who had to feed them, provide them with qāt, pay their daily wages and travel expenses (*masāfah*), and if necessary accommodate them overnight. These expenses were supposed to force a criminal to admit his crime, or a defaulter to pay outstanding fines or taxes. If a suspect was subsequently declared innocent, he was theoretically reimbursed these costs (though this could be difficult). But if he was guilty, then he or his group had to pay. If *tanfīdhs* failed to achieve their purpose, then the culprit was imprisoned until he complied.

The *tanfīdh* procedure strikingly resembles tribal modes of law enforcement in several respects. First, it constitutes a kind of legalization of the hospitality code. A pseudo-friendly relationship is created between suspects and officials; it is often necessary to slaughter an animal; and the two sides are bound by commensality, which would not be the case were a fine, for example, just paid at the door. Second, the police are directly reimbursed for their services, in an ad hoc way, just as *ḍumanā* are rewarded with the meat of slaughter-beasts and food trimmings, and their fees and expenses. Third, the culprit's costs escalate the longer he resists complying with the law, as do fines in *ʿurf*. It is not therefore surprising that Naẓīrīs assimilated *tanfīdhs* to the tribal procedure of coercive slaughtering in the following legend. This tells how an (unidentified) imām ordered a *tanfīdh* against an entire village, symbolized by a tree:

> The body of a man was discovered near a village. The imām asked the villagers who killed him, but they claimed ignorance. So the imām tied up a tree next to the village, and sent a *tanfīdh* to the tree. The policemen sat round it and demanded animals from the villagers, and they ate and ate until all their animals had been slaughtered. Then the villagers began to starve, and they delivered up the killer.

The *tanfīdh* system undermined the tribal law-enforcement procedures it resembled by partially usurping the functions of the *ḍumanā*. At the same time it underpinned the authority and power of shaykhs, who could summon police against a transgressor (or political rival) in their tribes, knowing that the *nāẓirah* would usually back them up without necessarily knowing the facts. By having *tanfīdh*s at their beck and call, shaykhs could flaunt their powers to their own constituents, while reassuring state officials that they respected their authority.

The *tanfīdh* system subdued and scared Rāziḥīs at this period, and could be abused, but it was not systematically deployed as ruthlessly as in non-tribal Lower Yemen, where it was a notorious instrument of extortion and persecution, and a major cause of resentment against the Ḥamīd al-Dīn imāms (Douglas 1987:13, 66). This, I suggest, is because the tribal system deterred tyrannical behavior. Tribes and their sub-groups could organize against shaykhly oppression, and resist it by defaulting on subscriptions, refusing orders, threatening defection, or even using force. It was therefore in the interests of a state which still depended on co-opting shaykhs and tribes to wield its (increased) powers of coercion with restraint, and for governors to show respect for tribal leaders and *ʿurf*. Imām Yaḥyā's first *nāẓirah* in Rāziḥ, Sayyid Muḥsin al-ʿAwāmī, was the epitome of such a governor in the nostalgic eyes of Shaykh Nāṣir of al-Naẓīr, who admiringly described how he employed *ʿurf* to defuse a potentially explosive situation after two Rāziḥīs and a Yemeni policeman were killed in a fight. What the shaykh particularly appreciated was not only that al-ʿAwāmī ordered tribal *diyah*s to be paid, and contributed from the treasury, but also and mainly that he required a bull and two sheep to be slaughtered as amends for each death.

> So that's what they did, and that put everything right and that was the end of it. *He* was a *real* governor (*ʿāmil aṣlī*). All we get now are the deaf and the blind (*ʿamā wa ṣamā*). Nowadays someone wounds someone, then just pays some *riyāl*s—and that's it!

Shaykh Nāṣir's final grumble contrasts al-ʿAwāmī's exemplary behavior, as he saw it, with that of certain republican governors who have failed to understand or respect tribal custom, especially the symbolic value of slaughtering. In the eyes of an old shaykh, money fines on their own are inadequate and insulting because, in contrast to ritual slaughter, they have no moral content and do not heal wounded relationships.

Taxation

Imāms Yaḥyā and Aḥmad strived to tighten their control over tax collection, to which end they sent tax supervisors to Rāziḥ from outside, presumably hoping that their loyalties would be primarily to the state, though they tended to settle and intermarry with leading local families. However, like all their predecessors, they also depended on local personnel to operate the system. Rāziḥī *sayyids*, mainly from Āl Muṭahhar (Bayt Abū Ṭālib), acted as tax inspectors and overseers (sing. *kāshif, murāqib*), did accounts, and maintained registers of tax payments and property sales (which were now taxed), for which they received an annual stipend. And shaykhs helped enforce the law against tax defaulters or cheats, using tribal methods, and oversaw various aspects of tax collection. For these and other services (*khidmah*), they continued to be paid a fraction of the *zakāt* of their tribes, still called the "return" (*marjūʿ*), which ranged from a twentieth to a fifth according to their political importance. In al-Naẓīr this was split half-and-half between the shaykh and *aʿyān,* and regarded as their wages (*ṣarf*). Under the supervision and guarantees of shaykhs and *aʿyān,* hamlet *amīn*s, who had intimate local knowledge of landholdings and cropping patterns, acted as assessors (sing. *ṭāyifī, mufaqqil*); they estimated yields before harvest-time, and oversaw the measuring out of the tithe on threshing floors. They then recorded the *zakāt* due from each taxpayer, checked payments, and made lists using the same well-worn methods as for collecting tribal subscriptions. Taxpayers had to deliver their taxes to designated government stores by donkey or camel on an appointed day. Some of the grain tax was centralized at al-Qalʿah in a huge government silo (*makhzān*), and the rest was stored in the household *madāfīn* of trusted men in different areas of Rāziḥ, for which they received a share of the grain. This avoided unnecessary transportation expenses, for the grain tax was, as usual, mostly distributed locally in salaries, in welfare payments, and in loans (sing. *ṣilfah*) during droughts which farmers repaid when harvests improved. Much of the grain tax was converted to cash by being sold on to grain traders, so the state often profited from droughts when prices soared. Many local people were therefore involved, in some capacity, in the taxation economy—as had always been the case—giving them a material interest in upholding religious rule.

Despite the fact that Imām Yaḥyā had condemned the Ottoman exaction of religiously illicit market taxes, he and his son did so too; as Ghaleb

FIGURE 10.5
Measuring grain with a wooden volumetric measure (*thumānī*), 1977

drily notes: "The need for funds to maintain the authority of any existing [Yemeni] government has always overshadowed the consideration of legality."[19] To Rāziḥī consternation, after the establishment of the Yemeni-Saudi border in 1934 Imām Yaḥyā established a customs post (*jumruk*) at nearby al-Ḍayʿah, and charged dues on all imports and exports at this important entrepôt. The tribes held a crisis meeting, and decided that four men from each tribe should beat up the customs officials and destroy the post. Imām Yaḥyā reacted by increasing the number of hostages, and Shaykh Nāṣir went to Sanaa to appeal. In the latter's self-aggrandizing account of this encounter, the imām declared: "You flailed the tax collector like you flail barley!" to which Nāṣir retorted, "And now we are going to *slaughter* him!" As a consequence of his heroic stand, Nāṣir claimed, the imām returned the extra hostages, and "replaced the *jumruk* with a really *simple* one."

What Shaykh Nāṣir omitted to mention is that, as always, tribal leaders collaborated in collecting revenues at al-Ḍayʿah. They counted loads going up and down the mountain, verified contents, arranged inspections, and assessed and collected the dues on different commodities. Overall charge of tax collection at the entrepôt was, however, farmed out—"sold" in local terms—to the highest bidder, who paid the government an agreed fixed sum and kept the surplus. This system enriched tax farmers, encouraged coercive extortion, and enabled the imām to dissociate himself from responsibility for his agents' excesses (although *tanfīdhs* were sent against tax defaulters). The first man to "buy al-Ḍayʿah" was an outsider, a *qabīlī* from Hamdān Ṣaʿdah, who came to Rāziḥ as a poor soldier with Imām Yaḥyā. People enviously retail his rags-to-riches story: "All he had was a gun, and even that didn't work." He bought land all over Rāziḥ, and married twenty-one times into prominent families, including eight times into shaykhly clans and twice into Ilt Faraḥ. He also married his children into leading Naẓīrī families, and during the Civil War even married a daughter to a cousin (FBS) of Imām al-Badr while the latter's entourage was staying in his well-furnished home. In old age he settled in al-Ḍayʿah, but many of his family—known as Bayt al-Hamdānī—still live in the large house he built in the *madīnah* of al-Naẓīr, facing *dīwān* al-shaykh. He thus joined a long line of state-appointed officials, stretching back centuries, who were sent to Rāziḥ from other *bilads*, got rich, and forged alliances with the local tribal elite, and whose descendants became naturalized Rāziḥīs. After al-Hamdānī relinquished the *jumruk,* it was "bought" in turn by the shaykh of al-Naẓīr, other prominent Rāziḥīs, and a *qabīlī* merchant from Khawlān.

The Civil War (1962–70)

In September 1962 Imām Aḥmad died of natural causes and was succeeded by his son, al-Badr Muḥammad, whom he had designated his heir apparent—again in contravention of Zaydī doctrine. A week later, on 26 September, al-Badr was ousted in a military coup backed by army officers, intellectuals, *ʿulamā,* Shāfiʿī merchants, and certain tribal shaykhs. In contrast to the coup of 1948, this variegated coalition sought to demolish the imāmate, not merely the dynastic monopoly of Bayt Ḥamīd al-Dīn, and to replace it with a modernizing republic. Al-Badr fled into the northern mountains, and the Yemen Arab Republic (YAR) was declared. The country then descended into an eight-year Civil War (*thawrah*) between "republicans" (supported by Egyptian ground and air forces), who desired a new order, and "royalists" (supported by Saudi Arabian money and arms), who sought to preserve a modified status quo.[20]

Rāziḥ was once more sucked into inter-state conflict because of its position. In late 1963 Imām al-Badr met foreign journalists at the foot of Jabal Rāziḥ to dispel rumors that he had perished, and to announce his intention of regaining power (Schmidt 1968:48). And in late 1964 he sheltered in caverns on Jabal Shidā and Jabal al-Naẓīr (Schmidt 1968:182, 275), though later he alternated between bases in the northern Tihāmah and ʿAsīr. The imām's officials stayed in post, meanwhile, at al-Qalʿah, which was garrisoned by soldiers from Khawlān al-Ṭiyāl, and continued to collect *zakāt* and administer *awqāf*. Most Rāziḥīs were therefore "royalist" by default as well as by conviction and contractual allegiance. But a small minority openly and actively supported the republicans, and others undoubtedly did so secretly, variously motivated by resentment of *sayyid* power and privilege, exasperation at al-Badr's inadequacies, and a yearning for the development promised by the republicans. Yet others were simply "bought."

Tribes and families were, therefore, as usual divided. As described in Chapter Four, the shaykh of al-Izid's desire to support the republicans provoked a threat of secession to al-Naẓīr by one of its wards (D1963; D1968a). And the shaykhly clan of al-Naẓīr, Ilt Faraḥ, included an active royalist (Shaykh Nāṣir) and two active republicans, including Sulaymān ʿAlī ʿĪsā, a son of the former shaykh, who later became prominent in the development movement. *Sayyids* obviously felt threatened by all these upheavals. Sayyid Zayd Abū Ṭālib, who was a royalist commander (*qā'id*) during the *thawrah*, recalled the flurry of pact-making which took place between the tribes and "their" *sayyids*. "They called them treaties of solidarity (*waraqāt al-taḍāmun*), and gave us copies. Then if anyone tried to ignore them, we could hold them to their commitments." In one such pact, written several months after the Civil War ended in March 1970, the shaykhs, elders, and leading *sayyids* of al-Naẓīr pledge to support one another and maintain security, to hold clans and Thirds responsible for dealing with offenders, and to protect the honor and land of *sayyids* and respect their *tahjīr* contracts (D1970c). Many inter-tribal alliances were also reaffirmed during this insecure period.

Egyptian aircraft bombed Rāziḥ early in the war, causing many to evacuate their homes; then in 1964 republican ground forces invaded from the *shawāmī*, a gatekeeping tribe having allegedly "opened up" for them. They took the *markaz* at al-Qalʿah in battle, killing the imām's *nāẓirah*, then occupied the heights against minimal resistance, invested forts on strategic peaks, and billeted soldiers in people's homes, where they allegedly behaved rudely according to Rāziḥī standards of "guest" behavior.

The imām's commander tried to coerce the Rāziḥīs into resisting this occupation by confiscating their property and other means, but Sayyid Zayd persuaded him that they needed help. The royalists in ʿAsīr therefore channeled arms, ammunition, money, and food to trusted local officials (including Sayyid Zayd and al-Hamdāni, the aforementioned customs agent). "The new guns were labeled with crossed swords and palm trees," Shaykh Nāṣir recalled. "There is no God but God, what wonderful arms they were! So I said, these are *all* for al-Naẓīr." But Sayyid Zayd had a more equitable solution. "The tribes were squabbling over who should get the guns. So I divided Rāziḥ into fifths according to an old method used when the whole region was fined, and I distributed them accordingly." The "fifths" in this particular fractional allotment were Ghamar, Munabbih, Izdī-and-Naẓīrī, ʿUqārib, and "the rest." Other Naẓīrīs remembered the imām giving SR100 and a gun to whoever would support him. Flour was also sent into Rāziḥ, and the imām's agents doled it out to local women who baked bread for the soldiers just as they do in tribal wars. Rāziḥīs were thus enabled and motivated to mount their resistance during the winter of 1964–65. Shaykh Nāṣir:

> Kohlānī [the *nāẓirah*] called up the shaykhs of Rāziḥ, and we pledged (*taʿāhadnā*) that if the imām "raised his head" [to support and lead them], we would strive together to expel the republicans. So we were *committed* (*rābiṭīn*) . . . and all the shaykhs [whom he named] pledged to mobilize their men on the same night.

After hauling ammunition and cannons up from the Tihāmah, the Rāziḥīs planned a concerted attack under cover of darkness on the forts invested by the republican soldiers and the houses in which they were billeted. "As soon as we agreed on the plan," Shaykh Nāṣir claimed, "I wrote to my allies in al-Naẓīr instructing them where to station themselves [to combat republican sympathizers]." Two days of fierce fighting ensued; many republican fighters defected, and others retreated. The royalists then besieged al-Qalʿah, but the republican commander, al-Sukkari, refused to surrender "until the first of Ramaḍān" two months later. He then emerged with his companions, and asked shaykhs from two *shawāmi* gatekeeping tribes to conduct him safely out of the massif. However, his escorts betrayed his trust, killed some of his group, and stole their guns, though he survived. A *sayyid* commented, "It was a huge disgrace (*faḍīḥah*). He thought they were peace-loving and honorable tribesmen, but he was terribly mistaken." Rāziḥ then returned to royalist "control" until after the Civil War, though there was little effective state government.[21]

It will have been noted that the structure of command in war replicated and reinforced that of peacetime administration. The operations in Rāziḥ were formally commanded, as on other royalist fronts, by "princes" of

Bayt Ḥamīd al-Dīn under the imām's authority. They in turn instructed leading local *sayyid*s whom they designated military leaders (sing. *qāʿid*), who included Zayd Abu Ṭālib, as mentioned, and ʿAlī b. ʿAlī Ḥusayn al-Ḥūthī, the son of the revered *ʿālim*. And these men, in turn, coordinated with local shaykhs who directed their respective tribesmen. The *thawrah* also bolstered the tribal system by increasing firearm ownership, activating customary methods of military mobilization, and empowering and enriching shaykhs. Like shaykhs elsewhere in Yemen (Dresch 1984b:169; Lichtenthäler 2003:57), those of Rāziḥ continued to receive gifts and trade concessions from Saudi Arabia after the Civil War. For example, Saudi officials in ʿAsīr gave Shaykh ʿAwaḍ Manṣūr of al-Naẓīr authority to award (or withhold) trading licenses for all Rāziḥīs. Such privileges helped shaykhs survive the transition into the republican period. However, they were not sufficient to magnify their power and influence on the national stage, as was the case with leading Ḥāshid and Bakīl shaykhs, who had larger followings, were based nearer the capital, and had sided with the republicans during the Civil War.

CHAPTER ELEVEN

The Republican Period

Rāziḥ Joins the Republic

Rāziḥīs realized they must accommodate to the republican state. But they still regarded the state-tribe relationship as subject to negotiation and contractual agreement, with reciprocal commitments. In early 1970, therefore, soon after the Civil War ended, they drafted the terms of their capitulation. These expressed their perennial political and economic concerns, all obviously intensified in the radical new circumstances. The government, they stipulated, should: rule justly according to the precepts of Holy Law; appoint only religious and reliable men, and dismiss corrupt ones; administer *waqf*s as their creators intended; extract only *zakāt,* not customs dues (*jamārik*) "lest people abandon the area"; appoint Rāziḥīs as police and border guards, and pay their wages and upkeep; and seek shaykhly permission to send *tanfīdh*s, and not overcharge for them. They also insisted that "the tribes of Rāziḥ" should be respected "like Ḥāshid-and-Bakīl and the rest of Khawlān ibn ʿĀmir," and that local *sayyid*s (referred to as *hijar*) should be as protected and respected as any other Rāziḥī. This was a highly sensitive issue after a revolution to eradicate their ascriptive privileges, and reflected the local reverence for *ahl al-bayt,* the close integration of *sayyid*s in local society, and the plethora of pacts they made with the tribes during the Civil War. Other demands express a longing for modern amenities—roads, schools, hospitals, water pumps, mechanical ploughs, a central telegraph system "so people with grievances can notify the authorities," and even a branch passport office in Rāziḥ "to facilitate travel to Saudi Arabia and elsewhere." Rāziḥīs had clearly grasped the fundamental difference between this modernizing state and the imāmate, which had obstructed development and provided negligible material services in return for taxes. Altogether, their utopian wish-list conveys a pragmatic willingness to create a cooperative relationship with a government they had recently violently opposed—on condition they benefited and their system was preserved.

Because of his age, experience, and reputation for toughness, Shaykh Nāṣir of al-Naẓīr was delegated to submit these terms, and in September 1971 he and his retinue sallied forth to meet the government's representative, Shaykh ʿAbdallāh al-Aḥmar, in a spot north of Ṣaʿdah specially selected with security in mind. In consequence of al-Aḥmar's huge following as "paramount shaykh" of all the Ḥāshid tribes, and his key role on the republican side during the Civil War, he had become speaker of the Consultative Council (*majlis al-shūrā*)—the legislative assembly of the Yemen Arab Republic established earlier that year.[1] Shaykh ʿAbdallāh purportedly addressed Shaykh Nāṣir with a wonderfully appropriate coffee metaphor: "Oh, Uncle Nāṣir, don't fill [the coffee pot] with husks" (*yā ʿamm Nāṣir, lā tilqimhā qishr*), meaning "use pure beans (*ṣāfī*)"—in other words, make me your best offer. Shaykh Nāṣir presented him with Rāziḥ's conditions, and he endorsed them (D1971a; D1971b). Thus did Rāziḥ formally and peacefully submit to the republican government. Pledges of allegiance presumably followed soon after.

The new government was weak, and preoccupied with building central institutions, so it made few changes to the former administrative divisions, and in the far north they remained much the same. They therefore continued to be based on tribal structures (Steffen et al. 1978:I/42, 45). The Province (*liwā*), later "governorate (*muḥāfaẓah*)," of Ṣaʿdah still encompassed Khawlān ibn ʿĀmir (plus Hamdān Ṣaʿdah, which is part of Bakīl); and greater Rāziḥ remained a sub-province (*qaḍā*). But Qaḍā Rāziḥ was now subdivided into two districts (sing. *nāḥiyah*): one comprised ʿUqārib and Jabal Rāziḥ, which (in a symbolic act of state appropriation) was renamed "Shidā and Ghumār" after the sites of the two government "centers" (sing. *markaz*); the other was "Ghamar." The *qaḍā* tier of administration was formally abolished in 1976, but Rāziḥīs had long internalized this government structure, and (as mentioned) continued to think of their region as "Qaḍā Rāziḥ" into the 1980s.

As before, senior posts were filled by a mixture of educated, high-status outsiders and men recruited locally, including *sayyids*. This was in conformity with the government's policy of "national reconciliation" after the Civil War, whereby they absorbed former royalists (excluding members of Bayt Ḥamīd al-Dīn) into their administrations (Stookey 1978:254–255). Governors (now called *ʿāmil* instead of *nāẓirah*) tended to be *qāḍis* or high-ranking *qabīlīs*, but many other important posts were filled by *sayyids*—notably members of Bayt Abu Ṭālib, who (as we have seen) became the *ḥākims* of Rāziḥ, and secured other leading positions within Rāziḥ and elsewhere in the Province of Ṣaʿdah. This was a consequence of the same factors that had always favored them—education, governmental experience, connections, and specialized local knowledge.

Below these upper administrative tiers, headed by government-appointed officials, were three lower tiers, named "sub-district" (*ʿuzlah*), "village" (*qaryah*), and "hamlet" (*maḥallah*), headed by locally chosen traditional leaders—shaykhs, *aʿyān*, and *umanā*. These smaller structures were imposed nationally, on paper, regardless of regional variations in settlement patterns and forms of organization. However, since each *ʿuzlah* was explicitly intended to comprise "a set of villages whose major inhabitants belong to one tribe (*qabīlah*) headed by a shaykh" (CPO 1974–75), in Qaḍā Rāziḥ there was a high degree of fit, and most of its *ʿuzlahs* correspond to tribes—apart from five which correspond to large wards. The term *ʿuzlah* did not, however, replace *qabīlah*, as appears to have happened elsewhere (Morris 1985; Tutwiler 1987).

The new regime, like the old, required shaykhs to supervise taxation, and to maintain order in their respective tribes by the application of tribal law, the legitimacy of which was explicitly upheld in successive national constitutions provided it did not contravene sharīʿah law.[2] Shaykhly stipends continued, and were initially based on a fraction of the *zakāt* of their tribes, as before, though they later took the form of monthly salaries. This change correlated with the decline in grain production and consequent reduction in grain tax, and the aid the government was receiving from Saudi Arabia, other foreign governments, and international agencies, which more than compensated for reduced tax revenues.[3] A Muslim government had to be seen to collect religious dues, however. So individuals were allowed to self-assess their *zakāt*—a custom called *bil-amānah* (see Messick 1978:171)—

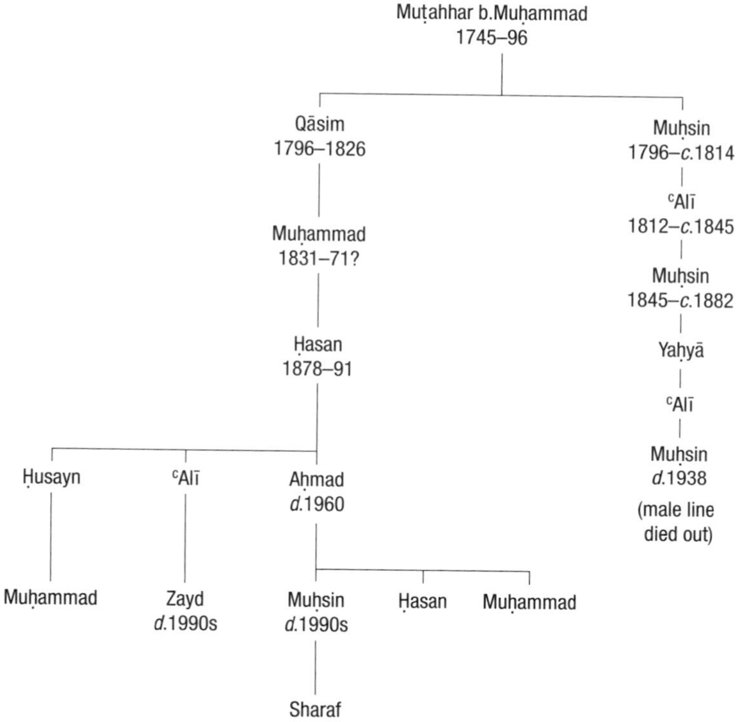

FIGURE 11.1
Simplified genealogy of part of Āl Muṭahhar/Bayt Abū Ṭālib, showing *sayyids* alive during fieldwork and mentioned in this work. Dates indicate when politically active

and on specified days announced in local sūqs Rāziḥīs paid their religious dues on agricultural produce and other earnings voluntarily, and mainly in money, directly to their local *amīns*; and they listed their contributions and sent them to Ṣaʿdah. The fiscal role of shaykhs was therefore reduced. The importance of customs dues, by contrast, greatly increased from the late 1970s, which particularly enriched and empowered the shaykhs of al-Waqir who controlled the Tiḥāmah entrepôt. The problems this created in Rāziḥ, culminating in the inter-tribal "War of al-Ḍayʿah" in 1985, were described in Chapter Eight. As we saw, this crisis exposed the state's relative impotence in solving inter-tribal conflicts, and the perennial desire of the tribes to preserve their efficacious procedures, as they see them, and keep the state at bay.

During the 1980s the government tightened its bureaucratic grip on shaykhs by insisting they collect their pay and activate other privileges through a "Department of Tribal Affairs" (*maṣlaḥah shu'ūn al-qabā'il*) in Sanaa (a branch later opened in Ṣaʿdah). This necessitated having their shaykhship contracts stamped by the governorates of Rāziḥ and Ṣaʿdah, and applying for an identity card confirming their shaykhly status. In addition, they were required to have all important *qawāʿid* endorsed at the local and provincial courts. Shaykhs were also symbolically assimilated into the state administration by being given uniforms with pips indicating rank, though only Ibn Ghalfān junior of al-Waqir ever wore this alien garb to my knowledge. While increasing its control of tribal leaders and activities, therefore, the republican government still upheld the principle of hereditary leadership, each tribe's right to choose its own leaders, and the contractual basis of tribal politics.

The first republican governors of Rāziḥ held little sway, and some just sat in al-Qalʿah doing token work and amassing fees and bribes. However, if they were too unjust and corrupt, or threatened local interests, shaykhs complained and sometimes got them replaced.[4] Governors were so weak in manpower and other resources that they had little choice but to allow shaykhs a relatively free hand in running their tribes, and as we have seen they generally complied with shaykhly requests for *tanfīdhs* against offenders or rivals. As under the imāmate, access to this instrument of coercion reduced shaykhly dependence on external guarantors to reinforce their internal positions and decisions (as mentioned in Chapter Ten), and also undermined the ability of shaykhs to restrain their peers—enabling some abuses. Shaykhs, at their best, acted as a buffer against greedy and exploitative government officials; at their worst they manipulated them to quash dissension and competition within their tribes, and increase their own power. Overall, the situation of state weakness strengthened shaykhs—particularly those with special clout such as the self-styled "shaykh" of Ghumār, from whose ward the Rāziḥī police were recruited as had been requested in the terms of capitulation, and the shaykhs of al-Naẓīr and al-Waqir, who controlled major markets.

The cooperation between state and tribes was regularly punctuated by disputes which revealed the tensions in their changing relationship. These were resolved by shaykhs and *sayyids* in customary ways. In one case during my fieldwork in the late 1970s, for example, a leading Rāziḥī shaykh fired at the Governor of the Province of Ṣaʿdah while the latter was visiting

Rāziḥ, not of course intending to hit him, but as a protest at his allegedly siphoning off money collected for road construction, and his insulting jibe that all *ahl* Rāziḥ were "like women." Many Rāziḥīs felt this act of symbolic violence had put a bad and tactless official in his place, shaykhs of several tribes met in the senior *ḥākim*'s *dīwān* in al-Naẓīr, and the crisis was quietly resolved by negotiation.

A year or so later a man from Banī Maʿīn visiting Ghumār accidentally rammed the governor's car—never a wise move. The culprit ran off to escape punishment, and a policeman fired a warning shot to stop him. Banī Maʿīn took umbrage, claiming this shooting infringed tribal law, and demanded a gun *rabākh* from Ghumār because the incident had taken place on its territory. However, the governor, a *qabīlī* from Ḥāshid, purportedly declared, "I'm familiar with tribal law, and all Ghumār needs to do to make amends is slaughter a sheep for Banī Maʿīn." Naẓīrīs admired this invocation of tribal procedures, but Banī Maʿīn were not mollified. They accused the governor of illegitimately ordering the shot to be fired, and he responded that he was only doing his job, and demanded that Banī Maʿīn produce witnesses and take oaths that their man had not been trying to evade justice. Hearing this, Sayyid Zayd of Bayt Abū Ṭālib, on leave from his post in Jumāʿah, sped off to al-Qalʿah and mediated between the governor and the tribe. Underlying such incidents was the desire of the tribes to defend their prerogatives and resources against the encroaching state and its often inadequate officials, and the desire of officials to assert their authority over the tribes and benefit financially from their temporary hardship postings in a remote and uncomfortable region.

The Development Movement

It was essential for the legitimacy of the fledgling YAR state that it deliver basic social and infrastructural projects to its glaringly undeveloped country. While government struggled to build central institutions to that end, impatient communities took matters into their own hands, and with typical Yemeni resourcefulness adapted traditional forms of ad hoc cooperation to more ambitious, "modernizing" goals. From the early 1960s, and most dramatically after the Civil War, scores of small, grassroots, self-help "Local Development Associations" (LDAs) (sing. *taʿāwun ahlī lil-taṭwīr*) sprang up spontaneously, and spread by example throughout the country, manifesting the popular desire for motor tracks, schools, health facilities, and water and electrification schemes.[5] Incapable of implementing such projects itself, the government encouraged these informal and diverse organizations and initially allowed them autonomy. Then in 1973 it appropriated and hierarchized them by incorporating them, through provincial Coordinating Councils chaired by provincial governors, into a nationwide umbrella organization called "The Confederation of Yemeni Development Associations (CYDA)," of which the President of the Republic was elected president.

CYDA became the government's instrument for dominating and regulating LDAs, and thereby extending state hegemony throughout the country. CYDA summoned LDA representatives from the provinces to large annual conferences in Sanaa, attended by ministers; it supervised and coordinated LDA projects; and it imposed rules and procedures on LDAs with regard to planning, auditing, and triennial elections. The government also encouraged LDA activities by exempting heavy equipment, such as bulldozers, from customs dues, and more important, by allowing half the local taxes, as well as state and foreign aid, to be channeled to LDAs via CYDA. This revenue was invested mainly in roads and schools, and was supplemented by government. This policy simultaneously encouraged tax payment and tapped the remittances of men working in Saudi Arabia; people were more inclined to pay up because they could see the benefits to themselves.[6]

The overall effect of the organization and financing of the Rāziḥ LDA was to reinforce the tribal system while accentuating inter-tribal disparities in wealth and influence, and predictably stimulating competition for control of funds and projects. Since the government had decreed that there be one LDA for each *nāḥiyah* or *qaḍā,* one was established for Qaḍā Rāziḥ. The tribal regions of ʿUqārib and Rāziḥ therefore continued to be joined in one state-defined administrative entity, and were not separated or fragmented for development purposes. Election methods, furthermore, underwrote tribes as the key local structures. CYDA rules decreed that each LDA have a policy-making committee, grandly titled a "General Assembly" (*jamʿiyyah ʿumūmiyyah*), constituted by electing one member from each five hundred to eight hundred of the population. In Rāziḥ this was organized on a tribal basis on instructions from above: "A government representative told us to choose about three or four members from each tribe, depending on its size." Tribes therefore held public meetings, and chose their assembly members by a show of hands. This method obviously favored the most populous tribes, as well as elite men with a sense of entitlement which their social subordinates were too diffident to challenge publicly. The outcome was that, at the first LDA elections in 1975 (the first "general election" in Yemen's history), fifteen or sixteen tribes of Qaḍā Rāziḥ chose forty-eight General Assembly members, of whom five came from al-Naẓīr. These men then (also according to the rules) elected from among themselves a nine-man Executive Committee (*hay'ah idāriyyah*) to organize the LDA and its projects—some as paid officials—and a president (*ra'īs al-ta'āwun*) to represent them on the Coordinating Council in Ṣa'dah.

This new electoral process for "modern" objectives maintained the traditional grip on community affairs of the tribal and religious elite, including members of Bayt Abū Ṭālib. At the same time, however, it tilted the balance of power toward their *shibāb,* and away from older power-holders. In particular, there was a discernible popular will to try to prevent shaykhs from increasing their power through control of LDAs, which happened elsewhere.[7] "Butchers," who presumably exercised self-exclusion, were not represented. Al-Naẓīr dominated the Rāziḥ LDA, which was first headed by a Naẓīrī merchant from a minor *sayyid* bayt, who had little effect, then by presidents (elected in 1975 and 1978) who were both Naẓīrī *qabīlī*s. The first was an ambitious young charismatic merchant, Ḥusayn 'Askar, who embodied the popular desire for a dynamic agent of change. His candidature was vigorously supported by fellow *shibāb* from leading *qabīlī* bayts, and by Bayt Abū Ṭālib, who wanted to block Ilt Faraḥ (the shaykhs of al-Naẓīr). His appointment aroused the jealous ire of Ilt Faraḥ, who—in shameful abuse of tribal and shaykhly values—resorted to criminal violence. This conflict was settled by slaughtering in the market, oath-taking, and eventually government intervention. When the second LDA president was elected, Ilt Faraḥ gained the influence they desired, for the successful candidate was Sulaymān 'Alī, the member of their clan who had supported the republicans during the Civil War, and had since held government posts in other provinces and, according to admirers, "emerged a poor man"—meaning he had not been corrupt. Because of his excellent links to the center, he was seen as a potentially influential broker of outside aid, which he proved to be.

While the institutional aspects of the Rāziḥ LDA were dominated by *shibāb* from leading *sayyid* and *qabīlī* bayts, its equally important, less formal, manifestations were dominated by the older guard of tribal leaders. Far from the tribal system's being a conservative obstruction to development projects, as anti-tribal stereotypes would have it (Burrowes 1987:60), it proved vital to their implementation. The drive to conserve political structures does not necessarily correlate with a desire to obstruct material improvement—especially when the latter is a popular cause. This was most conspicuously demonstrated with respect to the construction of motor tracks—the priority project for Rāziḥīs because of their trading interests. The construction of the main state-sponsored track from the eastern plateau to Rāziḥ, and through the Rāziḥ massif, proceeded in fits and starts, with often long delays caused by quarrels over the direction it should take, thieving bulldozer drivers, charges of embezzlement, and even sabotage. Whenever problems occurred, the shaykhs of the tribes concerned assumed that it was their duty and prerogative to try to solve them, and duly held meetings to sort things out with LDA and government officials and local notables, who sometimes acted as mediators. In 1977, for example, when the track had reached the border of Rāziḥ, a dispute broke out between Ghamar and Banī Asad about routing. The shaykhs of *shawāmī* Rāziḥ convened a large meeting in a tent at the roadhead, and invited Sayyid Zayd ʿAlī Abū Ṭālib to arbitrate a settlement. He later told me that this had been an easy problem to resolve compared with crises involving honor or spilled blood. The government might have seen "tribalism" as the problem, but they also saw that its traditional methods could deliver solutions.

Key tribal practices were also vital to "self-help" development. The direct contributions which communities were required to make toward government-sponsored motor tracks were organized on a tribal basis according to the principle of corporate subscription. Thus each tribe contributed, through the LDA, toward that segment of the track which passed through or skirted its territory. Furthermore, as the main trans-Rāziḥ track proceeded and was eventually completed (in 1981), each tribe, or sometimes ward or neighborhood, autonomously financed the construction of numerous branch tracks to their many settlements. The Naẓīrīs, for example, extended the main track from the *madīnah* down to their border with al-Waqir, near al-Ḍayʿah, at the foot of their mountain (as mentioned in Chapter Eight). These activities gave tribal leaders an important role outside the formal LDA structure. Not only did they regularly collect subscriptions from their own constituents toward hiring bulldozers and drivers and buying dynamite, but they also negotiated expense-sharing arrangements with neighboring tribes. When the Birkānīs wanted to build a branch track off the Naẓīrī-financed track, for example, Ilt Faraḥ negotiated a contribution from them toward al-Naẓīr's original outlay. Tribal principles of corporate subscription and mutual aid were also activated to buy land to build schoolrooms, top up the meager salaries of Yemeni and foreign teachers posted to Rāziḥ, and help the drivers of crashed or overturned cars. Each tribe also took responsibility for maintaining the tracks which ran through their respective territories, including clearing landfalls, for which passing drivers tipped them. Tribes and their members thus adapted to the challenges of radical infrastructural change, and functioned like organizations of "civil society" or state institutions. In the context of rapid development and all its attendant problems, therefore, tribal structures and practices were reinforced—first by being activated, and second by proving relevant, indeed indispensable, in fulfilling local needs.

President Ibrāhīm al-Ḥamdī (1974–77), who rose to power as head of CYDA, hoped to popularize and strengthen his rule by bypassing local notables and shaykhs (whose stipends he curtailed), and raising a new class of LDA-based functionaries—activist, modernist "youths" (*shibāb*) who would depend on government patronage (Burrowes 1987; Lutz 1992). However, he fatally underestimated the resilience of traditional elites, and the remarkable adaptability of the tribal system, not to mention individuals, to changing economic and political circumstances. His short-lived policy of trying to undermine the tribes, and exclude their leaders from state governance, was also counteracted by the Saudi government's policy of subsidizing tribal leaders in order to influence Yemeni politics—even as they simultaneously (and contradictorily) supported al-Ḥamdi's efforts to strengthen and centralize his state.[8] These subsidies have continued to the present, and are a major underlying factor in Yemeni politics.[9]

Al-Ḥamdī's policies predictably provoked dissension, and in summer 1977 plateau tribes (from Ṣaḥār and Sufyān) blocked the Sanaa-Ṣaʿdah road in protest. Rāziḥīs were feeling peripheral and neglected, and were anxiously awaiting bulldozers al-Ḥamdī had promised. The shaykh of al-Naẓīr therefore made an announcement in the sūq publicly dissociating his "peace-loving tribe" from the disruptive activities to the east. "That will get back to the government through the governor," a Naẓīrī commented. On National Day in September, Naẓīrī schoolchildren also paraded with Yemeni flags before local dignitaries. But nothing came of their efforts to ingratiate themselves with the government, for in October 1977 al-Ḥamdī was assassinated.

In 1978 an advisory "People's Constituent Assembly," which included tribal representatives, elected ʿAlī ʿAbdallāh Ṣāliḥ as president of the Yemen Arab Republic. Like his predecessors, he was also elected president

FIGURE 11.2
Rāziḥī dignitaries gathered for school celebrations on Republican Day, September 1977. From left to right: Sayyid Zayd Abū Ṭālib, Abū ʿAwthah (the shaykh of Banī Maʿīn), Sayyid Ḥasan Aḥmad Abū Ṭālib, Shaykh Ṣāliḥ Nāṣir (of al-Naẓīr), and Ḥusayn ʿAskar (head of the Local Development Association).

of CYDA. ʿAlī ʿAbdallāh was as aware as al-Ḥamdī had been of the organization's potential for legitimizing and strengthening the state. But he also realized that major shaykhs could not be excluded from power, and incorporated them into government. He then proceeded to exploit LDA election procedures to help build his nationwide power base, "The General People's Congress (GPC)," which later transformed into Yemen's dominant political party (Carapico 1998:38).

In 1980, Rāziḥ received its first official visitation by a republican delegation, and the excited Naẓīrīs arranged an impressive demonstration; they paraded placards inscribed with their wish list of projects; children recited religious texts; dignitaries delivered speeches; and the poet Muḥammad Yaḥyā Ibrāhīm read a poem (*qaṣīdah*) he had composed beseeching the government for aid. The Naẓīrīs treated the visitors to a lavish banquet followed by a qāt party, for which they collected subscriptions of SR100 from each adult male. Officials made promises, and a delegation of shaykhs went to Sanaa to chase them up. But little was forthcoming.

FIGURE 11.3
Ṣāliḥ Nāṣir of Ilt Faraḥ (*center*) provides hospitality for his supporters, 1980

Under the president's patronage, and fueled by remittances and aid, LDAs reached their zenith in the early 1980s when there were more than two hundred nationwide—roughly one for each *nāḥiyah*. But thereafter they declined. The government shifted responsibility for local projects onto provincial and local governors, presumably to empower them; and it co-opted LDA representatives into government, and made them automatic members of the General People's Congress, undermining their popular credibility. Finally, after legislation in 1985, cooperatives became subject to the policy directives of the Ministry of Local Administration in Sanaa. Thus was a vigorous grassroots movement stifled by the dead hand of central control.[10]

In May 1990, the territory of the Yemeni state expanded to almost its seventeenth-century extent when the Yemen Arab Republic merged with the People's Democratic Republic of Yemen to the south to form the Republic of Yemen. Major adjustments took place, but government administrative structures were unchanged in the north, although local governors were renamed "District Directors" (sing. *mudīr al-nāḥiyah*), and districts "Directorates" (sing. *mudīriyyah*). However, provincial staff increased, and started to assert government will and presence more forcefully.

Yemen faced serious economic problems as a result of world recession and several drought years in the late 1980s, and the crisis worsened after the government failed to condemn Iraq's 1990 invasion of Kuwait. In reaction western and Gulf states curtailed aid, and Saudi Arabia expelled its Yemeni guest-workers. Remittances stopped, unemployment soared, and the Yemeni riyal plummeted. It was in this context that ostensibly "religious" discord, which had been simmering in Rāziḥ for several years, came to the boil. As so often before, outside events exacerbated internal conflict, families and tribes were divided, the state displayed its might, and shaykhs and tribes reacted by asserting their powers and identities.[11]

A Clash of Fundamentalisms

During the 1970s and 1980s, certain men from the Ṣaʿdah region and Rāziḥ converted to Wahhabism while living and studying religion in Saudi Arabia, or fighting with the *mujāhidīn* against the Russians in Afghanistan. From the mid-1980s, leaders of this reformist, puritanical school of Sunnī Islam propagated their beliefs through lesson circles, mosques, and colleges in their native *bilāds* in explicit opposition to Zaydism. A Wahhabi teaching center developed near Ṣaʿdah, and Rāziḥī converts founded a religious college in the *madīnah* of al-Naẓīr, built or took over several mosques, and gained key posts in government schools. These activities were encouraged and financed, as elsewhere in Yemen, by the then Wahhabi-controlled Ministry of Religious Guidance (*irshād*), by Saudi and Yemeni business figures, and by the Yemeni Reform Grouping (*iṣlāḥ*)—a variegated coalition of tribal, religious, and mercantile figures, headed by Shaykh ʿAbdallāh al-Aḥmar, who were mainly united by their opposition to "secularist" socialism.[12]

One of the remarkable features of the Sunnī-Wahhabi movement was that it flourished in the birthplace and heartlands of Zaydī-Shīʿism. This was largely because it tapped a hitherto dormant resentment of key tenets of Zaydī doctrine still manifest there—especially the *sayyid* claim to religious authority and social superiority on the grounds of religious descent, which Wahhabis felt contravened Islamic ideals by promoting inequality.[13]

The most public and active converts to Wahhabism in Rāziḥ were *shibāb* from some *qabīli* and most "butcher" families. These young men, who were struggling to find work and marriage payments, and were traditionally subordinate to their elders and "betters," were attracted to Iṣlāḥ (which they equated with Wahhabism) by its welfare program, and to Wahhabism by its egalitarianism. They credited their education for their conversion. In contrast to their mostly illiterate fathers, who had depended on religious specialists for guidance, they had attended the first secondary schools (which opened in Rāziḥ in the 1980s), and had studied the Sunnī texts then flooding Yemen and formed their own opinions. One convert explained: "We could read books the imāms had forbidden and disparaged before the revolution. They prevented access to 'the truth' in order to maintain other people's inferiority." Some of these *shibāb* had also learned to deride certain Zaydī beliefs and practices as "superstitious" and "illogical" while working in Saudi Arabia. They also questioned the authenticity of *sayyid* pedigrees, and condemned *sayyid* marriage prohibitions as reinforcing social hierarchy.

Many Rāziḥī shaykhs also supported Wahhabi-Sunnīsm. They resented their unequal marriage relations with *sayyid*s, and being humiliatingly rebuffed when they applied to marry *sharīfah*s. They also hoped the pro-shaykh and anti-*sayyid* thrust of Iṣlāḥ would strengthen their positions and bring material benefits, as had happened among shaykhs in the Ṣaʿdah region (Lichtenthäler 2003). In contrast to the activism of the *shibāb,* however, their support for Wahhabism was prudently tacit and passive. It was also ambivalent. Their positions are underpinned, like those of *sayyid*s, by descent-based clans, hereditary entitlement, and strategic marriage alliances with other high-status families, including those of leading *sayyid*s to whom they had married daughters. They could therefore hardly embrace egalitarianism or renounce the descent principle. *Sayyid*s were quick to exploit this Achilles heel with taunts such as, "If you believe in equality so much, why don't you marry your daughter to a butcher?"

*Sayyid*s defended their refusal to marry their women "down" by citing the Islamic doctrine of *kafā'ah* (equality of marriage partners), and their fear that non-*sayyid*s might dishonor *sharīfah*s if allowed to marry them. They also reciprocally accused Wahhabis of heresy, of proselytizing a "foreign" *madhhab* for money, and of colluding with Saudi efforts to destabilize Yemeni society. Zaydism, they asserted, was the authentic "Yemeni" *madhhab,* and they its prime upholders. This marked a significant shift in the geographical construction of *sayyid* identity. Whereas they had formerly represented themselves as immigrant "northerners" (sing. *ʿadnānī*), and contrasted themselves with indigenous "southerners" (sing. *qaḥṭānī*), they were now emphasizing their "Yemeni" identity in order, presumably, to confirm that they were patriotic republicans.[14] This defensive adjustment should be understood against the general background of the growth of Yemeni nationalism, and in the specific context of Wahhabi claims (at least in Rāziḥ) that *sayyid*s were longing for the return of Imām al-Badr and the restoration of the imāmate—despite the fact that leading Zaydī scholars had taken the radical step of publicly renouncing the institution of the imāmate in 1990 (Bruck 1999; Haykel 1999:193). Other Zaydī loyalists insisted that it was unfair to vilify *sayyid*s indiscriminately, as many were admirable men. Overall, distinctions and qualifications emerged from the absolutist rhetoric; it was a debate.

In the difficult conditions during and after the 1960s Civil War, *sayyid*s had been unable to maintain their scholarly traditions (see Bruck 1999), leading to a dearth of religiously qualified *shibāb* from *sayyid* families. Into this vacuum stepped a number of charismatic young Zaydī *ʿulamā* of *qabīlī* background, who vigorously defended their beleaguered *madhhab* through teaching, preaching, and religious pamphleteering. Some of the leading lights of this Zaydī renaissance were from major *qabīlī* clans in al-Naẓīr, where they had begun their religious studies with Sayyid ʿAlī b. ʿAlī al-Hūthī and the *faqīḥ* Ḍayf Allāh Manṣūr before pursuing their studies in religious centers near Ṣaʿdah (see Haykel 1995; 1999). After al-Hūthī died in the late 1980s, Zaydī loyalists in al-Naẓīr enticed one of these scholars to return regularly from the *mashriq* to teach and preach by building him a house, for which they collected subscriptions, and by supporting him with charity (*ṣadaqah*). Many *ʿulamā* were similarly welcomed in the past when their succor and services were needed, though most such *muhājirīn* were *sayyid*s or *qāḍī*s. The fact that these new champions of Zaydism were *qabīli*s implicitly challenged *sayyid* dominance of religious scholarship. *Sayyid* supremacy was therefore threatened from within, as well as without, the Zaydī fold.

During this religious conflict, ritual became charged with immense symbolic and emotional significance—especially differences in Zaydī and Sunnī prayer methods previously dismissed as unimportant. Specific words and gestures became acts of mutual defiance and repudiation, leading to confrontations in mosques. And Wahhabis interpreted elements of Zaydī prayer as expressions of longing for an imām.[15]

From the mid-1980s, and in explicit reaction to the Wahhabi threat, Zaydīs began publicly celebrating ʿĪd al-Ghadīr—a profoundly significant feast-day for Shiʿites because it commemorates the Prophet's designation of ʿAlī ibn Abī Ṭālib as his successor (*khalīfah*).[16] The ceremony was held annually at Sūq Shaʿārah, the traditional tribal meeting-place in the center of the massif, "so that all the tribes could easily attend." As Zaydī-Wahhabi rivalry intensified the celebrations grew, and by the early 1990s hundreds of men were marching in procession from their respective tribes and congregating at Shaʿārah. There Zaydī *ʿulamā* gave rousing sermons extolling ʿAlī as their *khalīfah,* and men stomped in circles (sing. *ḥalīqah*), chanting *maghrads* and firing guns, to express their strength and solidarity. Religious loyalties were evidently being demonstrated in a tribal idiom, and tribal loyalties in a religious idiom, though Rāziḥīs saw these ceremonies (like the circumcision ceremonies they resemble) as predominantly religious.[17]

These clamorous gatherings unavoidably, and deliberately, flaunted Zaydī numbers and enthusiasm in the face of Rāziḥ's leading Wahhabi activist, Ibn Ḥayyān—an elder of Banī Rabīʿah who lived beside Sūq Shaʿārah. As the celebrations of June 1992 approached he waged an aggressive campaign to prevent them. On one occasion his supporters—including some from outside Rāziḥ—entered the Friday mosque of al-Naẓīr brandishing guns; Zaydī *shibāb* rushed for their weapons, and bystanders quickly intervened. People were outraged and frightened at "foreigners" "invading" Rāziḥ, not to mention mosques, with firearms. As the feast-day approached, shaykhs begged that the ceremony be canceled, but since they were suspected of Wahhabi sympathies, this only hardened Zaydī resolve.

The crisis then peaked. Just before the feast-day the son of Ibn Ḥayyān was murdered, and in a particularly disgraceful and cowardly way—anonymously and at night. The crime was also grossly disproportionate to the provocation. The situation was now explosive, and prominent Zaydīs rushed to Rāziḥ from their homes in Ṣaḥār to urge their co-religionists to cancel the celebrations and avoid further bloodshed. "They said the urgent thing was to placate the *dawlah.*" But their pleas fell on deaf ears, and the Zaydī activists defiantly congregated as planned—heavily armed to deter their opponents. To everyone's relief, however, the ceremony passed off peacefully, and the following day (Zaydī) "representatives of all the Rāziḥ tribes" descended on al-Naẓīr to celebrate.

In the following days several tribes, including al-Naẓīr, deposed their pro-Wahhabi shaykhs "for fomenting trouble," and replaced them with Zaydī loyalists. The hereditary principle prevailed; all the new shaykhs were chosen from shaykhly clans. The Naẓīrīs chose Shaykh ʿAwaḍ's son, Ṭayyib. Since leading Zaydīs lived in their tribe, they needed a strong leader who could defend them against accusations of being implicated in the disgraceful murder, and he had demonstrated the requisite qualities.

He had "offered proper hospitality on behalf of the tribe" when the Zaydī notables came from Ṣaḥār. And he had shown his mettle during the War of al-Ḍayʿah in 1985, when he had boldly confronted the enemy: "He was very brave then, and with no thought for the shaykhship."

In addition to the customary pledges of tribal unity, obedience to tribal and sharīʿah law, and allegiance to the state, Ṭayyib ʿAwaḍ's shaykhship contract (D1992a) contains new elements which reflect changes in the wider political environment. Yemen's first parliamentary elections were imminent, and, doubtless in reaction to the intensified democratic mood, the contract invokes a broad local electorate. Instead of recording that named tribal elders have chosen the new shaykh, as in imāmic times, it records that he has been chosen by "scholars, tribal leaders, and ordinary individuals" (*ʿulamā, aʿyān wa afrād*), and their hundreds of signatures are appended to the document, listed by category, in three long columns. The Naẓīrīs wanted to show the government that they had chosen Ṭayyib by a legitimate process which conformed with current national values, and to ensure that it would recognize his appointment and pay his stipend. At the same time their categorization of their tribal electorate affirmed both the traditional social hierarchy and the superiority of the religious elite, who appear under the heading "scholars" complete with the honorific *sayyid* prefixed to their names. However, this seemingly reactionary gesture also represents a shift in ideology and practice. The definition of *sayyid*s as "scholars" (*ʿulamā*) emphasizes the achieved, occupational aspect of their status. More significantly, their inclusion in the list of signatories casts them as participants in a key event of the tribal political process—the selection of a shaykh—in contrast to their neutral "outsider" role under the imāmate, when they only witnessed and ratified tribal agreements. Under local and national pressure, *sayyid*s were perhaps beginning to assimilate into the tribal system, and to relinquish (or at least downplay) claims to superiority based on holy descent.

The other significant new feature of Shaykh Ṭayyib's shaykhship contract are the endorsements, which graphically reveal the increased hierarchization and bureaucratization of the state since the 1980s. Instead of the agreement being simply endorsed by the judge (*ḥākim*) and/or the governor of Rāziḥ as before, it was processed and approved by no fewer than three government offices in addition to the *ḥākim*: the Ministry of Local Government in Ṣaʿdah, the Supreme Court of the Governorate of Ṣaʿdah, and finally the Department of Tribal Affairs in Sanaa, where it was filed. Like generations of his ancestors, the *ḥākim* of Rāziḥ, Muḥsin Aḥmad Abū Ṭālib, provided the crucial link between the grassroots appointment of a shaykh and its acceptance by the state with his authoritative confirmation based on local knowledge: "Shaykh Ṭayyib ʿAwaḍ has been chosen and elected by the agreement of the people."

A week later the new Rāziḥī leaders drew up an anti-Wahhabi defense pact, which is signed by "shaykhs, elders, and *ʿulamā,*" and is also (most unusually) thumbprinted—perhaps to avoid forgeries and false claims in this new era of photocopying machines. If this deliberately undated document (D1992b) was supposed to deter retaliation for the murder of Ibn Ḥayyān's son, it failed. Ibn Ḥayyān refused to accept *diyah,* fled Rāziḥ, and delayed his revenge until he had identified the culprit.

About six weeks later, in early August 1992, while several shaykhs were meeting in Shaʿārah to discuss the unresolved murder, they were astounded to behold twenty gun-mounted trucks and two armored cars rumbling along the narrow mountain track toward them. This was a flagrant breach of the usual courtesies; tribes expect government to warn them of important visits, and certainly before launching a military incursion. However, reassured that the vehicles were heading for the Saudi border (where there was international tension), they "allowed them to pass." Their true destination, however, was the *madīnah* of al-Naẓīr, where they parked in the marketplace before the new telephone exchange (the only government building), invested the surrounding buildings, and announced the reason for their unheralded "invasion." A rumor had reached them that Imām al-Badr (firmly retired in England since the Civil War) had "returned to Rāziḥ," and was being sheltered by Shaykh Ṭayyib. The government had evidently seized on this preposterous story (presumably propagated by Wahhabis) as an ideal pretext to flex its muscles in a peripheral region which had recently increased in importance because of border negotiations with Saudi Arabia. The Rāziḥīs responded by making a brave stand against state intimidation, and asserting their steadfast adherence to tribal values and leadership. The Naẓīrīs stationed armed men on rooftops with guns trained on the soldiers, though with reservations: "We were terrified that someone might fire their gun and shed blood, and that the government would send in troops or airplanes to wipe us out." And the participants at the Shaʿārah meeting, including Shaykh Ṭayyib, rushed through the mountains to al-Naẓīr in a convoy of vehicles bursting with armed tribesmen, and marched to the sūq yelling a *maghrad* extolling tribal solidarity:

> Our shaykh is the storm and we are his water channels
> The black-tressed [warrior] behind him should beware
> Worthless is he who opposes his fellow-tribesmen
> May the white [bitch] howl at his door

Despite a situation bristling with potential violence, both sides exercised restraint. No shots were fired, stalemate ensued, and as a Naẓīrī told it, "After three days we felt sorry for the soldiers, and gave them drinks and tough old chicken to eat!" Under this culinary offensive, and reassured that the rumor about the imām was false, the military retreated. In a parting gesture of state supremacy, however, they demanded that Shaykh Ṭayyib accompany them to Ṣaʿdah to help them with their enquiries into the murder of Ibn Ḥayyān's son. The Naẓīrīs were prepared to submit to state authority, but only on condition that tribal authority was reciprocally acknowledged—the age-old deal. They could not allow their shaykh to be ignominiously escorted from his domain by the army: "It would have insulted tribal honor, and they might have imprisoned him at al-Qalʿah on the way." They therefore insisted that he make his own way to Ṣaʿdah, and this was agreed. There he convinced officials that he was ignorant of the crime and was a compliant citizen and shaykh, and he returned to his tribe with his dignity intact and reputation enhanced.

After several months' investigations, Ibn Ḥayyān satisfied himself (rightly or wrongly) that his son's assassin was a *sayyid* from a minor branch of Bayt Abū Ṭālib who was employed as a policeman at al-Qalʿah. In deliberate contrast to the cowardly way his son had been murdered, he chose a moment when his suspect was on official duties, and shot him dead in front of the governor of Rāziḥ and several Rāziḥ shaykhs. Bayt Abū Ṭālib disowned their alleged criminal, and did not press charges. And the government exercised restraint. Eventually, the revenge killing was deemed to have equalized the original murder, and the matter was closed. Ibn Ḥayyān prudently emigrated to the *mashriq*.

Meanwhile, the religious conflict subsided. Both sides felt things had gone too far, and wanted to avoid provoking further government intervention. Partly for this reason, and partly because people were getting injured by celebratory gunfire, the ʿĪd al-Ghadīr celebrations became more muted and localized, and Wahhabis and Zaydīs concentrated on promoting their beliefs through religious colleges (Eagle 1995; Haykel 1995).

An important factor in the de-escalation of sectarian tension was that many of those divided by religion are closely linked in other ways. Leading Wahhabis are related by marriage to leading *sayyids*, including two with Bayt Abū Ṭālib; many families, houses, and hamlets also contain both Zaydī and Wahhabi activists. Those rent by religious belief in one situation therefore re-combined in others under different, overriding imperatives including duty to kin, neighbors, and fellow tribesmen—whatever their status category. This was evident even at the height of the religious conflict. During the armed confrontation in the mosque of al-Naẓīr, a Wahhabi convert defended his Zaydī uncles. When a Zaydī activist was imprisoned, a leading Wahhabi from the same tribe negotiated his release. And when a car full of *sayyid shibāb* from al-Naẓīr encountered a lone Naẓīrī "butcher" with Wahhabi connections being abused by government officials outside their *bilād,* they robustly stood up for him in the name of their shared "tribal honor." This was imperative, they explained, to show they came from a strong tribe, and to deter the officials from tampering with Naẓīrīs again. Though none involved in this incident were *qabīlīs*, in the context of state aggression they were united by common "tribal" values, and their awareness that their tribe is their safety net when the outside world turns hostile.

It is also interesting to note that the pattern of the Zaydī-Wahhabi conflict was typical of many tribal disputes. An escalating sequence of arguments and aggressive confrontations culminated in crises which, as soon as blood was shed or looked likely to be shed, were defused by people backing off or by third-party intervention. None of the aggressive or criminal actions which took place developed into serious or widespread disorder, despite their violent and escalatory potential. This manifestation of the Rāziḥī tribal ideal of the containment and resolution of conflict was contingent, in this instance, on the political context of an increasingly strong and encroaching state capable of delivering desired benefits or destructive punishment. No one wanted to deter state-bestowed development, nor to invite further state intrusions or curbs on local autonomy.

Tribal Conferences and National Elections

Shortly after unification in 1990, President ʿAlī ʿAbdallāh's new government sought to bolster its domestic legitimacy and power, and impress foreign governments and agencies, by liberalizing the press, allowing free political association, and increasing the democratization of the political process already begun with the LDA elections of the 1970s and 1980s. For a few heady years before the lid went back on the pressure cooker, people in all sectors of society enthusiastically explored their new freedoms.

Among these activities, in the early 1990s, were a succession of tribal conferences, the largest of which were attended by shaykhs representing scores of tribes. Speeches were delivered and poems read, and local shaykhs gave feasts and qāt parties. After these huge open-air gatherings, which sometimes lasted several days, proclamations were published. These expressed resentment of the government's playing tribe against tribe and provoking conflicts, and concern over selective and divisive Saudi patronage. Tribal leaders should, they asserted, be treated equally, without favoritism; and "foreign sources" should be prevented from subsidizing "certain shaykhs."[18] Some Rāziḥī shaykhs attended these conferences, which cannot fail to have boosted their confidence in the continuing legitimacy, relevance, and influence of "the tribes" in the republican state. They also joined networks of inter-tribal communication and understanding, the strands of which extended over most of North Yemen and into the South.

Following a national referendum on the constitution in 1991, the first national, multi-party parliamentary elections were held in 1993.[19] The country was divided into 301 constituencies (sing. *dā'irah*), each of which directly elected a delegate to the Council of Representatives (*majlis al-nuwwāb*), the single-chamber parliament in Sanaa. The boundaries of constituencies were supposedly drawn so that the numbers of eligible voters would be roughly equal, though were sometimes adjusted to favor the main parties. Whatever gerrymandering might have occurred elsewhere, however, the constituencies of the Province of Ṣaʿdah were based on its major tribal regions (apart from a separate constituency for the town of Ṣaʿdah).

The rules allowed any number of parties to compete, and any law-abiding citizen to stand. Fourteen candidates stood for Rāziḥ, of whom five secured party nominations while the rest stood as independents. All candidates were male *qabīlī*s from major clans of leading tribes—mostly from al-Naẓīr, Munabbih, and Maʿīnī-and-Asadī. Al-Naẓīr fielded the most candidates (five), of whom three were from Ilt Faraḥ. No *sayyid*s, low-ranking *qabīlī*s, or "butchers" stood for election, presumably realizing they stood no chance, or for fear of looking presumptuous. Women, of course, did not stand; nor did they vote, though officially allowed to. Because of social

FIGURE 11.4
Sūq al-Naẓīr in 1993. On the right is the new mosque, built in 1985, and at the far end the government telephone exchange. The new trans-Rāziḥ highway can be seen on the opposite mountainside.

pressures, therefore, the former religious elite kept a low profile, and the socially subordinate did not seize the opportunity to "get above themselves."

The election results reflected the burning local issues—mainly development, and the Zaydī-Wahhabi conflict—as well as tribal and personal loyalties which could not be publicly betrayed (voting secrecy was undermined by faulty balloting methods). It is noteworthy, in this light, that the victor and close runner-up were both development activists, and both from influential tribes in the *shawāmi* and *yamāniyah* respectively (Banī Maʿīn and al-Naẓīr). The victor was an active member of the ruling party, the Yemen President's General People's Congress, and people hoped by this connection that he would help Rāziḥ. The runner-up was Ḥusayn ʿAskar of al-Naẓīr, the above-mentioned former head of the Local Development Association, who had strong Zaydī and *sayyid* backing. He therefore split the vote with the official Zaydī candidate of the al-Haqq party, who was one of the new Zaydī *ʿulamā,* and from Ilt Faraḥ, the shaykhly clan of al-Naẓīr. Since other Zaydīs voted for the Yemeni Socialist Party candidate because of its anti-Wahhabi stance, the election confirmed the continuing dominance of Zaydism in the region. It also revealed that Wahhabis (most of whom can be assumed to have voted for Iṣlāḥ) constituted a sizeable minority.

The electoral innovations of the early 1990s did not challenge or undermine Rāziḥī tribal structures and their inequalities. In the delineation of constituencies, state and tribal geo-political conceptions remained congruent. The election also reinforced the notion of exclusive entitlement to high office of tribal elites, the inferior political status of weaker tribes and clans, and the continuing subordination of "butchers" and women. At the same time, the election reflected a major change: the political and religious eclipse of local *sayyids*. This overall picture was confirmed in the elections of 1997 and 2003.

The ideological significance of the elections for state-tribe relations in Rāziḥ was probably greater than their instrumental significance. The whole election process—the establishment of election committees, the definition of "constituencies," the registration of candidates and voters, and the implementation of complicated polling procedures—was a massive symbolic statement of state dominance. The state created and superimposed the structures and procedures, and the compliant populace submitted to them. By this participation, they re-acknowledged the republican state as the legitimate overarching power, and reaffirmed themselves as its loyal citizens. They also tied themselves more firmly to the center by another strand of dependency and obedience.

Conclusions

This work has identified the entities I have called "tribes," as the main units of governance in Rāziḥ. This key finding distinguishes the tribes of Rāziḥ from those in so-called "segmentary" systems, including the tribes of Ḥāshid and Bakīl, described by Dresch (1989:78), which have "no privileged level of organization that stands out in all circumstances." This study has also shown that the tribes of Rāziḥ can be regarded as sovereign polities within the tribal system. In this and other respects they are like micro states. They have well-defined territories with political borders and internal administrative divisions. Their populations comprise a mixture of natives, economic immigrants, defectors, and asylum seekers, and are socially and occupationally stratified. Tribes have permanent offices of leadership, and rituals and procedures for installing and rejecting leaders. Leaders administer and represent their tribes, have exclusive jurisdiction within them in matters of tribal law, control access to their domains, and mobilize men for defense or war. And tribes exist in a matrix of structurally equivalent, though politically unequal, mutually recognizing polities, and have intensive relations with one another which are contingent on proximity, interests, and economic and political circumstances. Tribes also enter into formal alliances to protect and promote their interests, and acknowledge supra-tribal courts of appeal. And all political relationships, at every level of the system, are based on written contracts, pacts, and treaties.

I mention these features in order to stress the governmental aspects of the tribes of Rāziḥ, but other politically important characteristics differentiate them from states. Most obviously they are part of states, and subject to their superior authority. They are tiny "face-to-face" polities with simple aims and administrations. Descent groups are fundamental structures, whereas modern states are more individuated. Their residents, groups, and settlements are closely interconnected by ties of kinship, affinity, and neighborhood. They are similarly structured and organized. And they share the same laws which generations of hereditary leaders have collaborated to formulate and uphold. This cultural and politico-legal homogeneity has profound and positive implications for mutual understanding and the resolution of conflicts, and has undoubtedly contributed to the remarkable longevity of this system of governance.

I have argued that the remarkable tribal system of Rāziḥ was shaped and sustained within a natural environment with good agricultural potential, the realization of which involves high costs and risks. We can speculate that, centuries ago, tribes formed in circumstances of population increase, pressure on land, and extensive terrace-building. When massive efforts are needed to construct and maintain resources, everyone's livelihood depends on them, and they are extremely vulnerable to natural disaster and social strife, then an effective regulatory system becomes imperative, though not of course inevitable, and a wide constituency has a vested interest in supporting it. Neither major investments in infrastructure nor permanent plantings are encouraged by endemic anarchy. Nor would traders embark on long treks, shoppers attend markets, or women venture out to work unless they could do so safely, and in confidence of redress if harmed. If rights in productive property are, furthermore, widely distributed, and the economy is organized by households, the system which emerges is more likely to be grassroots based, like that of Rāziḥ, than a top-down imposition by a powerful minority. It is in this context, we can suppose, that an ethos of cooperation and mutual aid developed which was formalized in a common law which places a material value on property and people, and exacts a price for harming them; that territorial polities formed, and institutionalized leadership became necessary to administer the law; and that a system of relatively consensual, highly participatory local governance emerged ideally geared toward the maintenance of order and security, the minimization and containment of violence, and the negotiated resolution of problems and conflicts.

Because of scarcity of land and the fragmentary effects of Islamic inheritance laws, tribal leaders were historically unable to accumulate sufficiently vast wealth to create powerful autocracies which could transcend the generations. Surpluses were sufficient, however, to sustain leadership hierarchies ideologically based on dynastic entitlement and popular choice, and materially based on ad hoc exactions from constituents and subsidies from rulers. Strong dynasties correlate with relatively weak leaders. This contributed to continuity in tribal governance, while simultaneously creating a perpetual tension between the peaceful interests of the majority, and the potentially disruptive interests of tribal leaders competing for influence, prestige, and the rewards of office. Though the power and wealth of leaders fluctuated, however, they always depended on the support of their constituents. When their autocratic or greedy ambitions threatened to undermine the very order they were charged with preserving, their peers and followers had recourse to various institutionalized means of protest and rejection. Any expansionist tendencies among leaders were also curbed by the realities of tribal administration within a rugged terrain where travel was, until recently, immensely difficult. No shaykhs, therefore, including structurally superior *maradd*s, seem ever to have risen above their tribal power-bases to claim much or all of Rāziḥ as their sovereign domain, nor do major amalgamations or "takeovers" of tribal domains appear to have taken place, though clans and wards occasionally seceded to other tribes. The names and number of Rāziḥ's tribes have therefore stayed remarkably constant over centuries, and they have remained small and apparently more or less within the same borders.

Shaykhs occasionally gained authority beyond the bounds of their own tribes through state patronage. *Maradd*s or other shaykhs were also appointed by their fellow shaykhs to act as supra-tribal arbitrators for the duration of inter-tribal disputes, or as spokesmen for all Rāziḥ with the government. Such ad hoc elevation should not, however, be confused with institutionalized political leadership; temporary administrative, mediatory, or representational authority must be distinguished from permanent rights of representation and jurisdiction over a sovereign domain. This is not always easy, partly because of the confusingly indeterminate use of the term *shaykh,* and because shaykhs themselves deliberately play on linguistic ambiguities in order to exaggerate their clout and attract state patronage. The potential for shaykhly aggrandizement has not, however, resulted in extreme or permanent disparities in shaykhly power in Rāziḥ, as has happened recently in the Ṣaᶜdah area, and over a longer period among the tribes of Ḥāshid-and-Bakīl.

I have further argued that the tribal system of Rāziḥ was also nurtured within a political environment of constant—but perpetually weak and poorly resourced—state rule. States were built from tribes, and all Rāziḥ's rulers until the end of the twentieth century depended on its tribal system to achieve their limited objectives of defending their territories and hegemony, collecting taxes, and maintaining law and order. All, therefore, superimposed their administrative structures onto the template of tribal structures, while sometimes dividing, aggregating, and recategorizing the latter for specific purposes. Each ruler introduced much the same kinds of judicial, tax, and law-enforcement officials, and these men coordinated in similar ways with tribal officials. Tribes and their wards were consistently treated as taxpaying units over the centuries, and under the Ḥamīd al-Dīn imāms, were additionally defined as hostage-giving units. Under republican rule, Rāziḥ also became a "development region," and an "electoral constituency," with its tribes in both cases continuing to be the main administrative units for state purposes. Throughout these changes, tribal institutions kept their "traditional" functions and identities, while being ascribed others by states.

Governors established and consolidated their rule by forging professional and marital relationships with the religious and tribal "establishment" of each region. They recruited selected *sayyids* for higher-level posts requiring religious learning—thereby defusing potential competition from locally revered men, and exploiting their local connections and knowledge. And this local religious elite was the key political link between the state at the apex of the pyramid of power, and the tribes at its wide base. States took tribes for granted as the main components of their "imperial" domains, recruiting shaykhs for lower-level administrative tasks, and rewarding them for their loyalty and services with a share of the taxes and other gifts. They thereby endowed tribes, incumbent shaykhs, and the ideology of hereditary leadership on which their dynastic monopolies were and are based, with impeccable religious legitimation, while creating co-dependent partnerships in the appropriation of surplus. Parallel religious and tribal dynasties were fused in this symbiotic relationship for centuries, the balance of power oscillating between them as *dawlah*s waxed and waned in wealth and power, foreign rulers threatened or attacked, and shaykhs exploited state conflicts to their own benefit.

It is important to appreciate that each state regime plugged into a tribal system which was *already organized* to fulfill similar goals to its own. It was not merely that the leadership hierarchies in each tribe could form a chain of downward command, but also that key tribal practices ideally suited rulers' needs. Because tribal law was geared toward maintaining the necessary order and security for the successful functioning of the local economy, it also protected the state's tax base—household-based agriculture and trade. More specifically, the tribal administrative methods of corporate subscription were ideally suited to the collection of taxes and (under the republic) the financing of development projects and the collection of census data. Customary methods for blockading and defending tribal domains, waging war, and compensating victims also served the purposes of militarily weak states under threat. Ironically, states even exploited the central tribal principle of collective responsibility in order to enforce their rule through the hostage system and *tanfīdhs*, and to punish tribes or their constituent groups for disloyalty or dissidence. In short, indirect rule—whether in collaborative or punitive mode—consistently supported and reinforced tribal structures and practices, while causing minor organizational, conceptual, and terminological modifications.

While states generally upheld the tribal system of Rāziḥ, ideologically and instrumentally, by taking its existence and legitimacy for granted, formally acknowledging its leaders as partners in governance, and exploiting its institutions and methods, they also periodically destabilized it. By rewarding shaykhs unequally according to their strategic positions and political circumstances, they created or enhanced disparities in wealth and influence between them, causing or exacerbating resentment and jealousy. And when states competed to control Rāziḥ or the adjacent Tihāmah and "bought" tribal allies, they inevitably created or widened rifts and enmities within and between tribes, sometimes provoking hostilities. In short, as Tapper (1991:52) has astutely remarked, while states sometimes had a "tribal problem," tribes sometimes had a "state problem."

The Rāziḥ case therefore challenges common assumptions about tribes and states in North Yemen, and the nature of their historical relationship. Yemeni rulers, and their officials and historians, have routinely portrayed "the tribes" as intrinsically anarchic, violent, and irreligious polities, and states as the only effective and legitimate sources of law and order, their attempts to govern constantly obstructed by fickle, warlike tribes inherently opposed to them. This must be understood as hegemonic propaganda. By their deride-and-rule stance, state regimes justified their subjection of tribes, while downplaying the extent of *state*-instigated violence, ignoring the religious ideals and governmental attributes of certain tribes such as those of Rāziḥ, and masking how profoundly rulers depended on them to achieve their administrative and military objectives.

Contrary to this typical anti-tribal propaganda, as I have shown, the tribes of Rāziḥ appear to have generally pragmatically accepted state rule, on condition rulers fulfill their religious and political ideals. This is partly because they believe Muslim states, like tribes, are ordained by God and part of the natural order of things; and because (until the republican era) they always had a religious overlord and believed in their religious obligations. Equally relevant to their submission to states are their environmental conditions. As cultivators they are tied to their land, and cannot retreat to territories beyond the pale of the state like nomads. Since they depend on trade, they must also accommodate to rulers who control their vital markets and trade routes. As significant in their compliance are the substantial rewards which shaykhs received for their cooperation with states. State recognition and material support gave religious legitimacy to shaykhly office, the tribal selection process, and the functions of tribal leaders, while simultaneously enhancing the power and influence of leaders, and their ability to implement state as well as tribal agendas.

Rāziḥī leaders and their constituents have therefore usually given their allegiance to rulers out of self-interested expedience as much as religious idealism; but they have also opposed those they regarded as unjust or illegitimate, or which flouted their principles or threatened their vital interests. The state-tribe relationship was a contract between two parties which shared the same political, religious, and legal culture (including "tribal law"), were well aware of each other's circumstances, and perfectly understood the reciprocal terms of their compact, and the possible repercussions of their breach. State vilification of tribal law as "heathen," and tribal dissension as irreligious and anti-state, was therefore disingenuous rhetoric.

Recent Trends

The tribal system of Rāziḥ persisted to the beginning of the twenty-first century because its legal and political functions remained locally relevant, and were not fatally undermined by the major economic and political changes of the 1970s–1990s—indeed, some were strengthened. The large-scale out-migration of young men to work in Saudi Arabia from the 1970s to 1990 posed a temporary challenge to the dominance of older men, but this was defused, among other ways, by inflated brideprices. Rich traders of all status categories emerged during that affluent period, but they did not collectively threaten the traditional leadership hierarchy; and the tribal (and *sayyid*) elite profited from trade and general prosperity too, including indirectly through fines and fees. Shaykhs and their associates also continued to be supported, materially and ideologically, by the republican state, which (like its predecessors) recognizes tribes as the key local polities with which it must articulate in order to maintain its rule and implement its agendas. Tribal leaders, for their part, assertively preserved their positions and methods, while adapting to, and exploiting, new situations. The drive to conserve political structures and practices does not necessarily correlate with a desire to obstruct material development, as some have assumed.

The power of *sayyid*s as a ruling class, by contrast, was destroyed by the 1960s political revolution. Individual Rāziḥī *sayyid*s maintained or gained official positions under the republic due to the same factors which always favored them—education, experience, and local and national connections. But the new state-sponsored ideology of egalitarianism, combined with the spread of literacy, caused a progressive, though uneven, erosion of the *sayyid* claims to superior status generally. The older generation of *qabīlī*s and butchers, raised in a culture of reverence for the Prophet's progeny, have been unable to discard their habits of deference. But many of the better-educated, better-traveled *shibāb* have more easily rejected such attitudes as old-fashioned and contrary to Islamic ideals—a process which was exacerbated by the surge of Wahhabism from the mid-1980s. Similarly, while older *sayyid*s cannot easily repudiate the duties and privileges of their birth or alter the associated behaviors, many younger *sayyid*s have conspicuously assimilated to ordinary *qabīlī* modes of dress and comportment—though some still retain a sense of social superiority and inherited religious duty. The social and political demotion of *sayyid*s, and the much-vaunted ideal of equality before God, has not, however, correlated with a promotion or eradication of the lowest social categories. The descent principle also continues to dominate social relationships, including marriage within and between social categories.

In the longer term, recent changes and trends must surely cause major transformations in the tribal system of Rāziḥ and the state-tribe relationship—particularly the development of transport, communications, and education, and the growth in state power. Rāziḥ is no longer a natural citadel in a remote, inaccessible province, days' or weeks' grueling travel from Ṣaʿdah or Sanaa. New roads mean that government officials and forces can now reach Rāziḥ within hours. The recent installation of a telephone network and modern surveillance apparatus also enables the center to keep well informed, and to issue instant instructions. The political significance of the dramatic topography in preserving Rāziḥ's relative isolation and independence has therefore substantially reduced. At the same time, oil wealth and foreign aid have greatly boosted the state's military capability. It could now easily blockade Rāziḥ's gateways, or enter the massif by force while maintaining its supply lines. It could also bombard it from the land or by air, as has happened in other regions—most recently in Ṣaḥār and Khawlān in 2004 and 2005.

As significant for the state's ideological and political penetration of Rāziḥ are the ubiquity of television, the establishment of state schools and health facilities, and the increased employment of Rāziḥīs locally and in other regions as (mostly low-level) government officials. Government control is also inexorably increasing. Shaykhs must now travel to Sanaa to collect their salaries. Local governors are exerting their will more forcefully, with central encouragement and backup. Censuses mean everyone is listed. And better policing at the local *markaz* and the frontier with Saudi Arabia means that customs dues, car registration, and other government demands can no longer be easily evaded. These changes have probably tilted the balance of power permanently toward the state, and bound the tribes of Rāziḥ more tightly to the center than ever before. In view of the continuing importance of tribes elsewhere in Yemen and the Middle East, however, it would be foolhardy to predict their imminent demise.

APPENDIX 1

Chronology of Events Affecting Rāziḥ: 1530s–1990s

1538–39	Ottomans seize Tihāmah. Start of coffee trade.
1540	Ottomans garrison Ṣaʿdah; probably occupy Rāziḥ.
1556–66	Khawlān Ṣaʿdah (*vilayet* Ṣaʿdah), including Rāziḥ, under the same Ottoman governor.
1566–72	Anti-Ottoman revolts.
1598	Imām al-Manṣūr al-Qāsim launches anti-Ottoman insurrection.
Early 1600s	Expansion of coffee trade in Ottoman empire; start of trade to Europe.
1606	Anti-Ottoman campaign in Khawlān south of Rāziḥ.
1613	Zaydīs expel Ottomans from Rāziḥ.
1618	Imām al-Qāsim appoints son Aḥmad "Abū Ṭālib" (d. 1655) to govern Khawlān Ṣaʿdah.
1622	Tax revolt in Khawlān Ṣaʿdah.
1626–27	Imām al-Mu'ayyad Muḥammad launches anti-Ottoman campaign; captures Abū ʿArīsh.
1635	Zaydīs expel Ottomans from all Yemen.
1644	Imām al-Mutawakkil Ismāʿil moves seat from northern highlands to south of Sanaa; appoints brother, Aḥmad "Abū Ṭālib," governor of Khawlān Ṣaʿdah.
1647–48	Zaydī imāmate embroiled in tax controversies.
mid-1600s	Expansion of coffee trade to Europe, Asia, and South America.
1654–60	Imām al-Mutawakkil Ismāʿil's expansionist campaigns in ʿAsīr and South Yemen.
1655	ʿAlī b. Aḥmad b. al-Qāsim succeeds father as governor of Khawlān Ṣaʿdah.
1676	ʿAlī b. Aḥmad resists Imām Ismāʿil's attempt to wrest control of Khawlān Ṣaʿdah; imām dies.
1677	Imām al-Mahdī Aḥmad confirms ʿAlī b. Aḥmad as governor of Khawlān Ṣaʿdah.

1686	"Al-Mutawakkil" ʿAlī b. Aḥmad of Ṣaʿdah proclaims his imāmate in opposition to Imām al-Mahdī Muḥammad; appoints his son Ḥusayn b. ʿAlī governor of Rāziḥ.
1690	Imām al-Mahdī Muḥammad appoints Sharīf of Mecca as his governor and tributary in ʿAsīr.
c. 1690	The Sharīf refuses to switch allegiance to Imām al-Mutawakkil ʿAlī of Ṣaʿdah, invades Rāziḥ, and is captured and taken to Ṣaʿdah. Zenith of the Yemeni coffee trade.
1691–93	Forces of Imām al-Mutawakkil ʿAlī of Ṣaʿdah revolt against Imām al-Mahdī Muḥammad, who captures Ṣaʿdah, then is expelled.
early 1700s	Europeans establish coffee-trading posts in Yemen.
1709	On father's death, al-Mu'ayyad Ḥusayn b. ʿAlī proclaims his imāmate in Ṣaʿdah in opposition to Imām al-Mahdī Muḥammad; appoints his son, Muḥammad Ḥusayn, governor of Rāziḥ.
1713/14	Al-Mu'ayyad Ḥusayn of Ṣaʿdah pledges allegiance to al-Manṣūr Ḥusayn of Shahārah, who is contesting the imāmate of al-Mahdī Muḥammad.
1714	Death of al-Mu'ayyad Ḥusayn of Ṣaʿdah; his son Muḥammad continues to govern Rāziḥ.
1720s	Yemen loses monopoly of international coffee trade; commerce hit as prices slump.
1728	Imām al-Manṣūr Ḥusayn of Sanaa appoints Sharīf Aḥmad b. Muḥ ammad b. Khayrāt of Abū ʿArīsh as governor of ʿAsīr Tihāmah.
1730	Sharīf Aḥmad of Abū ʿArīsh asserts his independence of Imām al-Manṣūr Ḥusayn.
1742	Sharīf Muḥammad b. Aḥmad of Abū ʿArīsh succeeds his father.
1745	Sharīf Muḥammad visits Muḥammad b. Ḥusayn of Rāziḥ; Muḥ ammad Ḥusayn dies, and is succeeded by his son, Ḥusayn Muḥ ammad "al-Sharafī."
1760s	Sharīf Muḥammad b. Aḥmad of Abū ʿArīsh conquers Yemeni Tihāmah.
1764	"Imām" Qāsim b. Yūṣuf of Ṣaʿdah tries to depose Ḥusayn "al-Sharafī" of Rāziḥ.
1765/6	Ḥusayn "al-Sharafī" crushes tax rebellion in Rāziḥ with help of Sharīf Muḥammad of Abū ʿArīsh.
1775	Ḥusayn b. ʿAli b. Qāsim becomes *dawlah* of Ṣaʿdah under Imām al-Manṣūr ʿAlī of Sanaa.
1776	The Banī al-Ḥurrāth threaten the Tihāmah entrepôt at al-Bār; Muṭahhar b. Muḥammad of Rāziḥ secures the support of Tihāmah *amīr*s (the Sharīfs of Abū ʿArīsh?).
1780	Violent conflict over Rāziḥī taxes between Ḥusayn "al-Sharafī" and his brother, Muṭahhar b. Muḥammad, allied with Ḥusayn ʿAlī Qāsim of Ṣaʿdah.

1790s	Sharīfs of Abū ʿArīsh control ʿAsīr Tihāmah and most of Yemeni Tihāmah.
1796	Death of Muṭahhar Muḥammad of *yamānī* Rāziḥ. Ḥusayn ʿAlī Qāsim of Ṣaʿdah and his forces enter Rāziḥ to control Ḥusayn "al-Sharafī."
1798	Major conflict between the *dawlah*s of *shawāmī* and *yamānī* Rāziḥ.
1801	Sharīf Ḥamūd "Abū Mismar" succeeds to sharīfate of Abū ʿArīsh, then loses it to the pro-Wahhabi Amīr of highland ʿAsīr (Abd al-Wahhāb "Abū Nuqṭah"), who appoints him as his governor.
1804–1805	Wahhabis occupy Tihāmah.
1805–1818	Sharīf Ḥamūd of Abū ʿArīsh controls most of Tihāmah, including Ḥodeidah; repeatedly harasses imāms of Sanaa.
c. 1807	Death of Ḥusayn "al-Sharafī," the *dawlah* of Rāziḥ. Tax rebellion in Rāziḥ.
1809	Ḥusayn ʿAlī Qāsim of Ṣaʿdah threatens both Rāziḥ *dawlah*s.
1811	Egyptians invade ʿAsīr; defeated by the pro-Wahhabi Amīr of highland ʿAsīr allied with the Sharīf of Abū ʿArīsh.
1815	Egyptians conquer ʿAsīr. Rāziḥīs shift their Tihāmah entrepôt from al-Bār to al-Ḍayʿah.
1817	Death of Sharīf Ḥamūd "Abū Mismar" of Abū ʿArīsh.
1818	Egyptians take Tihāmah with help of Sharīfs of Abū ʿArīsh; install ʿAli Ḥaydar as Sharīf.
1824–27	Egyptians under Ibrāhīm Pāsha take Tihāmah from Wahhabis, and cede it to Imām al-Mahdī ʿAbdallāh of Sanaa.
1832–38	Egyptian campaigns in ʿAsīr and Yemeni Tihāmah.
1835	Egyptians take Tihāmah with help of Ḥusayn b. ʿAlī Ḥaydar of Abū ʿArīsh.
1838	Ḥusayn ʿAli Ḥaydar succeeds to sharīfate of Abū ʿArīsh; claims ʿUqārib tribe of al-Waqir from the *dawlah* of Rāziḥ.
1840	Sharīf Ḥusayn ʿAlī Ḥaydar helps Amīr ʿĀyiḍ of highland ʿAsīr take Hodeidah and Mokha. Egyptians evacuate Yemen, ceding the Sharīf the Tihāmah.
1841	Sharīf Ḥusayn ʿAlī Ḥaydar makes an anti-British and anti-Ottoman alliance with Amīr ʿĀyiḍ.
1842	Sharīf Ḥusayn ʿAlī Ḥaydar submits to the Ottomans in return for overlordship of the Tihāmah.
1847	Imām al-Mutawakkil Muḥammad of Ṣanaa defeats Sharīf Ḥusayn ʿAlī Ḥaydar in the Tihāmah, and he retreats to Abū ʿArīsh.
1848	Sharīf Ḥusayn ʿAlī retakes towns and ports of Yemeni Tihāmah. Aḥmad b. Ḥāshim al-Waysi of Sāqayn (Khawlān) claims imāmate; Sayyid Muḥammad b. Qāsim of Āl Muṭahhar, Rāziḥ, pledges him allegiance.

1849	Ottomans capture the ʿAsīr and Yemeni Tihāmah and Sanaa. Establish *vilayet* of Yemen with center in Hodeidah.
1852	Ottomans appoint Sharīf Ḥaydar b. ʿAlī governor of Abū Arīsh, and take control of Jīzān.
1856	Conflict for control of the Tihāmah between Amīr ʿĀyiḍ of highland ʿAsīr, and the disputing sharīfs of Abū ʿArīsh.
1860	Anti-Ottoman uprising in ʿAsīr.
1863–65	Successful Ottoman campaigns against the sharīfs of Abū ʿArīsh and Amīr Muḥammad ʿĀyiḍ of highland ʿAsīr. Ottomans regain control of Jīzān and Abū ʿArīsh.
1869–70	Suez canal opens, facilitating Ottoman transportation. Anti-Ottoman campaigns in coastal and highland ʿAsīr.
1871–72	Ottomans occupy ʿAsīr and much of highland Yemen, but not Rāziḥ; Yemeni imāms submit; Yemen with ʿAsīr becomes an Ottoman *vilayet*.
1879	Imām al-Hādi Sharaf al-Dīn accedes to Zaydī imāmate; launches anti-Ottoman campaign.
1882	Rāziḥ gives allegiance to Imām al-Hādī.
1880s–1890s	Anti-Ottoman rebellions in ʿAsīr.
1890	Imām al-Manṣūr Muḥammad Ḥamīd al-Dīn accedes to Zaydī imāmate; launches anti-Ottoman campaign.
1896	Anti-Ottoman insurrections throughout Yemen, including the Tihāmah. Imām al-Manṣūr orders shifting of Rāziḥ's Tihāmah entrepôt from al-Ḍayʿah to al-Muhaymilah.
1897–1900	Rebellion in Rāziḥ against Imām al-Manṣūr.
1900–1905	Anti-Ottoman revolts in ʿAsīr led by Aḥmad ʿĀyiḍ in highlands and Muḥammad b. ʿAlī al-Idrīsī of Ṣabyā in the Tihāmah.
1904	Accession of Imām Yaḥyā b. Muḥammad Ḥamīd al-Dīn. Anti-Ottoman uprising in Yemen.
1907	Idrīsī uprising against the Ottomans.
1908	The Idrīsī proclaims his "imāmate."
1909	The Idrīsī launches anti-Turkish insurrections in coastal ʿAsīr, and expands his state into Yemeni Tihāmah and Khawlān ibn ʿĀmir, including Rāziḥ.
1910	The Idrīsī makes a "state visit" to Rāziḥ.
1911–12	Turco-Italian war; the Idrīsī supports Italians against the Turks, and receives arms, ammunition, and subsidies.
1911	Imām Yaḥyā launches anti-Ottoman uprising. Treaty of Daʿʿān: Ottomans cede Imām Yaḥyā annual subsidy and jurisdiction over Zaydī Yemen.
1913	(Dec.) Idrīsī forces including Rāziḥīs repel Imām Yaḥyā's attempt to conquer Rāziḥ.
1914	Conflict between forces of Imām Yaḥyā and the Idrīsī in the

	Tihāmah. Dec.–Jan.: Imām Yaḥyā captures Jabal Rāziḥ and part of ʿUqārib.
1917	By Feb./March: Rāziḥ's Tihāmah entrepôt has been shifted to Baẓaʿah. Sept.: fighting in Rāziḥ between the forces of Imām Yaḥyā and the Idrīsī.
1918	End of World War I. End of Ottoman rule in Yemen.
1919	Feb.: Imām Yaḥyā's son Aḥmad fights Idrīsī for the Yemeni Tihāmah and bordering mountains.
1920	Treaty between the Idrīsī and Ibn Saʿud.
1921	British cede Hodeidah to the Idrīsī.
1923	Death of Muḥammad b. ʿAlī al-Idrīsī. Succeeded by son ʿAlī.
1924	Competition between the Idrīsī and Imām Yaḥyā for control of the Tihāmah and ʿUqārib. Rāziḥ's Tihāmah entrepôt moves from Baẓaʿah to al-Muhaymilah, then to al-Ḍayʿah. Imām Yaḥyā captures Hodeidah from the Idrīsī.
1926	Ḥasan b. ʿAlī seizes the Idrīsī "imāmate." Oct.: Treaty of Mecca (published Jan. 1927) makes Idrīsī imāmate a protectorate of the Al Saʿud.
1927	June: hostilities in northern Tihāmah between Imām Yaḥyā and Ḥasan b. ʿAlī al-Idrīsī, who still holds part of ʿUqārib. Some Rāziḥīs side with the Idrīsī in battles with Imām Yaḥyā for Jabal Ḥibrah.
1930	Hostilities cease between the Idrīsī and Imām Yaḥyā, who gains control of the Yemeni Tihāmah up to Ḥaraḍ. Ḥasan b. ʿAlī al-Idrīsī abdicates sovereignty of ʿAsīr to Ibn Saʿūd.
1931	Imām Yaḥyā stations troops along northern Tihāmah frontier with ʿAsīr, including Jabal Rāziḥ; engages in hostilities against Ibn Saʿud in ʿAsīr.
1933	Imām Yaḥyā sends conscripts to his front, including Rāziḥ.
1934	Saudi-Yemeni war. Treaty of Ta'if agrees Yemen's northwest border along foothills of Rāziḥ on a twenty-year renewable basis.
1930s	Imām Yaḥyā consolidates his state.
1948	Feb.: Imām Yaḥyā assassinated; succeeded by his son, Imām al-Nāṣir Aḥmad (1948–62).
1948–62	Period of strong state control in Rāziḥ and Yemen.
1962	19 Sept.: death of Imām Aḥmad; succeeded by son, Imām al-Badr Muḥammad. 26 Sept.: Imāmate overturned in republican coup. Establishment of the Yemen Arab Republic (YAR). 10 Nov.: Imām al-Badr visits Rāziḥ to announce intention of regaining power.
1962–63	Egyptians bomb Jīzān and ʿAsīr.
1964	Unsuccessful Egyptian offensive in Ḥaraḍ, northern Tihāmah.

	Imām al-Badr moves headquarters to greater Rāziḥ. Egyptians bomb Rāziḥ.
1964–65	Republican forces occupy Jabal Rāziḥ, and royalists drive them out.
1966	Imām al-Badr moves to Saudi Arabia.
1967	Egyptian forces leave Yemen.
1969	March: Establishment of Yemeni parliament (*majlis al-waṭanī*) dominated by shaykhs.
1970	May: national reconciliation and end of the Civil War. Dec.: promulgation of national constitution.
1971	March: national elections establish Consultative Council (*majlis al-shūrā*), dominated by shaykhs and headed by Shaykh ʿAbdallāh al-Aḥmar. Sept.: Rāziḥ formally submits to the Republic.
1973	June: foundation of the Confederation of Yemeni Development Associations (CYDA), headed by Colonel Ibrāhīm al-Ḥamdī. Saudi Arabia agrees to fund YAR's budget deficit.
1974	June: Ibrāhīm al-Ḥamdī becomes head of state in bloodless coup.
1975	President al-Ḥamdī dissolves Consultative Council. First national elections to CYDA.
1975–77	Violent confrontations between plateau tribes and government, suppressed by air strikes.
1977	Oct. 11: President Ibrāhīm al-Ḥamdī assassinated.
1978	Establishment of the advisory People's Constituent Assembly, including tribal representatives. Assembly elects ʿAlī ʿAbdallāh Ṣāliḥ as President of the Republic.
1987	Dec.: Yemen begins to export oil.
1990	22 May: creation of the Republic of Yemen by unification of the People's Democratic Republic of Yemen (PDRY) and YAR. Aug.: Iraq invades Kuwait; Yemeni government fails to condemn; Saudi Arabia expels Yemeni migrant workers.
1991	National referendum on the constitution of the Republic of Yemen.
1993	May: first parliamentary elections of the Republic of Yemen.
1994	Civil war between North and South of the Republic of Yemen.
1997	April: second parliamentary elections of the Republic of Yemen.
2003	Third parliamentary elections of the Republic of Yemen.
2004–05	Government military action in Khawlān and Ṣaʿdah region against Zaydīs.

APPENDIX 2

Catalogue of Rāziḥī Documents

Note: Most documents are from the tribe of al-Naẓīr. For convenient reference, the Christian date is given first. Square brackets indicate identifications supplied by the author. Documents are referenced in the main text with the prefix D. A more detailed catalogue and copies of the documents can be consulted in the Oriental and India Office Collections, British Library. For reproductions of similar documents, see books by Abū Ghānim, al-Maqḥafī, and Sālim (1982).

1605 APRIL/MAY 1013 DHŪ AL-ḤIJJAH

Shaykh Faraḥ Ḥarbān al-Yūnisī buys a terrace [in al-Naẓīr]. Witnessed by a Birkānī and a Shāriqī.

1608 JANUARY/FEBRUARY 1016 SHAWWĀL

Aḥmad Ibrāhīm Faraḥ buys land [in al-Naẓīr]. [on reverse, undated]: list of proceeds from Ilt Ibrāhīm land in al-Muhaymilah.

1620A APRIL 1029 JUMĀDAH I

Shaykh Aḥmad Faraḥ [of al-Naẓīr] buys land with coffee in al-Naẓīr.

1628 APRIL/MAY 1037 SHAʿBĀN

Shaykh Aḥmad Faraḥ al-Yūnisī buys land. Witnessed by Qāsim Sarīʿ "the Izdī."

1654 JUNE/JULY 1064 SHAʿBĀN [DATE UNCLEAR; COULD BE 1074]

State official specifies dues on imports and exports, including coffee, at the market of *madīnat* al-Bār.

1657 MAY/JUNE 1067 SHAʿBĀN

Imāmic decree that al-Naẓīr should pay 100 silver *ḥarf* per month like the other *makātib* of the *yamāniyah* and Jabal Rāziḥ.

1658 AUGUST/SEPTEMBER 1068 DHŪ AL-ḤIJJAH

Qāsim Sarīʿ al-Yūnisī [of al-Izid?] sells a cistern; includes witnesses surnamed al-Wālī, Hayyān, and ʿIzzān.

1667 OCTOBER/NOVEMBER 1078/79 JUMĀDAH I

Diyah settlement between [al-Naẓīr and a tribe in Munbabbih al-Shām]. Imāmic official presides.

1668 JUN/JULY 1079 MUḤARRAM

Acceptance of the 1667 *diyah* settlement. Endorsed by imāmic official.

1690A FEBRUARY/MARCH 1101 JUMĀDAH I

Shaykhs of al-Naẓīr donate terraces to the mosque.

1746 JUNE/JULY 1159 JUMA¯DAH II (SEE FIGURE APPENDIX 2.1)

Sayyid Ḥusayn Muḥammad ["al-Sharafī," the *dawlah* of Rāziḥ] offers Ibn Jaʿfar [senior *maradd* of Ṣaḥār] an annual stipend for his support against "enemies" [presumably *dawlat al-mashriq*].

1759 FEBRUARY 1172 JUMĀDAH II

Ibn al-ʿAzzām [the *maradd* of Rāziḥ] and three other shaykhs guarantee to the *dawlah* that a man will not avenge a murder.

1762 OCTOBER/NOVEMBER 1176 RABĪʿ II

Ibn Jaʿfar secretly pledges Ḥusayn al-Sharafī his support.

1764 JULY 1178 MUḤARRAM

Register (*daftar*) of stipends due [or paid] by the *dawlah*s of *shawāmī* and *yamānī* Rāziḥ to officials and stipendiaries in the *mashriq,* Rāziḥ, and [the Tihāmah].

1766 JUNE–JULY 1180 MUḤARRAM

Settlement between al-Sharafī and Ibn Jaʿfar after a tax dispute.

1768 JUNE–JULY 1182 ṢAFAR

Tax-sharing agreement between al-Sharafī and his brother, Sayyid Muṭahhar Muḥ ammad [*dawlah* of *yamānī Rāziḥ*].

1775 JULY/AUGUST 1189 JUMĀDAH II

Sayyid Ḥusayn ʿAlī Qāsim [new *dawlat al-mashriq*] pledges support for Muṭahhar Muḥammad.

1776A JANUARY/FEBRUARY 1189 DHŪ AL-ḤIJJAH

Tax agreement between Muṭahhar Muḥammad and brother al-Sharafī.

1776B 1190

Six *amīrs* [in the Tihāmah] promise to support Muṭahhar Muḥammad against the Banī al-Hurrāth, and to accept his authority over Sūq al-Bār.

1780A JUNE 1194 JUMĀDAH II

Defense pact between six *sayyids* [probably from *dawlat al-mashriq*] and Muṭahhar Muḥammad against the sons of al-Sharafī

1780B JULY 1194 RAJAB (SEE FIGURE APPENDIX 2.2)

Defense pact between Ḥusayn ʿAlī Qāsim and Muṭahhar Muḥammad.

1780C JULY 1194 RAJAB

Letter from Ḥusayn ʿAlī Qāsim to Muṭahhar Muḥammad confirming the terms of their relationship.

1780D SEPTEMBER 1194 RAMAḌĀN

Settlement between the *dawlahs* [of *shawāmī* and *yamānī* Rāziḥ] after a tax dispute. *Maradds* of Khawlān ibn ʿĀmir guarantee.

1780E NOVEMBER 1194 DHŪ AL-QAʿDAH

After a one-year truce between [the *dawlahs* of *shawāmī* and *yamānī* Rāziḥ] expires, [*dawlat al-mashriq*] absolves guarantors of responsibility.

1793 JANUARY/FEBRUARY 1207 DHŪ AL-QAʿDAH

Inter-*sayyid diyah* settlement.

1796A MARCH /APRIL 1210 RAMAḌĀN

The shaykh and leading elders [of al-Naẓīr] pledge their military support to Muḥ sin Muṭahhar [the new *dawlah* of *yamānī* Rāziḥ].

1796B MARCH /APRIL 1210 RAMAḌĀN

Dawlat al-mashriq pledges the *dawlah* [of *yamānī* Rāziḥ] his support against [the *dawlah* of *shawāmī* Rāziḥ].

1796C MAY/JUNE 1211 RABĪʿAH I

Defense pact between [*dawlat al-mashriq*] and [the *dawlah* of *yamānī* Rāziḥ] against [the *dawlah* of *shawāmī* Rāziḥ].

1797 FEBRUARY 1211 SHAʿBĀN

[The shaykh of al-Waqir in ʿUqārib] pledges support for [the *dawlah* of *yamānī* Rāziḥ] against [the *dawlah* of *shawāmī* Rāziḥ].

1798A JANUARY/FEBRUARY 1212 SHAʿBĀN

Five tribes pledge support for Muḥsin Muṭahhar [the *dawlah* of *yamānī* Rāziḥ] and Ḥusayn ʿAlī Qāsim [*dawlat al-mashriq*]. Guaranteed by *maradd*s and shaykhs of Khawlān ibn ʿĀmir, Hamdān Saʿdah, and Jabal Baraṭ.

1798B DECEMBER/JANUARY 1213 RAJAB

*Dawlah*s of Rāziḥ agree to share the taxes of *madīnat* al-Bār.

1801 APR/MAY 1215 DHŪ AL-ḤIJJAH

Following a homicide, al-Naẓīr and al-Izid pledge to protect Sūq al-Bār and its access routes in cooperation with the Āl Hurrāth and the *dawlah*.

1807A AUGUST /SEPTEMBER 1222 /JUMĀDAH II

Tax-sharing agreement between the *dawlah*s of Rāziḥ; mediated by the shaykhs of six Rāziḥ tribes.

1807B DECEMBER 1222 SHAWWĀL

Tax-sharing agreement among Āl Muṭahhar.

1808 SEPTEMBER/OCTOBER 1223 SHAʿBĀN

Tax pledge by part of al-Shawāriq to Muḥsin Muṭahhar.

1809 JUNE/JULY 1224 JUMĀDAH I

Defense treaty between Āl al-Sharafī and Āl Muṭahhar against Ḥusayn ʿAlī Qāsim [*dawlat al-mashriq*].

1811A SEPTEMBER/OCTOBER 1226 RAMAḌĀN

Muḥammad ʿAlī Qāsim [new *dawlat al-mashriq*] affirms support for the *dawlah*s of Rāziḥ.

1812 NOVEMBER/DECEMBER 1227 DHŪ AL-QAʿDAH

Five Rāziḥ tribes pledge allegiance to Muḥsin Muṭahhar and son ʿAlī.

1814B OCTOBER/NOVEMBER 1229 DHŪ AL-QAʿDAH (SEE FIGURE APPENDIX 2.3)

Defense pact between three Rāziḥ tribes and "the people of al-Bār."

1815 JANUARY/FEBRUARY 1230 ṢAFAR

Sayyid ʿAlī Muḥsin [of *yamānī* Rāziḥ] affirms his authority over Sūq al-Ḍayʿah.

1821A JULY 1236 SHAWWĀL

Dispute settlement between members of [Āl Muṭahhar] and a *qabīlī* clan of al-Naẓīr.

1821B SEPTEMBER/OCTOBER 1237 MUḤARRAM

Defense pact between al-Naẓīr and Āl Muṭahhar over taxes.

1822A JANUARY/FEBRUARY 1237 JUMĀDAH I

Defense pact between al-Naẓīr and Āl Muṭahhar against [the *dawlah* of *shawāmī* Rāziḥ].

1822B OCTOBER/NOVEMBER 1238 ṢAFAR

Agreement among Āl Muṭahhar about using taxes for hospitality.

1825 1240

Āl Muṭahhar agree allocation of costs for war against Ghumār in which Bayt Faraḥ [shaykhs of al-Naẓīr] supported them.

1826 AUGUST /SEPTEMBER 1242 MUḤARRAM

Ibn al-ʿAzzām [shaykh of al-Shawāriq] sells part of his stipend from the *dawlah* to a member of Āl Muṭahhar.

1827A APRIL/MAY 1242 SHAWWĀL

Part of al-Shawāriq pledge their taxes to ʿAlī Muḥsin and his heirs.

1827B JULY/AUGUST 1243 MUḤARRAM

Part of al-Shawāriq pledge their taxes to female heirs of a member of Āl Muṭahhar.

1829B DECEMBER/JANUARY 1245 RAJAB

Defense treaty between four Rāziḥ tribes after a murder.

1830 DECEMBER/JANUARY 1246 RAJAB

Representatives of all the ʿUqārib tribes pledge their loyalty to the *dawlahs* of Rāziḥ, and acknowledge ʿAlī Muḥsin's authority over the sūq [al-Ḍayʿah].

1831A JANUARY 1246 SHAʿBĀN

Defense pact between the tribes of *shawāmī* and *yamānī* Rāziḥ and [their *dawlahs*] Āl al-Muṭahhar and Āl al-Sharafī regarding tax collection, and the resistance of Ibn Ghalfān [shaykh of al-Waqir] in al-Ḍayʿah.

1833A JANUARY/FEBRUARY 1248 RAMAḌĀN

Two Birkānī clans pledge their taxes to Āl Muṭahhar and their progeny.

1833C FEBRUARY/MARCH 1248 SHAWWĀL

Agreement between four tribes of *yamānī* Rāziḥ about vengeance and *diyah*.

1834A OCTOBER/NOVEMBER 1250 JUMĀDAH I

Inter-family agreement concerning fights and infringements of grazing rules.

1836A 1252

Al-Naẓīr and al-Izid agree *diyah* to be paid to Banī ʿAbīd.

1836B FEBRUARY 1252 MUḤARRAM

Muḥsin ʿAlī Muṭahhar affirms support for the shaykh of al-Naẓīr, and confirms it is [administratively] part of Khawlān ibn ʿĀmir.

1838A APRIL/MAY 1254/ṢAFAR (SEE FIGURE APPENDIX 2.4)

Agreement among Ilt Faraḥ about sharing their stipend from the *dawlah,* the taxes of al-Muhaymilah, and hospitality expenses.

1838B DECEMBER 1254 SHAWWĀL

Sharīf Ḥusayn ʿAlī Ḥaydar [of Abū ʿArīsh] asserts that al-Waqir is under him.

1841A APRIL/MAY 1257 RABĪʿ I

Naẓīrīs submit bonds to secondary guarantors from neighboring tribes.

1841B DECEMBER/JANUARY 1257

Naẓīrī clans renew pledges of loyalty to their shaykh after defecting.

1841C 1257

Naẓīrīs mediate between their shaykh and the *dawlah* in dispute over taxes, stipends, and expenses.

1844A JUNE/JULY 1260 JUMĀDAH I

Al-Naẓīr supports the claim of ʿAlī Muḥsin [the *dawlah* of *yamānī* Rāziḥ] to three-quarters of their tribe's taxes, the remaining quarter going to *dawlat al-mashriq.*

1844B NOVEMBER/DECEMBER 1260 DHŪ AL-QAʿDAH

Dispute settlement among Ilt Faraḥ about the *waqf* set aside for the upkeep of guests and Quran students.

1845A, 1845B, AND 1845C SEPTEMBER 1261 RAMADĀN (SEE FIGURE APPENDIX 2.5)

Al-Naẓīr (a), Banī Rabīʿah (b), and Banī Ṣayāḥ (c) pledge allegiance and taxes to Muḥsin ʿAlī of Āl Muṭahhar.

1846D SEPTEMBER/OCTOBER 1262 SHAWWĀL

List of *zakāt* payments by members of the three Thirds of al-Naẓīr.

1848A JANUARY 1264 ṢAFAR

Dispute settlement after someone from Āl Muṭahhar killed someone from Āl al-Sharafī.

1850A APRIL/MAY 1266 JUMĀDAH II

Agreement of mutual support and tax-sharing between Muḥsin ʿAlī of Āl Muṭahhar and Ibn Ghalfān of al-Waqir.

1852 MARCH/APRIL 1268 JUMĀDAH II

Naẓīrī agreement regarding offenders, and the extraction of subscriptions and fines.

1853A JANUARY/FEBRUARY 1269 RABĪʿAH II

Dispute settlement among Ilt Faraḥ concerning hereditary tax-collecting rights.

1853B FEBRUARY/MARCH 1269 JUMĀDAH I

Shaykh Jubrān Qāsim Faraḥ of al-Naẓīr pronounces to the Middle Third on taxes and dissension.

1855B DECEMBER/JANUARY 1272 RABĪʿ II

Al-Naẓīr affirms the protected status of the *qāḍīs* of Ilt al-Judhaynah.

1856 AUGUST 1272 DHŪ AL-ḤIJJAH

Defense pact between two parts of al-Izid.

1858 DECEMBER 1275 JUMĀDAH I

Dissident "imām" affirms Āl Muṭahhar and Āl al-Sharafī's tax rights and jurisdiction in Rāziḥ.

1859 JUNE 1275 DHŪ AL-QAʿDAH

Shaykh Jubrān Qāsim metes out penalties after dissension.

1860C SEPTEMBER/OCTOBER 1277 RABĪʿAH I

Tihāmah groups pledge taxes to Muḥsin ʿAlī [of Āl Muṭahhar].

1860D OCTOBER/NOVEMBER 1277 RABĪʿAH I

Part of al-Shawāriq pledge their taxes to Muḥsin ʿAlī.

1861 SEPTEMBER/OCTOBER 1278 RABĪʿ I

Alliance treaty between most of the tribes of Rāziḥ, Āl Muṭahhar, and Āl al-Sharafī.

1862 FEBRUARY 1278 SHAʿBĀN

Shaykh Jubrān Qāsim rules on the protection of visitors, Naẓīrī transgressions, and the collection and distribution of subscriptions.

1863A JUNE/JULY 1280 MUḤARRAM (SEE FIGURE APPENDIX 2.6)

Agreement between four Rāziḥī tribes on the protection of their respective territories against fugitives from justice.

1863B OCTOBER/NOVEMBER 1280 JUMĀDAH I

Shaykhs of all the tribes of Rāziḥ affirm an outsider died accidentally.

1864 MAY/JUNE 1280 DHŪ AL-ḤIJJAH

Agreement between Āl Muṭahhar and the Middle Third of al-Naẓīr about protection of *qifār*.

1867D FEBRUARY/MARCH 1283 SHAWWĀL

Agreement between clans of Banalqām about mutual help with labor, and not ganging up.

1867B APRIL/MAY 1283 DHŪ AL-ḤIJJAH

Al-ʿAzzām mediates between al-Izid and Banalqām over unintentional homicide.

1867C SEPTEMBER 1284 JUMĀDAH I

Agreement between Birkān and al-Naẓīr about *bāyis*.

1870A MARCH 1286 DHŪ AL-ḤIJJAH

Agreement between Izdī-and-Naẓīrī on one side, and al-Shawāriq on the other, affirming regulations concerning *kufalah* zones and *bāyis*.

1870B MARCH 1286 DHŪ AL-ḤIJJAH

Shaykh Jubrān Qāsim rules on distribution of liabilities and costs after war.

1871A OCTOBER/NOVEMBER 1288 SHAʿBĀN

Munabbih agrees to safeguard the *bāyis* and *kufalah* of al-Naẓīr according to prior treaties.

1871B NOVEMBER/DECEMBER 1288 RAMAḌĀN

Agreement between Birkān/Munabbih and Izdī-and-Naẓīrī about fugitives from justice.

1873A JANUARY 1289 SHAWWĀL

Tax agreement between Muḥsin ʿAlī of Āl Muṭahhar and the shaykh of al-Shawāriq.

1873C FEBRUARY/MARCH 1290 MUḤARRAM

Leaders of Banī Rabīʿah guarantee a *sayyid* tax pledge to Āl Muṭahhar.

1873D NOVEMBER/DECEMBER 1290 SHAWWĀL

A Banī Rabīʿah clan pledges taxes to Muḥsin ʿAlī of Āl Muṭahhar.

1873F MAY/JUNE 1290 RABĪʿ II

A *ḥākim* settles a dispute among Āl Muṭahhar over the revenues of al-Ḍayʿah.

1874A JUNE/JULY 1291 JUMĀDAH I

Shaykh Jubrān Qāsim decides on fees and fines, and allocates subscriptions toward injuries and guard duty expenses [after a war].

1874B JUNE/JULY 1291 JUMĀDAH I

Thirds of al-Naẓīr pledge bonds to Shaykh Jubrān Qāsim, and accept his subscription arrangements.

1875 DECEMBER/JANUARY 1292 DHŪ AL-ḤIJJAH

Claims and counter-claims in inter-tribal litigation case mediated by shaykh of al-Waqir.

1876A JANUARY/FEBRUARY 1293 MUḤARRAM

Izdī agreement not to shelter fugitives from justice.

1876B NOVEMBER/DECEMBER 1293 DHŪ AL-QAʿDAH

Shaykh Jubrān Qāsim allocates compensation and expenses after war.

1877B JUNE/JULY 1294 JUMĀDAH II

Shaykh Jubrān Qāsim allocates expenses and fines after a defection.

1878A APRIL/MAY 1295 RABĪʿ II

Banī Asad clans pledge to pay taxes directly to Muḥsin ʿAlī [of Āl Muṭahhar].

1878B AUGUST/SEPTEMBER 1295 RAMAḌĀN

Āl Muṭahhar make defense treaty against "*dawlah* or *amīr*."

1879A MAR/APRIL 1296 RABĪʿ II

Naẓīrī agreement on various war rules, hospitality, and tax shares.

1879E JUNE/JULY 1297 RAJAB

Sayyid ʿAlī Ḥusayn al-Ḥūthī settles a homicide case.

1880A MARCH/APRIL 1297 RABĪʿ II

Members of the Upper Third of al-Naẓīr accept *diyah* from the Lower Third for an unintentional killing.

1880B MARCH/APRIL 1297 RAJAB

Defense pact between al-Naẓīr and a branch of Āl Muṭahhar.

1880D OCTOBER/NOVEMBER 1297 QAʿDAH

Settlement of a dispute over tax and *diyah* by ʿAlī Ḥusayn [al-Ḥūthī].

1881C JULY 1298 SHAʿBĀN

Rulings by ʿAlī Ḥusayn al-Ḥūthī on claims after an inter-tribal conflict.

1882 APRIL/MAY 1299 JUMĀDAH II

Agreement between al-Izid and al-Naẓīr following accession of Imām al-Hādī Sharaf al-Dīn.

1884A FEBRUARY 1301 RABĪʿ II

Agreement between the Thirds of al-Naẓīr about offenders and intra-tribal homicides.

1887 MARCH/APRIL 1304 SHAWWĀL

Agreement between the "fifths" of the Middle Third of al-Naẓīr concerning subscriptions, the sustenance of the injured, guard duty, and rotation of hospitality duty.

1888 FEBRUARY/MARCH 1305 JUMĀDAH II

Nine Rāziḥī and ʿUqāribī tribes agree to support Shaykh Jubrān Qāsim and protect the sūq [unnamed].

1889 JUNE 1306 SHAWWĀL 1306

Tax agreement between ʿAlī Yaḥyā Muḥsin of Āl Muṭahhar and Ibn al-ʿAzzām, the shaykh of al-Shawāriq.

1890A JANUARY/FEBRUARY 1307 JUMĀDAH II

Birkānī shaykh and families pledge taxes to Sayyid Ḥasan Muḥammad Qāsim "their *dawlah*."

1890B JULY/AUGUST 1307 DHŪ AL-ḤIJJAH

Imām al-Mansūr endorses protected status of Ilt al-Judhaynah; later endorsement by Muḥammad ʿAlī al-Idrīs.

1891A MARCH/APRIL 1308 SHAʿBĀN

Defense pact between al-Izid and al-Naẓīr.

1891B JUNE/JULY 1308 DHŪ AL-QAʿDAH

Agreement between Birkān, al-Izid and al-Naẓīr about protecting *bāyis*.

1891D SEPTEMBER/OCTOBER 1309 ṢAFAR

Tax agreement between Banī Ṣayāḥ and Muḥsin ʿAlī of Āl Muṭahhar.

1892A MARCH/APRIL 1309 SHAʿBĀN

ʿAlī Ḥusayn al-Ḥūthī, on behalf of Imām al-Manṣūr, allocates the costs of an inter-tribal conflict.

1892B MAY/JUNE 1309 DHŪ AL-QAʿDAH

Agreement between al-Naẓīr and Birkān about the *kufalah* zone between them.

1893A SEPTEMBER/OCTOBER 1311 RABĪʿ I

Ilt al-Judhaynah negotiate protection terms (*tahjīr*) with Munabbih.

1893B OCTOBER/NOVEMBER 1311 RABĪʿ II

A member of Āl Muṭahhar attests that Ilt al-Judhaynah did not join in a conflict with Banalqām.

1893C NOVEMBER/DECEMBER 1311 JUMĀDAH I

ʿAlī Ḥusayn al-Ḥūthī judges a claim after an accidental inter-tribal homicide.

1895 [CIRCA; UNDATED]

Letter from Imām al-Manṣūr to Shaykh Jubrān Qāsim, with instructions about guards' pay at al-Ḍayʿah.

1896B APRIL/MAY 1313 DHŪ AL-QAʿDAH

The *ḥākim* of Rāziḥ agrees that Naẓīrīs can collect taxes at Sūq al-Muhaymilah.

1897 NOVEMBER 1315 JUMĀDAH II

Defense treaty between al-Izid and al-Naẓīr, with conditional loyalty pledges to Imām al-Manṣūr.

1898 SEPTEMBER/OCTOBER 1316 JUMĀDAH II

Note from Imām al-Manṣūr concerning claims dating from before his entry in 1308.

1900B JUNE 1318 ṢAFAR

ʿAlī Ḥusayn al-Ḥūthī adjudicates according to *ʿurf*.

1900D JULY 1318 RABĪʿ

Treaty of 1897 joined by Birkān.

1900E SEPTEMBER/OCTOBER 1318 JUMĀDAH II

Pact between al-Izid, al-Naẓīr, and Birkān with regard to Imām al-Manṣūr [the case of Ibn Karāmah].

1901 JULY/AUGUST 1319 RABĪʿ II

Ḥākim allocates costs of a rebellion against Imām al-Manṣūr after Ibn Karāmah killed a *sayyid*.

1902 APRIL 25 1320 MUḤARRAM

Unsuccessful appeal by al-Naẓīr for the fines [for the 1901 rebellion] to be reduced.

1904B MAY/JULY 1322 RABĪʿ

Defense pact involving six tribes about hostages on Jabal Ḥurum.

1905C NOVEMBER/DECEMBER 1323 SHAWWĀL

Shaykhs of al-Naẓīr agree to division of taxes and duties. Endorsed by ʿAlī Ḥusayn al-Ḥūthī.

1905A MARCH 25 1323 17 MUḤARRAM

Rival imām's official promises Āl Muṭahhar and Āl al-Sharafī stipends.

1905B APRIL/MAY 1323 ṢAFAR

The Thirds of al-Naẓīr agree to destroy property of a man who killed a guest from ʿUqārib.

1905C NOVEMBER/DECEMBER 1323 SHAWWĀL

Agreement among Ilt Faraḥ about division of taxes and duties.

1907B NOVEMBER/DECEMBER 1325 SHAWWĀL

Five Rāziḥ tribes support Āl Muṭahhar's claims to half the taxes, as under Imām al-Manṣūr.

1908C OCTOBER/NOVEMBER 1326 SHAWWĀL

Defense pact between the wards of al-Izid, affirming loyalty to rival imām.

1909A 1327

Letter to the shaykhs of al-Naẓīr and al-Izid from Muḥammad ʿAlī al-Idrīsī referring them to his governor in Rāziḥ.

1909B 1327

ʿAlī Ḥusayn al-Ḥūthī settles dispute among Ilt Faraḥ about funding their *dīwān* from *waqf* proceeds.

1914 25 NOVEMBER 1333 7 MUḤARRAM

Muḥsin ʿAlī of Āl Muṭahhar affirms the hostage duties of a member of Ilt Faraḥ.

1915 22 NOVEMBER 1334 13 MUḤARRAM

Loyalty pledge by al-Naẓīr to Imām Yaḥyā and his *nāẓirah,* Muḥsin al-ʿAwāmī.

1917 FEBRUARY/MARCH 1335 JUMĀDAH I

Shaykhship contract of Shaykh ʿAlī ʿĪsā Faraḥ of al-Naẓīr.

1918 JUNE 1336 RAMAḌĀN

Al-Naẓīr affirms its laws. Sharīʿah matters should go to the *nāẓirah.*

1919 NOVEMBER/DECEMBER 1338 ṢAFAR

Al-Izid and al-Naẓīr confirm tribal law on market and defense.

1921B OCTOBER 1340 ṢAFAR

Naẓīrīs agree on regulations for vengeance.

1924 MAY/JUNE 1342 SHAWWĀL 10

Government official confirms that regulations and taxes at al-Muhaymilah will be the same as at Baẓaʿah.

1925 OCTOBER/NOVEMBER 1344 RABĪʿ II

Al-Shawāriq and al-Izid promise the *nāẓirah*, al-ʿAwāmī, they will protect the guard posts in the foothills.

1930B DECEMBER/JANUARY 1349 SHAʿBĀN

Judgment by the *nāẓirah* of Sāqayn against Ilt Shārah of al-Naẓīr relating to the Idrīsī campaign two years before.

1931A JANUARY/FEBRUARY 1349 RAMAḌĀN

Ḥākim's judgment of Naẓīrī claims after war between the Idrīsī and Imām Yaḥyā and attack on al-Ḍayʿah. The period since 1923/1341 was considered.

1931B JUNE/JULY 1350 ṢAFAR (SEE FIGURE APPENDIX 2.7)

Hākim reports settlement of Ghumārī claims against *ahl al-yamāniyah* for injuries during the Idrīsī conflict.

1932B 1351

Naẓīrīs sue their shaykhs for levying excessive subscriptions.

1932D DECEMBER 27 SHAʿBĀN 1351

Naẓīrī complaint to the *nāẓirah* of Sāqayn and all Khawlān ibn ʿĀmir regarding property dispute with ʿAlī Ḥusayn al-Ḥūthī.

1933B 19 JUNE 1352 24 ṢAFAR

Following a tribal census, the Naẓīrīs redistribute men for subscriptions and hostage fees.

1934C NOVEMBER/DECEMBER 1353 SHAʿBĀN

Record of litigation among the Upper Third of al-Naẓīr over hostage fees and *tanfīdh*s.

1935B SEPTEMBER 1354 JUMĀDAH II

List of taxes paid by households in Banī Ṣayāḥ.

1936A JANUARY 7 1354 SHAWWĀL II

Shaykhship contract of ʿAlī ʿAlī ʿĪsā Faraḥ.

1936B JANUARY 7 1354 SHAWWĀL II

Naẓīrī agreement to pay *diyah* to a member of the Lower Third, and to comply with the *dawlah* regarding market dues at Sūq al-Khawbah [on the border with Saudi ʿAsīr].

1937A 19 SEPTEMBER 1356 13 RAJAB

Report on all the *sayyid* families of Rāziḥ by Muḥsin ʿAlī of Āl Muṭahhar, requested by Imām Yaḥyā.

1937B 1356

List of Naẓīrī men, by Thirds, for subscription purposes

1938B DECEMBER 26 1357 QAʿDAH 4

Imām's official concludes complaints by Shaykh ʿAlī ʿĪsā against Shaykh Nāṣir Manṣūr are unfounded.

1939A JANUARY 1357 28 DHŪ AL-QAʿDAH

Naẓīrīs confirm tribal laws on injuries and homicides. Endorsed by a government official.

1941 MAY/JUNE 1360 JUMĀDAH I

Ḥākim's judgment on a dispute among Ilt Faraḥ about hostage fees.

1947 1366 SHAʿBĀN

List of Naẓīrī subscribers to hostage fees, ordered by the *nāẓirah*.

1948 1367

Al-Naẓīr pledge loyalty to Imām Aḥmad Ḥamīd al-Dīn, with conditions.

1950 FEBRUARY – APRIL 1369 JUMĀDAH I AND II AND RAJAB

List of subscribers to hostage dues in the Lower Third of al-Naẓīr.

1955 AUGUST /SEPTEMBER 1375 MUḤARRAM

Shaykhship contract of ʿAwaḍ Manṣūr Faraḥ of al-Naẓīr.

1963 SEPTEMBER/OCTOBER 1383 JUMĀDAH 1

Izdīs complain about their shaykh to the shaykh of al-Naẓīr, threatening defection.

1969B 1389 24 JUMĀDAH II/8 SEPTEMBER

Pact between part of Birkān and al-Naẓīr.

1971A 13 SEPTEMBER 1391 22 RAJAB

Rāziḥī conditions for capitulation to the Republic.

1971B 28 SEPTEMBER 1391 27 RAJAB

Rāziḥī conditions for capitulation to the Republic.

1978/9 1399

Inter-clan defection contract.

1979B NOVEMBER 1400 MUḤARRAM

Inter-tribal defection contract.

1979A 1 DECEMBER 1400 10 MUḤARRAM

Record of the litigation and settlement of the Qullat Ḥajar dispute between al-Naẓīr and Birkān.

1980B FEBRUARY 4 1400 RABĪʿ I

Inter-tribal defection contract.

1985A – F 1405 – 06

Record of litigation and settlement of War of al-Ḍayʿah.

1992A 22 JUNE 1412 20 DHŪ AL-ḤIJJAH

Shaykhship contract of Ṭayyib Manṣūr Faraḥ of al-Naẓīr.

1992B [UNDATED]

Anti-Wahhabi pact.

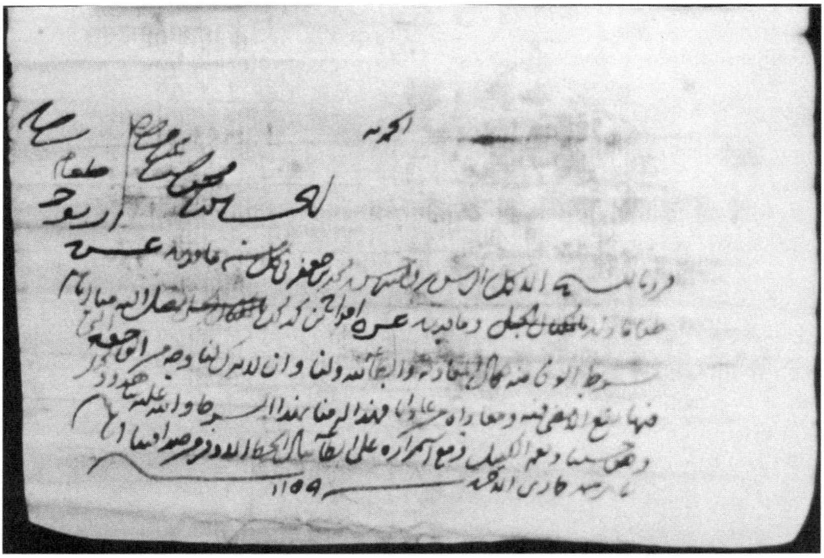

APPENDIX 2.1

1746 June/July 1159 Jumādah II

Sayyid Ḥusayn Muḥammad Ḥusayn ["al-Sharafī," the *dawlah* of Rāziḥ] offers Shaykh Ḥasan Muḥammad Jaʿfar [the senior *maradd* of Ṣaḥār] an annual stipend of grain and coffee in return for his support against "enemies" [presumably *dawlat al-mashriq*].

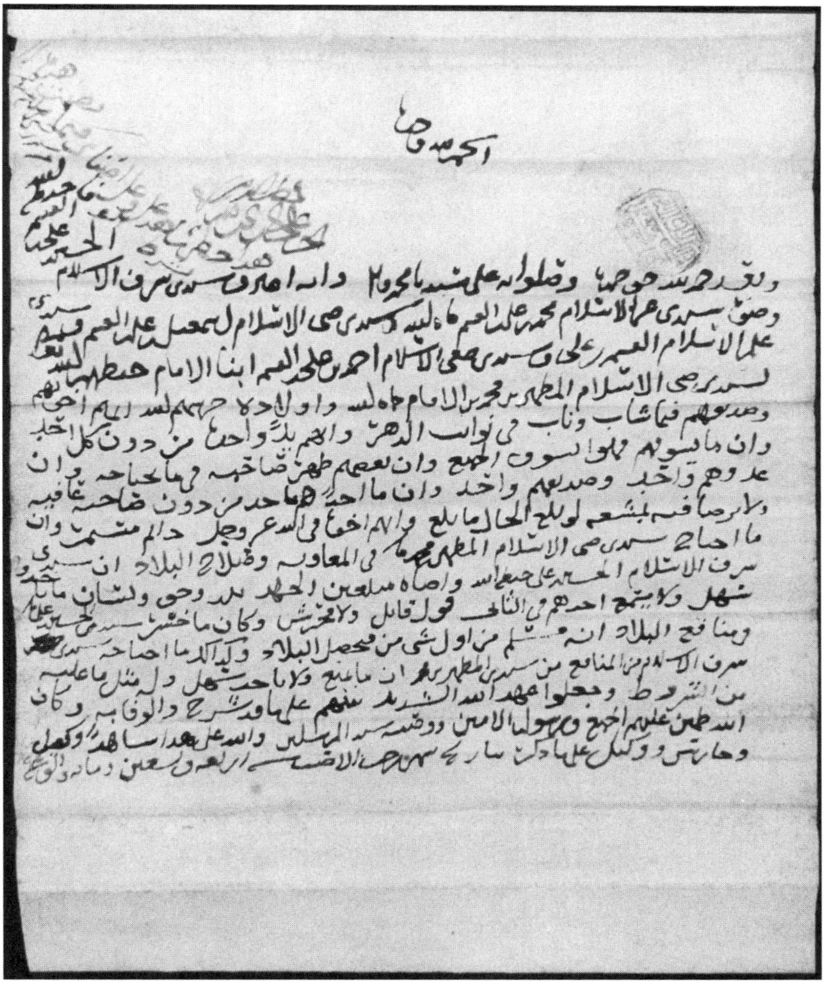

APPENDIX 2.2

1780b July 1194 Rajab

Defense pact between Sayyid Sharaf al-Islām Ḥusayn ʿAlī Qāsim [*dawlat al-mashriq*] and his brothers, and Sayyid Muṭahhar Muḥammad [the *dawlah* of *yamānī* Rāziḥ].

APPENDIX 2.3

1814b October/November 1229 Dhū al-Qaʿdah

Defense pact between representatives of al-Naẓīr, al-Izid, Banī Rabīʿah, and the people of al-Bār [the Tihāmah entrepôt]. They agree that if they cannot resolve their disputes by tribal means [arbitration], they will resort to their *dawlah,* Sayyid ʿAlī b. Muḥsin Muṭahhar, whose authority over the suq and tribes they affirm. Primary guarantors from the same tribes; secondary guarantors (*jidhū*) from other Rāziḥ tribes [including al-Shawāriq and Banī Maʿīn].

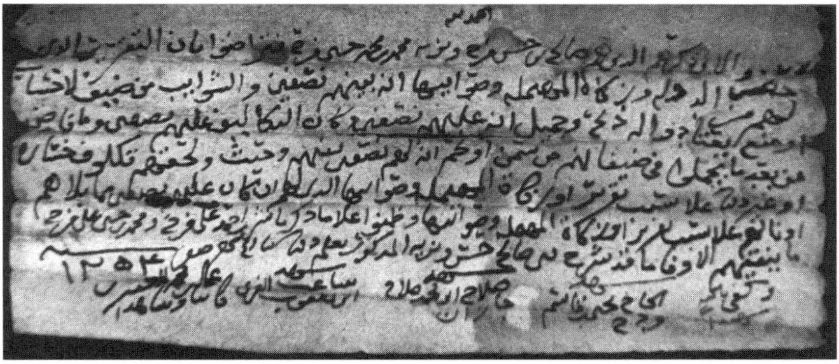

APPENDIX 2.4

1838a April 1254 Ṣafar

Agreement between two members of Ilt Faraḥ [the shaykhly clan of al-Naẓīr] to divide between them, half each, their stipends from the *dawlah,* the *zakāt* of al-Muhaymilah, and their hospitality and other expenses. Guaranteed by other members of Ilt Faraḥ; witnessed by elders from the three wards ("Thirds") of al-Naẓīr.

APPENDIX 2.5

1845a Sept 1261 Ramaḍān

Shaykh Nāṣir Qāsim ʿAlī Faraḥ pledges the allegiance and taxes of *qabīlat* al-Naẓīr to their *dawlah,* Sayyid Muḥsin ʿAlī, and his descendants, and pledges to uphold previous agreements.

APPENDIX 2.6.

1863a June/July 1280 Muḥarram

Agreement between representatives of Banī Rabīʿah, al-Naẓīr, al-Izid, and Birkān to protect their respective domains from fugitives from justice, aggressors, and thieves, and not to harbor criminals. Guarantors: elders of the four tribes; witnesses include a *sayyid* from Āl Muṭahhar [the *dawlah* of *yamānī* Rāziḥ].

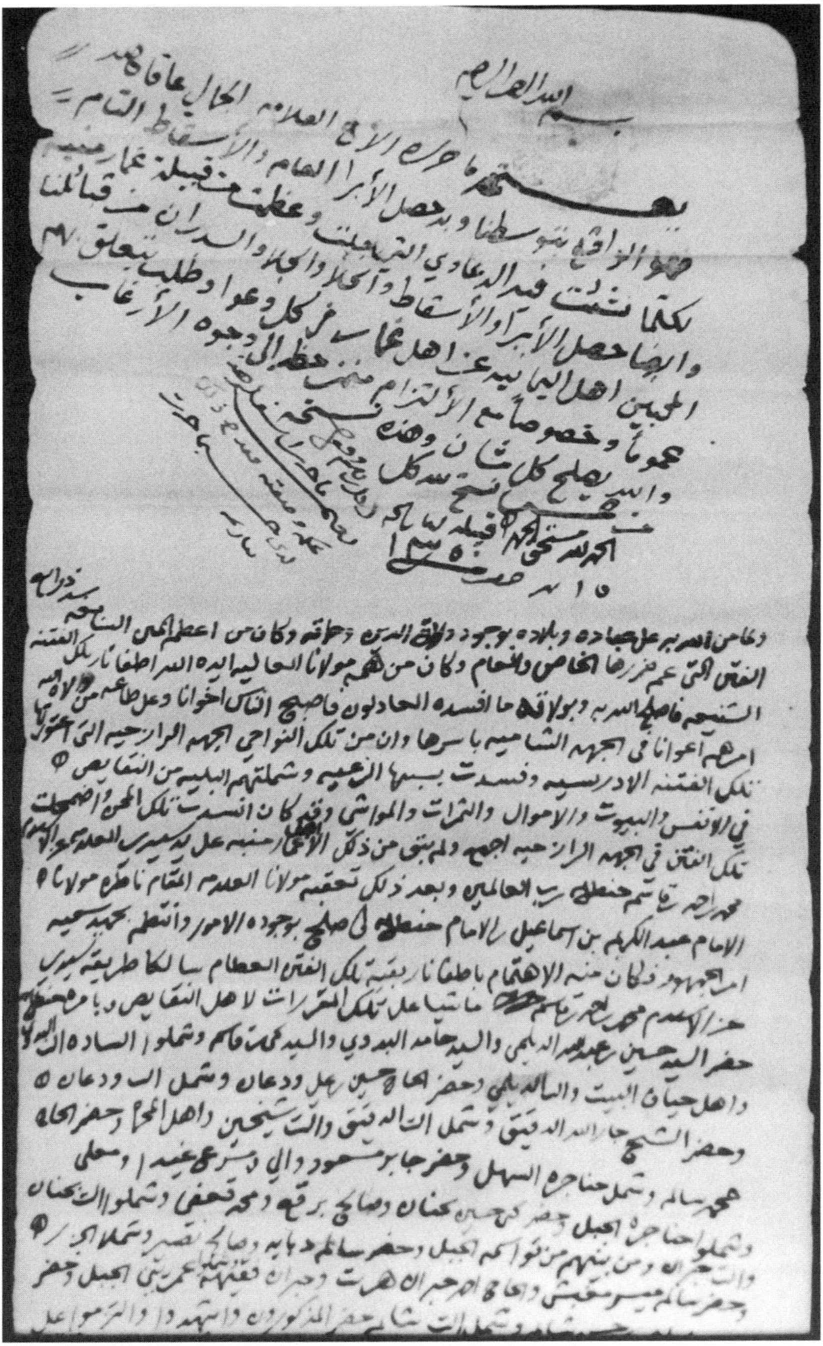

APPENDIX 2.7

1931b June/July 1350 Ṣafar

Part of a report by the *ḥākim* of Rāziḥ that *ahl al-yamāniyah*, named as al-Izid, al-Naẓīr, Birkān, al-Shawāriq, Banalqām, and Banī Rabīʿah, have settled all claims against them by Ghumār in Munabbih for injuries and losses the latter sustained during the war against the Idrīsī. Endorsed at the head by the local governor (?).

Notes

Introduction

1. Tapper 1983:1, 42; 1991; 1997:5–10; see also Helm 1968.

2. Dresch 1989; Gingrich 1993.

3. Mundy 1995; Blumi (2003, 2004) is particularly vehement in denying the validity of the category "tribe."

4. On all these basic issues see Tapper 1983:9, 43–48, 66; 1997:6, and Eickelman 2002:117, 119.

5. See Hartley 1961; Mitchell et al. 1978; Adra 1982; Bédoucha 1987; Dresch 1989; Gingrich 1987, 1989a, 1993; Gingrich and Heiss 1986; Meissner 1987; Tutwiler 1987; Mundy 1995; Boxberger 2002.

6. Dresch 1981:77; 1984a; 1989:125, 330–338. For other idealist, structuralist analyses which downplay the significance of geographical or economic factors, see Chelhod 1985:39–62; Meissner 1987.

7. Evans-Pritchard 1940:142; Gellner 1969:41–42, 1981; Lindholm 1981, 1986; Dresch 1988; Eickelman 2002:75 and Chap. 6.

8. Gellner 1981:41, 81, 120–121; Serjeant 1977.

9. See Dresch 1986 and Caton 1987 and 1991 with regard to Yemen; Hammoudi 1980, Munson 1989 and 1993, and H. Roberts 2002 and 2003 with regard to Morocco and Algeria.

10. Robin 1982a:1; Daum 1988:9–13; Müller 1988:49.

Chapter 1

1. Philby 1952:612; Gingrich and Heiss 1986:76; Gingrich 1989a.

2. Agriculture expanded after the introduction of pump irrigation in the 1980s.

3. These attitudes are common throughout Yemen (Swanson and Hebert 1982:43).

4. Jabal Fayfah in Saudi Arabia, just north of Rāziḥ, receives 12 percent of its annual rainfall during these months (Abdulfattah 1981:40).

5. On the recent decline in grain cultivation see Weir 1985a, 1987.

6. Pump irrigation has recently caused dramatic expansion of cultivation (Lichtenthäler 2000).

7. Steffen et al. 1978:I/62, 70. These estimates include men then working abroad. The population has grown markedly since then, but more recent censuses are purportedly inaccurate.

8. Tritton 1925:118; Dresch 1989:280

9. Varisco 1982:239; Tutwiler 1987:126–127; Messick 1978:162–168.

10. See Varisco 1982:Chap. 6; Mundy 1989 and 1995:65.

11. This custom is widespread in Yemen (Dostal 1974; Messick 1978:357–358; Varisco 1982:247ff; Meissner 1987:259; Lichtenthäler 2003:45, 204).

12. See Weir 1985a for a more detailed description of landholdings in Rāziḥ ("al-Jabal" in the article).

13. See Messick 1978:374; Mundy 1979, 1995; Tutwiler and Carapico 1981:62; Dresch 1984b:156; Tutwiler 1987:55–57.

14. See Messick 1978:153, 359, 377; Mitchell, Escher, and Mundy 1978; Tutwiler and Carapico 1981:23, 58ff; Tutwiler 1987:129; and Dresch 1989:102.

15. Dresch 1989:205–208; Gingrich 1993.

16. Messick 1978:149, 160; Swanson 1982:50; Dresch 1989:Chap. 6.

17. Philby 1952:424; Muhammad al-Zulfa, pers. comm.

18. D1620a; D1620b; D1627. On the Yemeni coffee trade see Van Arendonk 1974; Tuchscherer, Schaeffer, and Geoffroy, in Tuchscherer (ed.), 2001:72.

19. Philby 1952:424; Muhammad al-Zulfa, pers. comm.

20. See Gingrich and Heiss 1986:78–85; Weir 2007.

21. D1653 and D1896b; Philby 1952:312 and 473–474; Weir 1975; Baldry 1982.

22. Tutwiler and Carapico (1981:27) make a similar argument.

23. I found no evidence of Hindu Indians (Banians) or Hadramis dominating trade in Rāziḥ as they did elsewhere in Yemen (Messick 1978:269; Serjeant 1983b; Morris 1985:65; Meissner 1987:142).

24. Robin 1982a:29; al-Yāqūt 1866–71, Vol I:463. I am grateful to Francine Stone for the latter reference.

25. Al-Malāḥīṭ is in the territory of the Banī al-Ḥurrāth of the Tihāmah (see Schweizer 1985; Gingrich and Heiss 1986:76).

26. The earliest documentary mention of "the mosque of al-Naẓīr" is in D1690.

27. Five were members of the religious elite (*sayyid*s), twelve of "tribal" (*qabīlī*) status, and six of the lowest, "butcher" category. There were also seven families or individuals who had recently immigrated from elsewhere in Yemen.

28. See for comparison Tutwiler 1987:106ff; Mundy 1995.

29. Fractional ownership of rooms as a result of population pressure has also been noted for Ibb (Messick 1978:37, 375) and Jabal Ḥufāsh (Maclagan 1993:44).

30. Steffen et al. 1978:I/62; CPO 1978:68–85.

31. This is common in Yemen, though there are exceptions (Dorsky 1986:53, 95; Mundy 1979; Varisco 1982:92).

32. This has also been stressed by Tutwiler and Carapico 1981:25; Tutwiler 1987:53, 75; Dorsky 1986:107, 171–172; and Maclagan 1993.

33. This arrangement is similar to that elsewhere in the northern highlands at the same period (Messick 1978:149, 156; Tutwiler and Carapico 1981:59, 62, 149; Varisco 1982:255–258; Morris 1985:133; Tutwiler 1987:135–136; Mundy 1995:68–69; Donaldson 2000).

34. Mitchell, Escher, and Mundy 1978; Messick 1978:155–160; Myntti 1983:98.

35. For commercial partnerships in the town of Ibb, see Messick 1978:342ff.

36. For descriptions of delayed or generalized reciprocity elsewhere in Yemen see Tutwiler and Carapico 1981:19; Varisco 1982:344; Tutwiler 1987:116.

37. For a similar custom in al-Maḥwīt see Tutwiler 1987:136.

Chapter 2

1. Gerholm (1980) suggests that daggers are phallic symbols, but Rāziḥīs denied this interpretation.

2. Maclagan (1993:161–162) also makes this point.

3. For more detailed and nuanced accounts of the above aspects of rural women's lives see Dorsky 1986; Walters 1987; Maclagan 1993; and Mundy 1979 and 1995.

4. In Jabal Ḥufāsh only about 7 percent of marriages are between FBD/FBS (Maclagan 1993:172–174).

5. Maclagan (1993:89, 102) paints a similar picture for Jabal Ḥufāsh.

6. Early accounts are over-generalized, but for more locally specific descriptions see Bujra 1971; Gerholm 1977:109–138; Stevenson 1985:93–105; Adra 1982; Meissner 1987:Chaps. 3, 4; Dresch 1989:Chap. 4; Gingrich 1993.

7. These estimates are based on my 1980 census in the tribe of al-Naẓīr, which probably has more *sayyid* and butcher residents than other tribes. See Bruck (1991:91; 1993:85) for similar estimates for the whole of the former YAR.

8. In the *madīnah* of al-Naẓīr in 1980, 18.6 percent (163) of the population were *sayyids*, 66.4 percent (582) *qabīlīs*, and 15 percent (132) "butchers." For different breakdowns in similar highland "towns," see Meissner 1987:205; Morris 1985.

9. See Meissner 1987:245, 250; Messick 1993:41–42.

10. Leaders occasionally referred to the largest clans as one "flesh" (*laḥmah*), but this term is uncommon in Rāziḥ and probably a borrowing from other regions (see Meissner 1987:235).

11. Early Islamic historians invoked this dual ancestry to conceptualize the evolution and distribution of Arabian tribes and states in a genealogical idiom (see G. Rentz, "Djazīrat al-ʿArab," EI:I 544–545; Dresch 1988).

12. Most North Yemenī *sayyids* claim descent from Ḥasan b. ʿAlī b. Abī Ṭālib, and a minority from his brother Ḥusayn (Bruck 1991:78).

13. Serjeant 1969:297. On such one-sided characterizations, see Bruck 1991:37.

14. Meissner 1987:225; Bruck 1991:209, 241; Marchand 2001.

15. Chelhod 1970; Gerholm 1977:117; Dresch 1989:133, 156; Mundy 1995:13.

16. Mundy 1983:531n13; Meissner 1987:189, 198; Dresch 1989:120; Gingrich 1989c; Bruck 1991:129; Abū Ghānim 1991:236.

17. For a similar picture in al-Sharafayn, see Meissner 1987:140, 196.

18. See Bruck 1991:247.

19. On the status symbolism of daggers elsewhere in Yemen, see Gerholm 1980; Mundy 1983:532n20; Dresch 1989:38–39; and Bruck 1991:115–116, 143n41.

20. For more detailed accounts of Yemeni dress distinctions, including turban symbolism, see Mundy 1983; Dresch 1989:136, 155n28; Bruck 1991:142–143.

21. On the relaxation of these marriage restrictions elsewhere under the republic see Bruck 1991:287ff and 1992/3; Maclagan 1993:172.

22. Bujra 1971:95; Meissner 1987:187; Maclagan 1993:171.

Chapter 3

1. Messick 1978:50; Dresch 1989:280; Boxberger 2002.

2. Yaḥyā b. al-Ḥusayn 1968, Vol I:427–428.

3. Such longevity is typical of North Yemen (Wilson 1981, 1989:9; Meissner 1987:22, 242; Dresch 1984a; 1989:32, 89, 320–321; Gingrich 1989c; Heiss 1998; Smith 2002:207n25).

4. Mundy (1995:61) makes the same point for Wādī Ḍahr near Sanaa.

5. The same applies in other North Yemeni tribes (Bédoucha 1987).

6. This applies throughout North Yemen (Dresch 1984a:34, 1989:314n12; Morris 1985; Meissner 1987:177; Gingrich 1989c).

7. Ilt ʿAṭās is first mentioned in D1627 and last mentioned in D1918.

8. The name Qayyāl is first mentioned in D1608, and Wālī in D1658.

9. The concept of tribal sovereignty has also been mentioned or implied by other writers on Yemen, but not developed (Labaune 1981:15; Chelhod 1985:135n8; Dresch 1984b:158, 163 and 1989:343, 348; Gingrich 1993; Mundy 1995:31–32).

10. The polysemy of *bayt* is common throughout Yemen (Stevenson 1985:67; Maclagan 1993:44; Mundy 1995:93), although some areas have distinct terms for "household" or "family" (*usrah*) or "clan" (*laḥmah*) (Meissner 1987:235), neither of which is Rāziḥī usage.

11. The term *shaʿb* was similarly used for different levels of grouping in pre-Islamic Arabia, which made Beeston (1972) reluctant to translate it as "tribe" (Bédoucha 1987).

12. Dresch 1984b, 1989:111n4; Gingrich 1993.

13. The term *qabīlah* appears to be used in a similarly polysemic way in al-Sharafayn (Meissner 1987:232) and among the Ḥāshid and Bakīl tribes (Dresch 1986:322n5), which makes Dresch's statement (1989:7) that by "tribe" he is simply translating *qabīlah* confusing.

14. This principle is centrally important throughout North Yemen (Meissner 1987:253; Dresch 1984a:41; 1989:131, 210–211; Mundy 1995).

15. Serjeant 1977; Meissner 1987:243; Dresch 1989:91.

16. D1863a; D1876a; D1971b:8.

17. This contrasts with the Ḥāshid and Bakīl region (Dresch 1989:88–89).

18. On the more ad hoc and unstable structures of guarantee among the tribes of Ḥāshid and Bakīl, see Dresch 1989:96; 1990.

19. Montagne (1930:157 and 1973:46) uses a similar argument to explain the size of the fractions or "cantons" of the sedentary Berber tribes of the High Atlas of Morocco.

20. Meissner (1987:232) makes a similar point for al-Sharafayn.

21. This is common throughout Yemen (Hartley 1961; Meissner 1987:233; Wilson 1989:16).

22. The wards of Munabbih are also referred to as *majālis* in D1871a, a term which has similar administrative connotations to *makātib*.

23. An Izdī elder said that the "fifths" of Rāziḥ were Ghamar; Banī Maʿīn and Banī Asad; Munabbih and Birkān; Banī Rabīʿah, al-Izid, and al-Naẓīr; and al-Shawāriq, Banalqām, and Banī Ṣayāḥ. Such statements are invariably ahistorical, although they derive from specific political and historical circumstances. The "fifths" of Khawlān ibn ʿĀmir were Ṣaḥār, Khawlān, Rāziḥ, Jumāʿah, and Munabbih al-Shām (the region north of Rāziḥ, not the Rāziḥī tribe of the same name). This shows that Munabbih al-Shām was once administered as a separate region, and not as part of Jumāʿah as it is today.

24. Montagne (1930:152) came to a similar conclusion about the "subfractions" (*moudaʿ*) of the fractions or "cantons" of the Berbers.

25. Leaders sometimes referred to wards (and clans) by the common Arabic term *fakhdh* (literally "thigh"), which is not common Rāziḥī usage. This term also means no more than "part of a whole," which the researcher must determine.

26. The same applies elsewhere in tribal North Yemen (Caton 1990:69, 245; Dresch 1984b:158; 1989:79, 343; Meissner 1987:227, 257–258).

27. I earlier mistakenly transcribed this term as *guflah* (Weir 1986).

Chapter 4

1. These are still called "the graves of the Ṣaḥārīs." I mistakenly described these as deriving from another conflict in Weir 1986.

2. The shaykhs in the Ḥāshid and Bakīl region are similarly conceived as order-importing immigrants (Dresch 1984a:36–37).

3. An Ibn ʿUrayj is mentioned as a stipendiary in D1764, and as a shaykh in D1848a, around the time of this story.

4. A "shaykh" Aḥmad Nāṣir appears in D1855a, and D1855b, where he is clearly subordinate to Shaykh Jubrān Qāsim. D1860b records that Aḥmad Nāṣir was injured in a dispute with Shaykh Jubrān Qāsim.

5. The eponymous ancestor of Ilt Ibrāhīm is mentioned in D1666 with the title "shaykh."

6. Labaune (1981) describes a similar system.

7. My census of 429 married men in the tribe of al-Naẓīr, including the *madīnah,* showed that 93 percent (400) had one current wife, 5 percent (22) two, 0.9 percent (4) three, and only 0.7 percent (3) had four (among whom were Shaykh ʿAwaḍ Manṣūr and the judge, Sayyid Muḥsin Abū Ṭālib).

8. Compare and contrast Meissner 1987:246–247; and Dresch 1989:108.

9. *Maʿnā fī sīrah wa jīrah, wa mā ʿalayhim ʿalaynā wa mā ʿalaynā ʿalayhim ḥīn abtalū.*

10. *Hum min jumlah ahl al-Naẓīr ʿām bi ḥarb wa qatil wa tanṣīb wa marāqīm wa furūq yisallimū maʿnā.*

11. There are similar customs in al-Sharafayn, and among the Hāshid and Bakīl tribes (Meissner 1987:265–266; Dresch 1989:109).

12. D1841b. Shaykh Jubrān Qāsim prosecutes a similar case in D1877b.

Chapter 5

1. The tribes of Ḥāshid and Bakīl have similar concepts (Dresch 1984a:33). Such symbolic use of kinship terms goes back to pre-Islamic times (Beeston 1972).

2. Wilson 1989:16–17; Heiss 1998. Yemeni historians and compilers of tribal lists have repeated al-Hamdāni's genealogical formulations as though they are historically valid descriptions of ancestral origins rather than symbolic statements of political relations (see for example al-Jirāfī 1987:61; al-Maqḥafī 2002).

3. Ṣaʿdah was already some kind of "government" center for "Khawlān" (meaning today's Khawlān ibn ʿĀmir) by the third to fourth century AD (Heiss 1987).

4. Al-Hamdānī 1963:203, 323, 348, 350. None of the other names al-Hamdānī cites as "sons" of Khawlān corresponds to any of today's major tribal regions, however (see Heiss 1998:184, 237); nor do any of his "sons" of Rāziḥ correspond to the names of present-day tribes of Rāziḥ (al-Hamdānī 1963:323, 352). I am grateful to Robert Wilson, André Gingrich, and Johann Heiss for information on al-Hamdānī's genealogical schemes, for which see Robin 1982a; Wilson 1989; Heiss 1998; and Gingrich 1993.

5. *Al-sūq āmin bī amān Allāh wa amān ḍumanāhōh min Izdī-wa-Naẓīrī.* Izdī-and-Naẓīrī also shared protection of the Tihāmah entrepôt when it was at al-Bār, just inside Naẓīrī territory (D1801).

6. For tribal protection of markets elsewhere in Yemen, see Chelhod 1985; Dresch 1989:124ff and 1990.

7. I did not discover why the shaykh of Banī ʿAbīd is the senior shaykh of ʿAbīdī-wa-Ṣafwānī, where there is no market.

8. For similar pacts elsewhere in Yemen see Dresch 1989:350–351.

9. Similar structures are found throughout tribal North Africa and eastern Asia (Montagne 1930:162ff and 1973:37; Tapper 1983:49, 79n47; Lindholm 1996).

10. The term *ḥilf,* however, means "alliance," and *jihwaz* is perhaps a cognate of *jihāz* for "set" or "equipment"—especially, in Yemen, the dagger set.

11. Fernea (1970:87) suggests a similar system of shaykhly roles in southern Iraq.

12. These titles go back to the time of the Prophet (Serjeant 1964:13).

13. Schmidt 1968:170–171; O'Ballance 1971:123; Dresch 1989:101–102, 105; Gingrich, pers. comm.; Lichtenthäler 2003:45.

14. See Lichtenthäler 2003:42. Moieties apparently exist elsewhere in Yemen too (Chelhod 1985:149–151; Gingrich 1993). Ḥāshid-and-Bakīl perhaps function similarly, since their constituent tribes are also territorially discontinuous (Dresch 1989).

15. Rāziḥīs also equate the moieties of the tribal region of Munabbih to their north, called Furūd and Ahāniyah, with Ḥilfī and Jihwazī respectively (see Philby 1952:493, 502–503, 561; Gingrich 1993).

Chapter 6

1. See Hoebel 1954; Llewellyn and Hoebel 1961:284; Pospisil 1971:43–96.

2. See Obermeyer 1981a; Caton 1990:26–27. As Gingrich (1997:157) points out, this renders useless any distinction between "high" and "low" Islam.

3. See Serjeant 1969:11 and 1979; al-Abdin 1975:196; Mundy 1979 and 1995; al-ʿAmrī 1985:122; Meissner 1987:272; Dresch 1989:227; Haykel 2003:65. For Quranic references to *ṭāghūt,* see Rossi 1948:11–16 and Chelhod 1985:142n19. For the political significance of state condemnations of *ʿurf* as equivalent to *ṭāghūt,* see Obermeyer 1981a.

4. Serjeant 1983a:79; al-Abdin 1975:174, 181; Dresch 1984b:164.

5. Donaldson 2000:46–48.

6. See Adra 1982:166; Mundy 1995.

7. Messick 1993:301n23 makes a similar point.

8. For terminology elsewhere in Yemen see Rossi 1948; Rathjens 1951; Serjeant 1977 and 1982; Chelhod 1985:132; Obermeyer 1981a; Adra 1982:163–165; Mundy 1995:51.

9. This contrasts with the Ḥāshid and Bakīl region, where Dresch says there is "no formal doctrine of precedent" (1989:116n36).

10. *Wa kān mā bi yid al-shaykh min al-ẓunnāt wa al-fuṣūl innahum ṣaḥāḥ qadīm wa akhīr ḥasbamā fīhim min al-ʿadd wa al-dhikr wa al-ḍumān.*

11. Dresch 1989:108, 122. Donaldson (2000:188–189) gained a similar impression of sparse document production in Lower Yemen.

12. Glaser 1884:174; Rossi 1948:17–18; Rathjens 1951; al-Abdin 1975:196; Serjeant 1982:44n118; Adra 1982:168ff; Chelhod 1985:146; Mundy 1995:230, 312; Meissner 1987:272–273; Abū Ghānim 1991:363–385; Laila al-Zwaini, pers. comm.

13. On the concept and institution of *hijrah* in Yemen, see Puin 1984; Dresch 1989:136, 143ff, 159; Albergoni and Bédoucha 1991; Bruck 1991; al-Akwaʿ 1996; Lichtenthäler 2003.

14. This distinction is noted by Chelhod 1985:155; Mundy 1983:65; and Dresch 1989:80, 124, and Chap. 2.

15. The same applies in Wādī Ḍahr (Mundy 1995:34), but it is more widely distributed among Ḥāshid and Bakīl tribes (Dresch 1989:112n16).

16. D1848a; D1900d; D1919. In the late 1970s, the tribal *diyah* for murder was YR60,000 (YR45,000 for a woman), and for unintentional manslaughter YR48,000. By 1980 it had doubled to YR120,000 (informants; Dresch 1989:48), presumably because the riyal devalued. These sums are much higher than those recorded for Wādī Ḍahr (Mundy 1995:34, n34).

17. This is common in Yemen (Mundy 1995:32, 34).

18. For an interesting discussion, see Maclagan 1993:295.

19. These relative values are the reverse of those described for other areas (Rathjens 1951:184; Rossi 1948:30; Adra 1982:162; Dresch 1989:60).

Chapter 7

1. A similar preference has been noted by Obermeyer (1981a) and Meissner (1987:271).

2. This has also been noted by Meissner (1987:267, 270) and Messick (1993:157, 182–184).

3. This is the case throughout Yemen (Messick 1993:Chap. 9).

4. See Messick 1993:175 on this distancing process in Ibb.

5. On sureties elsewhere in Yemen see Chelhod 1985:150; Dresch 1989:51.

6. Another expression for this is "he has his day" (*yawmōh lōh*).

7. In dialect, *jāhī naḥāk bō ṭībit nafsak.*

8. Some, though not all, have been mentioned by Chelhod 1985:155, 180n24; Dresch 1989:50–55 and 72n15; and Mundy 1995:249, 253n17.

9. D1836a; D1848b; D1853b; D1870a; D1874a; D1878c; D1884a; D1886b; D1891b; D1892b; D1892c; D1921b; D1985a–e.

10. Rossi (1948:30–32) and Meissner (1987:216 and 267) also mention these methods.

Chapter 8

1. *Mā baqī lī aḥad ya ʿṣub wa law ma ʿ waladeh aw ʿammeh* (D1918:16); *kān man ḥaḍar al-khuṣmah bayn ithnayn inn kān al-thālith farā ʿ* (D1834a).

2. Dostal (1974), Serjeant (1977), Dresch (1989:68), and Gerholm (1977) have also stressed the importance of intervention in Yemen, though not I think that it is a legal obligation.

3. *Wa yawm yakhtaṣimū ithnayn min al-thalāth al-qubul wa ahl al-Bār, fa kān al-thālith farā ʿ, wa kān mā aḥadan ya ʿṣab ma ʿ [spelled mā] al-thānī ilā farā ʿīn baynhim* (D1814b).

4. I followed this dispute closely, attended, photographed, and tape-recorded key meetings, interviewed participants, and later translated the associated documents (D1979a, D1979b, and D1980b).

5. Their defection contract, D1979b, is quoted in Chapter Four.

6. For comparable litigation in a sharīʿah court in Ibb, see Messick 1993:175–177.

7. *Anḥā qāṭaʿīn bōkum, nakhlā wa nibrā minnakum man ṭalaʿ.*

8. D1891a; D1897.

9. This contrasts with sharīʿah law (*qiṣāṣ*) on homicides, which decrees that the killer be executed (Surah 2.178; Hallaq 1997 : 86n7).

10. The same applies among the tribes of Ḥāshid and Bakīl (Dresch 1989 : 114n27). My definition of "feud" follows Peters 1990 : 59.

11. Black-Michaud 1975 : 11; Lindholm 1981; Dresch 1989 : 49, 79; Peters 1990 : 59.

12. D1856; D1879a; 1887; D1891a.

13. D1862. Similar conventions obtain among the Ḥāshid and Bakīl tribes (Dresch 1984b:162, 169; 1989 : 81).

14. After this war Ghamar is said to have severed its connections with the Banī Baḥr tribe in Khawlān because it failed to contribute to its *diyah* liabilities, and redefined itself as one of the tribes of Rāziḥ.

15. I am grateful to Aḥmad Muḥammad Jubrān for his recordings and photographs of the peacemaking.

Chapter 9

1. Zaydism is named after Zayd b. ʿAlī b. Ḥusayn b. ʿAlī b. Abī Ṭālib (d. 740), the grandson of the Shīʿite martyr of Karbala. The following summary is based on van Arendonk 1960; Strothmann, "al-Zaidīya," EI:I, and 1971; Madelung 1971; Serjeant 1969, 1983a:77–78; Gochenour 1984; Eagle 1994; Haykel 2003.

2. On recent radical revisions of this ideology see Bruck 1999; Haykel 1999.

3. Others were al-Maḥwīt province (Tutwiler 1987 : 214–233), Kawkabān (Haykel 2003 : 30), and Jabal Baraṭ (Stookey 1978 : 92; Serjeant 1983a:79–82; al-ʿAmrī 1985 : 52; Dresch 1989 : 134, 138, 199, 212–214).

4. For example, tribes on Jabal Munabbih north of Rāziḥ, on Jabal Yāfiʿ in the South, and some in the arid east (Stookey 1978 : 146; Gingrich 1993 and pers. comm.; Flagg Miller, pers. comm.).

5. The *zakāt* is 10 percent on rain-fed crops, and 5 percent on artificially irrigated crops. Other categories of *zakāt* are the annual poll tax (*fiṭrah*) paid at Ramaḍān, the wealth tax on savings (*bāṭin*), and the *jizyah* collected from non-Muslims (Jews and Hindu Banians) categorized as "protected" (*dhimmī*) under Islamic law (al-Abdin 1975 : 206; Meissner 1987 : 142).

6. On *mukūs* and *maʿūnah* see references in Serjeant and Lewcock (eds.) 1983.

7. Al-Abdin 1975 : 205–206; Serjeant 1983a:82.

8. Al-Abdin 1975 : 43; Varisco 1982 : 33; Mundy 1995 : 212n41.

9. Meissner (1987 : 98) and Tutwiler (1987 : 63) have made similar points.

10. Al-ʿAmri 1985 : 122–123; Meissner 1987 : 107; Haykel 2003:Chap. 2.

11. Niebuhr 1774 : 184–186; Al-ʿAmri 1985 : 20, 23.

12. Stookey 1978 : 137; Blackburn 1980 : 64; Tuchscherer 2000.

13. D. 314, fol. 6b, Topkapi Archives, by courtesy of Salih Ozbaran (pers. comm). See also Sahillioglu 1985; Ozbaran 1994.

14. Sālim 1974; Stookey 1978:138; Blackburn 1979:291ff; Tuchscherer 2000.

15. Yaḥyā b. Ḥusayn 1968 Vol. 2:799; Tritton 1925:20, 28, 48–50, 56–58, 61, 69.

16. Brouwer 1988; Tuchscherer 1993, 1997, and 2001; Khan 2001.

17. Serjeant 1983a:80, 82; Haykel 2003:Chap. 2.

18. Al-ʿAqīlī 1982:481; Serjeant 1983a:83–105; al-ʿAmri 1985, 1993; Klaric 2001; Haykel 2003:34.

19. Tritton 1925:76; Stookey 1978:66–67, 147; al-ʿAqīlī 1982:481; Serjeant 1983a:80–82; al-ʿAmri 1993; Klaric 2000; Haykel 2003:43–44.

20. Al-Shawkānī, *al-Badr* I:30–31, quoted by Klaric 2000:24–25; Zabārah 1957, I:572–573; al-ʿAqīlī 1982:374; Tuchscherer 1992:24.

21. Al-ʿAqīlī 1982:374–375; 481; Klaric 2000, 2001.

22. D1657. On the term *maktab* (pl. *makātib*) for government tax unit or office see Messick 1978:169; Dresch 1989:235n29.

23. Zabārah 1957, I:572–573; D1937a; Niebuhr 1774:235–236.

24. Serjeant 1983a:84–91.

25. Niebuhr 1774:235–236; D1762. Niebuhr misspells Ṣaḥār as Sahān.

26. See Lichtenthäler 2003:42.

27. D1766 refers back to this tax-collecting arrangement.

28. D1746; D1762; D1764; D1766.

29. D1775; 1776a; 1776b; D1780d; D1780e; D1793.

30. Playfair 1970 (1859):127–143; Serjeant 1983a:88; al-ʿAmrī 1985:93; al-Zulfa 1987:30–38, 111; Bang 1996:14.

31. D1812; D1814b (quoted in Chapter Eight).

32. Al-Zulfa 1987:109.

33. Al-ʿAmrī 1985:93.

34. The date of this document is unclear, and could also be 1244 (1828).

35. I earlier (Weir 1991) mistakenly stated that the designated area was just the immediate hinterland of the sūq, when it is, in fact, the whole of al-Waqir. This makes better sense in tribal law, according to which (as we have seen) each tribe is responsible for protecting trade routes within its borders.

36. Serjeant 1983a:89b; Al-Zulfa 1987:30-54; Al-ʿAmrī 1993:192; Farah 2002:29-31, 39.

37. Playfair 1970 (1859); EI:ʿAsir, Djayzan; Baldry 1976a; Serjeant 1983a:89; al-ʿAmri 1993:192; al-Zulfa 1987:33, 53, 56–57.

38. Serjeant 1983a:89–91; Farah 2002:58ff; Haykel 2003:187–189.

39. Playfair 1970 (1859):152–155; Serjeant 1983:89; al-Kibsī n.d. I am grateful to Zayd al-Wazir for sending me a copy of the relevant page of this manuscript.

40. For stipends among the Ḥāshid and Bakīl tribes, see Dresch 1989:228–229.

Chapter 10

1. Al-ʿAnsī, forthcoming: 297–298; Farah 2002:157.

2. Al-ʿAnsī, forthcoming; D1890b; D1892a; Blackburn 1980:78; Serjeant 1983a:72; al-ʿAmrī 1985:49.

3. See al-ʿAnsī, forthcoming; Bang 1996:33; Farah 2002:157; D1888.

4. Undated letter catalogued as D1895.

5. D1896b. Al-Muhaymilah is where Ilt Faraḥ and Ilt Ibrāhīm of al-Naẓīr still have joint landholdings.

6. D1904d; D1905a; D1905c; D1908c.

7. Baldry 1973; al-ʿAqīlī 1982: Vol I; Bang 1996; Farah 2002:240–246.

8. Al-ʿAqīlī 1982:660–661; Bang 1996:87; D1909a; D1911.

9. Wenner 1967:47–48; Serjeant 1983a:96; Farah 2002, Annex J: 297–298 gives the terms of the treaty.

10. Baldry 1973:38; Dresch 1989:224–225.

11. D1924; D1931a.

12. D1925; D1930b; D1931a; D1931b; Baldry 1973:187; Bang 1996:126.

13. Obermeyer 1981b; Peterson 1982:53, 70; Serjeant 1983:100b, 152; Bruck 1991:173, 187–188; 1999:183; Messick 1993:108; Haykel 2003:200–210.

14. Rihani 1930b:104, 222.

15. The provincial center presumably shifted from Sāqayn to Ṣaʿdah after the Saudi-Yemenī war of 1934. Later Imām Yaḥyā made the Province of Ṣaʿdah a "Qaḍā" under the "principality" of Sanaa, and redefined Rāziḥ as a *nāḥiyah*.

16. British Admiralty 1946:329–333, 357–358; Lombardi 1947.

17. Imām Yaḥyā pursued this policy nationwide (Bruck 1991:208). The document lists about twenty *sayyid* families or clans then resident in Rāziḥ, five of which are named as stipendiaries of the Qāsimī *dawlah* in D1764.

18. These principles are manifested in D1937b and D1947.

19. Ghaleb 1979:99; see also Scott 1942:163–177; Messick 1993:278n51.

20. Saudi forces did not engage in Yemen, but were sometimes mobilized at the border (Gause 1990:58; 61–62).

21. During this period, al-Badr held a huge rally of tribal supporters in Rāziḥ, and in September/October 1966 his *nāẓirah* re-endorsed the 1948 Naẓīrī pledge of allegiance to Imām Aḥmad (D1948).

Chapter 11

1. Al-Abdin 1975:133; Stookey 1978:257; Peterson 1982:108; Gause 1990:95; Dresch 2000:126.

2. Al-Abdin 1975:Chap. 3; Stookey 1974:Chap. 3; Adra 1982:166; Varisco 1982:227–228, 259, 357; Donaldson 2000; Messick 1993:223; Iris Glosemeyer, pers. comm.

3. Al-Abdin 1975:155–156; Stookey 1978:262; Messick 1978:221; Peterson 1982:144; Tutwiler 1987:308.

4. Corruption at the local government level was and remains endemic in Yemen (al-Abdin 1975:163; Messick 1993:195–198).

5. For an overview, see Carapico 1998:Chap. 5.

6. See Abduldaim 1992:29–31 and Lutz 1992:45–46; Lutz points out that *zakāt* revenue consequently multiplied between 1973 and 1976, although agricultural production hardly increased.

7. Dresch 1981:203; Lutz 1992:43, 51; see also Swanson and Hebert 1981; Tutwiler 1984; Stevenson 1985; Morris 1985; Swagman 1988; and, for a summary of the varied outcomes, Carapico 1998:110–114.

8. Saudi policy was consistently inconsistent (Burrowes 1987:60; Gause 1990:111; 115–117; 120).

9. Dresch 1989:19, 35n20, and 2000:124.

10. Lutz 1992:50; Piepenburg 1992:58ff, 64–65; Burrowes 1987:66–70; Abduldaim, Lutz, and Peipenburg in al-Saidi (ed.) 1992; Carapico 1998:Chap. 5.

11. I earlier published a shorter account of the following case (Weir 1997) which contains some inaccuracies introduced by the editor.

12. Dresch and Haykel 1995; Haykel 2003:225–229; Carapico 1998:42, 124; Bruck 1999.

13. The ʿAlawī-Irshādī conflict in Indonesia in the first half of the twentieth century had a similar basis (Bujra 1971:130–133).

14. I am grateful to Gabriele vom Bruck for alerting me to the significance of this shift.

15. Prayer rituals have gained similar significance in the past (see Serjeant 1983a:86, 91; Meissner 1987:40; Haykel 1995, 2003:41, 93, 175).

16. On ʿĪd al-Ghadīr see Vaglieri 1983:993–994; Gochenour 1984:131–132; Meissner 1987:31; Mermier 1991:177–180; Bruck 1999:186; Haykel 2003:39–40.

17. The tribalistic aspects of this ritual have also been noted by Gochenour (1984:131–132) and Mermier (1991:177–180).

18. On tribal conferences, see Dresch 1995:44–54 and Carapico 1998:163–166.

19. See Glosemeyer 1993 and 1998; Detalle 1993; Glosemeyer 1993, 1998; Kostiner 1996:55, 71–73; Carapico 1998:Chap. 6. I am grateful to Dr. Glosemeyer for providing me with details of the Rāziḥ elections from her unpublished research data.

Glossary

Note: Rāziḥī meanings are given, which sometimes differ from elsewhere.

abū father
ahl al-ḥuqūq tax officials
ahl al-naqṣ bereaved family
ahl al-ṣaḥab allies; co-signatories of a pact; secondary guarantors
akh pls. *akhwah, akhwān* brother; ally
āl people of; descendants of
amin security
amīn pl. *umanā'* hamlet headman
amr order; summons; government rule
amīr ruler (esp. in ʿAsīr); "prince" in imamate
arsh compensation for injury
aṣlī original; authentic
aʿyān al-qabīlah tribal elders, notables
ʿabd pl. *ʿabīd* slave; henchman
ʿālim pl. *ʿulamā'* scholar of religious "sciences"
ʿāmil pls. *ʿāmilīn, ʿummāl* tax collector; governor
ʿaqīrah pl. *ʿaqāyir* slaughter-beast
ʿār potential source of male disgrace
ʿarḍ pl. *aʿrāḍ* honour; locus of honour
ʿaṣabiyyah ganging-up
ʿayb pls. *ʿayūb, ʿawāyib* wrong; disgrace; penalty
barāḥah female expedition to collect wood or fodder
barakah God's blessing; rain
bayʿah oath of allegiance
bāyis pl. *bawāyis* specially protected categories
bayt pl. *buyūt* house; family; clan (pl. *abyāt*)
bilād territory; homeland

daʿwah proclamation of claim (to the imamate)
dawlah sayyid ruling dynasty; government; state
dīwān reception room; business room; imam's court
diyah compensation for homicide
ḍaʿīf socially weak person
ḍamīn pl. *ḍumanā'* guarantor, guardian
ḍayfah official hospitality
faqīh pl. *fuqahā'* religious scholar, jurist, Quran teacher
farq pl. *furūq* tribal subscription
fataḥ/yiftaḥ to allow access to a tribal territory
gharāmah pls. *gharāmāt, aghrām* expenses, often food
ghārim pl. *gharrāmah* male member of a tribe, lit. contributor to expenses
hajar judicial slaughter-beast
hajjar/yihajjir to slaughter as an apology
hijrah pl. *hijar* religious person or place under special tribal protection
ḥadd pl. *ḥudūd* border; *ḥudūd-wa-sudūd:* territory of tribe
ḥakam/yiḥkum (bayn) to adjudicate; to govern
ḥākim pl. *ḥukkām* judge
ḥakkam/yiḥakkim to appoint an arbitrator; to slaughter for judicial reasons
ḥamīlah pl. *ḥamāyil* woman married into another tribe
ḥaqq pl. *ḥuqūq* rights; *ḥuqūq Illāh,* God's dues ie the canonical taxes
ḥasab pl. *aḥsāb* wife's brother; affine
ḥukum pl. *aḥkām* law; judgement; judicial slaughter-beast; government rule
ibn pls. *abnā, banī* son; descendant; men/men of
ijrah pls. *ijārah/ajāyir* fee; hostage stipend
ilt followers of; descendants of
imām pl. *a'immah* Zaydi ruler; prayer leader in mosque
ʿīd religious festival
ʿilm religious "sciences"
jabal pl. *jibāl* hill; mountain; massif
jāhiliyyah ungoverned, without order; pre-Islamic period
jambiyyah pl. *janābī* dagger
jār pl. *jīrān* neighbour; client; new immigrant; person of "weak" social status
jār wa qarār all the residents of a tribe, new and old
jazzār pl. *jazr* butcher; member of the "butcher" status category
jidhū secondary guarantors
jidd pls. *judūd, ajdād* grandfather; ancestor
jihād Holy War
kabīr pl. *kubār* leader; tribal elder
kufalah pl. *kufal* security zone at tribal border
khamīs pl. *akhmās* fifth (fraction of tribe or region)
khārij abroad (another tribe)
madfan pl. *madāfin* underground grain silo
madhhab school of law

madīnah town
maghrad pl. *maghārid* high-pitched rhyming chant
maghrib west
makhzan, makhzān pl. *makhāzin* government tax store or treasury
maktab pls. *makātib, makātīb* government tax /administrative unit
maqṣad pl. *maqāṣid* gesture of entreaty
maradd senior (appeal) shaykh (syn. *marji*ʿ)
maraq soup; compensation for injury
*marjū*ʿ shaykh's fraction of taxes
markaz pl. *marākiz* government centre
mashīkh shaykhship
mashriq east
maʿūnah assistance; government tax to fund *jihād*
mīʿād pl. *mawāʿīd* tribal meeting
mijrān threshing floor
muhājir pl. *muhājirīn* wandering scholar
muhajjar pl. *muhajjarīn* religious elite with special protection; victims for whom animals are slaughtered
muhajjir pl. *muhajjirīn* one who orders judicial slaughter
muḥakkam pl. *muḥakkamīn* victims for whom animals are slaughtered
muḥakkim pl. *muḥakkimīn* arbitrator; one who orders or carries out judicial slaughter
muqaddam pl. *muqaddamīn* representatives
nāḥiyah district (state administrative unit)
nasab pl. *ansāb* ancestor; pedigree, descent; agnatic kin; relative
nāẓirah governor of sub-province under imamate
qabīlah pls. *qubul, qabāyil* tribe; (rhetorical) other tribal political groups
qabīlī pl. *qabāyil* man of the 'tribal' status category
qaddām pls. *qaddāmīn, qaddāmah* representative
qaḍā sub-province
qāḍī pl. *quḍāh* jurist-administrator under imamate
qafarah pl. *qifār* uncultivated land; wilderness
qāʿidah pl. *qawāʿid* tribal agreement, pact, treaty
qāt *Catha edulis* Forskk., shrub with mildly stimulant leaves
rabākh surety
rahīnah pl. *rahāyin* hostage
riddat lil-barā declaration of stand-off or war
ritib pl. *artāb* defence; guard duty
sahal coastal plain (Tihāmah)
sayyid pls. *sādah, sādāt* male descendant of the Prophet
silf pls. *aslāf, sawālif* tradition; (pl) ancestors
sūq pl. *aswāq* market
shabb pl. *shibāb* youth
shām north

sharaf dignity, integrity; nobility
sharīʿah Islamic law
sharīf pl. *shurafāʾ* male descendant of the Prophet (in ʿAsīr and Hijaz)
sharīfah pl. *sharāyif* female descendant of the Prophet
shawāmī northern district of Rāziḥ
shaykh pl. *mashāyikh* leader; head of a tribe
shaykh al-shamil senior shaykh
ṣadaqah alms
ṣaḥab alliance
ṣāḥib pl. *aṣḥāb* fellow tribesman; supporter, ally
ṣulḥ pl. *aṣlāḥ* negotiated settlement; reconciliation
taghlīq closure of tribal borders, blocking access
takālīf expenses, damages
tanfīdh pl. *tanāfidh* coercive billeting
thilth pl. *athlāth* third (ward/fraction of tribe)
ṭāʿah obedience (to the imam)
ṭāghūt pagan law
ʿurf pl. *aʿrāf* tribal law, common or customary law
ʿuzlah pl. *ʿuzal* sub-district (state administrative unit)
wādī water course, valley, gorge
wajh pls. *wujīh, wujūh* face; honor; authority; (pl.) tribal authorities
wājibāt canonical taxes
waqf pl. *awqāf* religious endowment
yaman south
yamānī, al-yamāniyah southern district of Rāziḥ
yamīn oath
zakāh, zakāt canonical taxes

Bibliography

Abbreviations

AA: American Anthropologist
EI: Encyclopaedia of Islam
IJMES: International Journal of Middle East Studies
J.Anth.Research: Journal of Anthropological Research
JRAI: Journal of the Royal Anthropological Institute
MERIP: Middle East Research and Information Project
SOAS: School of Oriental and African Studies

al-Abdin, al-Tayyib Zayn. 1975. *The Role of Islam in the State: Yemen Arab Republic (1940–1972).* Ph.D. thesis, University of Cambridge.

Abduldaim, Dirar. 1992. "The cooperative movement in North Yemen: Beginnings and development," in al-Saidi (ed.) 1992: 22–39.

Abdulfattah, Kamal. 1981. *Mountain Farmer and Fellah in ʿAsīr, Southwest Saudi Arabia: The Conditions of Agriculture in a Traditional Society.* Erlangen: Erlanger Geographische Arbeiten.

Abū Ghānim, Faḍl ʿAlī Aḥmad. 1990. *Al-qabīlah wa al-dawlah fīl-Yaman.* Cairo: Dār al-Manār.

———. 1991 (1985). *Al-bunyat al-qabaliyyah fīl-Yaman bayn al-istimrār wa al-taghayyur.* (2nd ed.) Sanaa: Dār al-Kalimah al-Yamaniyyah.

Abu Lughod, Janet. 1989. "Zones of theory in the anthropology of the Arab world." *Annual Revue of Anthropology* 18: 267–306.

Adra, Najwa. 1982. *Qabyala: The Tribal Concept in the Central Highlands of the Yemen Arab Republic.* Ph.D. thesis, Temple University, Philadelphia.

———. 1985. "The concept of tribe in rural Yemen," in Saad Ibrahim et al. (eds.), *Arab Society: Social Science Perspectives.* Cairo: American University of Cairo, 275–285.

al-Akwaʿ, Ismāʿil. 1996. *Les hijra et les forteresses du savoir au Yémen.* Trans. B. Marino. Sanaa: Centre Francais d'Études Yémenites.

Albergoni, Gianni, and Bédoucha, Geneviève. 1991. "Hiérarchie, médiation et tribalisme en Arabie du Sud: la hijra yéménite," *L'Homme* 118, 31/2: 7–36.
al-ʿAmrī, Ḥusain. 1985. *The Yemen in the 18th and 19th Centuries: A Political and Intellectual History*. Durham: Ithaca.
———. 1993. "Yemen in the 18th and 19th centuries: The reign of the Āl Qāsim b. Muḥammad dynasty," in Gingrich et al. 1993:185–198.
al-Ansī, ʿAbd Allāh b. ʿAlī. Forthcoming. *Nukhbat al-fikr wa nuzhat al-naẓar,* ed. Zayd al-Wazir, Sanaa: Markaz al-turāth wa al-buḥūth al-Yamanī.
al-ʿAqīlī, Muḥammad b. Aḥmad b. ʿĪsā. 1982. *Ta'rīkh al-Mikhlāf al-Sulaymānī,* Riyadh: Dār al-Yamāmah lil-baḥth wa al-tarjamah.
Al Rasheed, Madawi. 1991. *Politics in an Arabian Oasis*. London: I. B. Tauris.
Asad, Talal. 1986. *The Idea of an Anthropology of Islam*. Washington, D.C.: Center for Contemporary Arab Studies, Georgetown University.
Baldry, John. 1973. "The Idrisi imāmate of south-west Arabia." Unpublished manuscript.
———. 1976a. "Al-Yaman and the Turkish occupation, 1849–1914," *Arabica* 23: 156–196.
———. 1976b. "The Turkish-Italian war in the Yemen, 1911–12," *Arabian Studies* III: 51–65.
———. 1977a. "Anglo-Italian rivalry in Yemen and ʿAsir, 1900–1934," *Die Welt des Islams,* XVII, 1–4: 156–193.
———. 1977b. "Imām Yaḥyā and the Yamani uprising of 1904–1907," *Abr Nahrain* Vol. XVIII: 33–73.
———. 1982. "Imām Yaḥyā and the Yamani uprising of 1911," *Annali,* Vol. 42: 425–459.
Bang, A. K. 1996. *The Idrīsī State in 'Asīr' 1906–1934*. Bergen University: Bergen Studies on the Middle East and Africa Series: Vol. 1.
Barnard, Alan, and Jonathan Spencer (eds.). 1998. *Encyclopedia of Social and Cultural Anthropology*. London: Routledge.
Becker, Hans, V. Hohfeld, and H. Kopp. 1979. *Kaffee aus Arabien*. Wiesbaden: Franz Steiner Verlag.
Bédoucha, Geneviève. 1987. "Une tribu sédentaire: La tribu des hautes plateaux yémenites," *L'Homme* 102, XXVII: 139–150.
Beeston, F. 1972. "Kingship in ancient South Arabia," *J. of the Economic and Social History of the Orient,* Leiden: Brill, Vol. 15: 257–268.
Behnstedt, Peter. 1985. *Die Nordjemenitischen Dialekte*. Teil 1: Atlas, Wiesbaden: Ludwig Reichert.
———. 1987. *Die dialekte der gegend von Ṣaʿdah*. Wiesbaden: Harrassowitz.
Benet, F. 1957. "Explosive markets: The Berber highlands," in K. Polanyi et al. (eds.), *Trade and Markets in Early Empires,* 188–217. Glencoe: The Free Press.
Blackburn, J. Richard. 1979. "Arabic and Turkish source materials for the early history of Ottoman Yemen, 945/1538–976/1568," in *Sources for the History of Arabia: Proceedings of the First International Symposium on Studies in the History of Arabia*. Riyad: University Press, Vol. 2: 202–205.

———. 1980. "The collapse of Ottoman authority in the Yemen, 968/1560–976/1568," *Die Welt des Islams,* XIX, i–iv: 119–176, Berlin.

Black-Michaud, Jacob. 1975. *Cohesive Force: Feud in the Mediterranean and the Middle East.* New York: St. Martin's Press.

Blukacz, Francois. 1993. "Le yémen sous l'autorité des imāms zaidites au XVIIe siècle: une ephemère unité," *Revue du Monde Musulman et de la Méditerranée,* 67:39–51.

Blumi, Isa. 2003. *Rethinking the Late Ottoman Empire: A Comparative Social and Political History of Albania and Yemen, 1878–1918.* Istanbul: Isis Press.

———. 2004. "Shifting loyalties and failed empire: A new look at the social history of late Ottoman Yemen, 1872–1918," in *Counter-Narratives: History, Contemporary Society and Politics in Saudi Arabia and Yemen.* M. Al Rasheed and R. Vitalis (eds.): 103–117. New York: Palgrave.

Bohannan, P. 1967. *Law and Warfare: Studies in the Anthropology of Conflict.* New York: Natural History Press.

———. 1977 (1964). "Anthropology and the Law," in Sol Tax and Leslie Freeman (eds.), *Horizons of Anthropology*: 290–299.

Bonnenfant, Paul (ed.). 1982. *La Péninsule Arabique d'Aujourd'hui,* 2 vols., Paris: Centre National de la Recherche Scientifique.

Bourdieu, Pierre. 1965. "The sentiment of honour in Kabyle society," in J. G. Peristiany (ed.), *Honour and Shame: The Values of Mediterranean Society.* London: Wiedenfeld and Nicholson.

Boxberger, Linda. 2002. *On the Edge of Empire: Hadhramawt, Emigration, and the Indian Ocean, 1880s–1930s.* New York: State University of New York Press.

British Admiralty (Naval Intelligence Division). 1917. *A Handbook of Arabia.* Vol. I. London: HMSO.

———. 1946. *Western Arabia and the Red Sea.* London.

Brouwer, C. G. 1988. *Cowha and Cash: The Dutch East India Company in Yemen.* Amsterdam: D'Fluyte Rarob.

Bruck, Gabriele vom. 1991. *Descent and Religious Knowledge: "Houses of Learning" in Modern San'ā, Yemen Arab Republic.* Ph.D. thesis, University of London.

———. 1992/3. "Enacting tradition: The legitimation of marriage practices amongst Yemeni sadah," *Cambridge Anthropology* 16, 2: 54–68.

———. 1993. "Réconciliation ambigue: Une perspective anthropologique sur le concept de la violence légitime dans l'imāmat du Yémen," in E. Le Roy and T. V. Trotha (eds.), *La Violence et l'État: Formes et Évolution d'un Monopole,* Paris: L'Harmattan: 85–103.

———. 1999. "Being a Zaydī in the absence of an Imām: Doctrinal revisions, religious instruction, and the (re-)invention of ritual," in Leveau, Mermier, and Steinbach 1999 (eds.), *Le Yémen Contemporain,* 169–192.

Bujra, Abdalla. 1971. *The Politics of Stratification: A Study of Political Change in a South Arabian Town.* Oxford: Clarendon Press.

Burrowes, Robert D. 1987. *The Yemen Arab Republic: The Politics of Development, 1962–1986*. Colorado: Westview Press.

Carapico, Sheila. 1998. *Civil Society in Yemen: The Political Economy of Activism in Modern Arabia*. Cambridge University Press.

Caton, Steven C. 1985. "The poetic construction of self," *Anthropological Quarterly* 58(4): 141–151.

———. 1986. "*Salām taḥīyah*: Greetings from the highlands of Yemen," *American Ethnologist* 13(1): 290–308.

———. 1987. "Power, persuasion and language: A critique of the segmentary model in the Middle East," *IJMES* 19: 77–102.

———. 1990. *Peaks of Yemen I Summon: Poetry as Cultural Practice in a North Yemeni Tribe*. Berkeley: University of California Press.

———. 1991. "Anthropological theories of tribe and state formation in the Middle East: Ideology and the semiotics of power," in Khoury and Kostiner (eds.): 74–108.

Chelhod, Joseph. 1970. "L'organisation sociale au Yémen," *L'Ethnographie,* New Series, No. 64: 61–86.

———. 1985. "L'organisation tribale," in Chelhod (ed.) 1985: 39–62.

———. 1985. (ed.) *L'Arabie du Sud: Histoire et Civilisation. 3. Culture et Institutions du Yémen*. Paris: Maisonneuve et Larose.

Cornwallis, Sir Kinahan. 1976 (1916). *Asir before World War I*. Cambridge: Oleander Press.

CPO (Central Planning Organization of the YAR). 1974–75. *Statistical Yearbook,* Sanaa.

———. 1978. *Al-Tawzīʿah al-Sukkānī fī Muḥāfaẓah Ṣāʿdah*. Sanaa.

Daum, Werner (ed.). 1988. *Yemen: 3000 Years of Art and Civilisation in Arabia Felix*. Innsbruck: Pinguin-Verlag.

Davis, J. 1987. *Libyan Politics: Tribe and Revolution*. London: Tauris.

Detalle, Renaud. 1993. "The Yemeni elections up close," *MERIP* 185, Vol. 23, Nov.–Dec.

———. 2000 (ed.). *Tensions in Arabia: The Saudi-Yemeni Fault Line*. SWP-Conflict Prevention Network, Baden-Baden: Nomos Verlagsgesellschaft.

Dole, Gertrude. 1968. "Tribe as the autonomous unit," in Helm (ed.) 1968: 83–100.

Donaldson, William. 2000. *Sharecropping in the Yemen: A Study in Islamic Theory, Custom and Pragmatism*. Leiden: Brill.

Dorsky, Susan. 1986. *Women of ʿAmran: A Middle Eastern Ethnographic Study*. Salt Lake City: University of Utah Press.

Dostal, Walter. 1974. "Sozio-ökonomische Aspekte der Stammesdemokratie in Nordost-Yemen," *Sociologus* 24 (1):1–15.

———. 1983. *Ethnographic Atlas of ʿAsīr: Preliminary Report*. Vienna.

———. 1996. "The special features of the Yemeni weekly market system: An attempt at an anthropological interpretation," *New Arabian Studies* 3, University of Exeter Press.

Douglas, Leigh. 1987. *The Free Yemeni Movement, 1935–62*. American University in Beirut.

Dresch, Paul. 1981. "The several peaces of Yemeni tribes," *J. of the Anthropological Society of Oxford*, 12/2:73–86.

———. 1984a. "The position of shaykhs among the northern tribes of Yemen," *Man*, 19/1:31–49.

———. 1984b. "Tribal relations and political history in Upper Yemen," in Pridham (ed.) 1984:154–174.

———. 1986. "The significance of the course events take in segmentary systems," *American Ethnologist* 13 (2): 309–324.

———. 1987. "Placing the blame: A means of enforcing obligations in Upper Yemen," *Anthropos* 82: 427–443.

———. 1988. "Segmentation: Its roots in Arabia and its flowering elsewhere," *Cultural Anthropology* 3 (1): 50–67.

———. 1989. *Tribes, Government, and History in Yemen*. Oxford University Press.

———. 1991. "The tribes of Ḥāshid-wa-Bakīl as historical and geographical entities," in Jones (ed.) 1991:8–24.

———. 1995. "The tribal factor in the Yemeni crisis," in J. al-Suwaidi (ed.) 1995: 33–55.

———. 2000. *A History of Modern Yemen*. Cambridge University Press.

Dresch, Paul, and Bernard Haykel. 1995. "Stereotypes and political styles: Islamists and tribesfolk in Yemen," *IJMES*, 27/4: 405–431.

Eagle, A. B. D. R. 1994. "Al-Hādi Yaḥyā b. al-Ḥusayn b. al-Qāsim (245–98/859–911): A biographical introduction and the background and significance of his imāmate," *New Arabian Studies* 2, University of Exeter Press: 103–122.

———. 1995. "Yemeni Zaydīs: The imāmate and its aftermath," *Middle East International*, June.

Eickelman, Dale F. 2002. *The Middle East and North Africa: An Anthropological Approach* (4th edition). New Jersey: Prentice Hall.

Evans-Pritchard, E. E. 1940. *The Nuer: A Description of the Modes of Livelihood and Political Institutions of a Nilotic People*. Oxford University Press.

———. 1949. *The Sanusi of Cyrenaica*. Oxford: The Clarendon Press.

Farah, Caesar E. 2002. *The Sultan's Yemen: Nineteenth-Century Challenges to Ottoman Rule*. London: I. B. Tauris.

Fernea, Robert. 1970. *Shaykh and Effendi: Changing Patterns of Authority among the El Shabana of Southern Iraq*. Cambridge: Harvard University Press.

Fernea, R., and James M. Malarkey. 1975. "Anthropology of the Middle East and North Africa: A critical assessment," *Annual Review of Anthropology*, 4.

Fried, Morton H. 1968. "On the concepts of 'tribe' and 'tribal society,'" in Helm (ed.) 1968:3–20.

Gause, F. Gregory III. 1990. *Saudi-Yemeni Relations: Domestic Structures and Foreign Influence*. New York: Columbia University Press.

Gavin, R. J. 1975. *Aden under British Rule, 1839–1967*. London: Hurst.

Gearing, Fred. 1968. "Sovereignties and jural communities in political evolution," in Helm (ed.) 1968: 111–119.
Gellner, Ernest. 1969. *Saints of the Atlas*. London: Weidenfeld and Nicholson.
———. 1981. *Muslim Society*. Cambridge University Press.
———. 1983. "The tribal society and its enemies," in Richard Tapper (ed.), *The Conflict of Tribe and State in Iran and Afghanistan,* 436–448.
———. 1985. "The roots of cohesion," *Man* 20 (1): 142–155.
———. 1991. "Tribalism and the state in the Middle East," in Khoury and Kostiner (eds.): 109–126.
———. 1995. "Segmentation: Reality or myth?" *JRAI* (NS) 1: 821–829.
———. 1996. "Reply to critics," in *The Social Philosophy of Ernest Gellner,* ed. J. A. Hall and J. A. Jarvie, Amsterdam: Rodopi, 639–656.
Gerholm, Tomas. 1977. *Market, Mosque and Mafraj: Social Inequality in a Yemeni Town*. Stockholm University Press.
———. 1980. "Knives and sheaths: Notes on a sexual idiom of social inequality in North Yemen," *Ethnos* 1–2: 82–91.
Ghaleb, M. A. 1979 (1960). *Government Organisations as a Barrier to Economic Development in Yemen*. University of Texas.
Ghanem, Isam. 1981. *Yemen: Political History, Social Structure and Legal System*. London: Probsthain.
———. 1988. *Arbitration in the Yemen Arab Republic*. Devon: Merlin Books.
Gilsenan, Michael. 1982. *Recognizing Islam*. London: Croom Helm.
Gingrich, André. 1987. "Die Banū Munebbih im nordlichen Khawlān: Einige vorläufige Ergebnisse ethnologischer Feldforschung im Nordwesten der AR Yemen," *Sociologus*: 89–93.
———. 1989a. "Les Munebbih du Yémen percus par leurs voisins: Description d'une société par le corps et sa parure," *Techniques et Culture* 13: 127–139.
———. 1989b. "The guest meal among the Munebbih: Some considerations on tradition and change in *ʿaish wa milḥ* in Northwestern Yemen," *Peuples Mediterraneens* 46: 129–149.
———. 1989c. "How the chiefs' daughters marry: Tribes, marriage patterns and hierarchies in north-western Yemen," in A. Gingrich, S. Haas, and G. Paleczek (eds.), *Kinship, Social Change and Evolution*. Vienna: Ferdinand Berger, 75–85.
———. 1993. "Tribes and rulers in Northern Yemen," in A. Gingrich, S. Haas, G. Paleczek, and T. Fillitz (eds.), *Studies in Oriental Culture and History: Festschrift for Walter Dostal*. Vienna: Peter Lang, 253–280.
———. 1997. "Inside an "exhausted community": An essay on case-reconstructive research about peripheral and other moralities," in *The Ethnography of Moralities,* ed. Signe Howell, London: Routledge, 152–177.
Gingrich, André, and Johann Heiss. 1986. *Beitrage zur Ethnographie der Provinz Ṣaʿda (Nordjemen)*. Vienna: Verlag der Osterreichischen Akademie der Wissenschaften.

Glaser, E. 1884. "Meine Reise durch Arḥab und Ḥāschid," *Petermanns Mitteilungen* 30: 170–183, 204–213.

Gledhill, John. 2000. *Power and Its Disguises: Anthropological Perspectives on Politics* (2nd edition). London: Pluto Press.

Glosemeyer, Iris. 1993. "The first Yemeni parliamentary elections in 1993," *Orient* 34: 439–451.

———. 1998. "Parliamentary elections in Yemen, 1997," in S. Behrendt and C. Hanelt (eds.), *Elections in the Middle East and North Africa,* Munich/Gutersloh: Bertelsmann Foundation.

Gochenour, David Thomas. 1984. *The Penetration of Zaydī Islam into Early Medieval Yemen,* Ph.D. thesis, Harvard University.

al-Ḥajrī, M. A. 1984. *Majmūʿ buldān al-yaman wa qabā'ilihā.* Sanaa: Wizārat al-iʿlām wa al-thaqāfah.

Hallaq, Wael. 1997. *A History of Islamic Legal Theories.* Cambridge University Press.

al-Hamdānī, Ḥasan b. Aḥmad. 1963. *Kitāb al-Iklīl* Vol. I. (ed.) Oscar Lofgren, 1954/1965, Uppsala-Wiesbaden; (ed.) Muḥammad b. ʿAlī al-Akwaʿ al-Hiwāli, 1963, Cairo: al-Maktabat al-Yamaniyyah.

Hammoudi, A. 1980. "Segmentarity, social stratification, political power and sainthood: Reflections on Gellner's theses," *Economy and Society* 9 (3): 279–303.

Hamnett, I. (ed.). 1977. *Social Anthropology and Law.* A.S.A. Monograph 14. London: Academic Press.

Hart, David. 1989. "Rejoinder to Henry Munson, Jr.: On the irrelevance of the segmentary lineage model in the Moroccan Rif." *AA* 91: 765–769.

———. 1996. "Segmentary models in Morocco," *JRAI* 2 (4): 721–722.

Hartley, John G. 1961. "The political organization of an Arab tribe of the Hadhramaut," Ph.D. thesis, University of London.

Haykel, Bernard. 1995. "A Zaydī revival?" *Yemen Update* 36, Winter–Spring.

———. 1999. "Rebellion, migration or consultative democracy? The Zaydīs and their detractors in Yemen," in Leveau, Mermier, and Steinbach 1999 (eds.): 193–201.

———. 2003. *Revival and Reform in Islam: The legacy of Muḥammad al-Shawkānī.* Cambridge University Press.

Heiss, Johann. 1987. "Historical and Social Aspects of Ṣaʿdah, a Yemeni Town," *Proceedings of the Seminar for Arabian Studies* 17: 63–80.

———. 1998. *Tribale Selbstorganisation und Konfliktregelung: Der Norden des Jemen zur Zeit des ersten Imāms (10 Jahrhundert).* Ph.D. thesis, University of Vienna.

Helm, June (ed.). 1968. *Essays on the Problem of Tribe.* Seattle: University of Washington Press.

Heyworthe-Dunne. 1958. "The Yemen," *Middle Eastern Affairs* 9 (January).

Hoebel, E. A. 1954. *The Law of Primitive Man.* Cambridge: Harvard University Press.

al-Hubaishi, H. A. 1988. *Legal System and Basic Law in Yemen*. London: Sphinx.

Ibn Khaldun. 1967. *The Muqaddimah: An Introduction to History*. London: Routledge and Kegan Paul.

Jamous, Raymond. 1992. "From the death of men to the peace of God: Violence and peace-making in the Rif," in J. Peristiany and J. Pitt-Rivers (eds.), *Honour and Grace in Anthropology*. Cambridge University Press.

al-Jirāfī, ʿAbdallāh. 1987 (1951). *Al-muqtaṭaf min ta'rīkh al-yaman*. Cairo: ʿĪsā al-Bābī al-Ḥalabī.

Jones, Alan (ed.). 1991. *Arabicus Felix, Luminosus Britannicus: Essays in Honour of A. F. L. Beeston on his Eightieth Birthday*. Reading: Ithaca Press.

Kay, H. C. 1882. *Yaman, Its Early Medieval History*. London.

Khan, Iftikhar Ahmad. 2001. "Coffee trade of the Red Sea: First half of the 18th century," in Tuchscherer 2001 (ed.):319–331.

Khoury, Philip, and Joseph Kostiner (eds.). 1991. *Tribes and State Formation in the Middle East*. London: Tauris.

al-Kibsī, Muḥammad Ismāʿil. n.d. *Al- ʿināyah al-tāmmah*. Unpublished manuscript in the library of the Yemen Heritage and Research Centre, Richmond, UK.

Klaric, Tomislav. 2000. *Pouvoir et successions au sein de la dynastie qāsimide (XVII siécle)*. Masters thesis, University of Aix-Marseille.

———. 2001. "Chronologie du Yémen (1045–1131/1635–1719)," *Chroniques Yéménites,* Centre Francais de'Archéologie et de Sciences Sociales, Sanaa.

Kopp, Horst. 1981. *Agrargeographie der Arabischen Republik Jemen*. Erlangen.

Kopp, H., and G. Schweizer (eds.). 1984. *Entwicklungsprozesse in der Arabischen Republik Jemen*. Wiesbaden: Reichert.

Korotayev, Andrey. 1993. "*Bayt*: Basis of Middle Sabaean social structure," *Revista degli Studi Orientali,* vol. LXVII, no. 1–2:55–63.

Kostiner, Joseph. 1996. *Yemen: The Tortuous Quest for Unity, 1990–94*. London: Royal Inst. of International Affairs.

Kuczynski, Liliane. 1977. "La vie paysanne dans un village du Nord-Yémen," *Objets et Mondes* 17:155–174.

Labaune, Patrick. 1981. "Democratie tribale et systeme politique en Republique Arabe du Yémen," *L'Afrique et l'Asie Moderne,* no. 129, 12–32.

Lambert, Jean. 1997. *Le Médecine de l'Âme: Le Chant de Sanaa dans la Société Yéménite*. Nanterre: Société d'Ethnologie.

Leveau, Remy, Franck Mermier, and Udo Steinbach (eds.). 1999. *Le Yémen Contemporain*. Paris: Editions Karthala.

Lewellen, Ted C. 1992. *Political Anthropology: An Introduction*. (2nd edition.) Westport, Conn.: Bergin and Garvey.

Lichtenthäler, Gerhard. 2000. "Power, politics and patronage: Adaptation of water rights among Yemen's northern highland tribes," *Études Rurales,* July–December: 143–166.

———. 2003. *Political Ecology and the Role of Water: Environment, Society and Economy in Northern Yemen*. Aldershot: Ashgate Publishing Ltd.

Lindholm, Charles. 1981. "The Structure of Violence among the Swat Pukhtun," *Ethnology* 20: 147–156.

———. 1986. "Kinship Structure and Political Authority: The Middle East and Central Asia," *Comparative Studies in Social History* 45 (1): 19–32.

———. 1995. "The new Middle Eastern ethnography," *JRAI* 1 (4), December: 805–820.

———. 1996. *The Islamic Middle East: An Historical Anthropology*. Oxford: Blackwells.

Llewellyn, K. N., and E. A. Hoebel. 1941. *The Cheyenne Way*. Norman: University of Oklahoma Press.

Lombardi, N. 1947. "Divisioni amministrative del Yemen con notizie economiche e demografiche," *Oriente Moderno*, XXVII. Rome.

Lutz, Eberhard. 1992. "The Local Development Associations and their socio-political relevance," in al-Saidi (ed.) 1992:41–54.

Maclagan, Ianthe. 1992. "Food and gender in a Yemeni community," in S. Zubeida and R. Tapper (eds.), *Culinary Cultures of the Middle East,* Centre for Near and Middle Eastern Studies, SOAS, London.

———. 1993. *Freedom and Constraints: The World of Women in a Small Town in Yemen*. Ph.D. thesis, University of London.

Madelung, Wilferd. 1971. "Imāmah," *EI*[2] (new edition).

———. 1986. "Al-Hamdānī's description of northern Yemen in the light of chronicles of the 4th/10th centuries," in ʿAbdallāh, Yūṣuf (ed.). *Al-Hamdāni: A Great Yemeni Scholar (Lisān al-Yaman)*. Sanaa: University of Sanaa, 129–137.

———. 1988. "Islam in Yemen," in Daum (ed.) 1988:174–177.

———. 1991. "The origins of the Yemenite *hijra,*" in Jones (ed.) 1991:25–44.

Maine, Henry. 1986 (1861). *Ancient Law*. Tucson: University of Arizona Press.

Mair, Lucy. 1962. *Primitive Government*. Harmondsworth: Penguin (Pelican).

al-Maqḥafī, Ibrāhīm. 2002. *Muʿjam al-buldān wa al-qabāʾil al-yamaniyyah*. Sanaa: Dār al-Kalimah.

Marchand, Trevor. 2001. *Minaret Building and Apprenticeship in Yemen*. Richmond: Curzon Press.

Marx, Emanuel. 1967. *Bedouin of the Negev*. University of Manchester Press.

———. 1977. "The tribe as a unit of subsistence: Nomadic pastoralism in the Middle East," *AA* 79: 343–363.

Meeker, Michael. 1979. *Literature and Violence in North Arabia*. Cambridge University Press.

Meissner, Jeffrey. 1987. *Tribes at the Core: Legitimacy, Structure and Power in Zaydī Yemen*. Ph.D. thesis, Columbia University.

Meneley, Anne. 1996. *Tournaments of Value: Sociability and Hierarchy in a Yemeni Town*. Toronto University Press.

Mermier, Franck. 1985. "Patronyme et hiérarchie sociale à Sanaa (République Arabe du Yémen)," in *Peuples Méditerranéens,* no. 33, Oct.–Dec.: 33–41.

———. 1991. "Récit d'origine et rituel l'allégeance: Le jour de *ghadīr khumm* et la cérémonie du *nushūr* au Yemen," *Peuples Méditerranéens,* no. 56–57, Jul.–Dec.: 177–180.

———. 1993. "La commune de Ṣanʿā: Pouvoir citadin et legitimité religieuse au XIX siècle," in Gingrich et al. 1993 : 242–252.

———. 1994. "Le ʿÂqil de quartier à Sanʿā." *Maghreb Machrek Monde Arabe,* 143: 17–18.

———. 1997. *Le Cheikh de la Nuit. Sanaa: Organisation de Souks at Société Citadine.* Arles: Sindbad/CNRS.

Messick, Brinkley. 1978. *Transactions in Ibb: Economy and Society in a Yemeni Highland Town.* Ph.D. thesis, Princeton University, New Jersey.

———. 1983. "Legal documents and the concept of restricted literacy," *International Journal of the Sociology of Language* 4 : 41–52.

———. 1988. "Kissing hands and knees: Hegemony and hierarchy in shariʿa discourse," *Law and Society Review* 22 (4): 637–659. The Law and Society Association.

———. 1989. "Just writing: Paradox and political economy in Yemeni legal documents," *Cultural Anthropology* 4 (1): 26–50.

———. 1990. "Literacy and the law: Documents and document specialists in Yemen." In *Law and Islam in the Middle East,* ed. Daisy Dwyer, 75–90. New York: Bergin and Garvey.

———. 1993. *The Calligraphic State: Textual Domination and History in a Muslim Society,* University of California Press.

———. 2003. "Evidence: From memory to archive," *Islamic Law and Society* 9(2):231–270.

Mitchell, Brigitta, Hermann Escher, and Martha Mundy. 1978. *A Baseline Socio-Economic Survey of the Wādī Mawr Region.* Washington: World Bank.

Montagne, R. 1930. *Les Berbères et le Makhzen dans le Sud du Maroc.* Paris: Felix Alcan.

———. 1973 (1931). *The Berbers: Their Social and Political Organisation,* trans. D. Seddon. London: Frank Cass.

Moore, Sally Falk. 1978. *Law as Process: An Anthropological Approach.* London: Routledge.

Morris, Tim. 1985. *Adapting to Wealth: Social Change in a Yemeni Highland Community.* Ph.D. thesis, University of London.

Müller, Walter W. 1988. "Outline of the history of ancient southern Arabia," in Daum (ed.) 1988 : 49–54.

Mundy, Martha. 1979. "Women's inheritance of land in highland Yemen," *Arabian Studies* V: 161–187.

———. 1983. "Sanʿā' dress, 1920–75," in Serjeant and Lewcock (eds.) 1983 : 529–541.

———. 1989. "Irrigation and society in a Yemeni valley: On the life and death of a bountiful source," *Peuples Méditerranéens* 46(1): 97–128.

———. 1995. *Domestic Government: Kinship, Community and Polity in North Yemen.* London: I. B. Tauris.

Munson, H. Jr. 1989. "On the irrelevance of the segmentary lineage model in the Moroccan Rif." *AA* 91, 765–769.

———. 1993. "Rethinking Gellner's analysis of Morocco's Ait ʿAtta," *Man* (NS) 28 (2): 267–280.

———. 1995. "Reply to Gellner: 'Segmentation: reality or myth?'" *JRAI* (NS) 1, 829–832.

Myntti, Cynthia. 1979. *Women and Development in the Yemen Arab Republic.* GTZ, Eschborn, Germany.

———. 1983. *Medicine in Its Social Context: Observations from Rural North Yemen.* Ph.D. thesis, University of London.

Nader, Laura. 1965. "The anthropological study of law," *AA* 67:3–32.

Niebuhr, Carsten. 1774. *Description de l'Arabie.* Amsterdam.

Niewohner-Eberhard, Elke. 1985. *Saʿda: Bauten und Bewohner in einer traditionellen islamischen Stadt* (Beihefte zum Tübinger Atlas des Vorderen Orients, No. 64), Wiesbaden: Dr. Ludwig Reichert Verlag.

O'Ballance, Edgar. 1971. *The War in the Yemen.* London: Faber and Faber.

Obermeyer, Gerald J. 1981a. "Ṭāghuut, manʿ, and sharīʿa: The realms of law in tribal Arabia," in *Studia Islamica: Festschrift for Ihsan Abbas,* ed. W. Kadip, 365–371.

———. 1981b. "Al-Iman and al-Imām: Ideology and the state in the Yemen, 1900–1948," in *Intellectual Life in the Arab East,* ed. Marwan R. Buheiry. American University of Beirut, 176–192.

Ozbaran, Salih. 1994. "The Ottoman budgets of the Yemen in the sixteenth century," in S. Ozbaran (ed.), *The Ottoman Response to European Expansion.* Istanbul: The Isis Press.

Peters, Emrys. 1990. *The Bedouin of Cyrenaica: Studies in Personal and Corporate Power* (ed. J. Goody and E. Marx), Cambridge University Press.

Peterson, J. 1982. *Yemen: The Search for a Modern State.* London: Croom Helm.

Philby, H. St. John. 1952. *Arabian Highlands.* New York: Cornell.

Piepenburg, Fritz. 1992. "The cooperative movement of Yemen: Developments after 1985," in al-Saidi (ed.) 1992:55–66.

Playfair, R. L. 1970 (1859). *A History of Arabia Felix.* Westmead: Gregg International Ltd.

Pospisil, Leopold. 1971. *Anthropology of Law: A Comparative Theory.* New York: Harper and Row.

Pridham, B. R. (ed.) 1984. *Contemporary Yemen: Politics and Historical Background.* Croom Helm London.

———. (ed.) 1985. *Economy, Society and Culture in Contemporary Yemen.* Croom Helm London.

Puin, Gerd-R. 1984. "The Yemeni *hijrah* concept of tribal protection," in T. Khalidi (ed.), *Land Tenure and Social Transformation in the Middle East.* Beirut: AUB, 483–494.

Rathjens, Carl. 1951. "Taghut gegen scheriʿah," *Jahrbuch des Linden-Museums,* Stuttgart.

Rentz, G. "Djazīrat al-ʿArab," EI[1].

Riches, David. 1986. "The phenomenon of violence," in *The Anthropology of Violence,* ed. David Riches, Oxford: Blackwell.

Rihani, Ameen. 1930a. *Around the Coasts of Arabia*. London: Constable.

———. 1930b. *Arabian Peak and Desert*. London: Constable.

Roberts, Hugh. 2002. "Perspectives on Berber politics: On Gellner and Masqueray, or Durkheim's mistake," *JRAI* 8(1): 107–126.

———. 2003. "De la segmentarité a l'opacité: A propos de Gellner et Bourdieu et les approches théoriques à l'analyse du champ politique algérien," *Insāniyāt: Revue algérienne d'anthropologie et de sciences sociales* 19–20 Vol. VII, 1–2: 65–95.

Roberts, Simon. 1979. *Order and Dispute: An Introduction to Legal Anthropology*. Penguin.

Robin, Christian. 1982a. *Les Hautes-Terres du Nord-Yémen avant l'Islam. Vol. 1. Recherches sur la géographie tribale et religieuse de Khawlān Quḍāʿa et du Pays de Hamdān*. Istanbul: Nederlands Historisch-Archaeologisch Instituut.

———. 1982b. "Esquisse d'une histoire de l'organisation tribale en Arabie du sud antique," in Bonnenfant (ed.) 1982, Vol. II, 17–30.

Rossi, E. 1948. "Il diritto consuetudinario delle tribu arabe del Yemen," *Revista degli Studi Orientali,* 23: 1–36.

Rouland, Norbert. 1994 (1988). *Legal Anthropology*. Trans. P. B. Planel. Stanford University Press.

Sālim, Muṣṭafā. 1974. *Al-fatḥ al ʿuthmāni al-awwal lil-Yaman*. Cairo: Matbaʿt al-Jabalāwi.

———. 1982. *Wathāʾiq yamaniyyah*. Cairo: Maṭbaʿat al-Fanniyyah.

Sahillioğlu, Halil. 1985. "Yemen'in 1599–1600 yili bütçesi," in *Ord. Prof. Yusuf Hikmet Bayur'a Armağan*. Kurumu/Ankara: Türk Tarih.

al-Saidi, Muhammad (ed.). 1992. *The Cooperative Movement in Yemen and Issues of Regional Development*. New York: Professors World Peace Academy.

Schacht, J. 1964. *An Introduction to Islamic Law*. Oxford University Press.

Schmidt, Dana Adams. 1968. *Yemen: The Unknown War*. New York: Holt, Rinehart and Winston.

Schofield, Richard. 2000. "The international boundary between Yemen and Saudi Arabia," in Detalle (ed.) 2000.

Schuman, L. O. 1962. *Political History of the Yemen at the Beginning of the Sixteenth Century*. Groningen.

Schweizer, Günther. 1985. "Social and economic change in the rural distribution system: Weekly markets in the Yemen Arab Republic," in Pridham (ed.) 1984: 107–121.

Scott, Hugh. 1942. *In the High Yemen*. London: Murray.

Serjeant, R. B. 1962. "Ḥaram and ḥawṭah, the sacred enclave in Arabia," in *Melanges Taha Husain,* ed. A. al-Badawī, Cairo: Dār al-Maʿārif, 41–58.

———. 1964. "The 'constitution of Medina,'" *The Islamic Quarterly,* VIII: 3–16.

———. 1969. "The Zaydīs" in A. J. Arberry (ed.), *Religion in the Middle East,* Cambridge University Press: 285–301.
———. 1977. "South Arabia," in C. van Nieuwenhuijze (ed.), *Commoners, Climbers and Notables,* Leiden: Brill, 226–247.
———. 1978. "The sunnah jāmiʿah, pacts with the Yathrib Jews, and the taḥrīm of Yathrib: Analysis and translation of the documents comprised in the so-called "constitution of Medina,"" *Bull.SOAS,* XLI:1–42.
———. 1979. "The Yemeni poet al-Zubayri and his polemic against the Zaydī Imāms," *Arabian Studies* V, London: Hurst, 87–130.
———. 1981. *Studies in Arabian History and Civilisation.* London: Variorum Reprints.
———. 1982. "The interplay between tribal affinities and religious (Zaydī) authority in the Yemen," *Al-Abhath* XXX, Beirut: American University of Beirut.
———. 1983a. "The post-medieval and modern history of Ṣanʿāʾ and the Yemen, ca. 953–1382/1515–1962," in Serjeant and Lewcock (eds.) 1983: 68–107.
———. 1983b. "Ṣanʿāʾ the 'protected,' Hijrah," in Serjeant and Lewcock (eds.) 1983: 39–43.
Serjeant, R. B., and Ismāʿil al-Akwaʿ. "The statute of Ṣanʿaʾ (*qānūn* Ṣanʿāʾ)," in Serjeant and Lewcock (eds.) 1983: 179–232.
———. 1991. *Customary and Sharīʿah law in Arabian Society.* London: Variorum Reprints.
Serjeant, R. B., and R. Lewcock. 1983. *Sanʿāʾ: An Arabian Islamic City.* London: World of Islam Festival Trust.
Sharaf al-Din [Sharafaddin], Ahmad b. Husayn. 1961. *Yemen: "Arabia Felix."* Taʿizz.
———. 1964. *Al-Yaman ʿabr al-taʾrīkh.* Cairo: Maṭbaʿat al-Sunnat al-Muḥammadiyyah.
Smiley, David. 1975. *Arabian Assignment.* London: Leo Cooper.
Smith, Clive. 2002. *Lightning over Yemen: A History of the Ottoman Campaign 1569–71,* translation of work by Quṭb al-Dīn al-Nahrawālī. London: I. B. Tauris.
Smith, G. Rex. 1988. "The political history of the Islamic Yemen down to the first Turkish invasion (1–945/622–1538)," in Daum (ed.) 1988: 129–139.
Starr, June, and Jane F. Collier (eds.). 1989. *History and Power in the Study of Law: New Directions in Legal Anthropology.* Ithaca: Cornell University Press.
Steffen, H., et al. 1978. *Final Report on the Airphoto Interpretation Project of the Swiss Technical Co-operation Service,* Berne. Zurich.
———. 1979. *Population Geography of the Yemen Arab Republic.* Wiesbaden: Ludwig Reichart.
Stevenson, Thomas. 1985. *Social Change in a Yemeni Highlands Town.* Salt Lake City: University of Utah Press.
Stewart, Frank H. 1987. "Tribal Law in the Arab World," *IJMES* 19: 473–490.
Stookey, Robert W. 1974. "Social structure and politics in the Yemen Arab Republic," Parts I and II, *Middle East Journal* 28, No. 3: 248–260, 409–418.

———. 1978. *Yemen: The Politics of the Yemen Arab Republic.* Colorado: Westview Press.

Strothmann, R. 1908–1938. "Al-Zaidīya," *EI* I, 1196–1198.

Suwaidi, Jamal S (ed.). 1995. *The Yemeni War of 1994: Causes and Consequences.* London: Saqi Books.

Swagman, Charles. 1988. *Development and Change in Highland Yemen.* Salt Lake City: University of Utah Press.

Swanson, Jon, and Mary Hebert. 1982. *Rural Society and Participatory Development: Case Studies of Two Villages in the Yemen Arab Republic.* Cornell University: USAID/Y Project.

Tapper, Richard. 1983. "Introduction," in R. Tapper (ed.), *The Conflict of Tribe and State in Iran and Afghanistan.* Beckenham: Croom Helm, 1–82.

———. 1991. "Anthropologists, historians and tribespeople on tribe and state formation in the Middle East." In Khoury and Kostiner (eds.), 48–73.

———. 1997. *Frontier Nomads of Iran: A Political and Social History of the Shahsavan.* Cambridge University Press.

Tritton, A. S. 1925. *The Rise of the Imāms of Sanaa.* Oxford University Press.

Tuchscherer, Michel. 1992. *Imāms, Notables et Bédouins du Yémen au XVIII siècle: Ou Quintessence de l'Or du Regne de Cherif Muḥammad b. Aḥmad (Chronique de ʿAbd al-Raḥman b. Ḥasan al-Bahkalī).* Cairo: Institut Francais d'Archéologie Orientale du Caire, TAEI XXX.

———. 1993. "Le commerce en mer Rouge aux alentours de 1700: Flux, espaces et temps," *Les Orientales* V: 159–178.

———. 1997. "Des épices au café: Le Yémen dans le commerce international (xvie–xviie siècle)," in *Chroniques Yéménites,* Centre Francais de'Archéologie et de Sciences Sociales, Sanaa.

———. 2000. "Chronologie du Yémen (1506–1635)," *Chroniques Yéménites,* Centre Francais de'Archéologie et de Sciences Sociales, Sanaa.

———. 2001. "Commerce et production du café en mer Rouge au XVI siècle," in Tuchscherer (ed.) 2001.

Tuchscherer, M. (ed.). 1994. *Le Yémen: Passé et Present de l'Unité, Revue du Monde Musulman et de la Méditerranée,* No. 67, Edisud: Aix-en-Provence.

———. (ed.). 2001. *Le Commerce du Café avant l'ère des plantations coloniales: espaces, reseaux, sociétés (XVe–XIXe siècle).* Cairo: Institut Francais d'Archéologie Orientale.

Tutwiler, Richard. 1984. "Taʿāwun Maḥwīt: A case study of a Local Development Association in Highland Yemen," in L. Cantori and I. Harik (eds.), *Local Politics and Development in the Middle East,* Boulder: Westview.

———. 1987. *Tribe, Tribute and Trade: Social Class Formation in Highland Yemen.* Ph.D. thesis, New York: Binghamton.

Tutwiler, Richard, and Sheila Carapico. 1981. *Yemeni Agriculture and Economic Change,* American Institute for Yemeni Studies.

Vaglieri, L. Veccia. 1983. "Ghadīr Khumm," in *EI* II.

Van Arendonk, C. (revised by K. N. Chaudhuri). 1960. *Les debuts de l'imāmat Zaidite au Yemen*. French trans.: J. Ryckmans. Leiden: Brill.

———. 1974. "Ḳahwa," EI: II.

Varisco, Daniel Martin. 1982. *The Adaptive Dynamics of Water Allocation in al-Ahjur, Yemen Arab Republic*. Ph.D. Thesis, Ann Arbor, Michigan.

———. 1994. *Medieval Agriculture and Islamic Science: The Almanac of a Yemeni Sultan*. Seattle: University of Washington Press.

Varisco, Daniel Martin, and Najwa Adra. 1981. "Affluence and the concept of the tribe in the central highlands of the Yemen Arab Republic," in Richard Salisbury et al. (eds.), *Affluence and Cultural Survival,* American Ethnological Society.

Vincent, Joan. 1990. *Anthropology and Politics: Visions, Traditions and Trends*. Tucson: University of Arizona Press.

Walters, Delores. 1987. *Perceptions of Social Inequality in the Yemen Arab Republic*. Ph.D. thesis, New York University.

al-Wāsiʿī, ʿAbd al-Wāsiʿ b. Yaḥyā. 1947 (1366). *Ta'rīkh al-Yaman*. Cairo: al-Maṭbaʿah Hijāzī.

Watson, J., B. Glover Stalls, K. A. al-Rāziḥī, and S. Weir. 2006. "The language of Jabal Rāziḥ: Arabic or something else?" *Proceedings of the Seminar for Arabian Studies,* London.

Weber, Max. 1947 (1922). *The Theory of Social and Economic Organization*. Trans. A. M. Henderson and Talcott Parsons. New York: The Free Press.

Weir, Shelagh. 1975. "Some observations on pottery and weaving in the Yemen Arab Republic," *Proceedings of the Seminar for Arabian Studies,* Vol. 5: 65–76.

———. 1985a. "Economic aspects of the qāt industry in North-West Yemen," in Pridham (ed.) 1985: 64–82.

———. 1985b. *Qat in Yemen: Consumption and Social Change*. London: British Museum Publications.

———. 1986. "Tribe, hijrah and madinah in North-West Yemen," in *The Middle Eastern City in Comparative Perspective,* London: Ithaca, 225–239.

———. 1987. "Labour migration and key aspects of its economic and social impact on a Yemeni highland community," in R. Lawless (ed.), *The Middle Eastern Village: Changing Economic and Social Relations,* Croom Helm, 273–296.

———. 1991. "Trade and tribal structures in North West Yemen," in *Arabie du Sud: Le Commerce comme facteur dynamisant des changements économiques et sociaux*. Paris: Cahiers de Gremamo, 10, 88–101.

———. 1996. "Documents from Razih as anthropological and historical sources," in *Proceedings of the Seminar for Arabian Studies,* 26: 167–173.

———. 1997. "A clash of fundamentalisms: Wahhabism in Yemen," *MERIP* 204 Vol. 27, no. 3.

———. 2007. "The contemporary softstone industry in Jabal Rāziḥ, north west Yemen," in St. J. Simpson and Carl Phillips (eds.), *Softstone in Arabia and Iran*. Oxford: Archaeopress.

Wenner, Manfred W. 1967. *Modern Yemen 1918–1966*. Baltimore: Johns Hopkins University Press.

Wilson, Robert. 1981. "Al-Hamdānī's description of Ḥāshid and Bakīl," *Proceedings of the Seminar for Arabian Studies*, Vol. 11: 95–104.

——. 1989. *Gazetteer of Historical North-West Yemen in the Islamic Period to 1650*. New York: Georg Olms Verlag.

Wyman Bury, G. 1915. *Arabia Infelix or the Turks in Yamen*. London: Macmillan.

Yaḥyā b. al-Ḥusayn. 1968 (1866–71). *Ghāyat al-Amānī fī akhbār al-quṭr al-yamānī*, ed. S. ʿĀshūr. Cairo: Dār al-Kitāb al-ʿArabī.

Yāqūt al-Ḥamawī, ʿAbdallāh. 1955 (1866–73). *Muʿjam al-buldān*. Beirut.

Yemen Arab Republic. 1971. "The Permanent Constitution of the Yemen Arab Republic," *Middle East Journal* 25(3): 389–401.

Zabārah, Muḥammad. 1957/1376. *Nashr al-ʿArf*. Cairo (3 Vols).

al-Zulfa, Muḥammad ʿAbdallāh. 1982. "Village communities in Bilād Rufaydah: Their political and economic organization," *Arabian Studies* VI:77–94.

——. 1987. *Ottoman Relations with ʿAsīr and the Surrounding Areas: 1840–72*. Doctoral thesis, Cambridge University.

Index

The page numbers of maps and photographs are in bold. Page numbers of tables are in italics.